AF575929

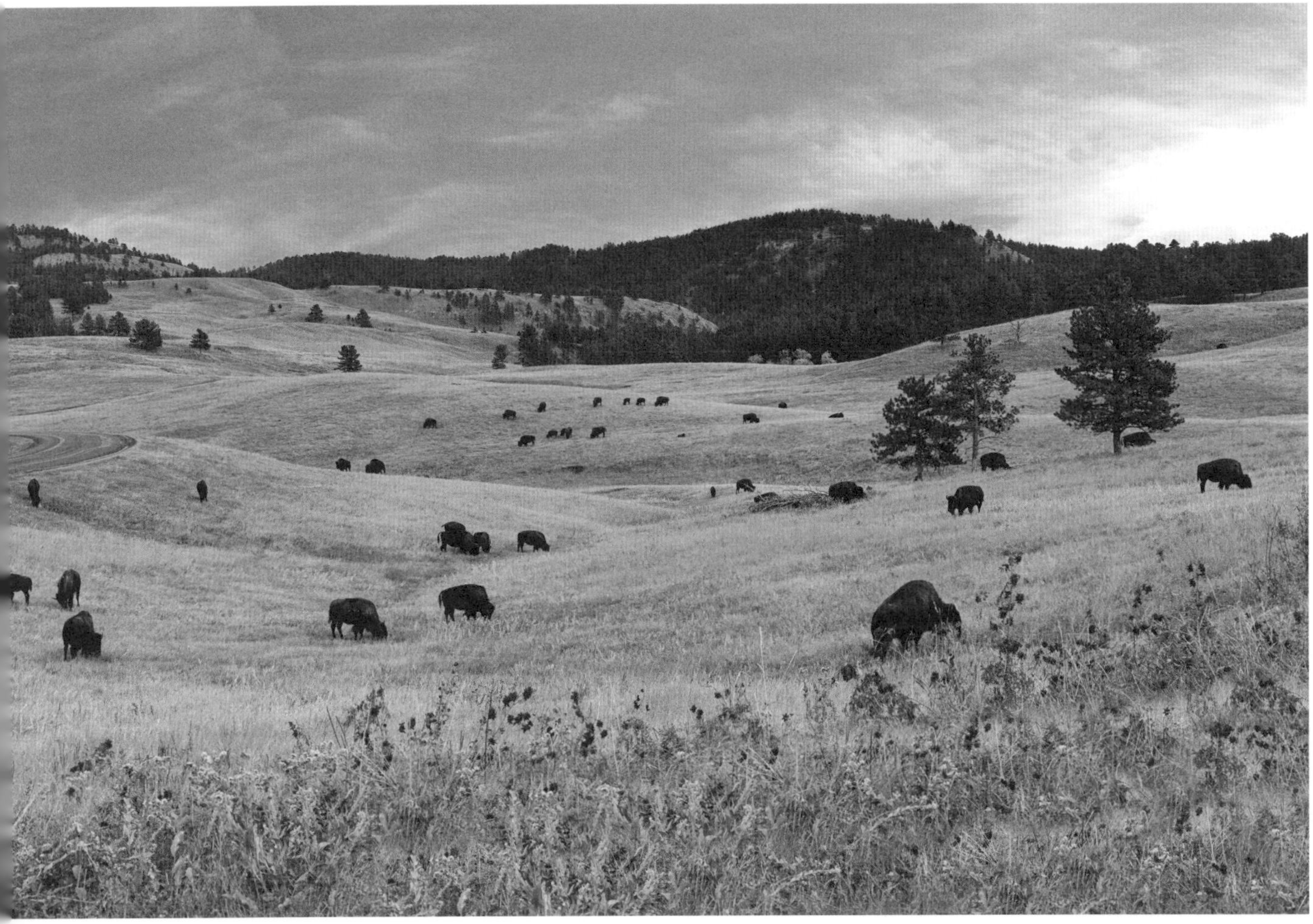

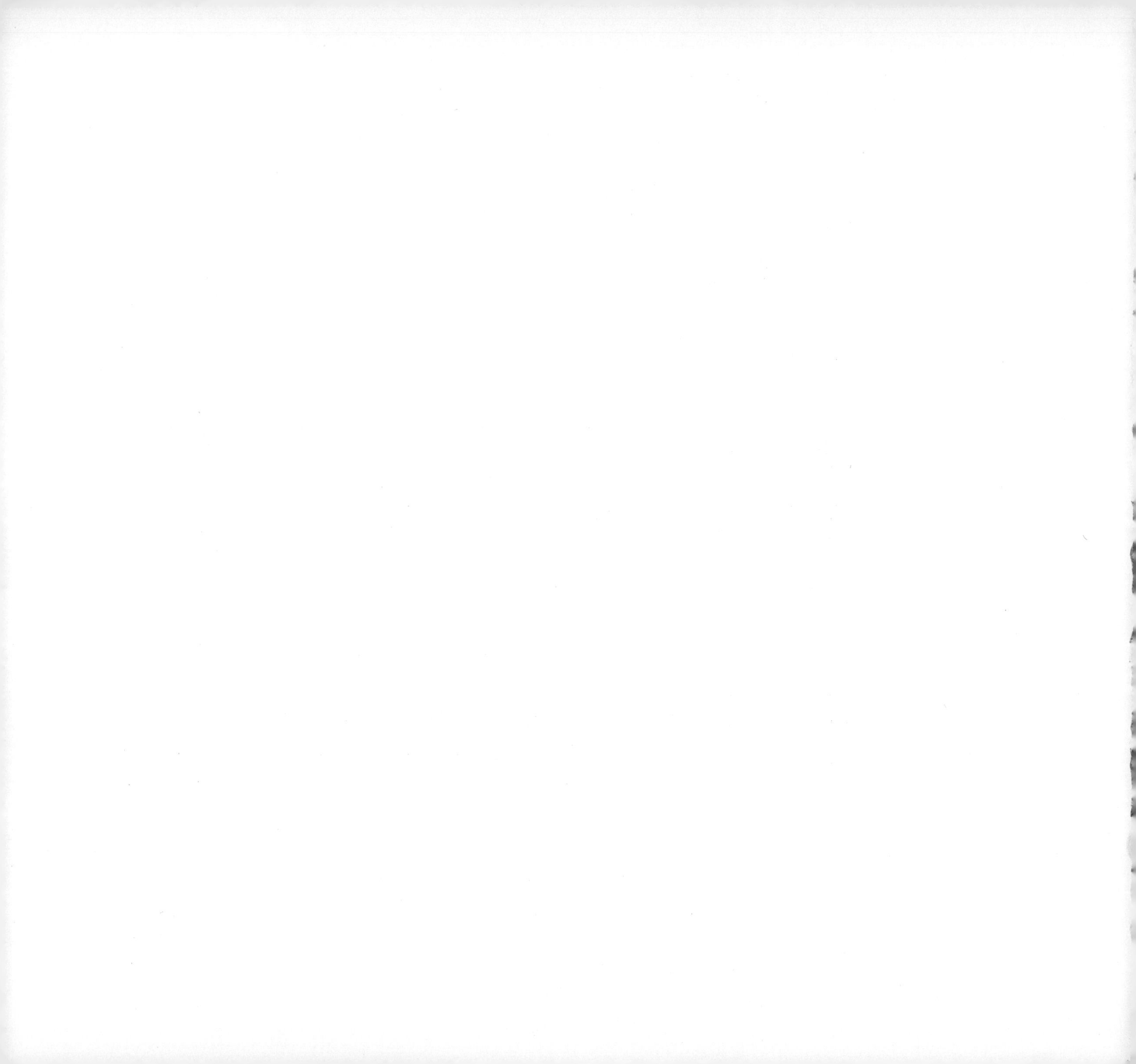

BACK ROADS OF THE GREAT PLAINS

OKLAHOMA, KANSAS, NEBRASKA, AND THE DAKOTAS

Photographs by David Skernick

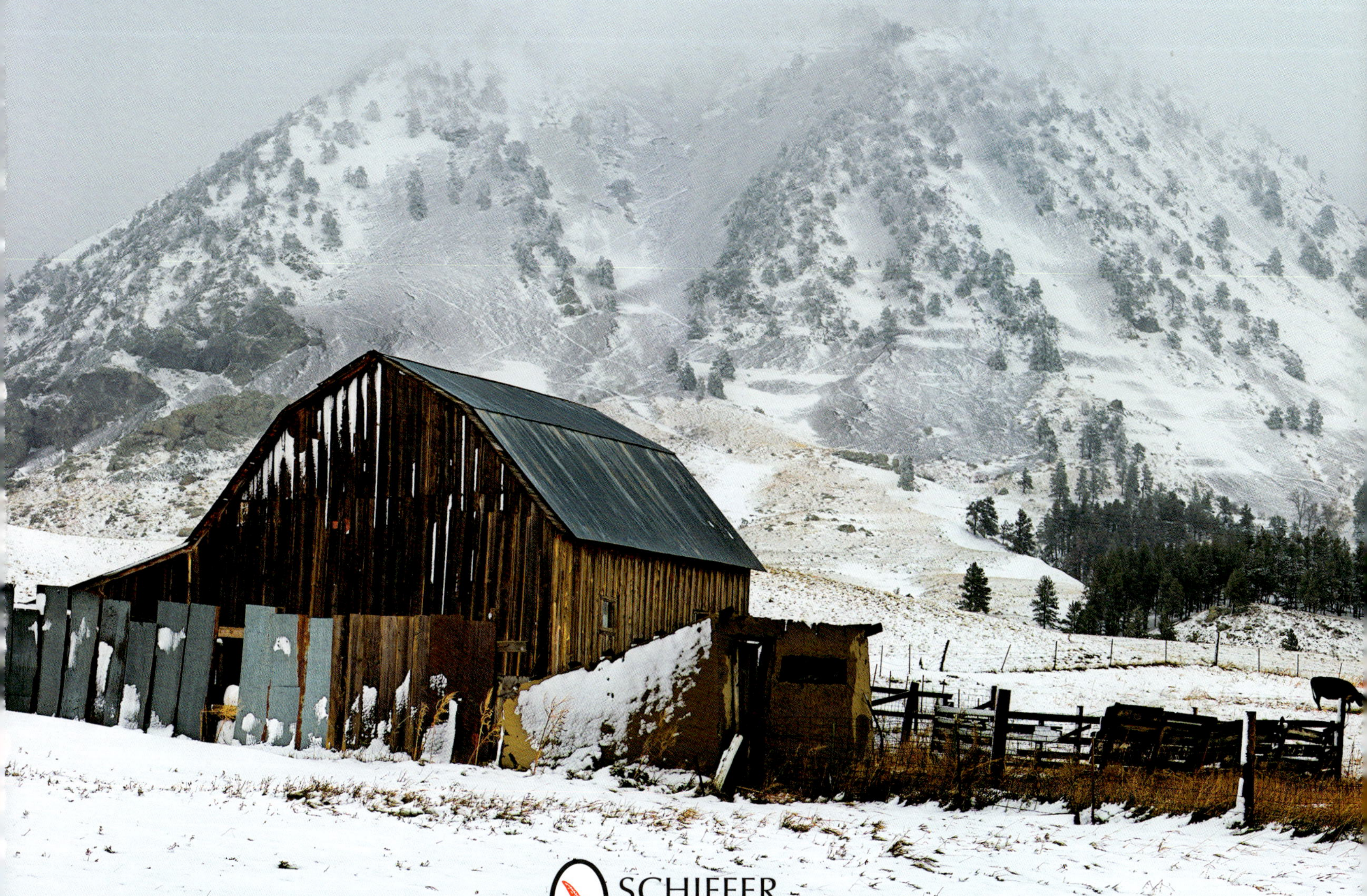

SCHIFFER PUBLISHING

4880 Lower Valley Road • Atglen, PA 19310

Other Schiffer Books by David Skernick

Back Roads of Northern California,
ISBN 978-0-7643-5762-6

Back Roads of Southern California,
ISBN 978-0-7643-5763-3

Back Roads of the Southwest,
ISBN 978-0-7643-5858-6

Library of Congress Control Number: 2020943640

Designed by Justin Watkinson
Cover design by Justin Watkinson

Type set in Proxima Nova

ISBN: 978-0-7643-6186-9
Printed in China

Published by Schiffer Publishing, Ltd.
4880 Lower Valley Road
Atglen, PA 19310
Phone: (610) 593-1777; Fax: (610) 593-2002
E-mail: Info@schifferbooks.com
Web: www.schifferbooks.com

To the farmers, cowboys, and field workers of the Great Plains. I hope some of you see this book and rediscover the beautiful places where you live and work, and I thank all of you for the food!

As to scenery (giving my own thought and feeling), while I know the standard claim is that Yosemite, Niagara Falls, the Upper Yellowstone, and the like afford the greatest natural shows, I am not so sure but the prairies and plains, while less stunning at first sight, last longer, fill the esthetic sense fuller, precede all the rest, and make North America's characteristic landscape.

—Walt Whitman

FOREWORD

In 1983, when our daughter Shelby was about to turn thirteen, she requested a "grown-up" camera for her birthday. Finding the camera was easy; figuring out what to do with it was another matter. At the time, we lived in the San Fernando Valley and so began the hunt for the best possible instructor willing to come to our Sherman Oaks home every week for Shelby's lessons. We soon found that all roads led to David Skernick. And while we expected David would teach Shelby the ins and outs of her equipment and the art of photography, we had no idea his lessons were really about the art of life.

Through the ensuing years, David became Shelby's mentor. He harvested her curiosity and turned her natural talent into a passion. So much so that Shelby became an award-winning photographer in high school. During this time I was developing my own interest in photography, but I didn't dare ask David if he would accept me as a student until Shelby was off to college. You can bet that the same day we waved goodbye after she settled into her dorm room, I booked my first lesson. And so, I embarked on a decades-long journey during which David became not only a lifelong "family member" but my most important teacher.

David spent time teaching me the basics of my camera equipment before my first field lesson. He took me to a western ranch back lot at one of the local movie studios. Set among a rambling pioneer ghost town was an old hitch wagon with huge wagon wheels. I couldn't wait to start shooting. But, before I could attach a lens to the camera body, David stopped me, asking what exactly caught my eye. I had to really think about the answer. And once I realized it wasn't the entire scene but rather the angle of the hitch wagon with the sun lighting up the back wheel, I began to understand the importance of identifying what moved me, so I could capture the essence of the shot. I've never forgotten that lesson.

While David's private lessons were invaluable, it was when I joined his photo trips that I began to truly understand the genius behind his work. David is innately curious, and his images are so absorbing and compelling because they are so personal. He is also a master at finding the light—manipulating its color, quality, and direction. Even in bad-light situations, I've seen David shape and direct the light that's present to produce magnificent impressions.

A master storyteller, David produces images that are so powerful, it takes only a few seconds to see the layers of stories in each one. In these pages, David has compiled an extraordinary portrait of five remarkably diverse states bound together by their geographic location. The 400 million acres stretching from Canada to Mexico once had an abundance of wildlife unmatched anywhere else in North America. But today, the Great Plains are one of the most threatened, the most altered, and least protected habitats in North America. David's images remind us that we cannot shrink from the responsibility of restoring a healthy Great Plains environment for future generations.

Studying David's images, I am reminded of what Eliot Porter said about truly creative photographers. "Before all else, a work of art is the creation of love. Love for the subject first and for the medium second. Love is the fundamental necessity underlying the need to create, underlying the emotion that gives it form, and from which grows the unfinished product that is presented to the world."

Barbara Balik
a.k.a. Shotgun
Napa Valley

INTRODUCTION

This book is part of a series of books of photographs taken all over the United States—a collection of places and things I see as I drive along. I travel 50,000 miles or so every year along the back roads of the United States. I call this getting lost on gray roads. On the maps you can get at your local AAA office, gray is the color of the smaller, two-lane winding roads.

Being lost is not about losing one's way, but rather the utter pleasure of being nowhere specific. Gray roads ramble across the landscape as if they have only a vague idea where they are going, hunting for clues of cardinality in small towns and railroad crossings.

As I crisscrossed the back roads of what some people call "the flyover states," I found little gems everywhere. Once, I stopped in a tiny store to pick up a bag of ice in a little tiny town called Protection, Kansas. When a man there heard I was photographing the area, he offered to lead me to his farm, where they were cutting sorghum. We jumped into our pickups and he led me along dirt road after dirt road to his farm. I took several photographs, which appear in this book. The man's name was Mitch. Timing is everything. Talking to people is rarely a mistake. What a great day.

I have experienced southern hospitality—it's a real thing. The Great Plains has its own flavor of hospitality. Driving down a dirt road between farms in North Dakota, I saw a farmer sitting by the side of the road and looking glum. After a mile or so, I turned around to see if he was okay. It turns out that Jim Olsen's sprayer had broken down, and he was waiting for his nephew to bring him the part he needed to get it going. I mentioned that his sprayer, even broke down, looked cool to me and that I'd like to photograph it. I explained about panoramic photos and he insisted on opening out the arms so the shot would be better. They opened out to something like 100 feet, and it made the shot! You can see for yourself toward the end of the book.

These chance meetings are what keep me wanting to be on the road. Although I travel mostly alone, I am never lonely. We may be divided by politics and religion, but we all love our country and want to show it off. Ready to spend some time on the back roads of the Great Plains? Let's go!

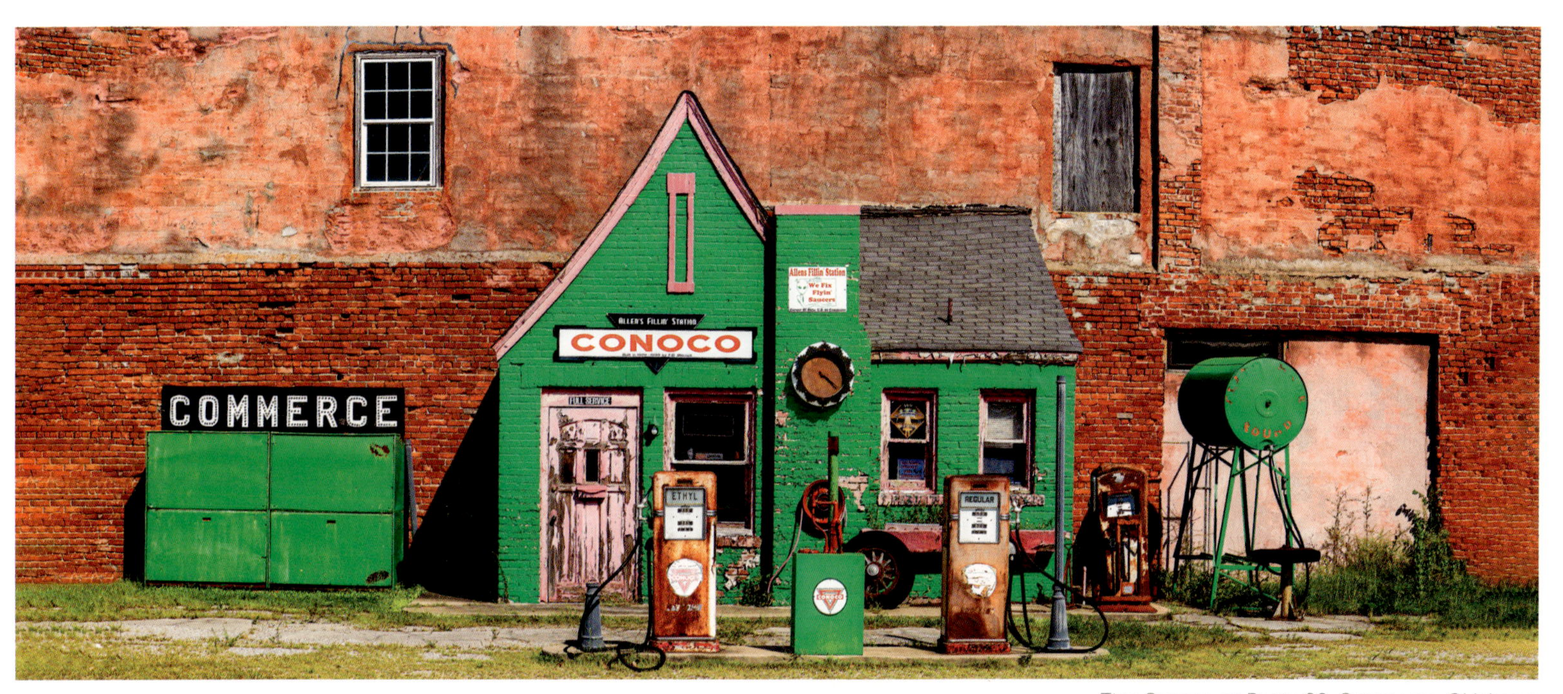

Tiny Conoco on Route 66, Commerce, Oklahoma

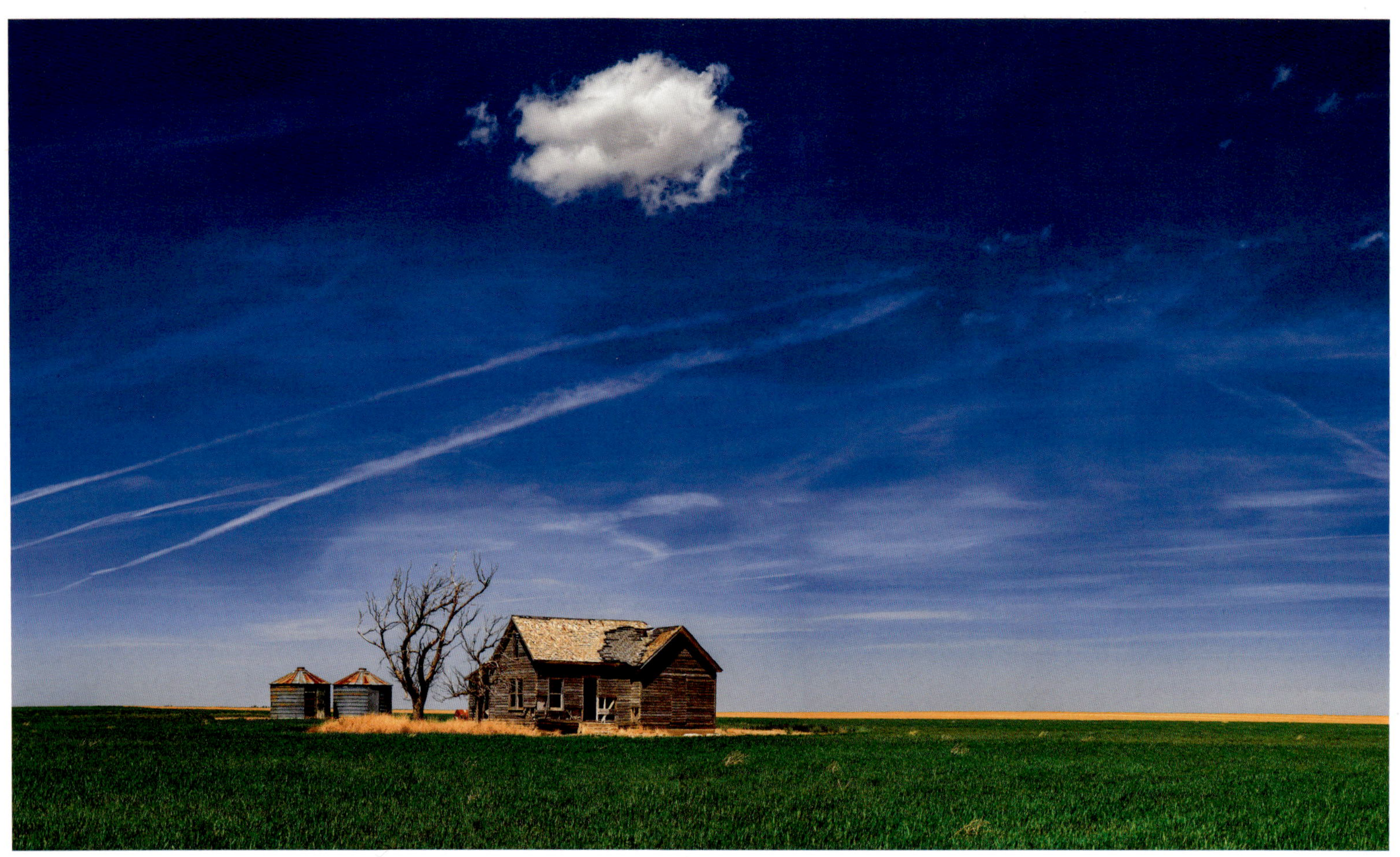

Homestead off Oklahoma State Highway 171

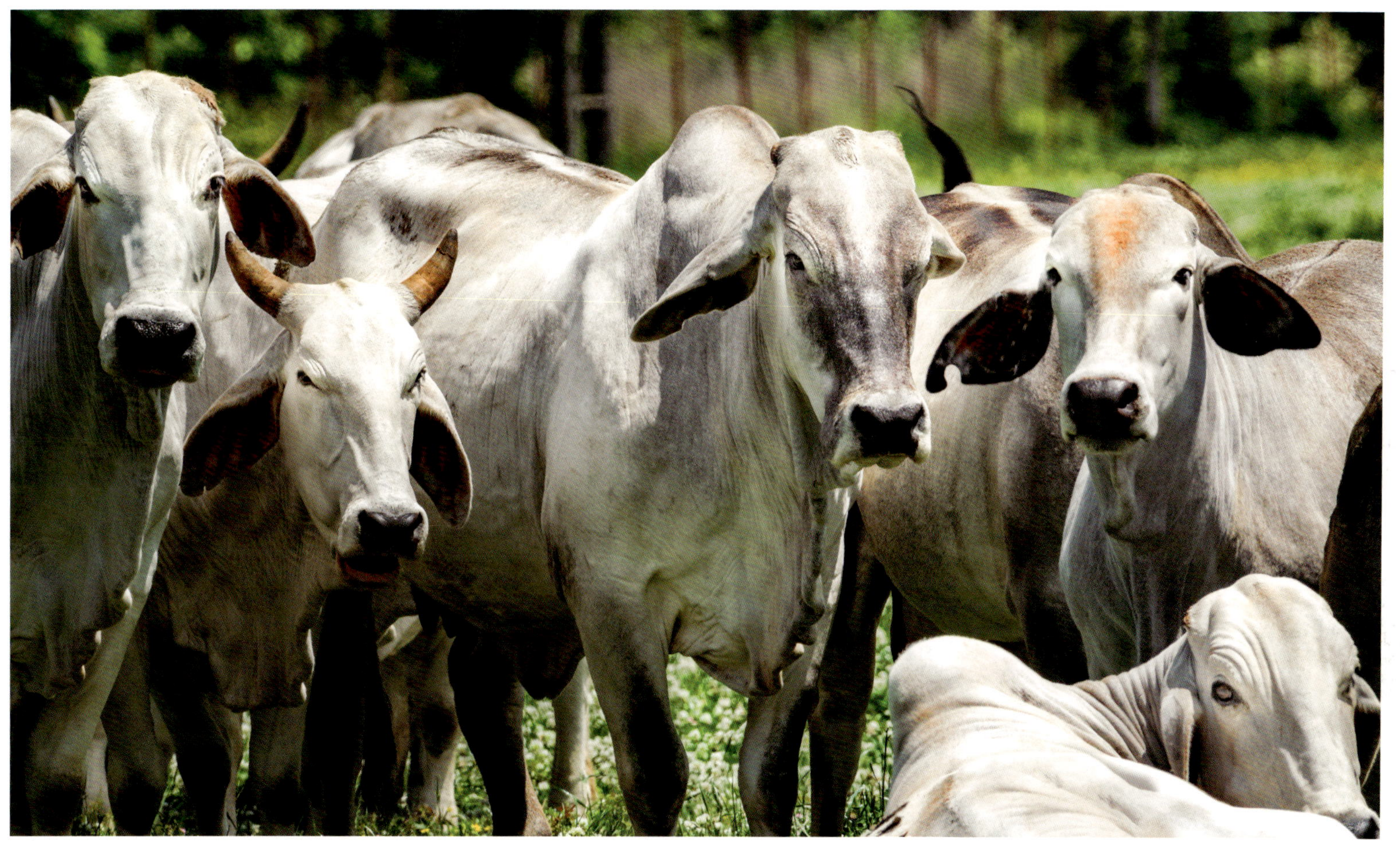

Brahman cattle, Oklahoma

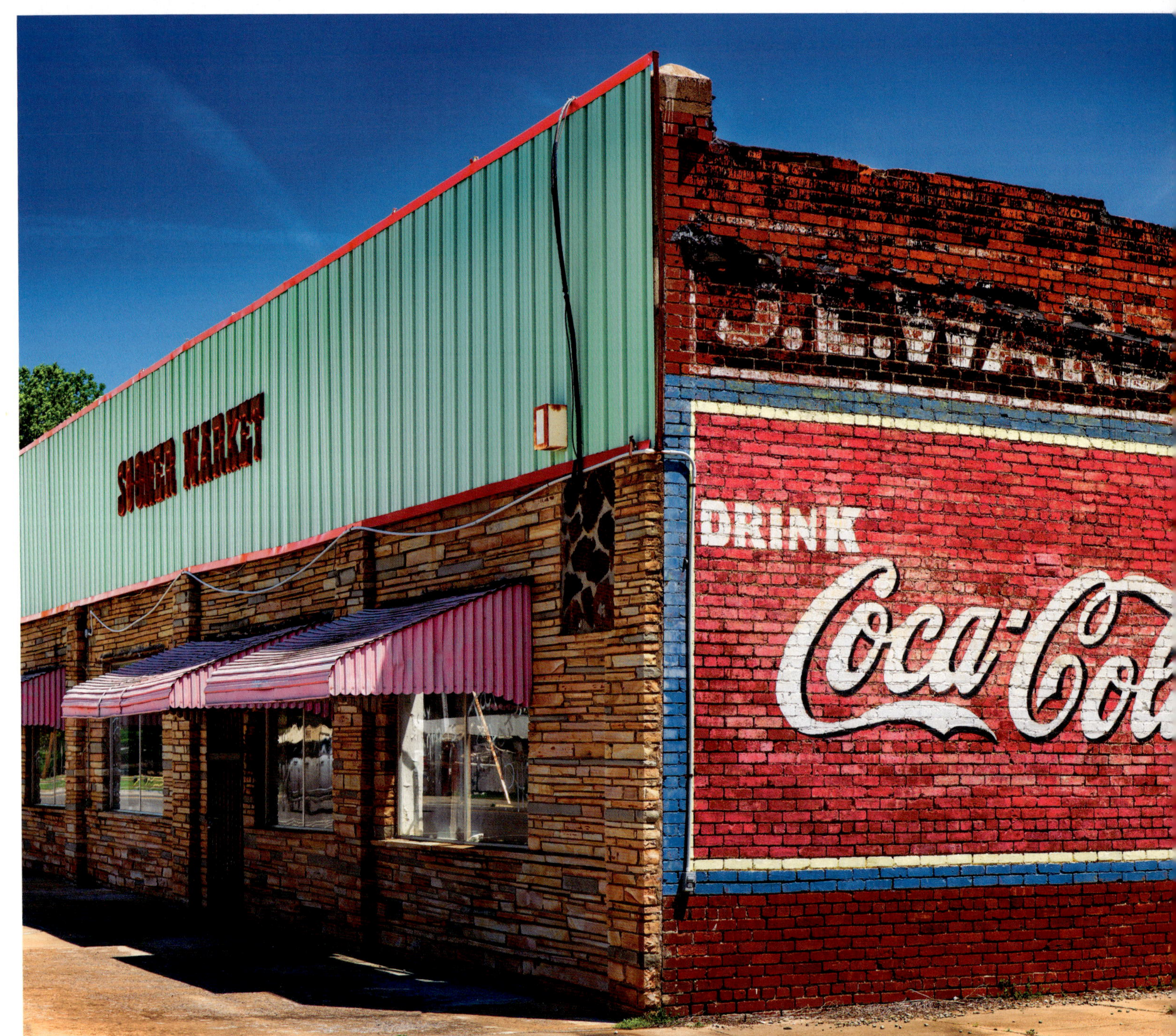

Sooner Market, Porum, Oklahoma

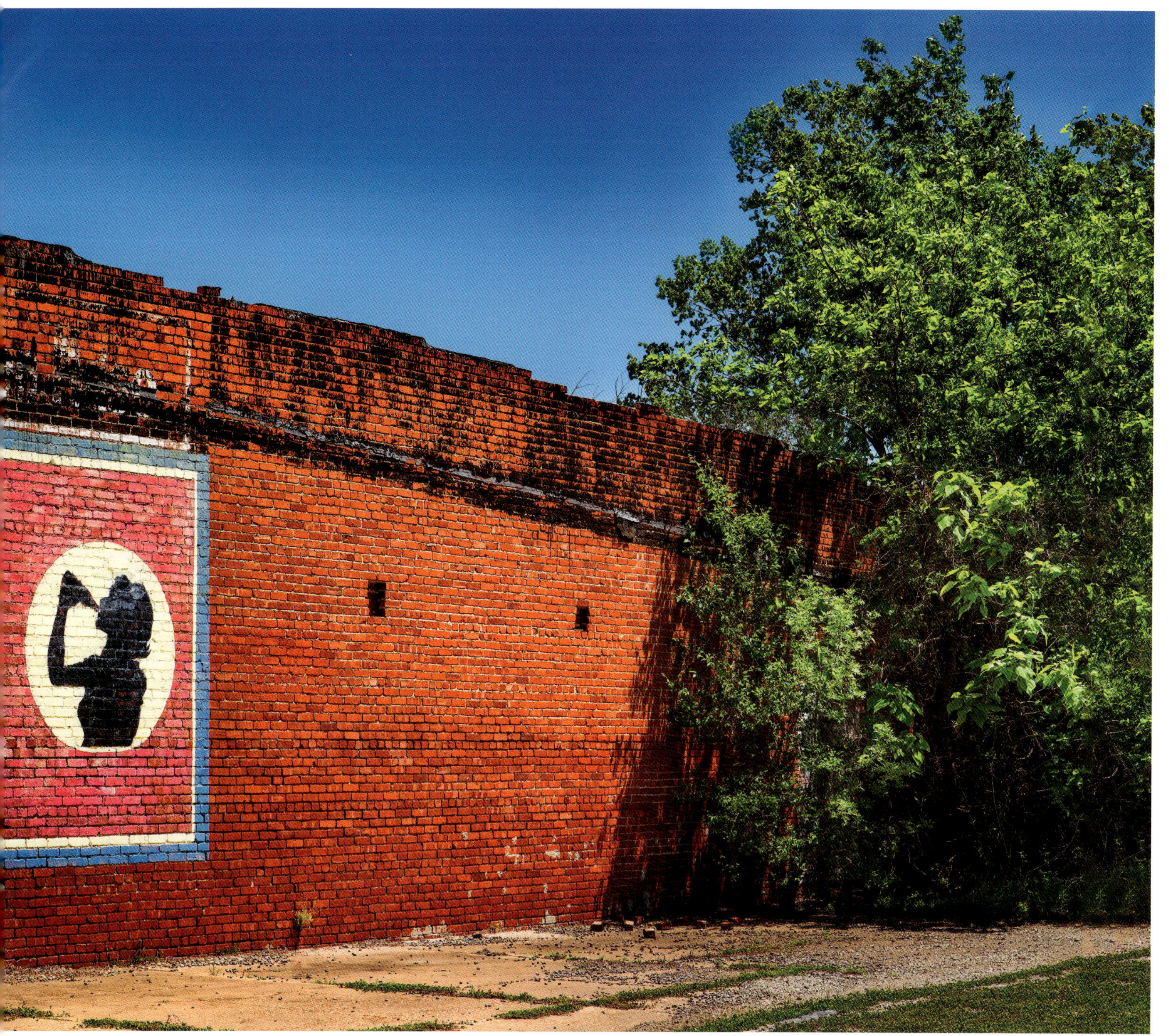

After I shot this, I went in and bought a Coke.

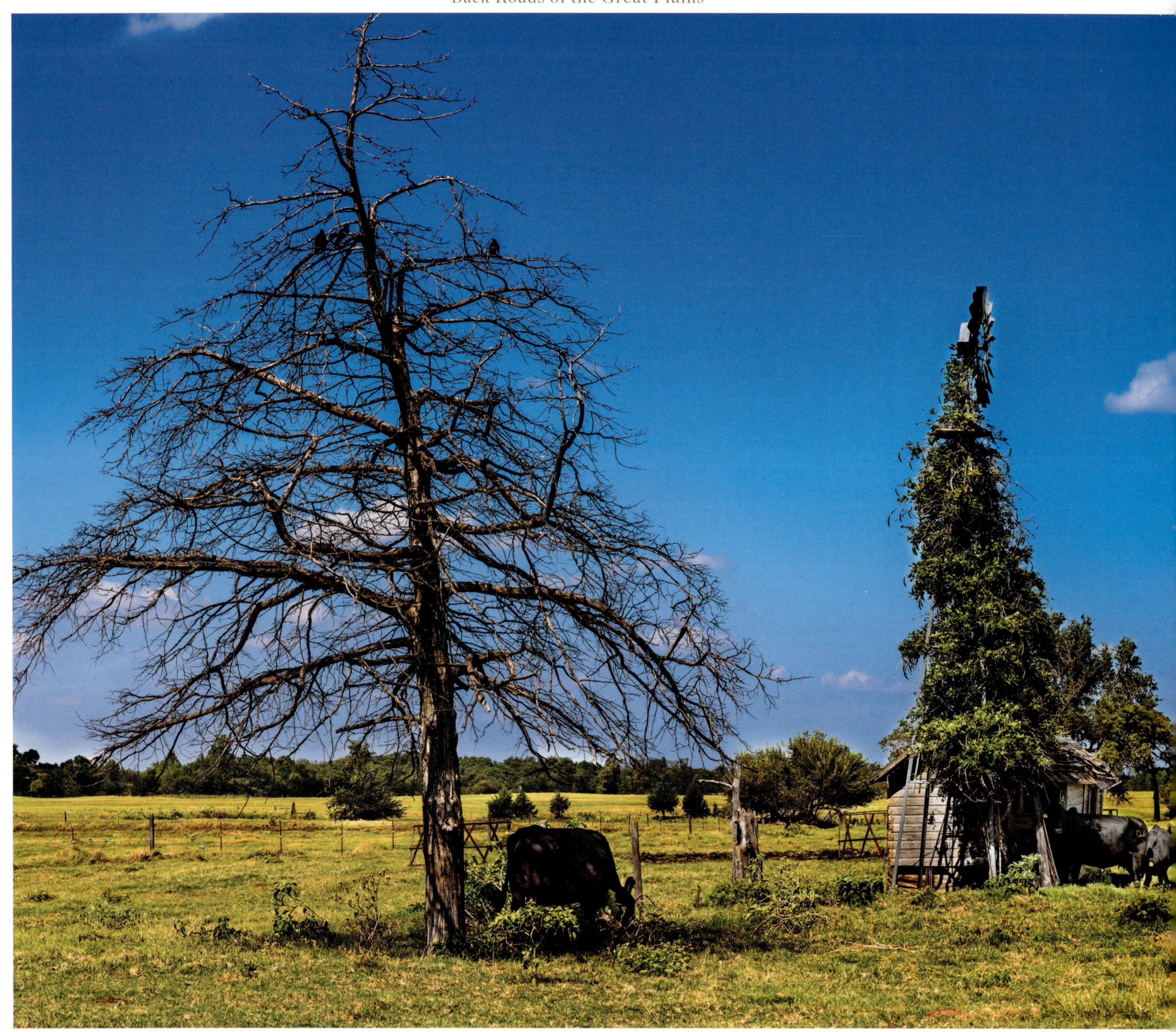

Old house in Salt Plains National Wildlife Refuge, Oklahoma

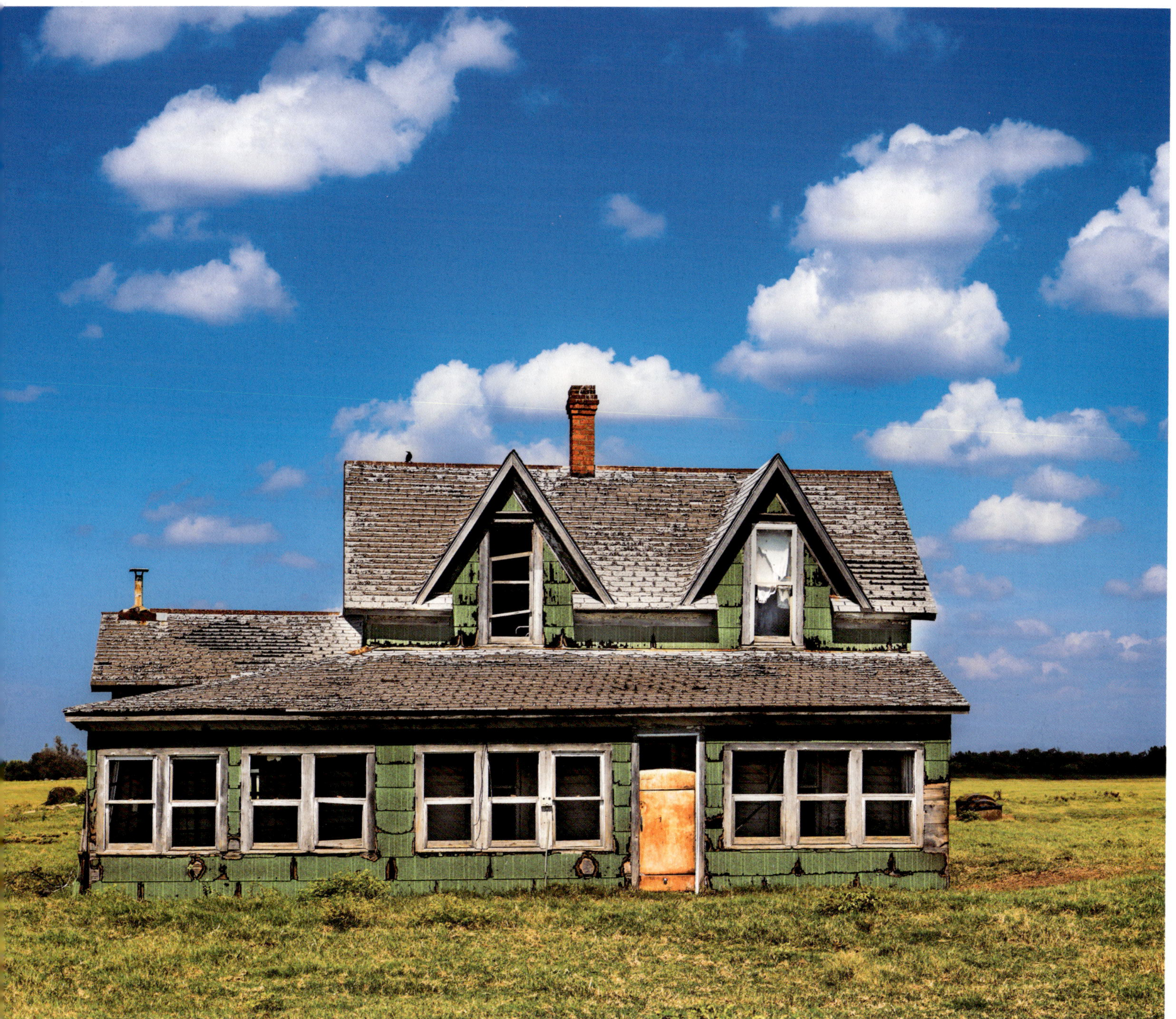

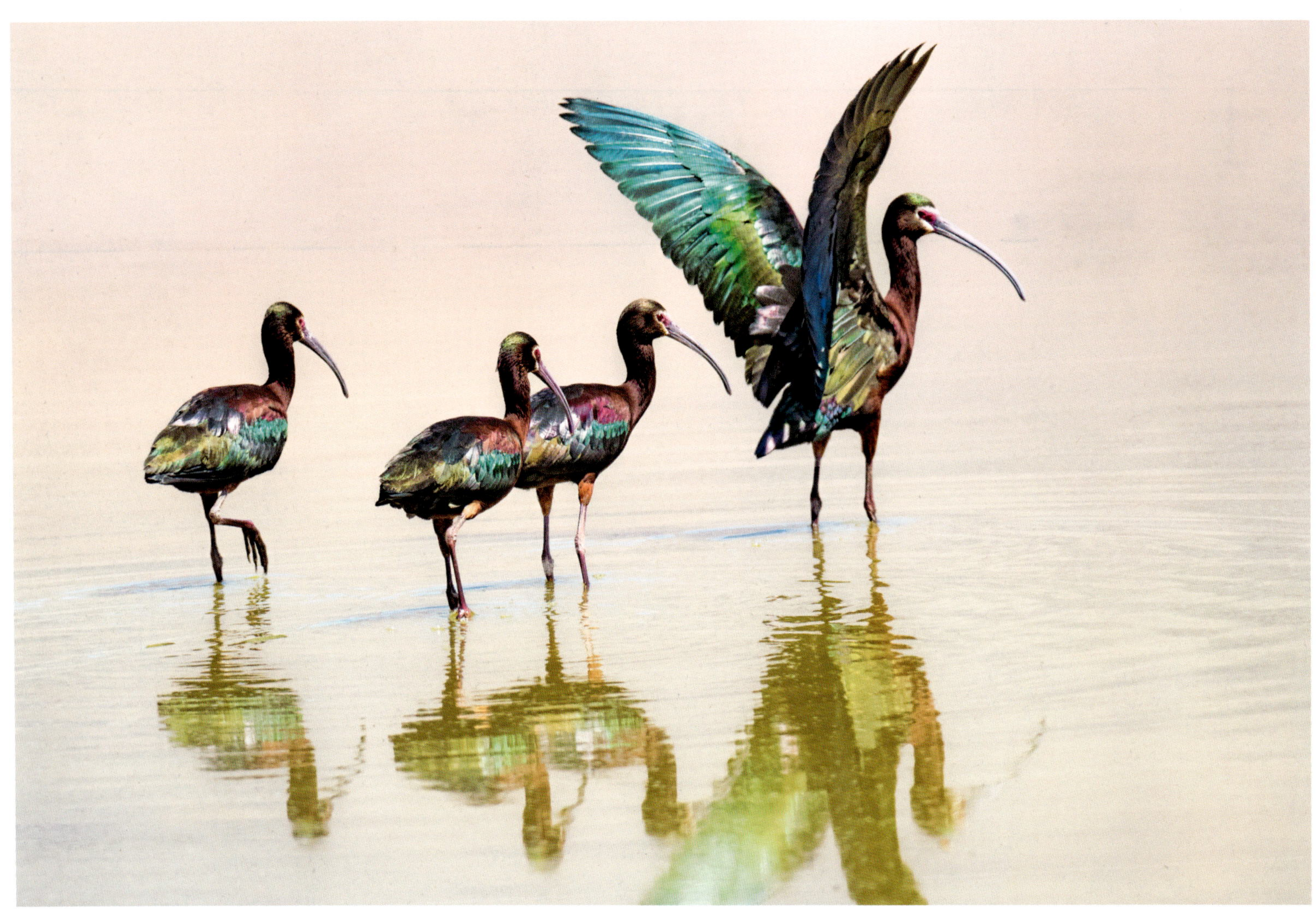

Glossy ibis, Wichita Mountains National Wildlife Refuge, Oklahoma

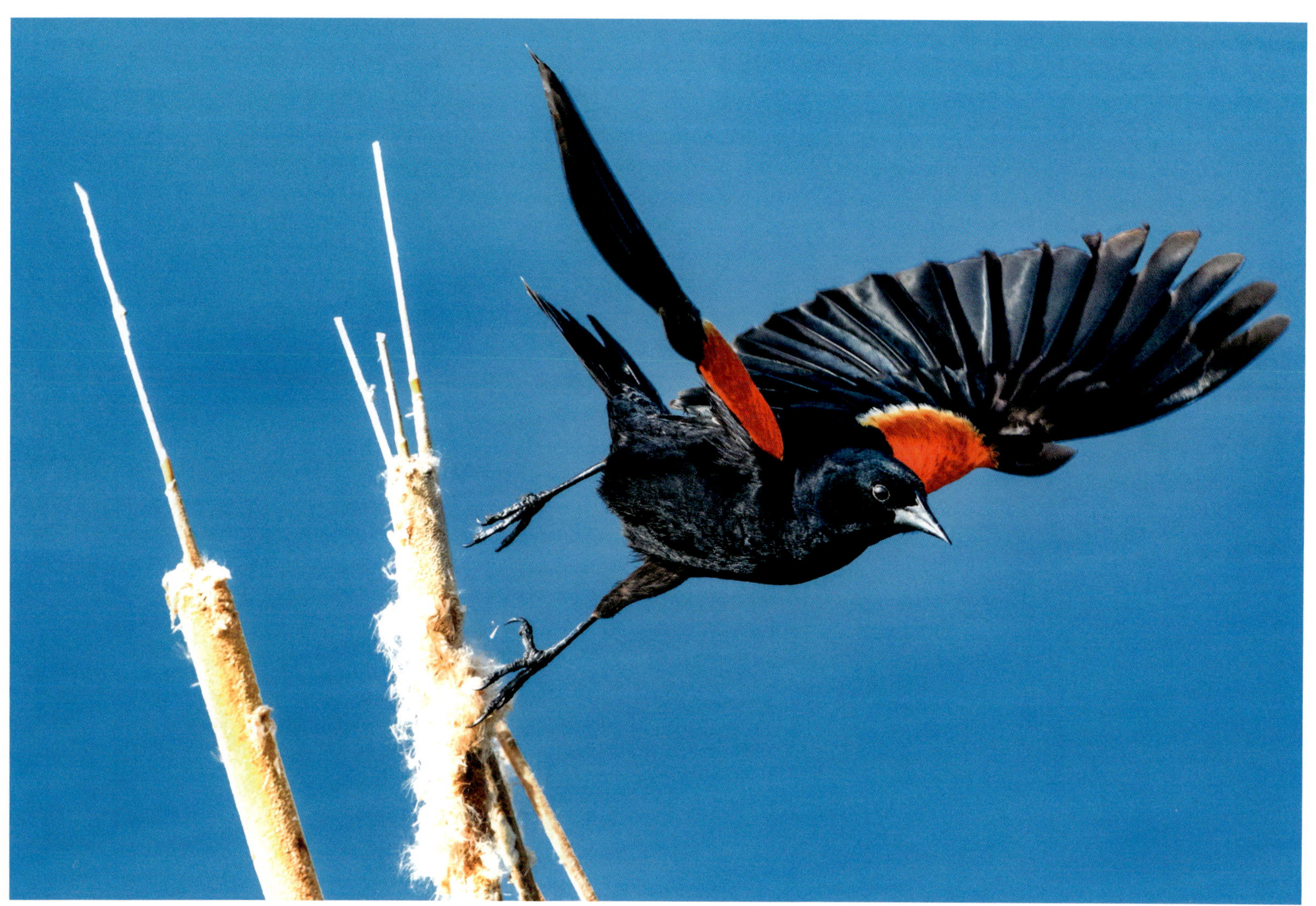

Red-winged blackbird, pond on Harris Road, Oklahoma

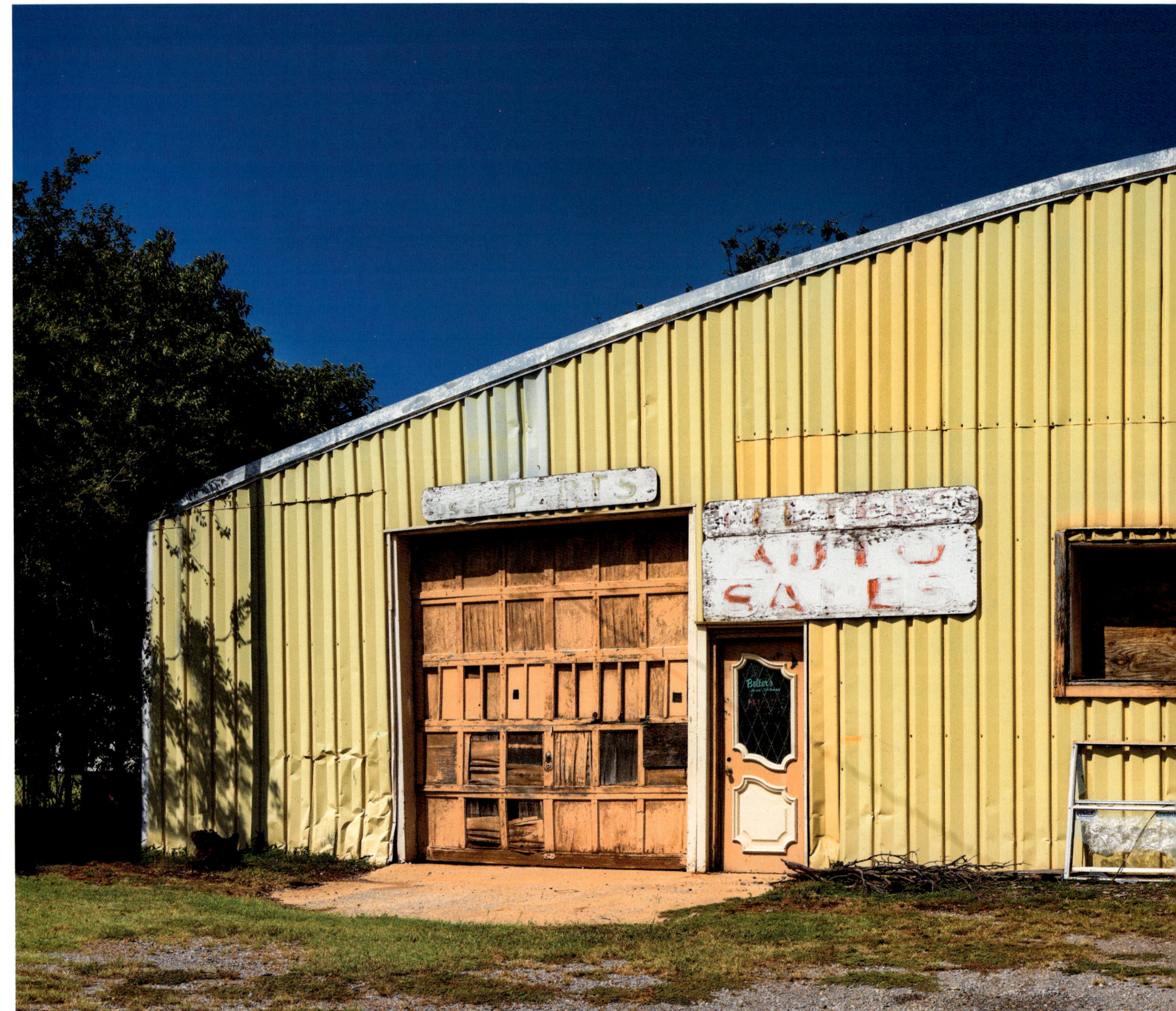

Belter's Auto Salvage, Route 66, Clinton, Oklahoma

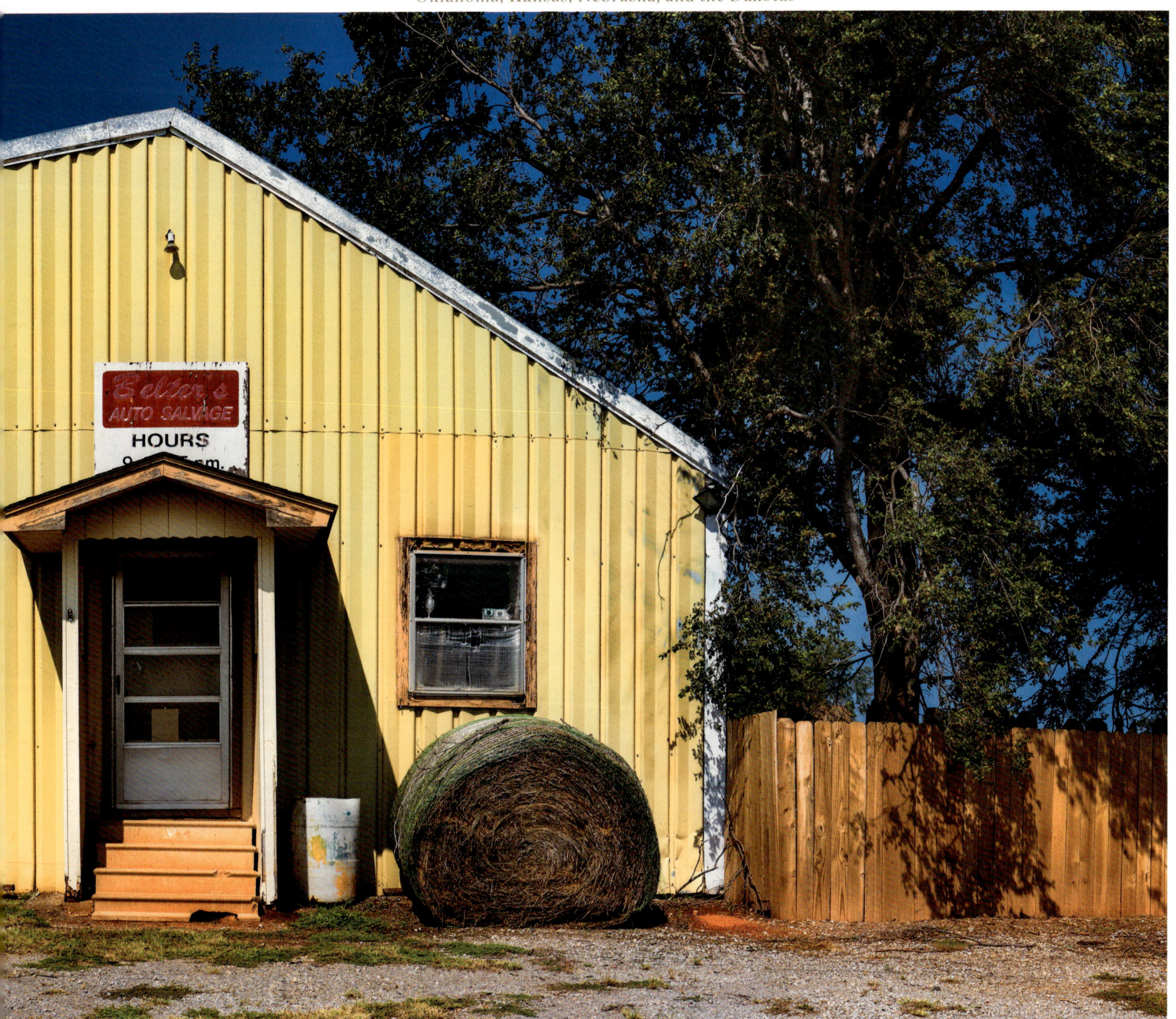
AUTO SALVAGE
HOURS

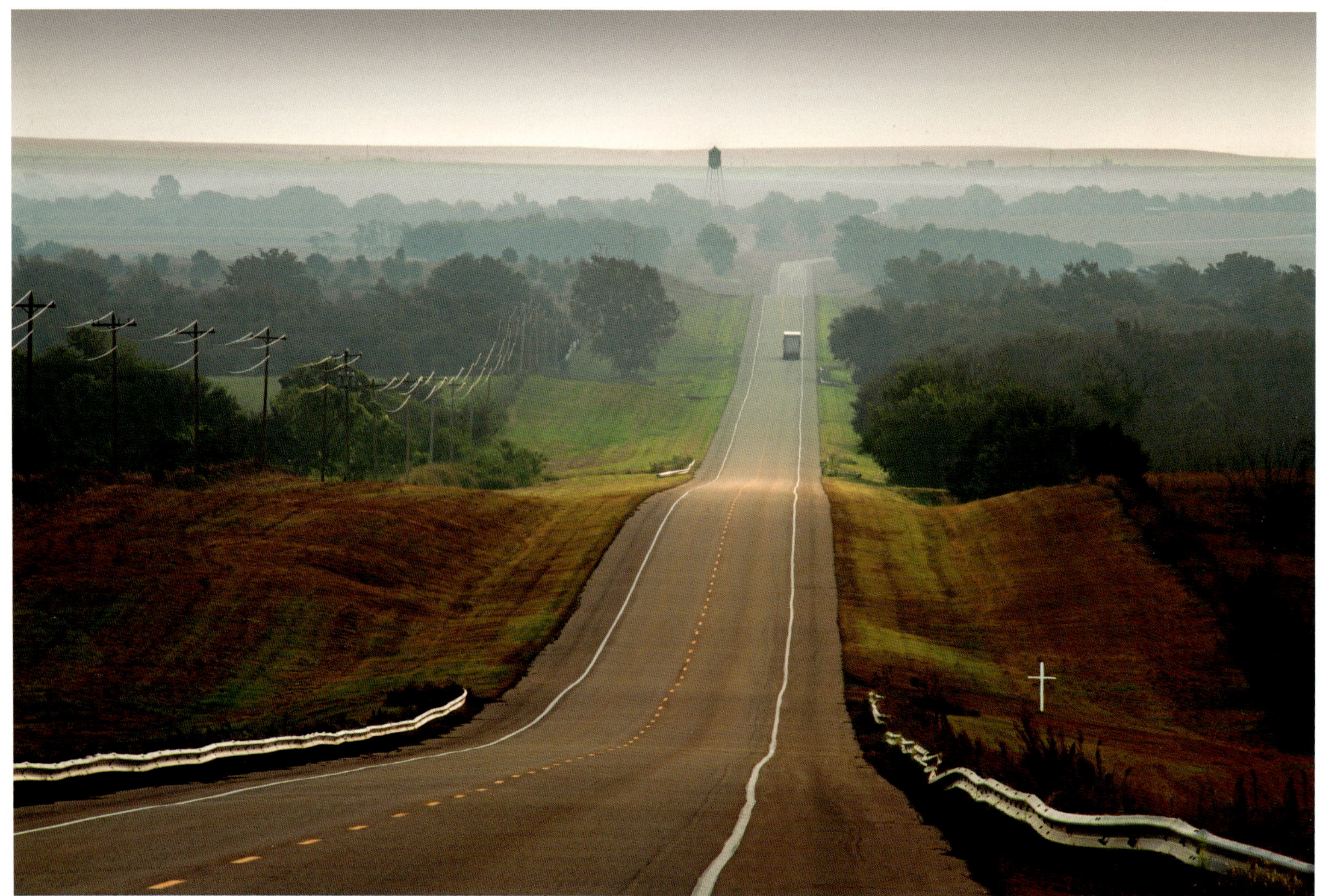

Oklahoma State Highway 60

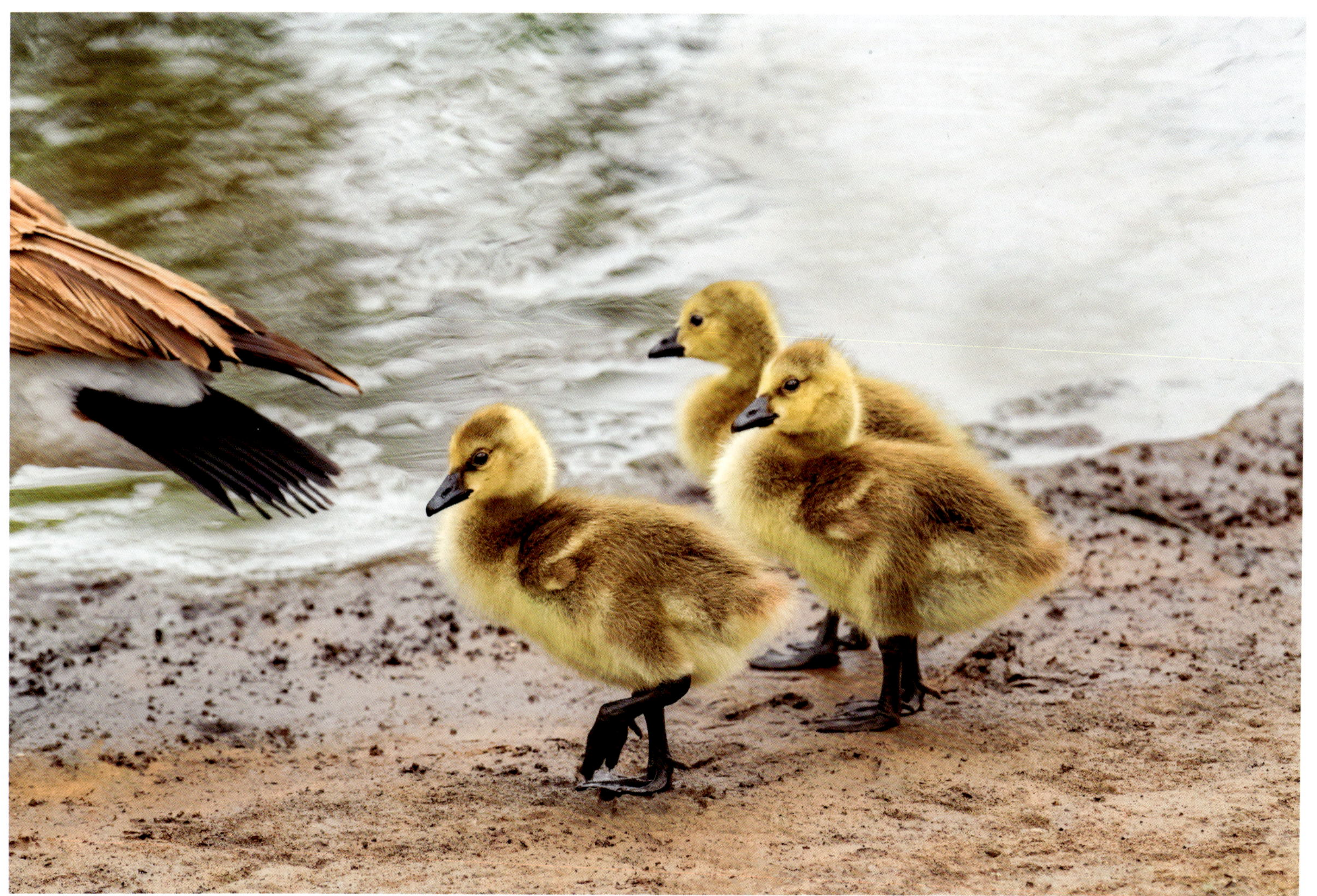

Canada goslings, Salt Plains National Wildlife Refuge, Oklahoma

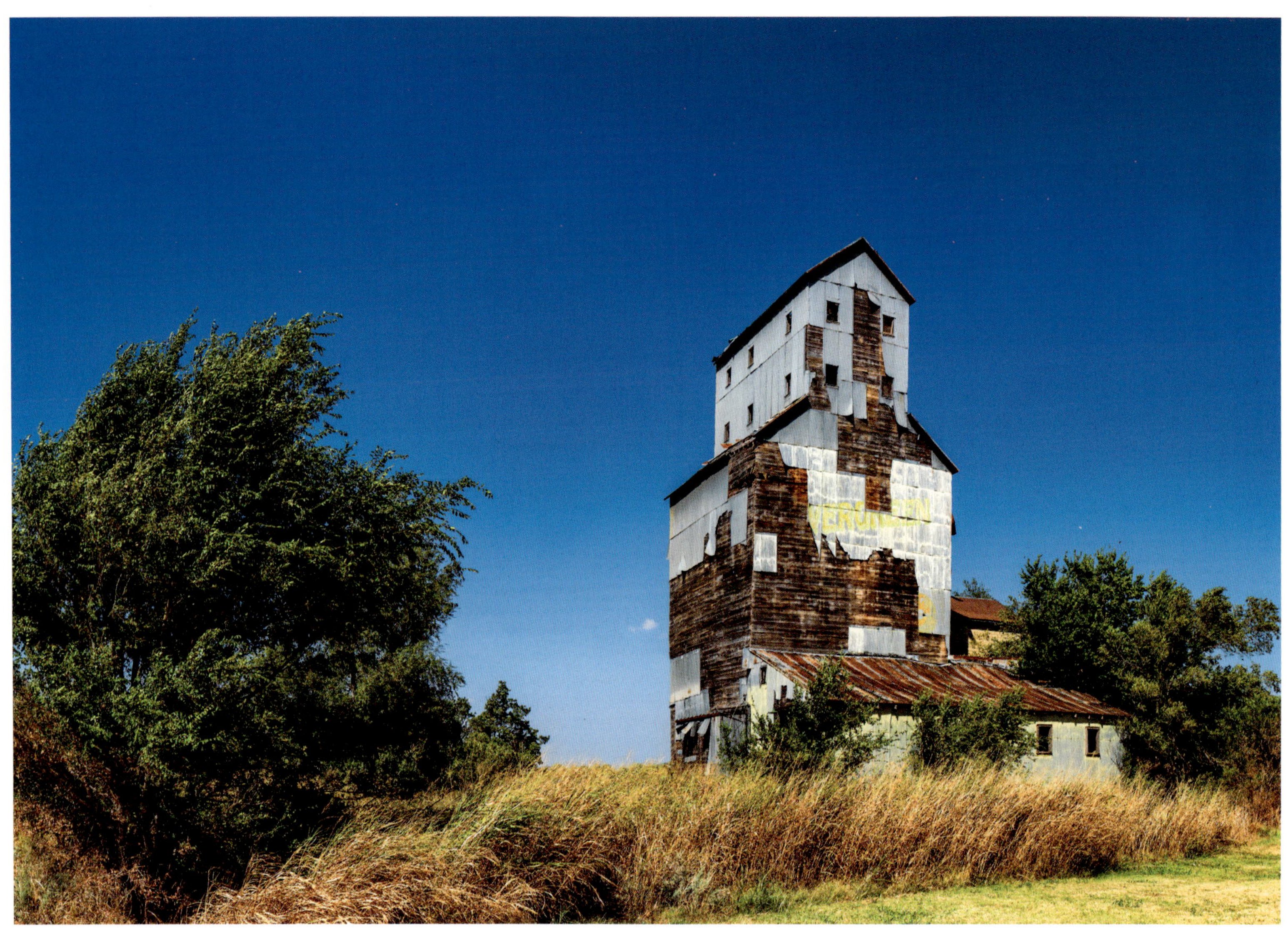

Old granary, Cherokee, Oklahoma

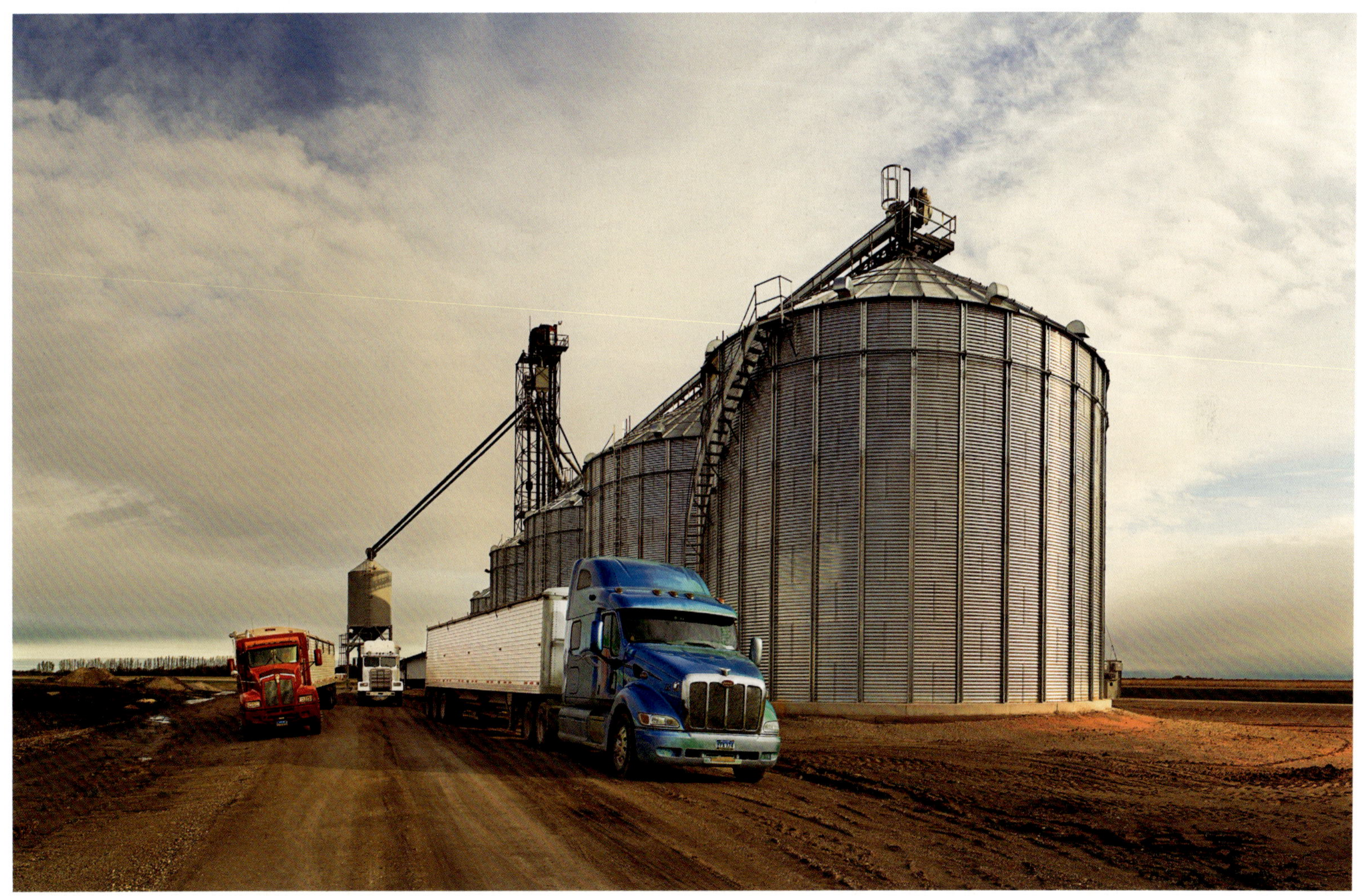

Silos and trucks on the Great Plains

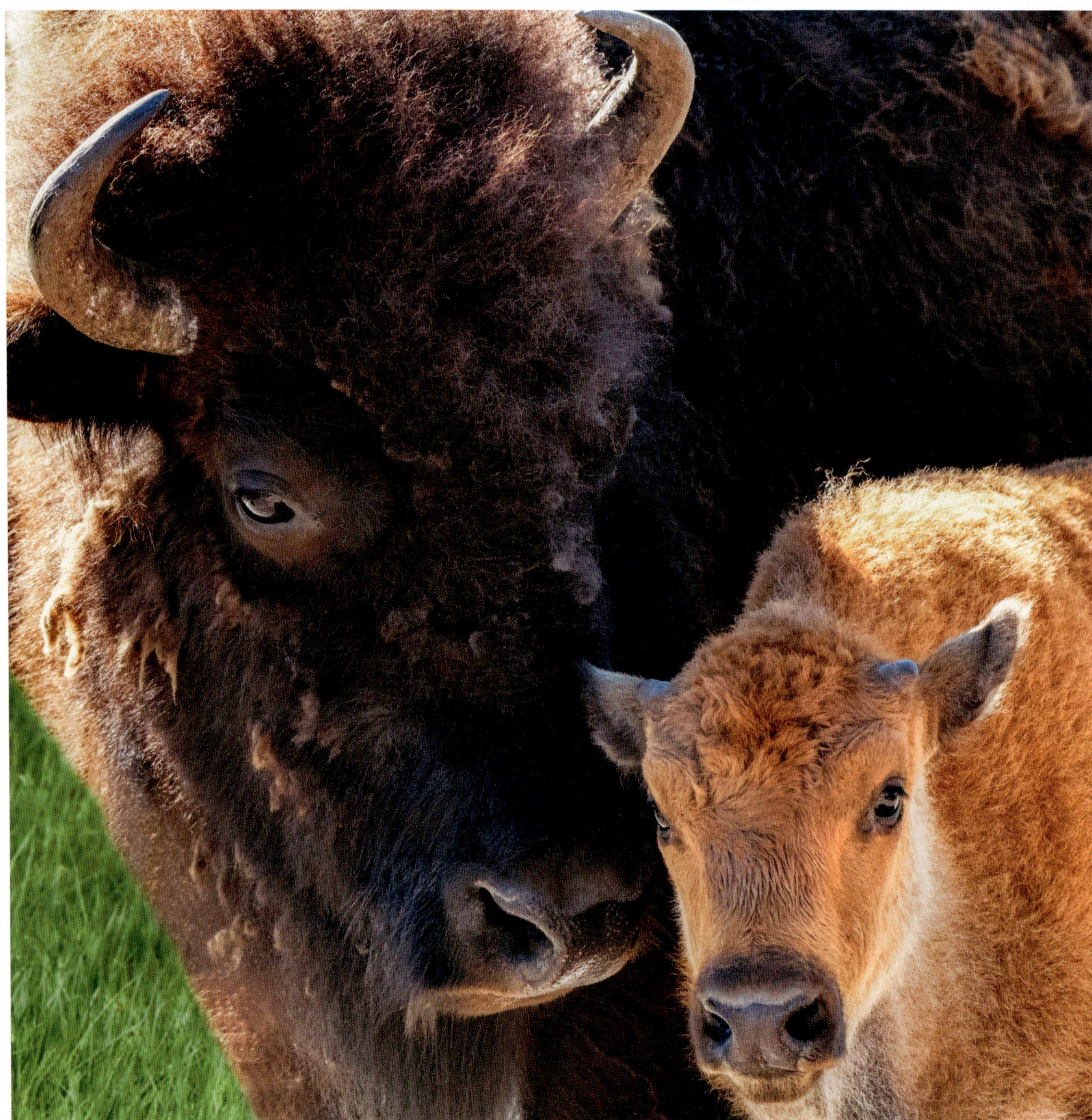

Bison cow and calf, Wichita Mountains National Wildlife Refuge, Oklahoma

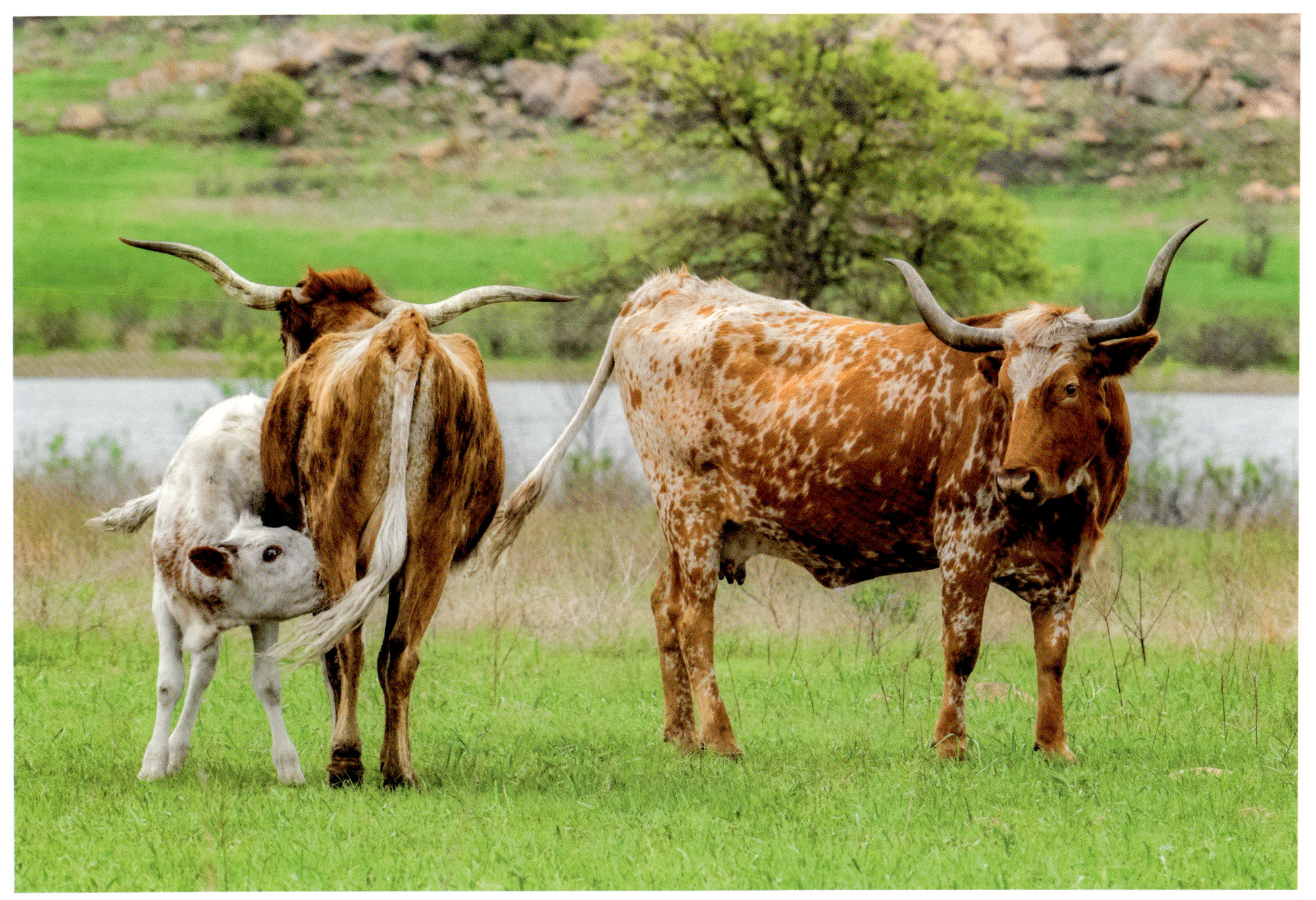

Longhorn cattle, Wichita Mountains National Wildlife Refuge, Oklahoma

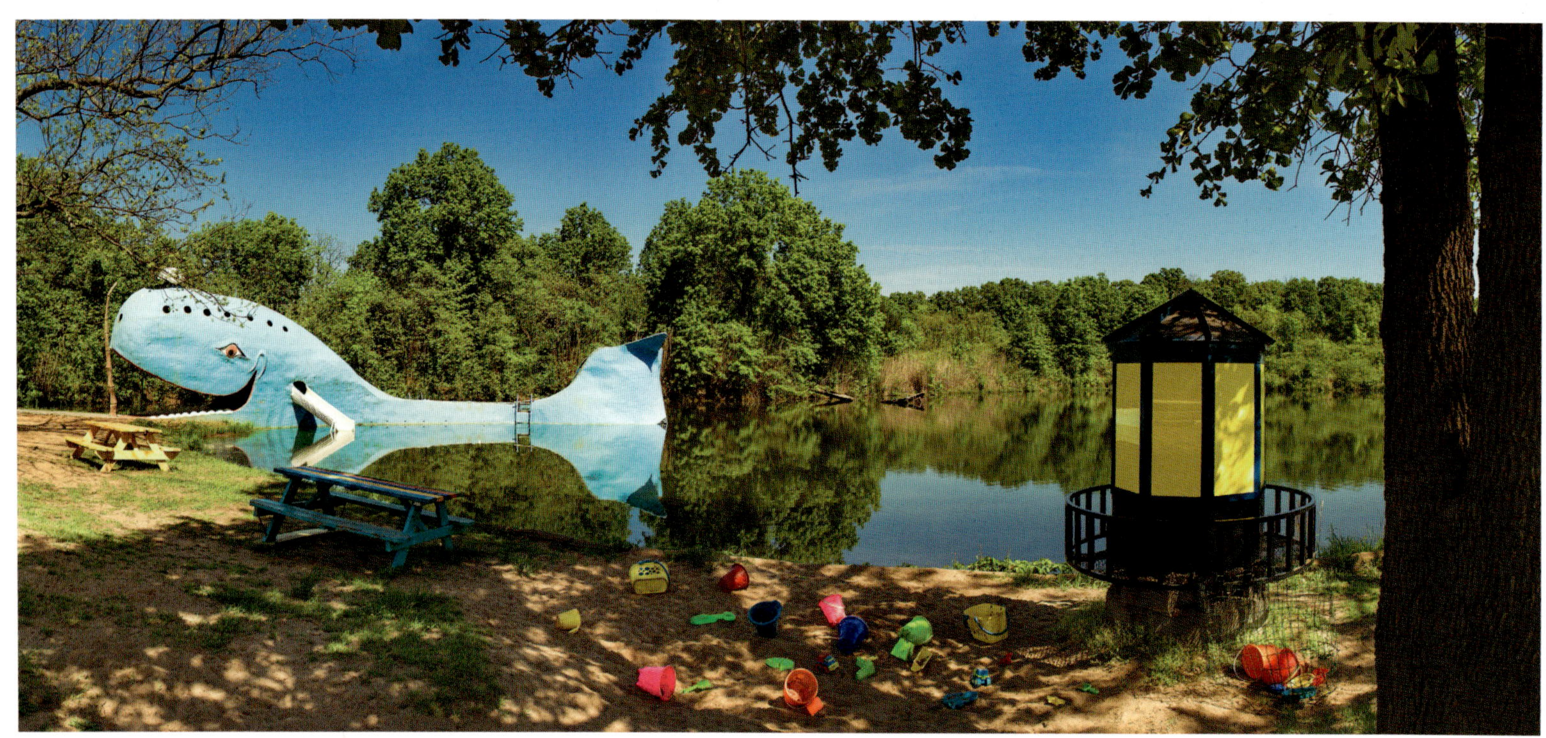

Blue whale of Catoosa, Route 66, Oklahoma

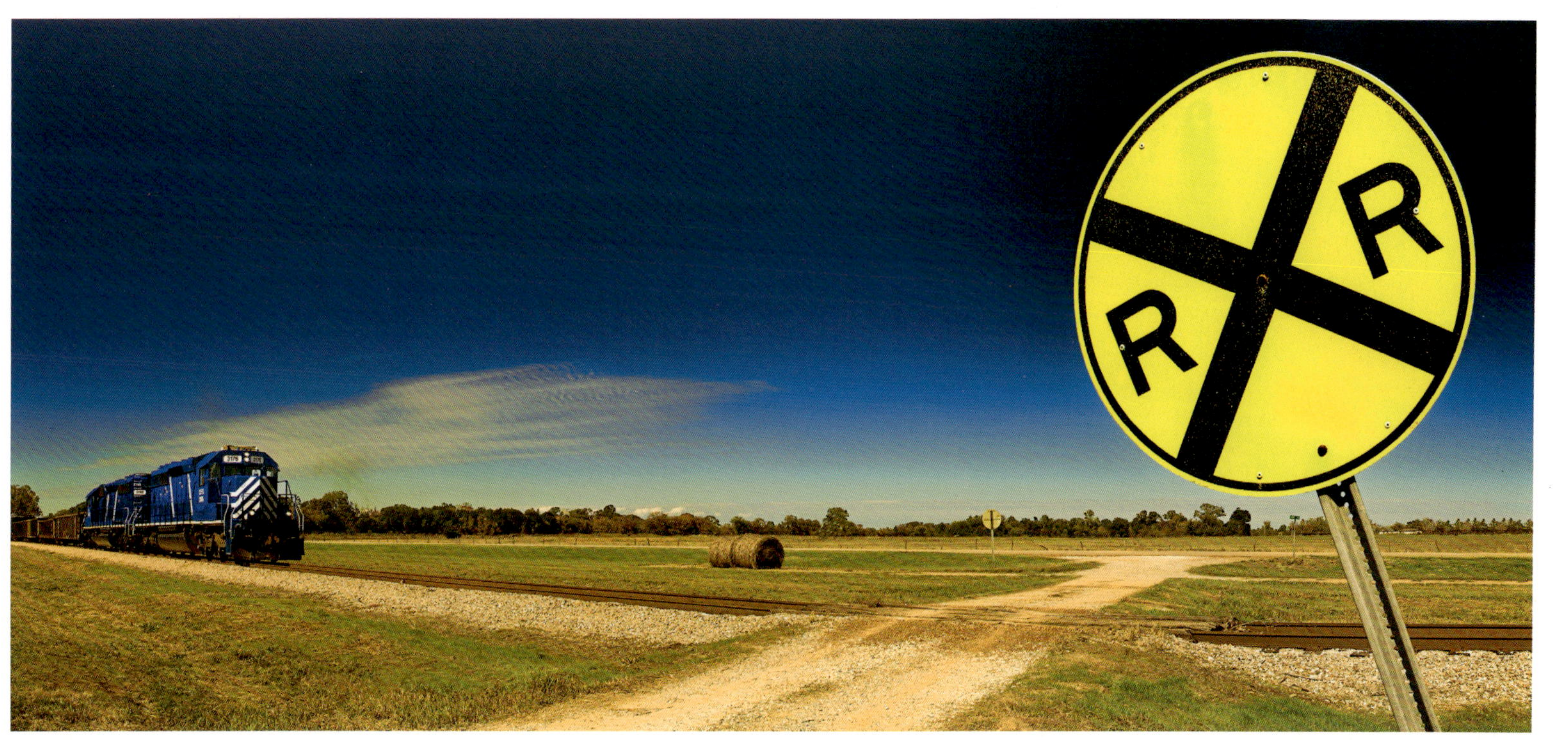

Train along Oklahoma State Highway 70

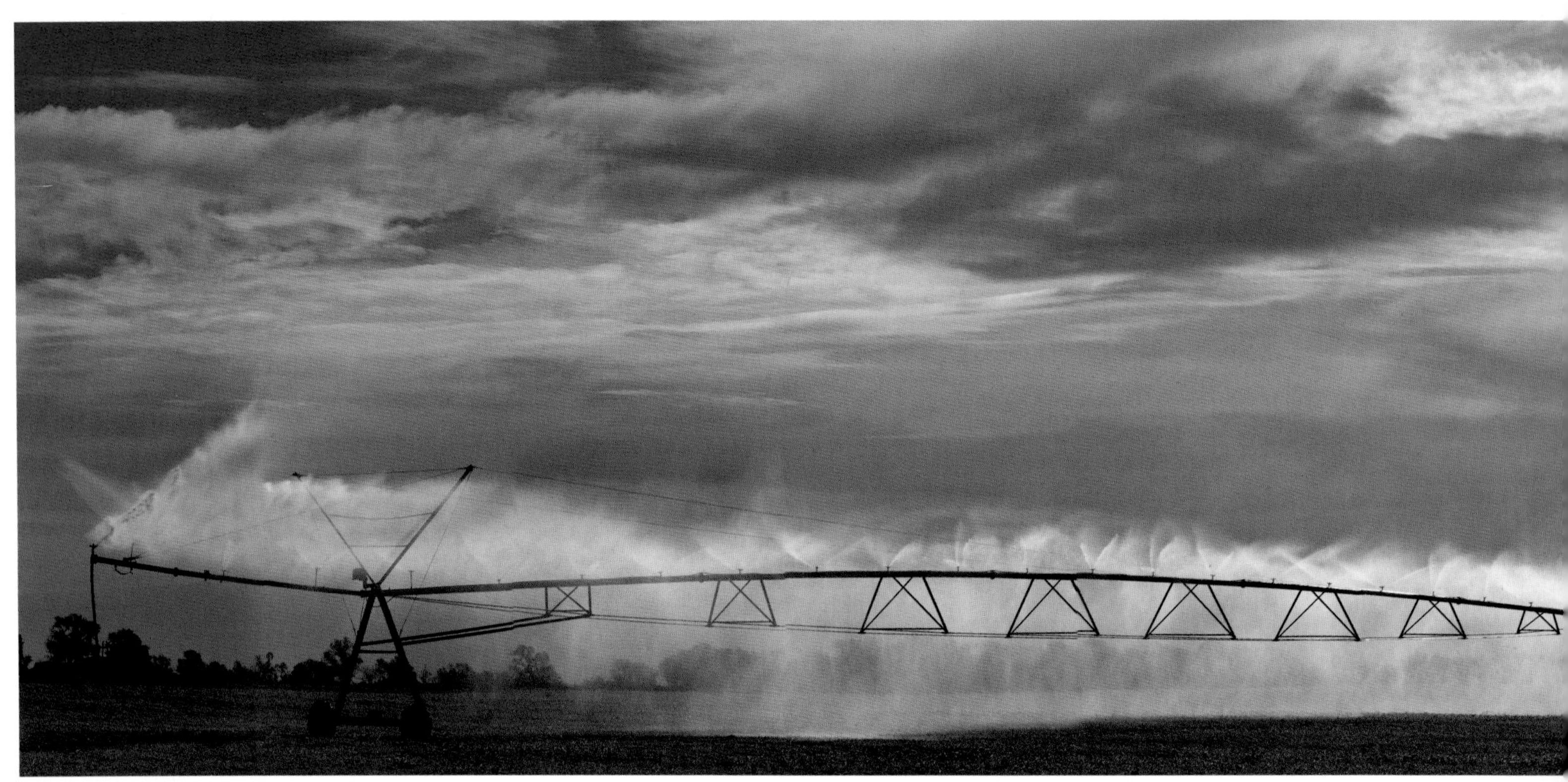

Sprinklers on a stormy day, Oklahoma

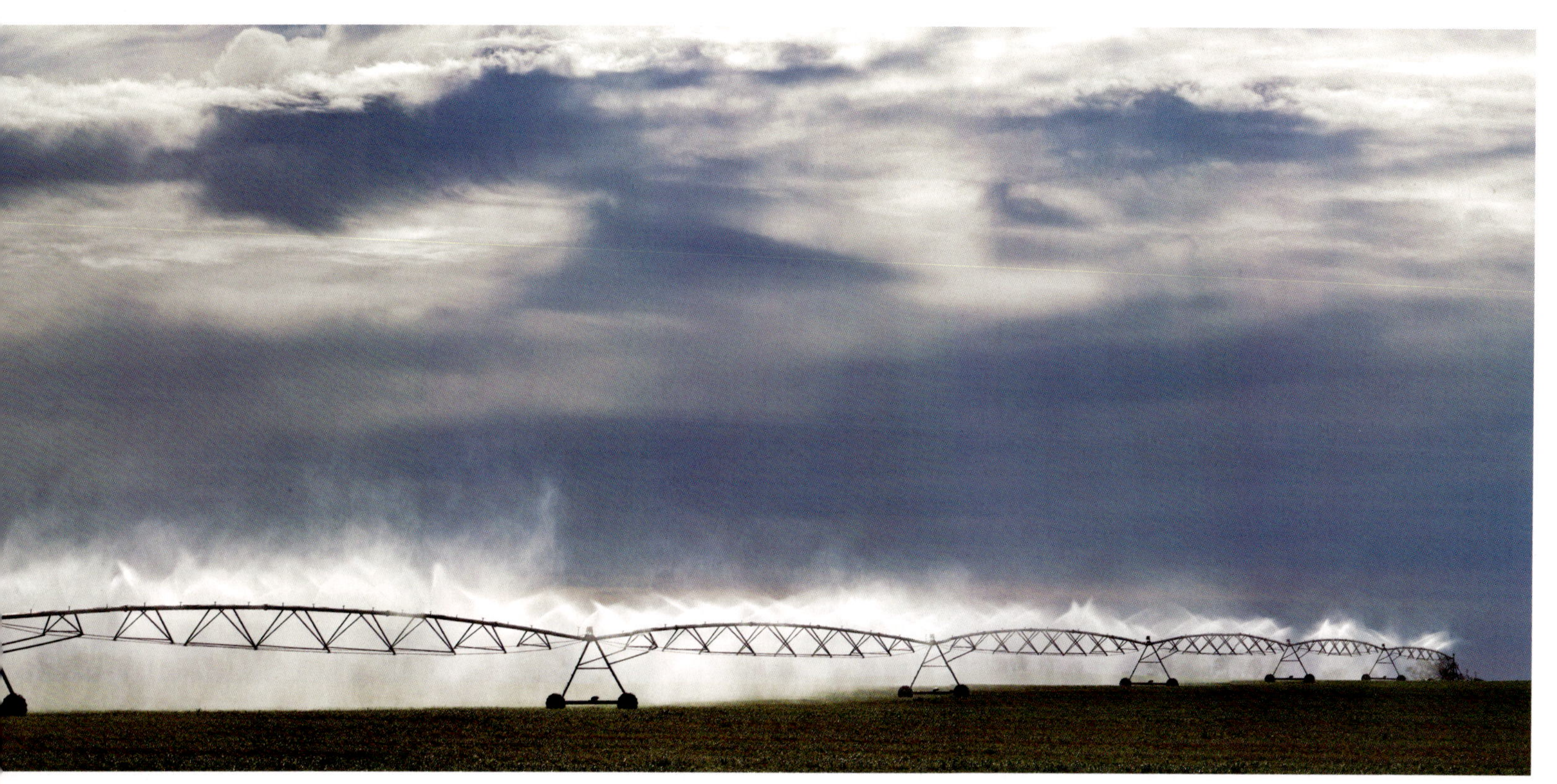

These irrigation systems always catch my attention. The light and the wind made this one worth the stop.

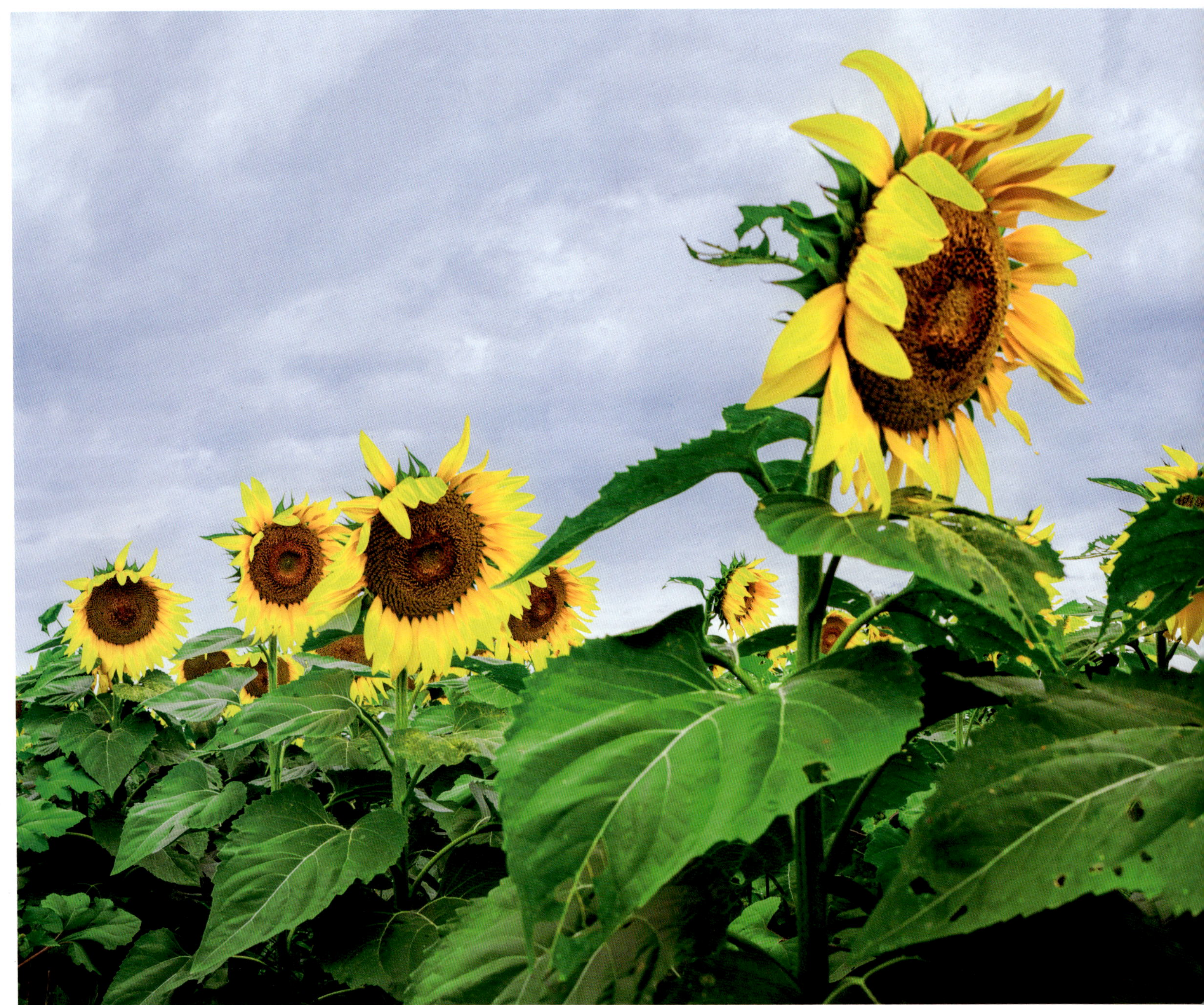

Sunflower field, Kansas

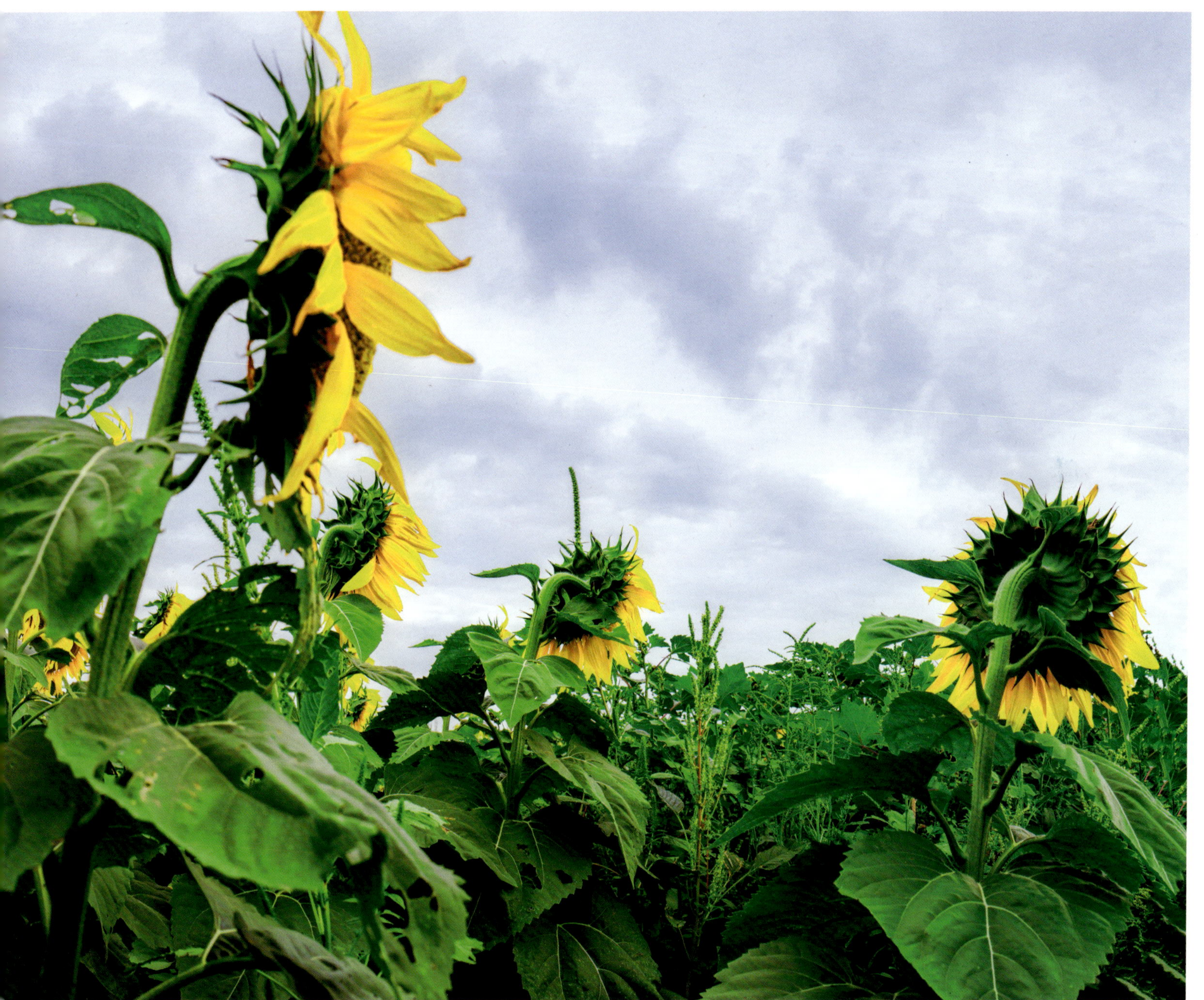

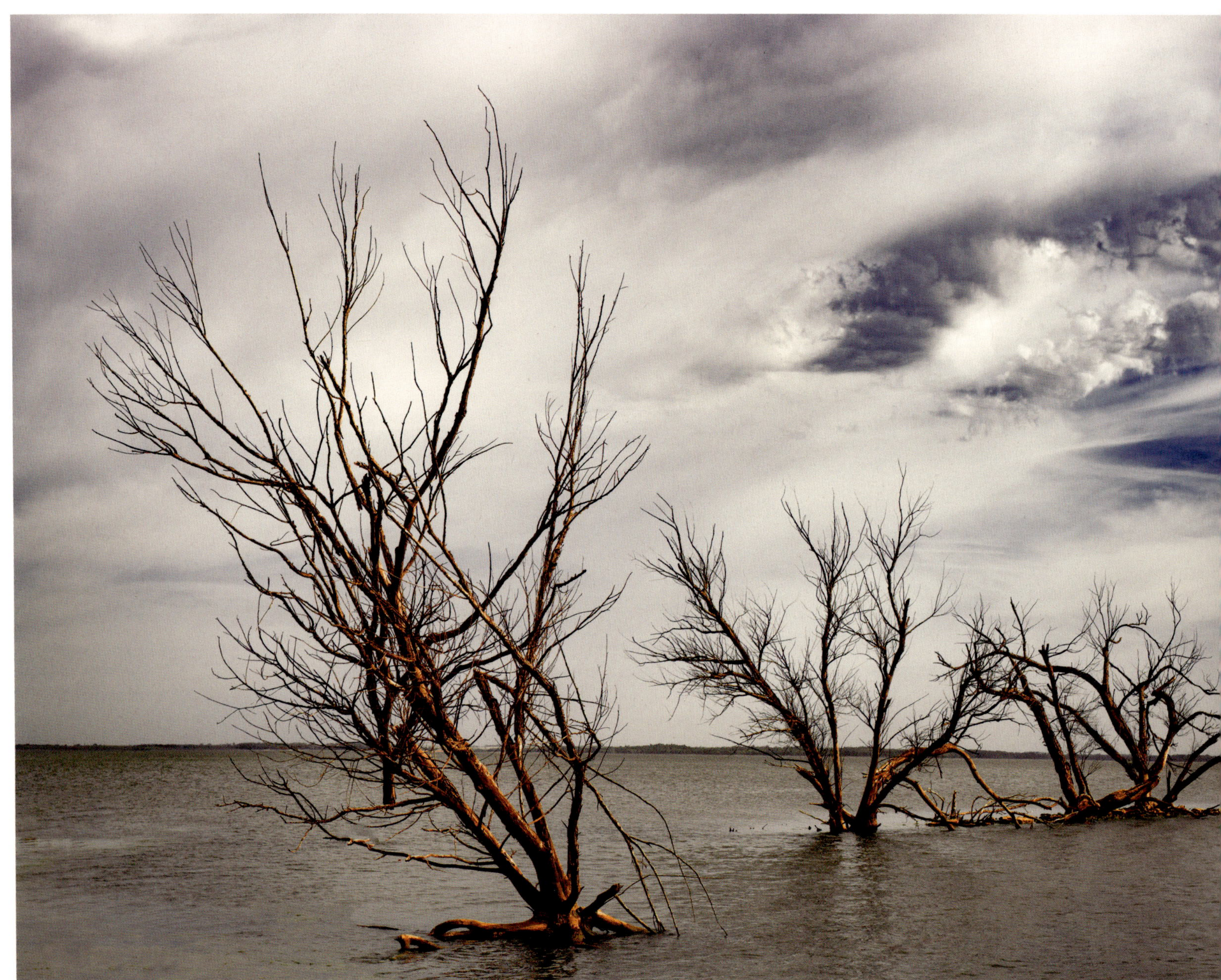

Otter Creek, John Redmond Reservoir, Kansas

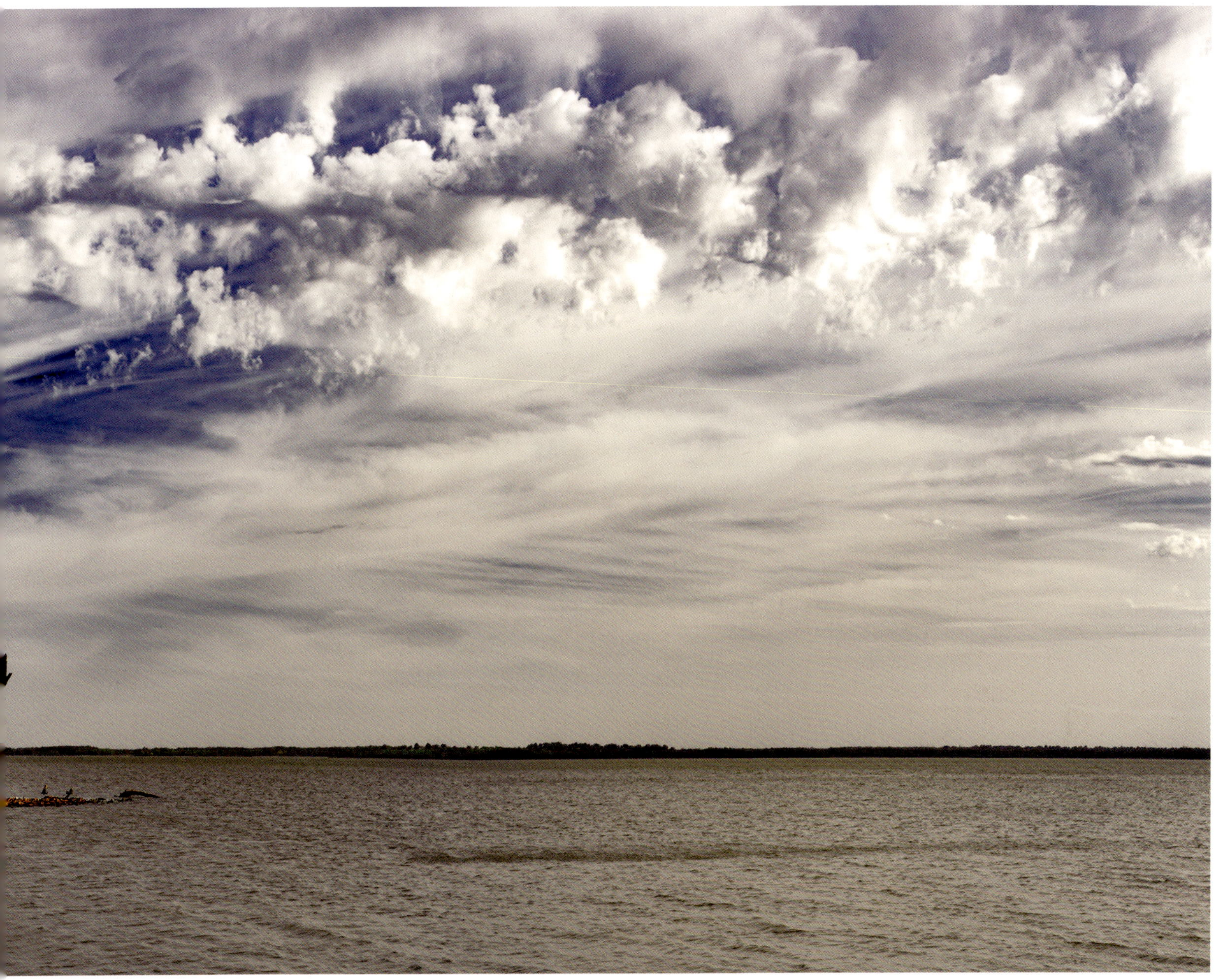

I was so happy to find something to photograph in the foreground of that cloud that I was sort of whooping. A couple of fishermen came over to make fun of me, but when I pointed out the cloud, they "got it" and we all whooped together.

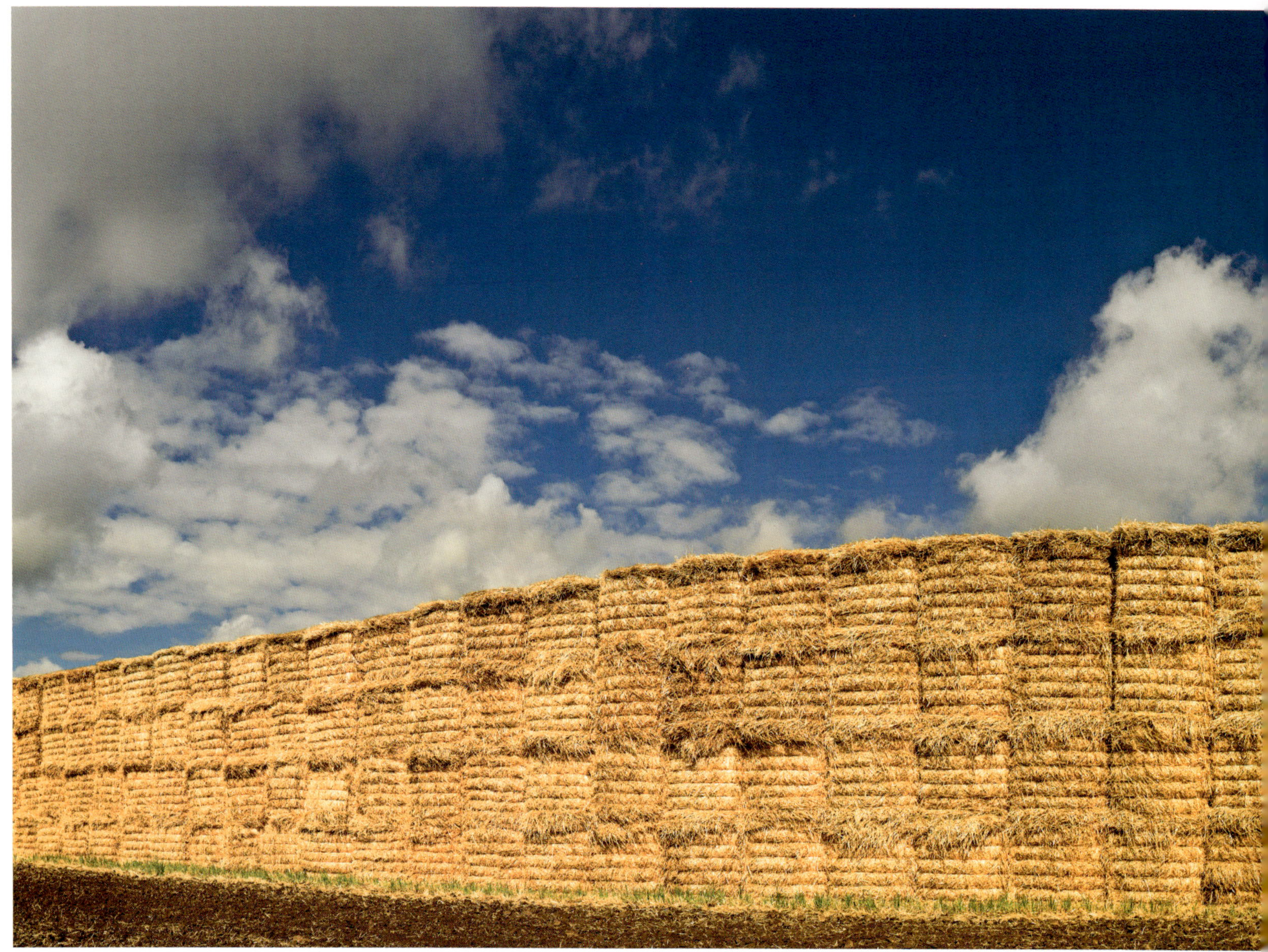

Giant haystacks, Kansas

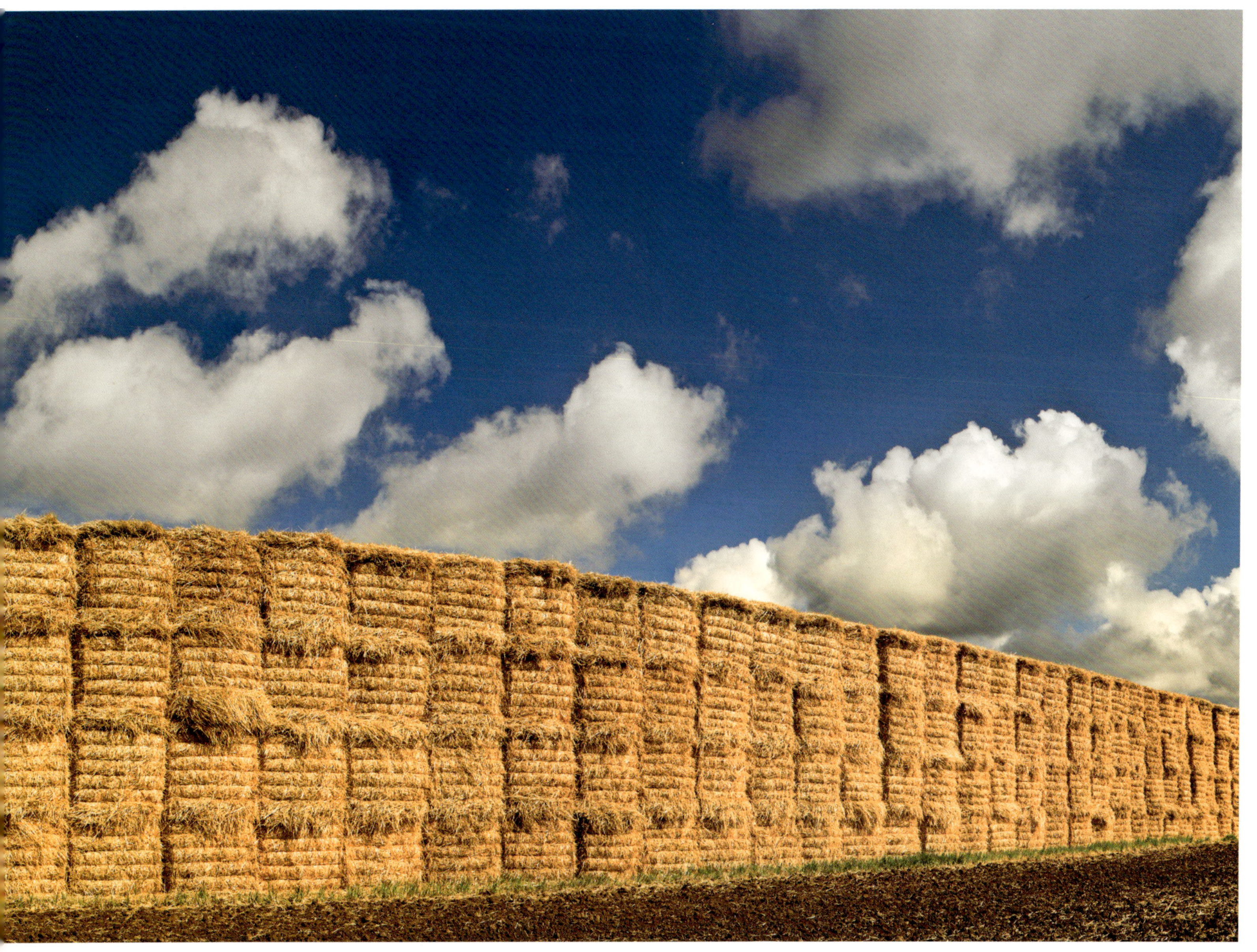

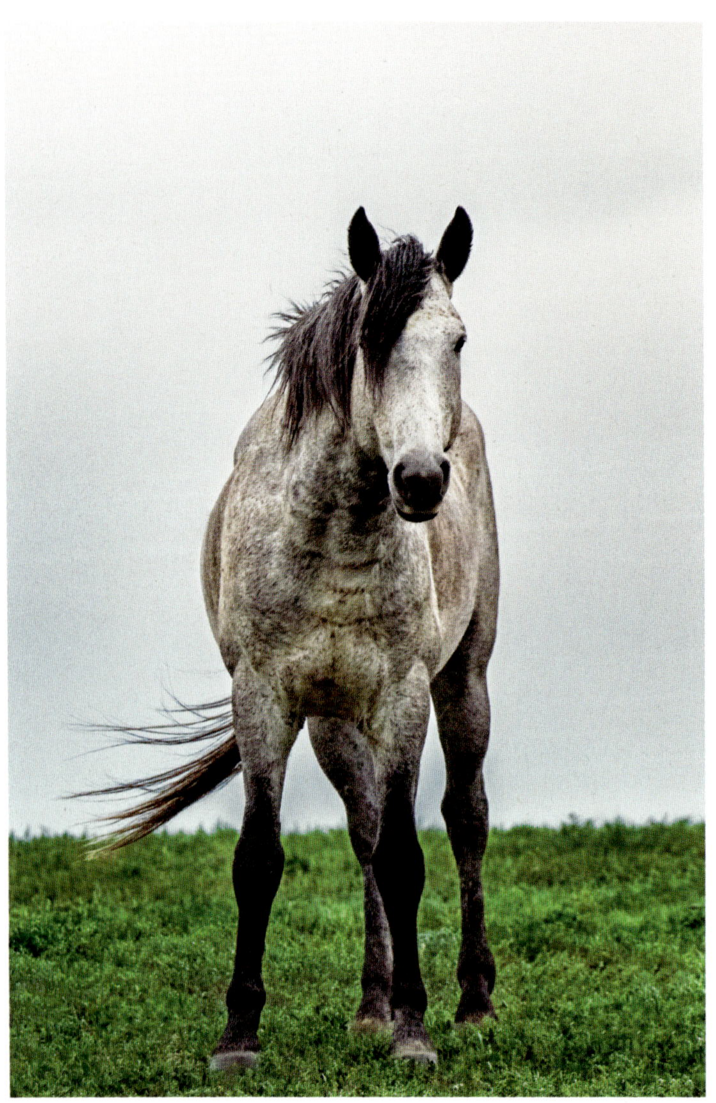

Wild horse, Theodore Roosevelt National Park, North Dakota

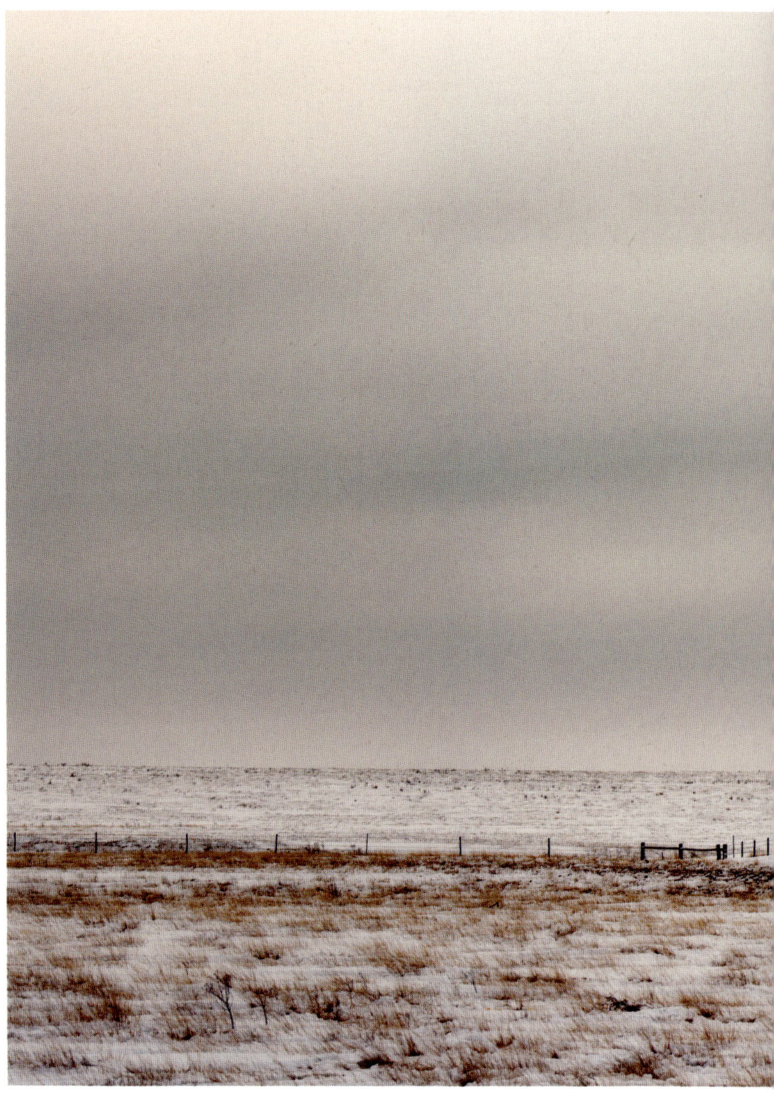

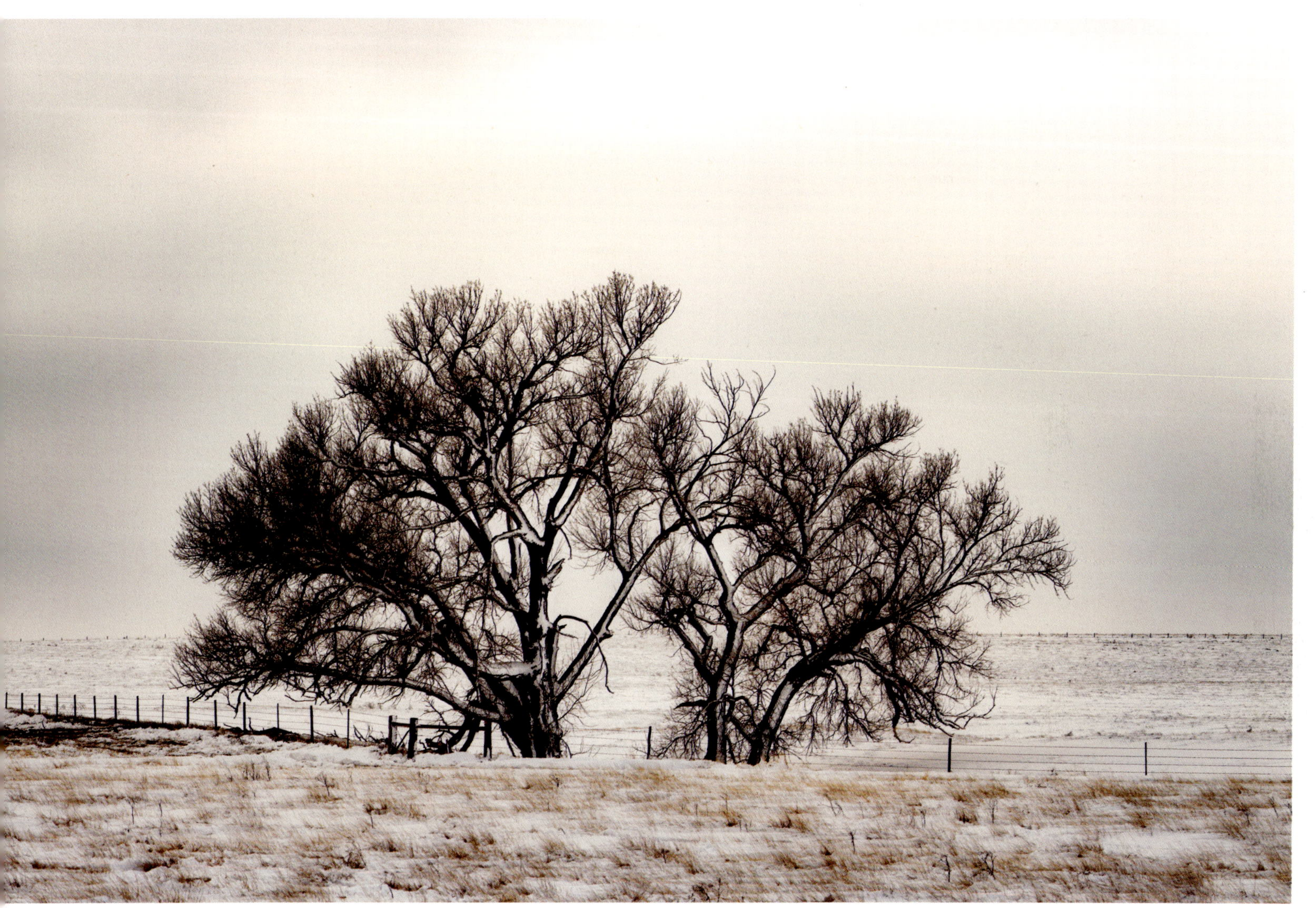

Tree and fence, Kansas State Highway 23

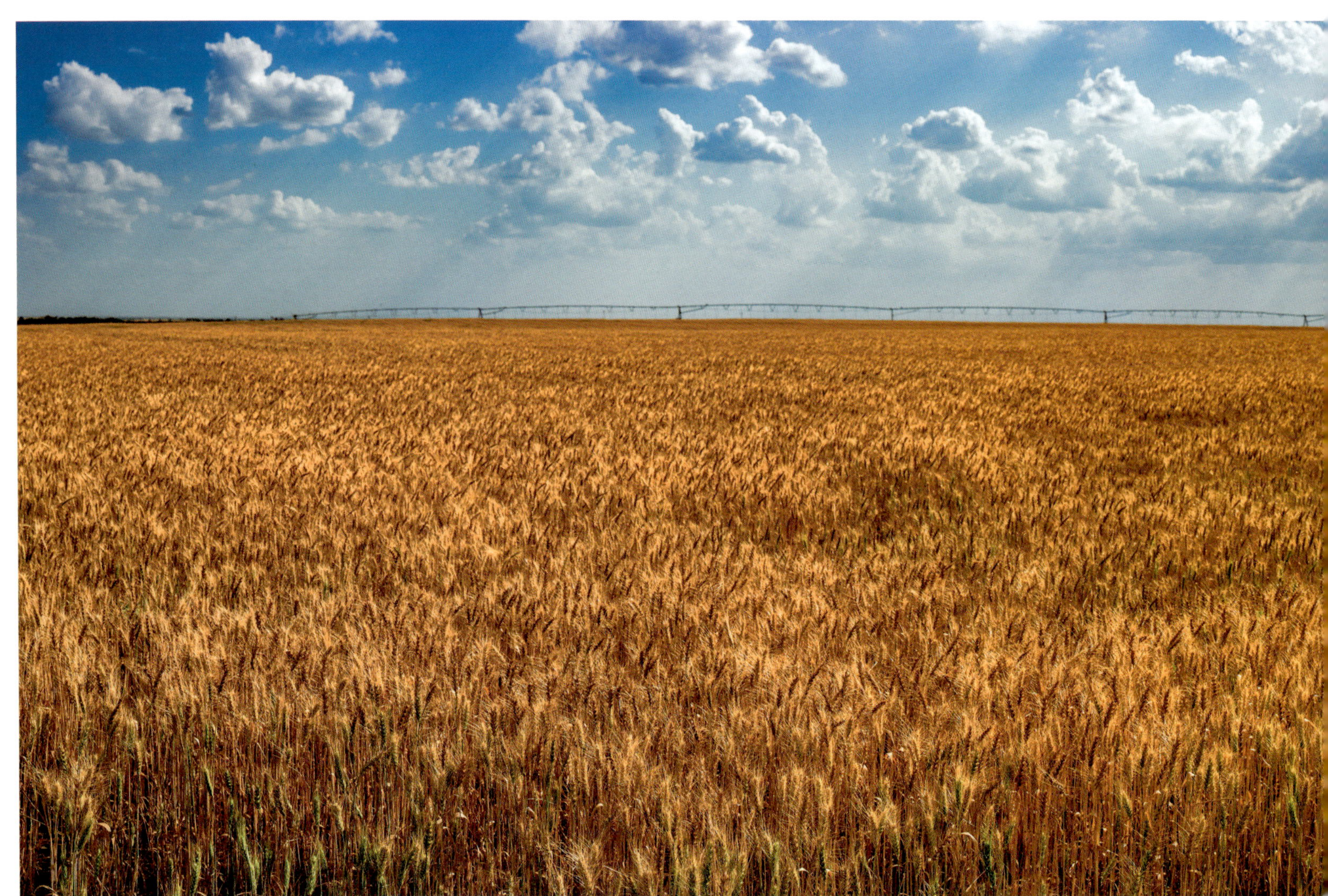

Wheat field, 180th Street, Minneapolis, Kansas

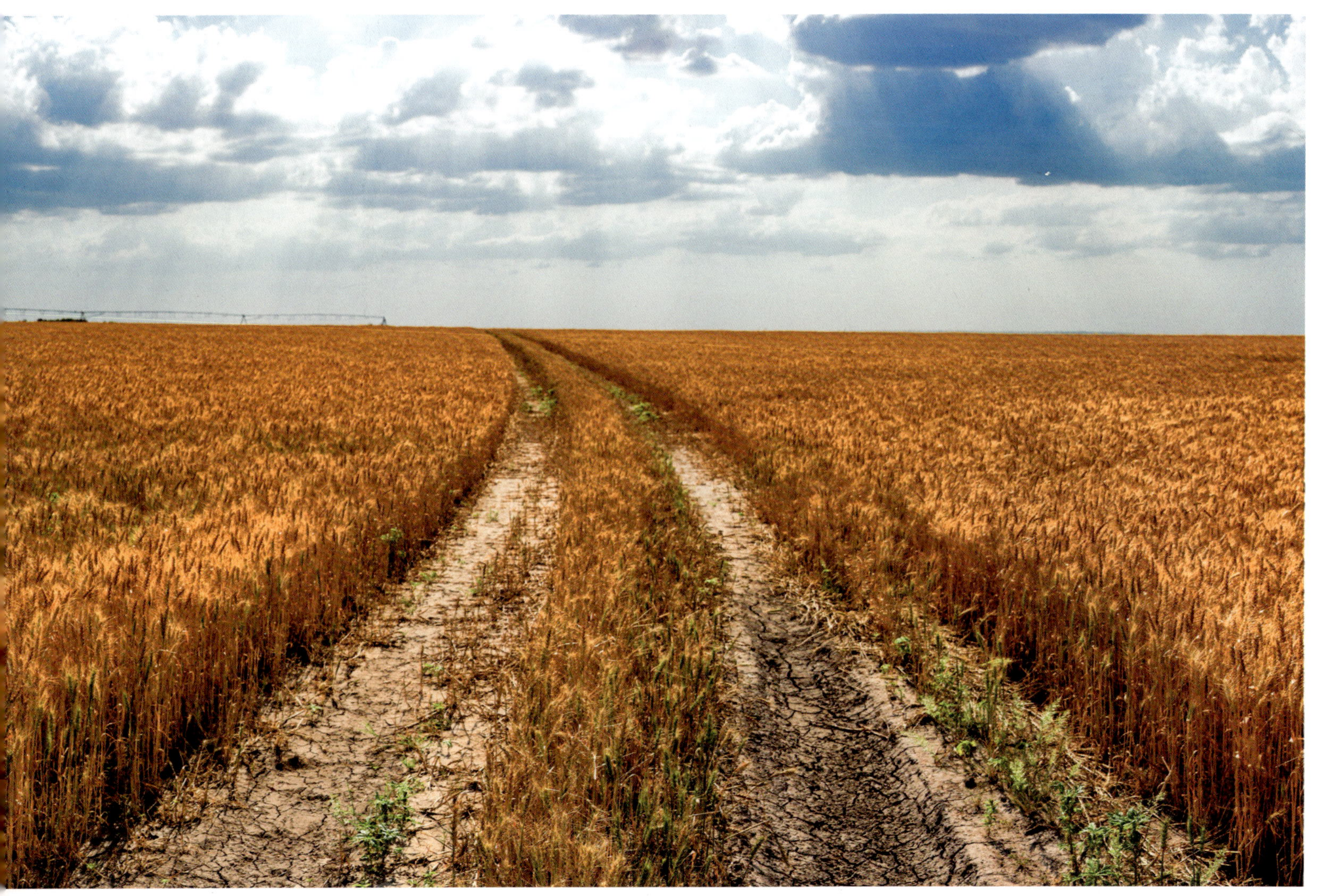

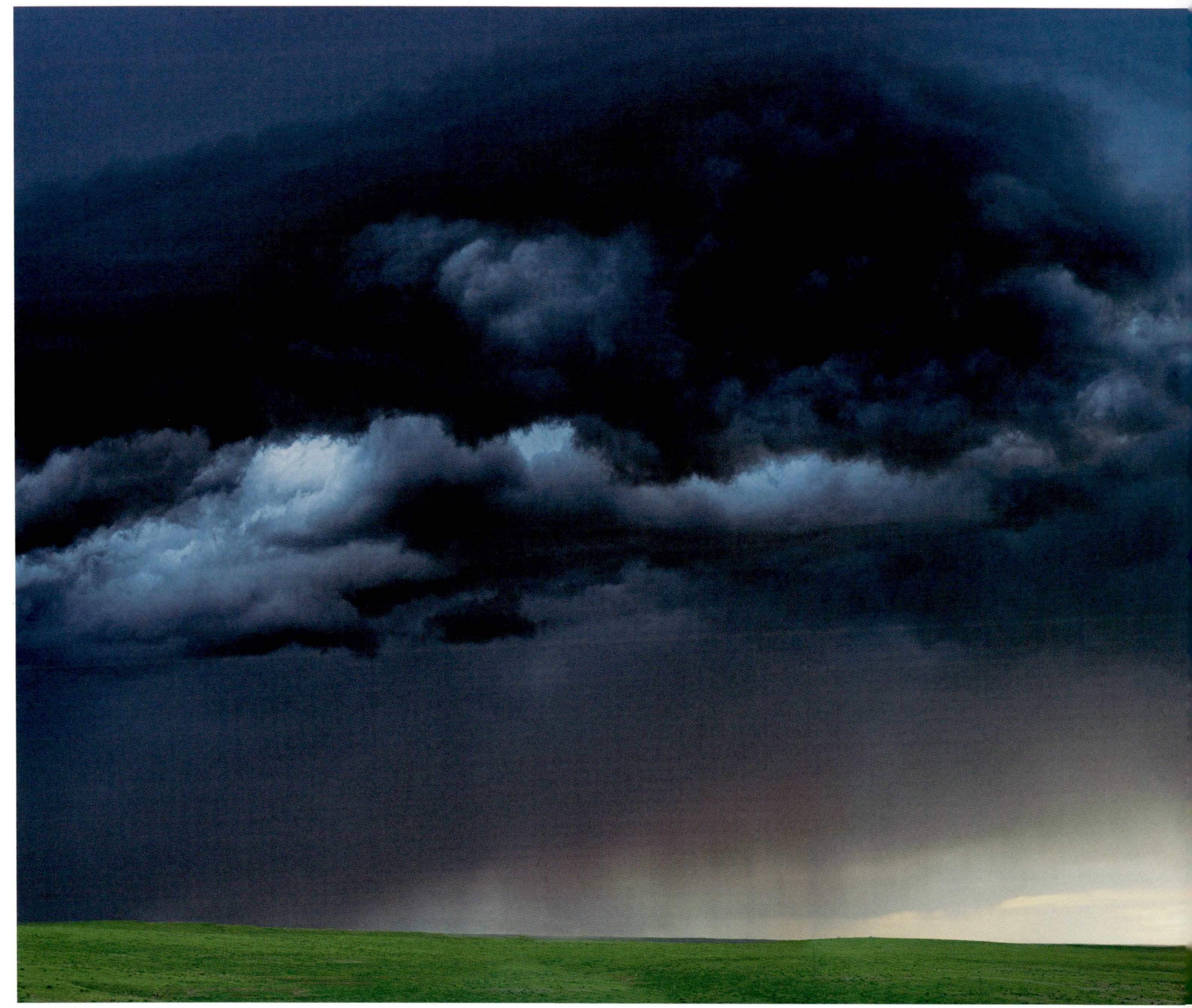

Storm over the Great Plains

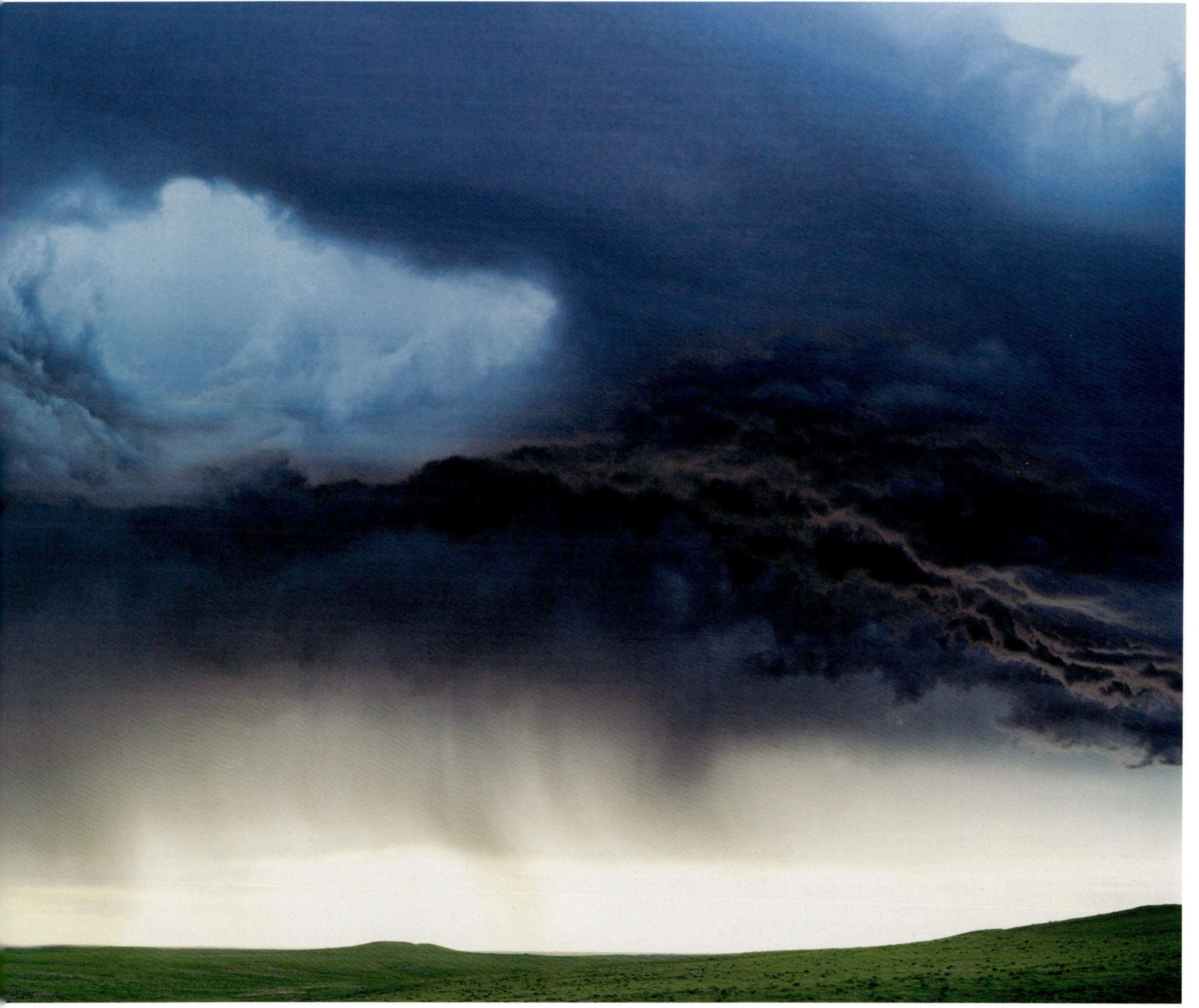

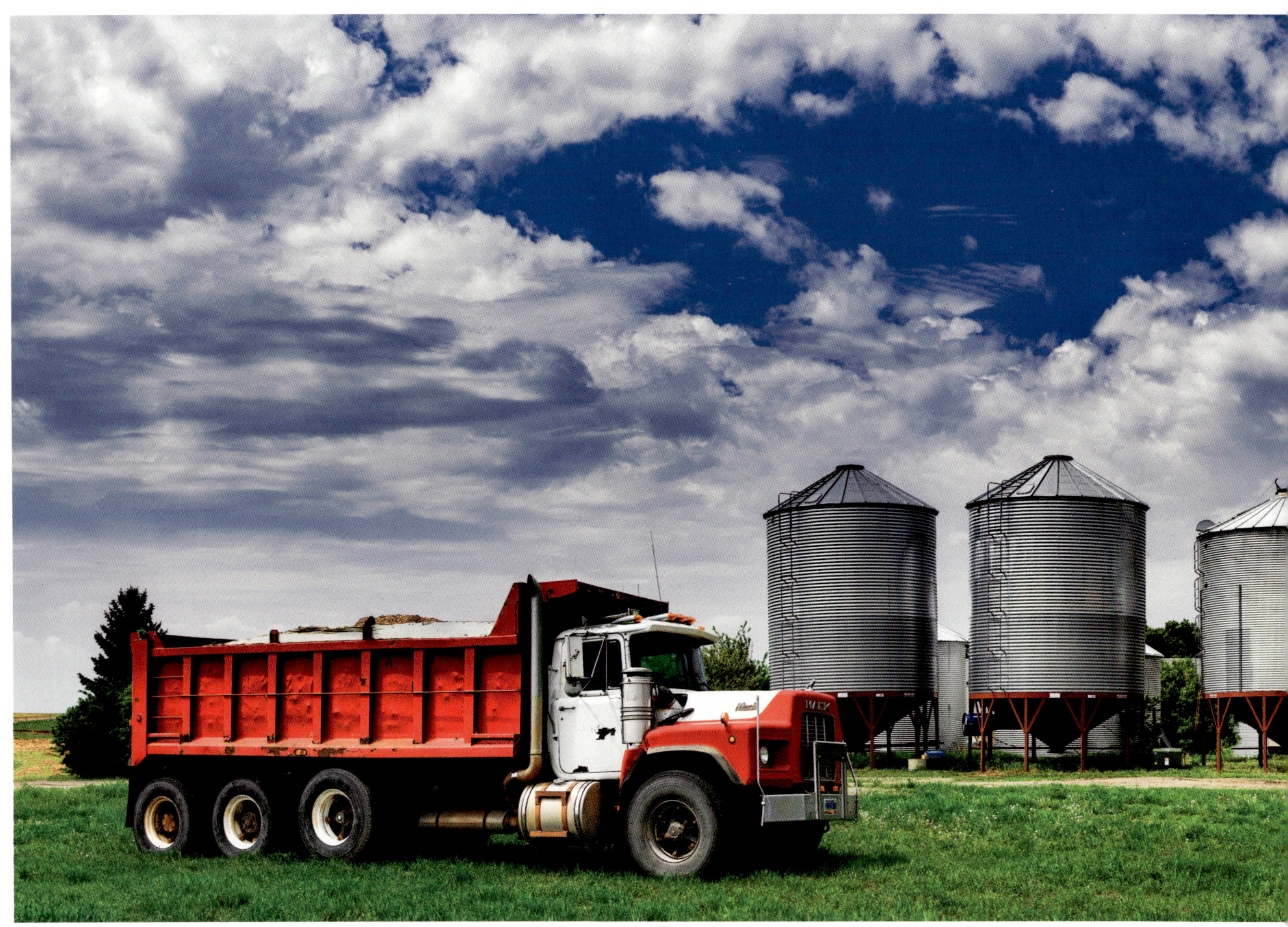

Trucks and silos, Kansas

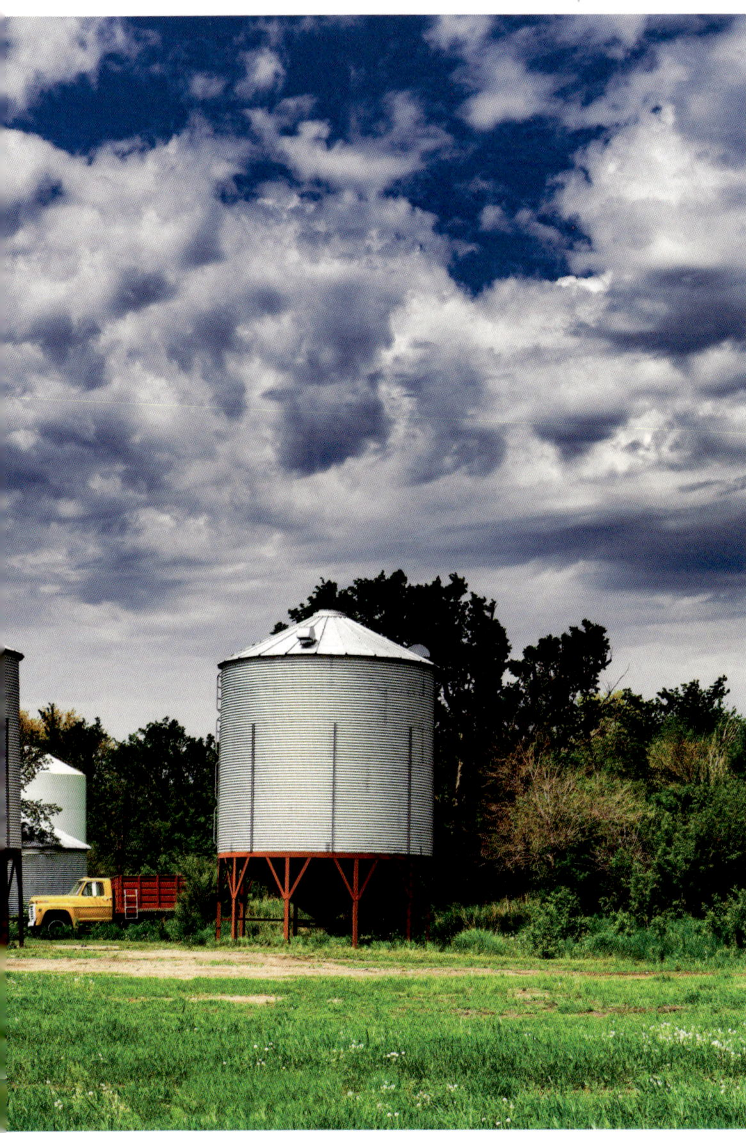

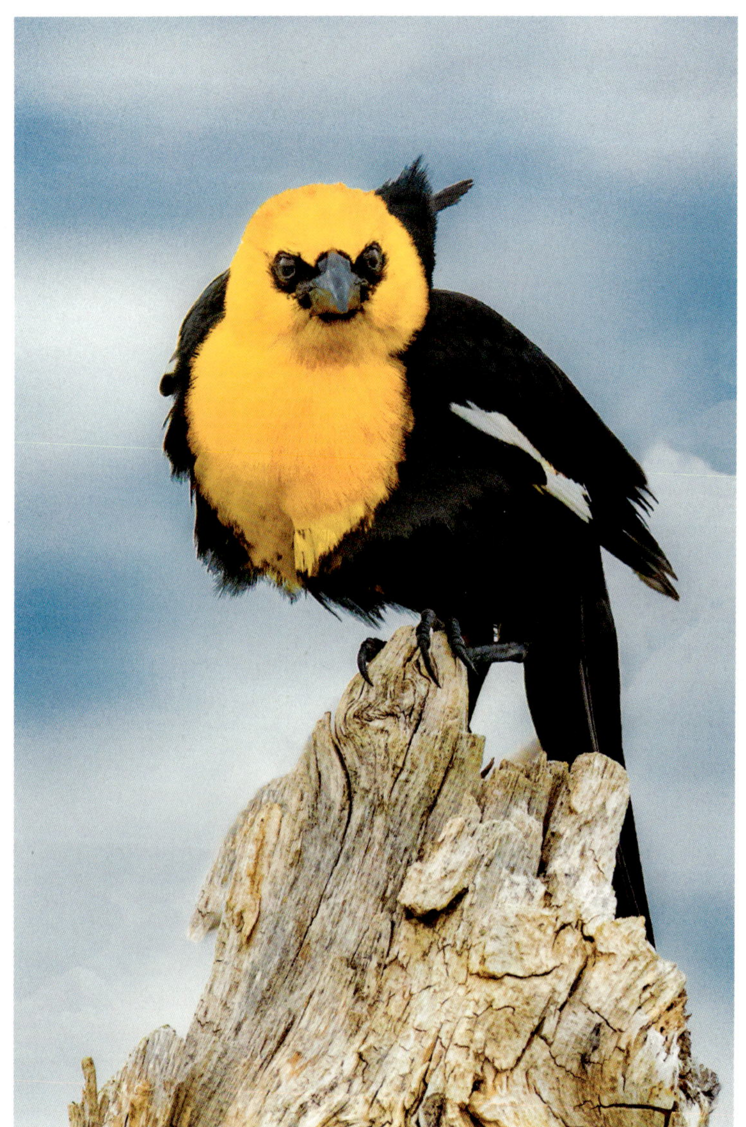

Yellow-headed blackbird, Kansas

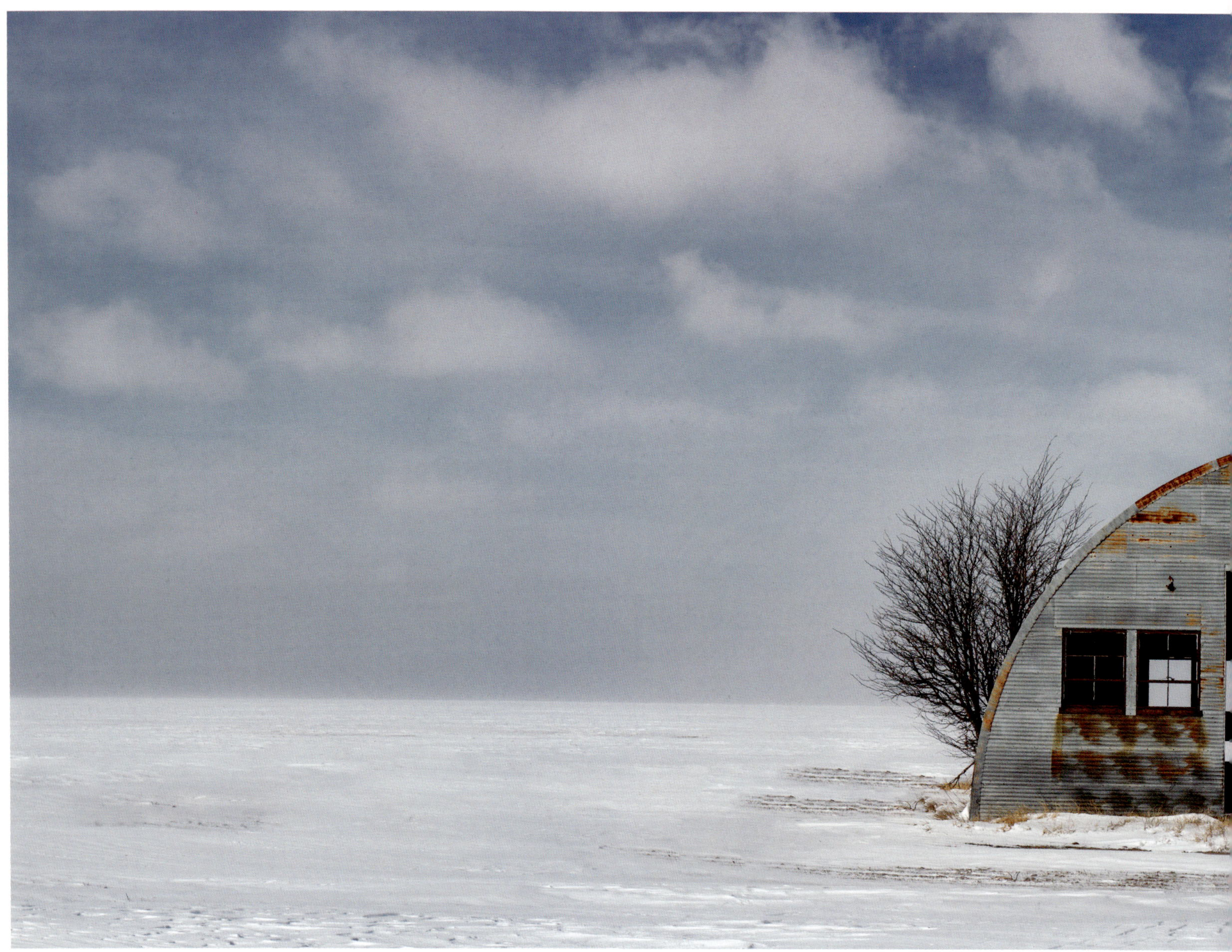

Frozen barn, Kansas State Highway 25

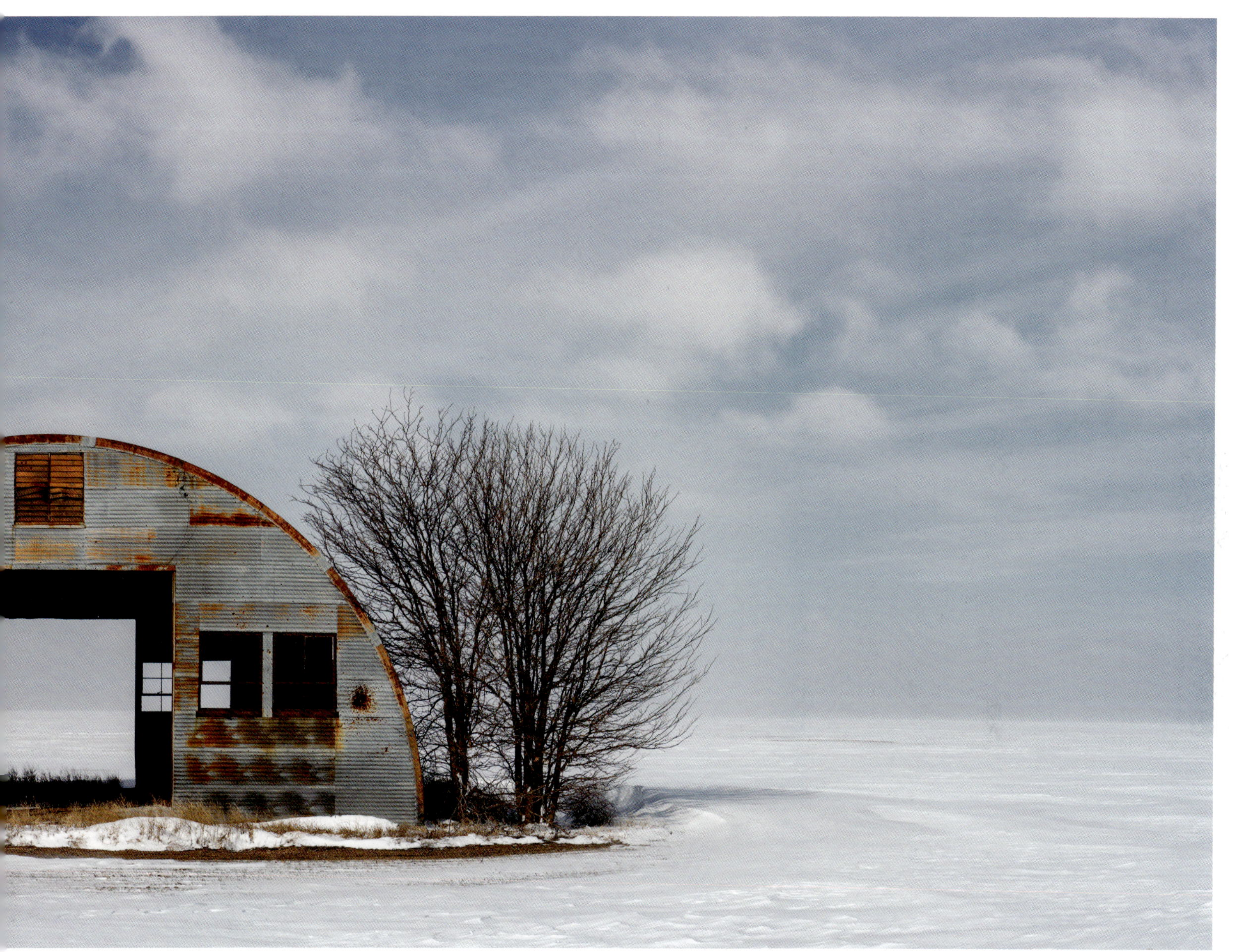

It was cold, minus 16 degrees. I think it needs to be that cold to look that cold.

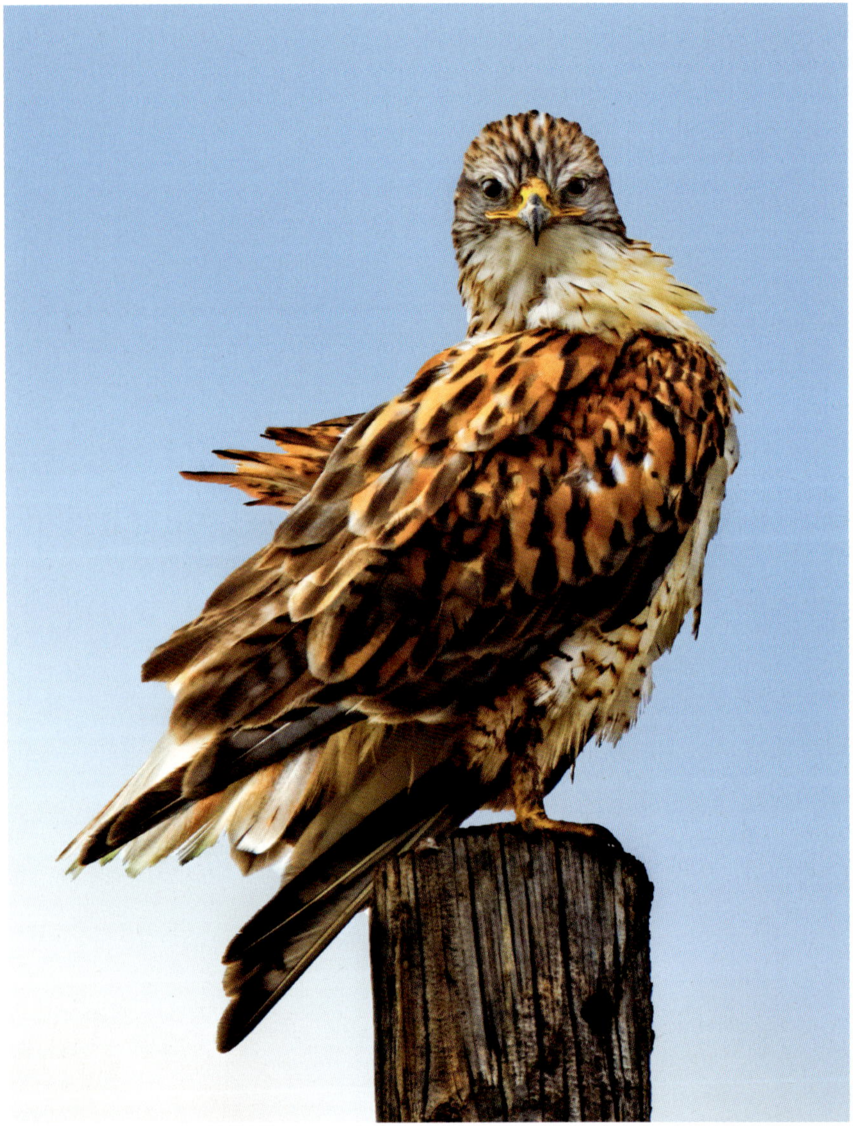

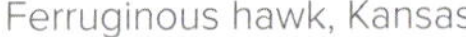

Ferruginous hawk, Kansas

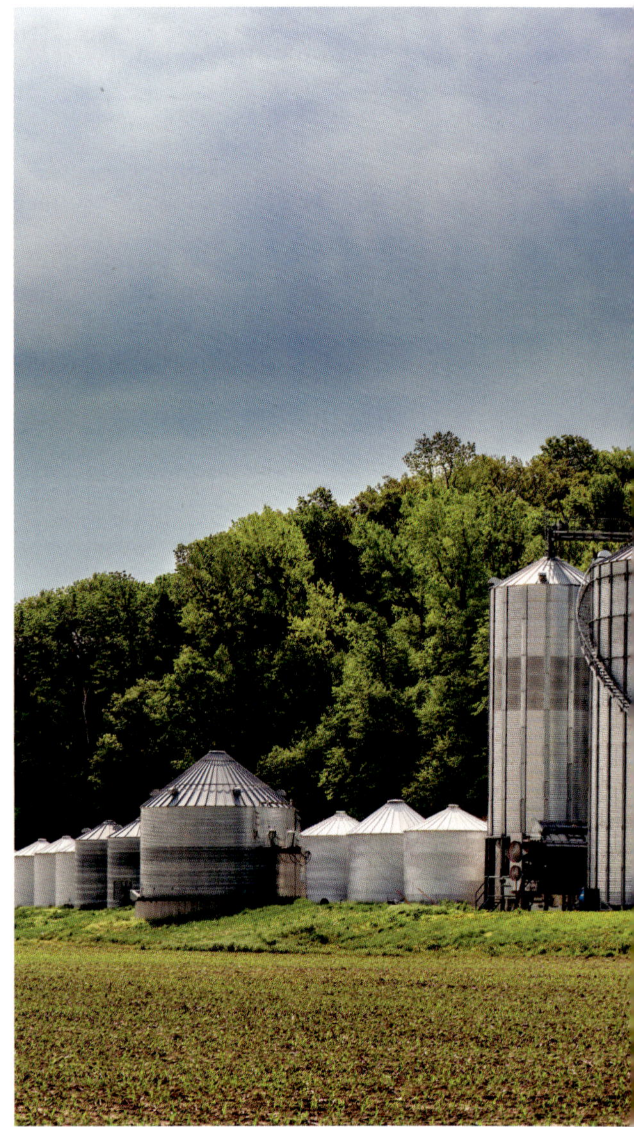

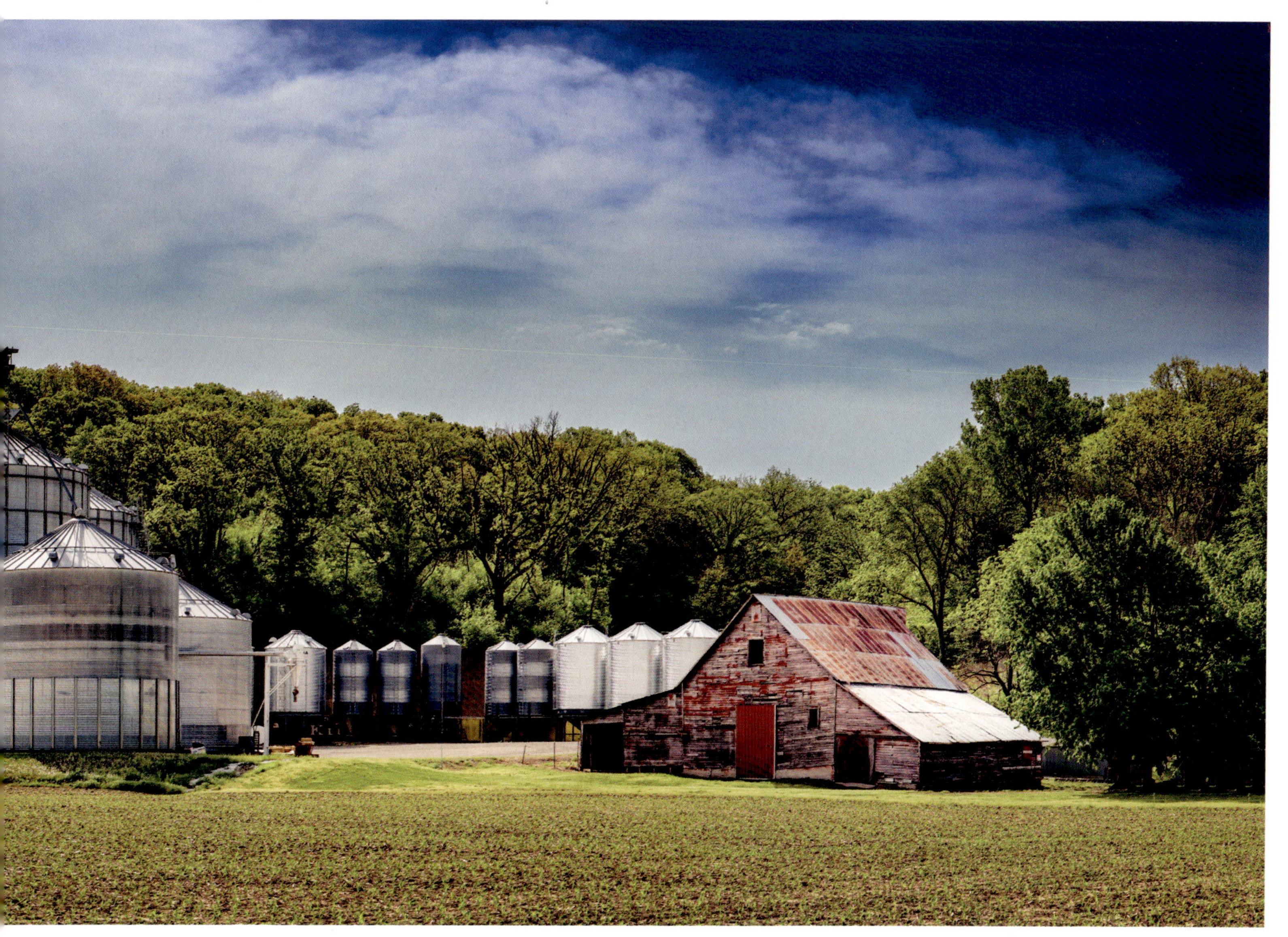

Barn and silos, White Cloud, Kansas

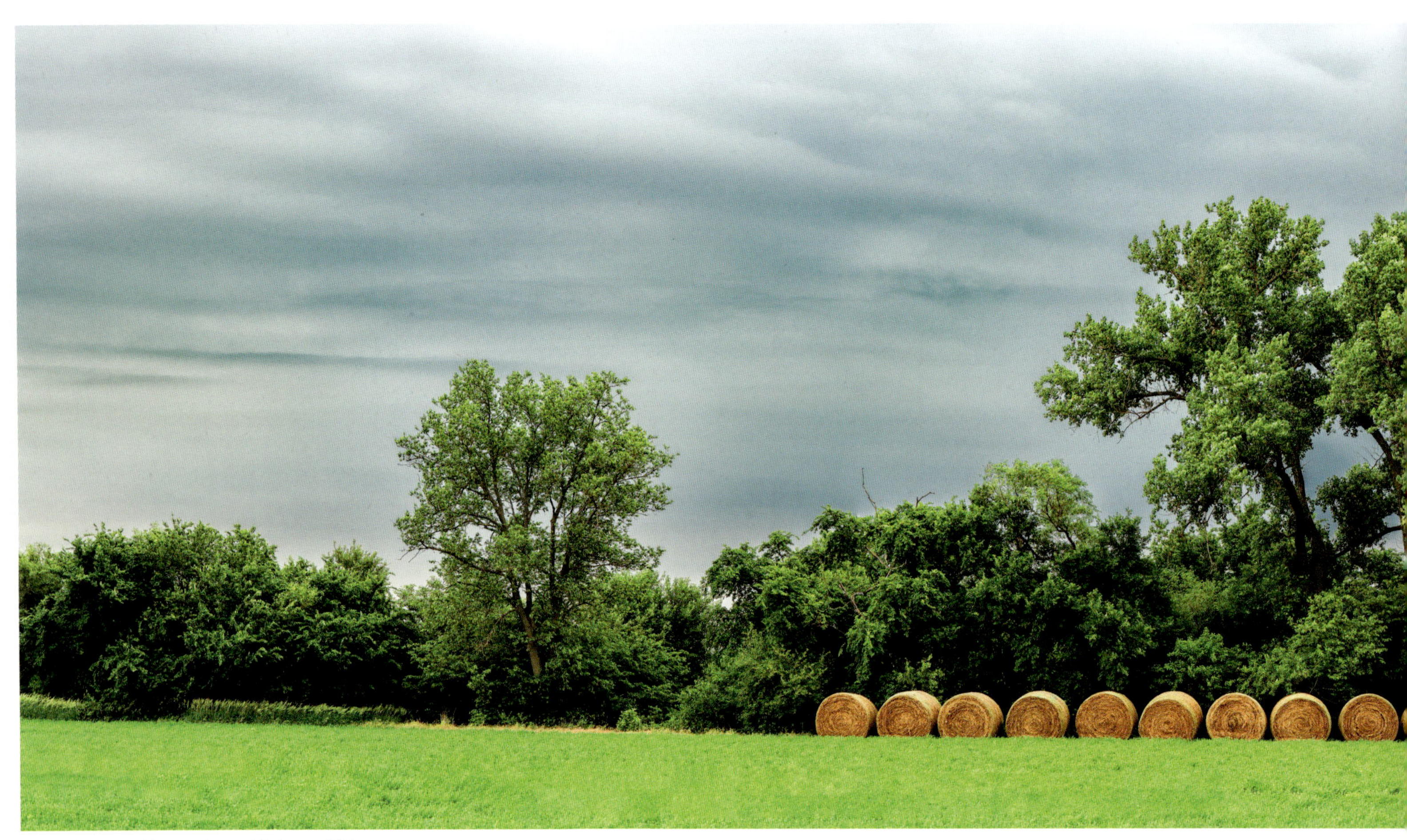

Hay rolls along Kansas State Highway 284

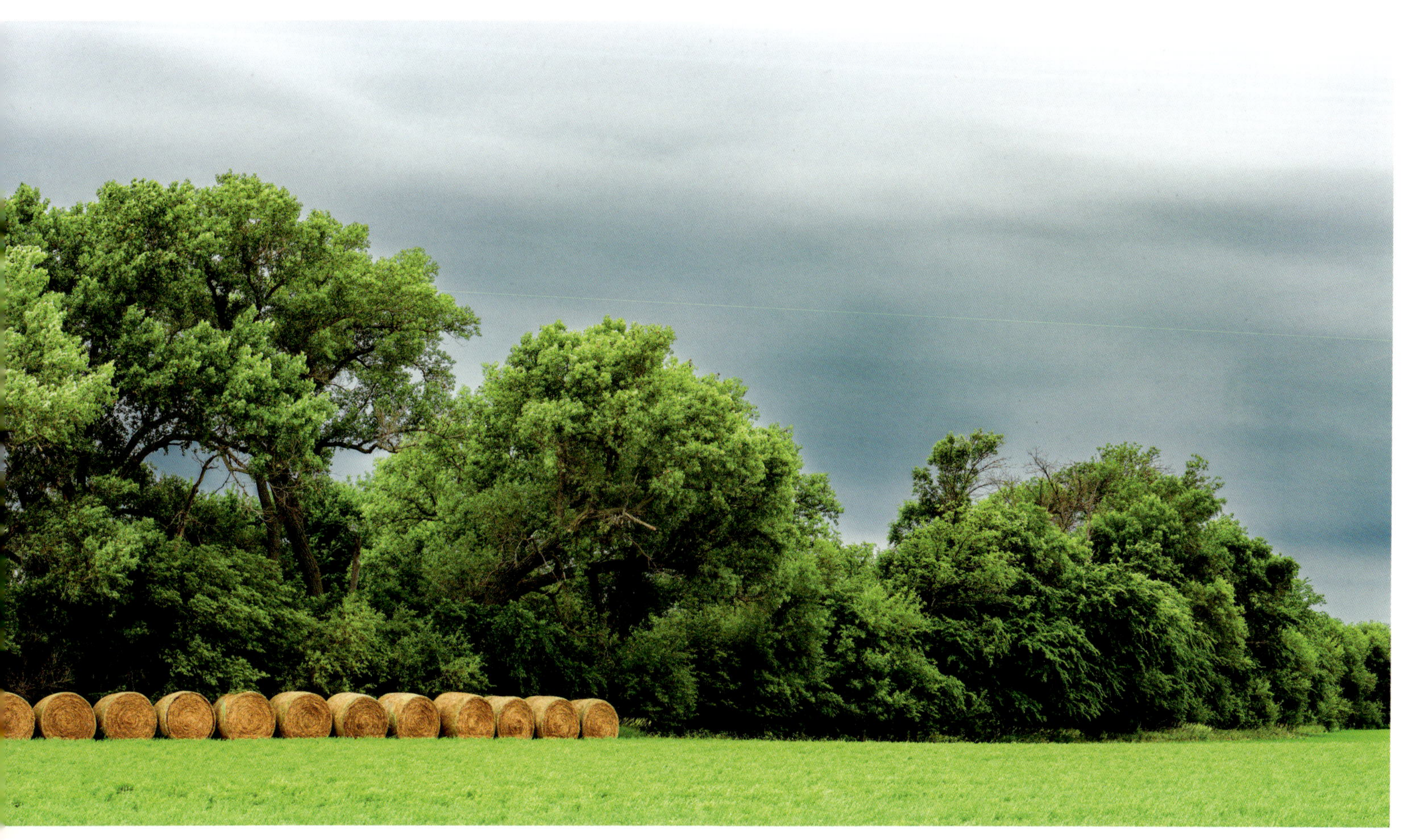

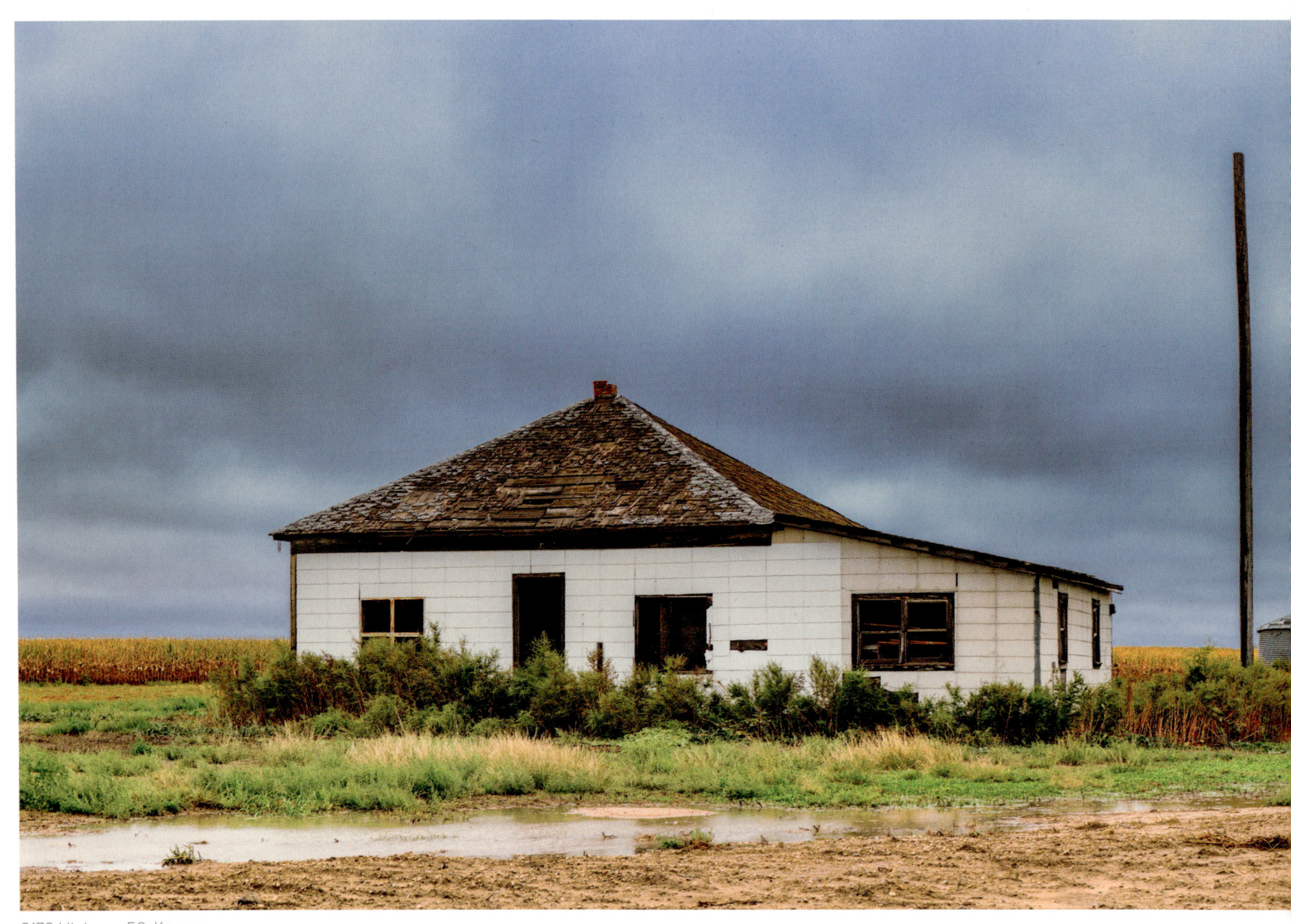

2178 Highway 50, Kansas

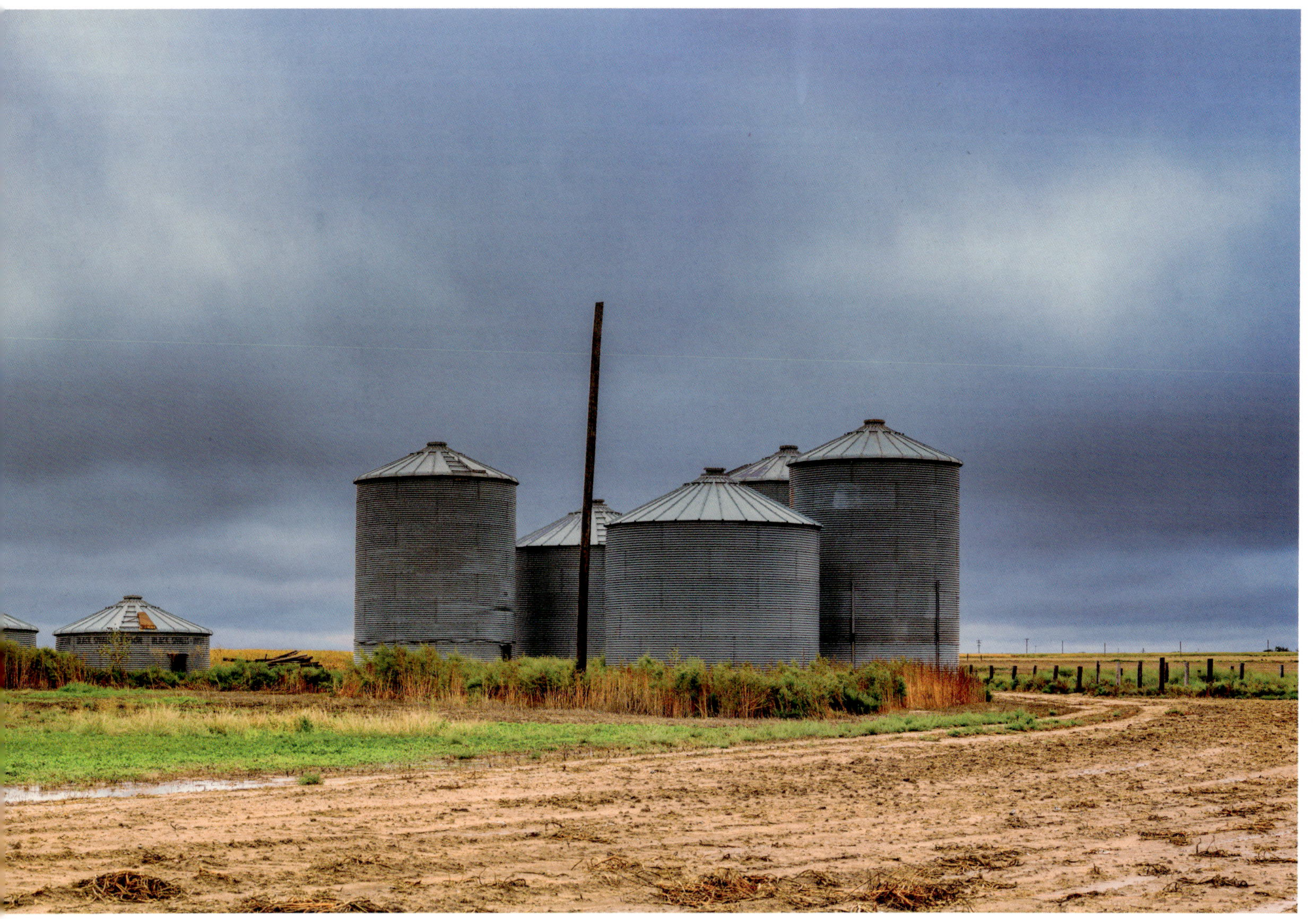

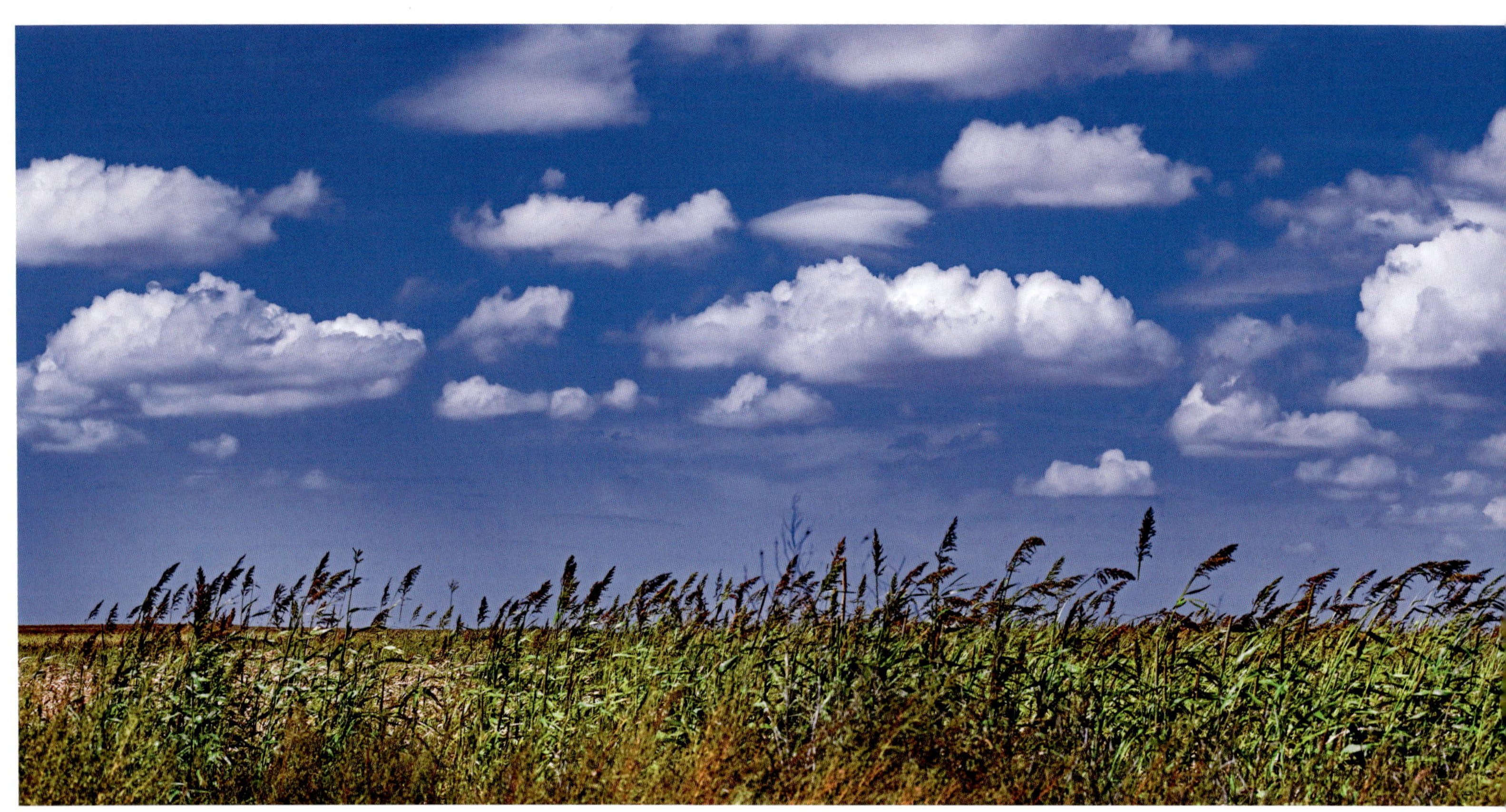

Johnson grass along Kansas State Highway 1

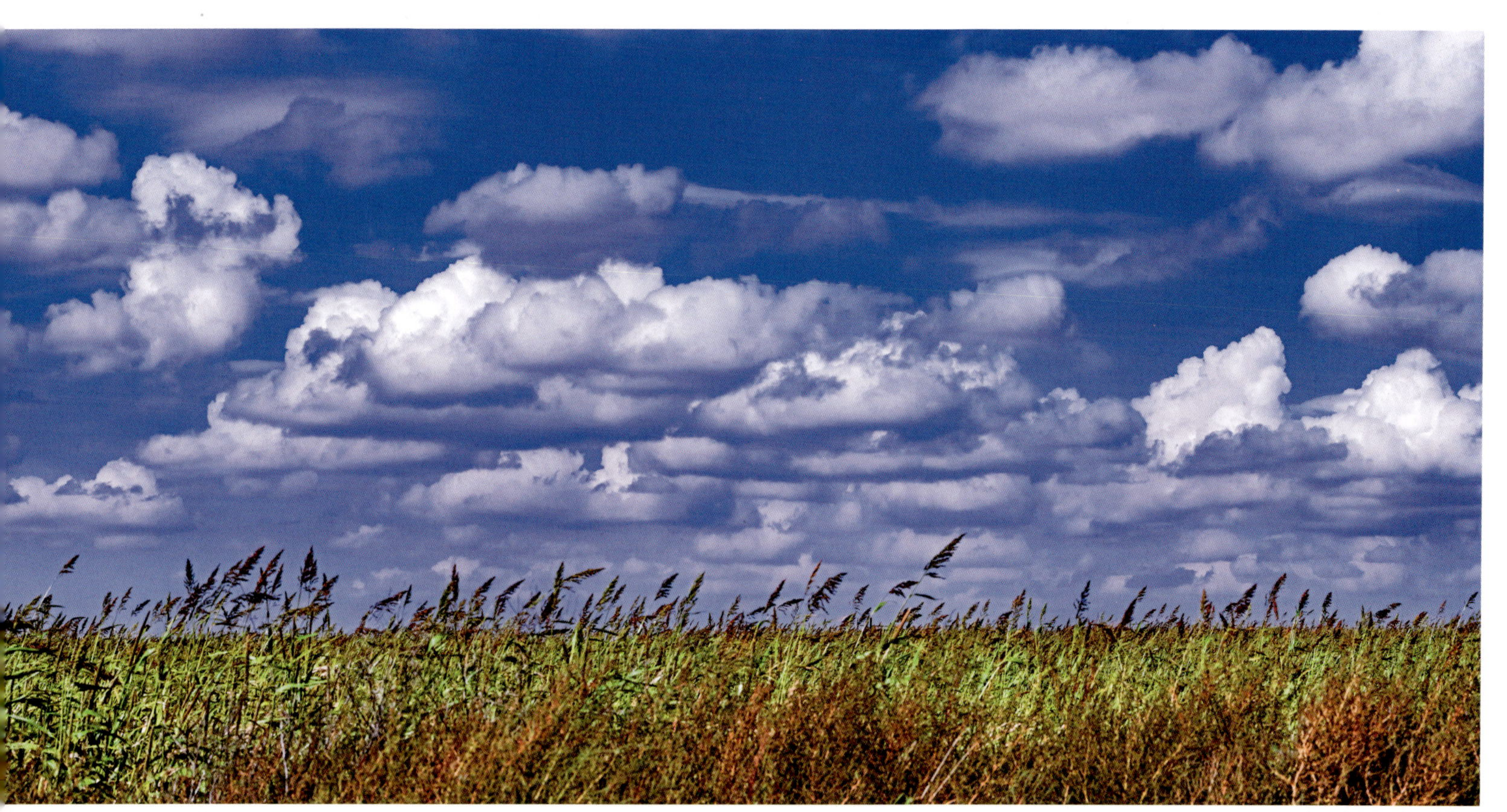

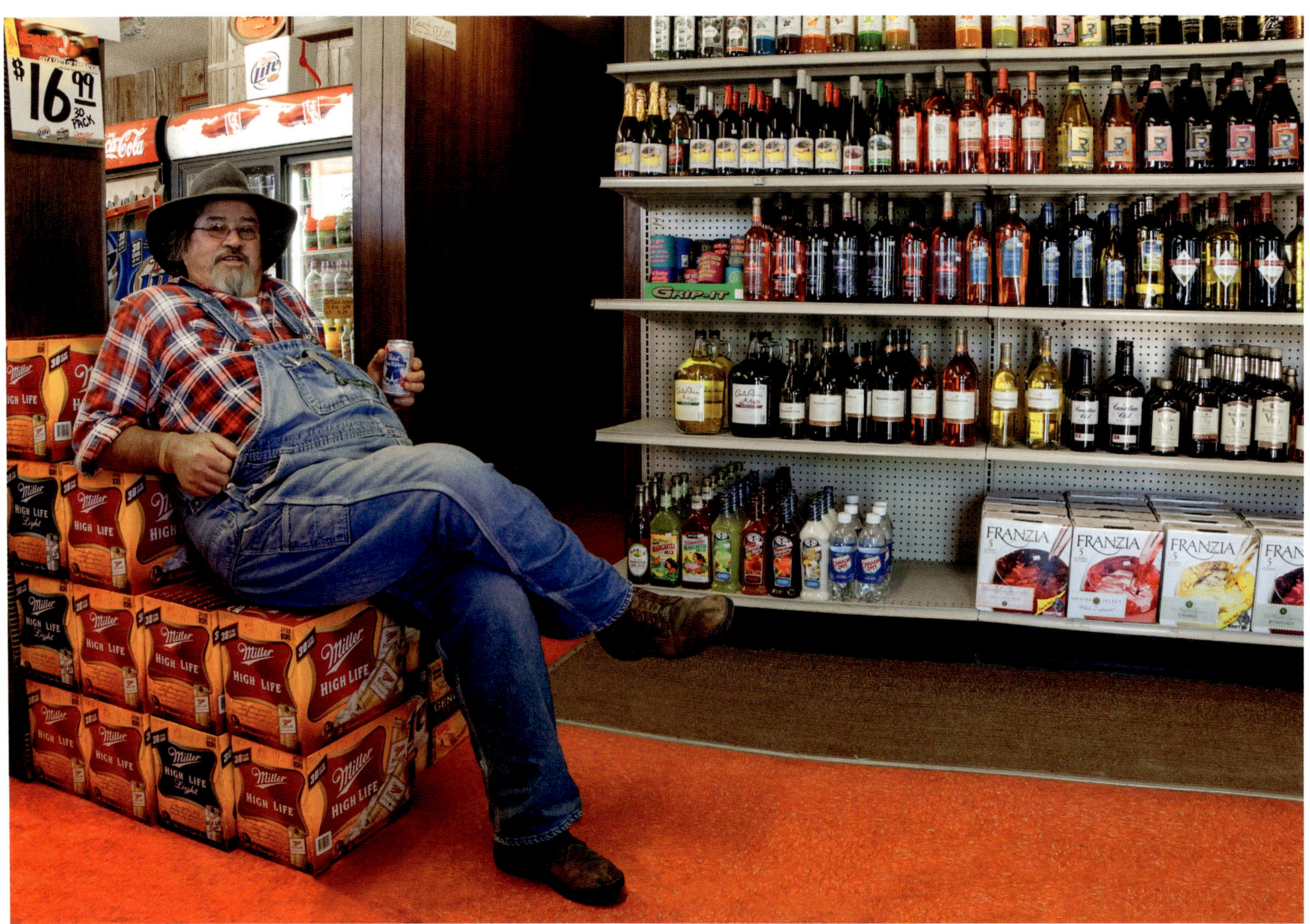

George Moody, Kansas

He was sitting just like that when I went to pay for gas. I went back to my truck for my camera and was happy to find him still there and willing to pose when I returned.

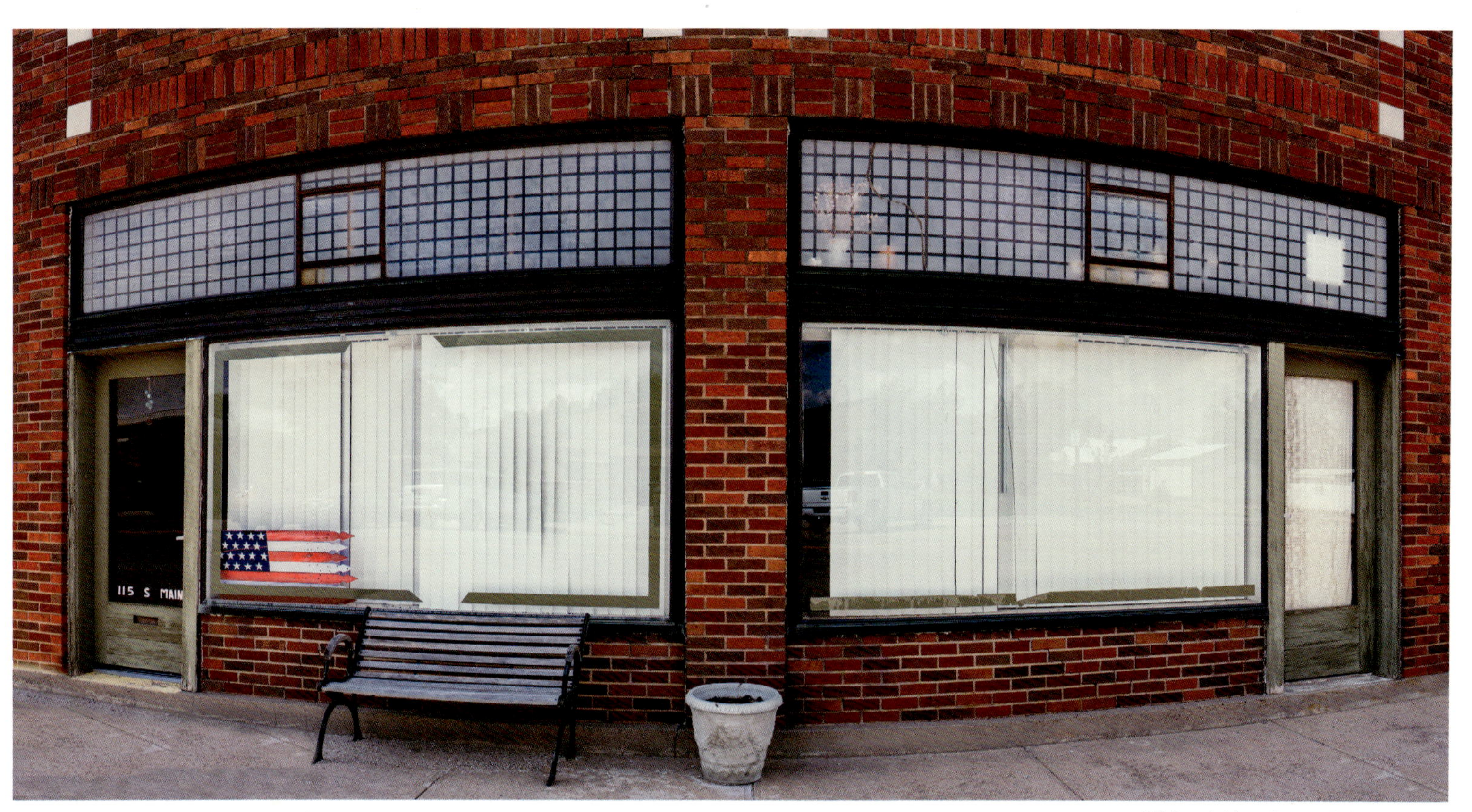

115 South Main Street, Buklin, Kansas

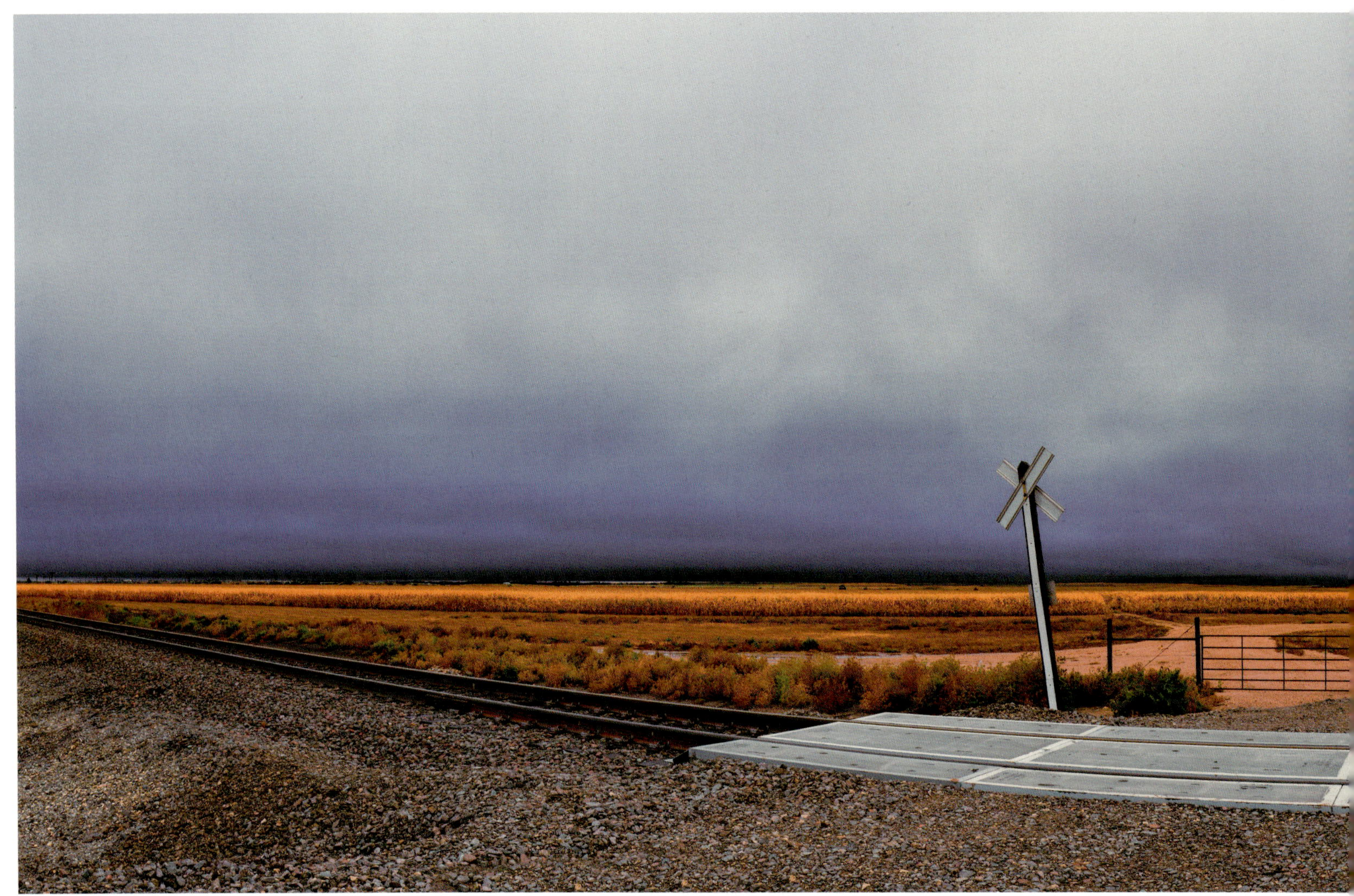

Train tracks along US 50, Kansas

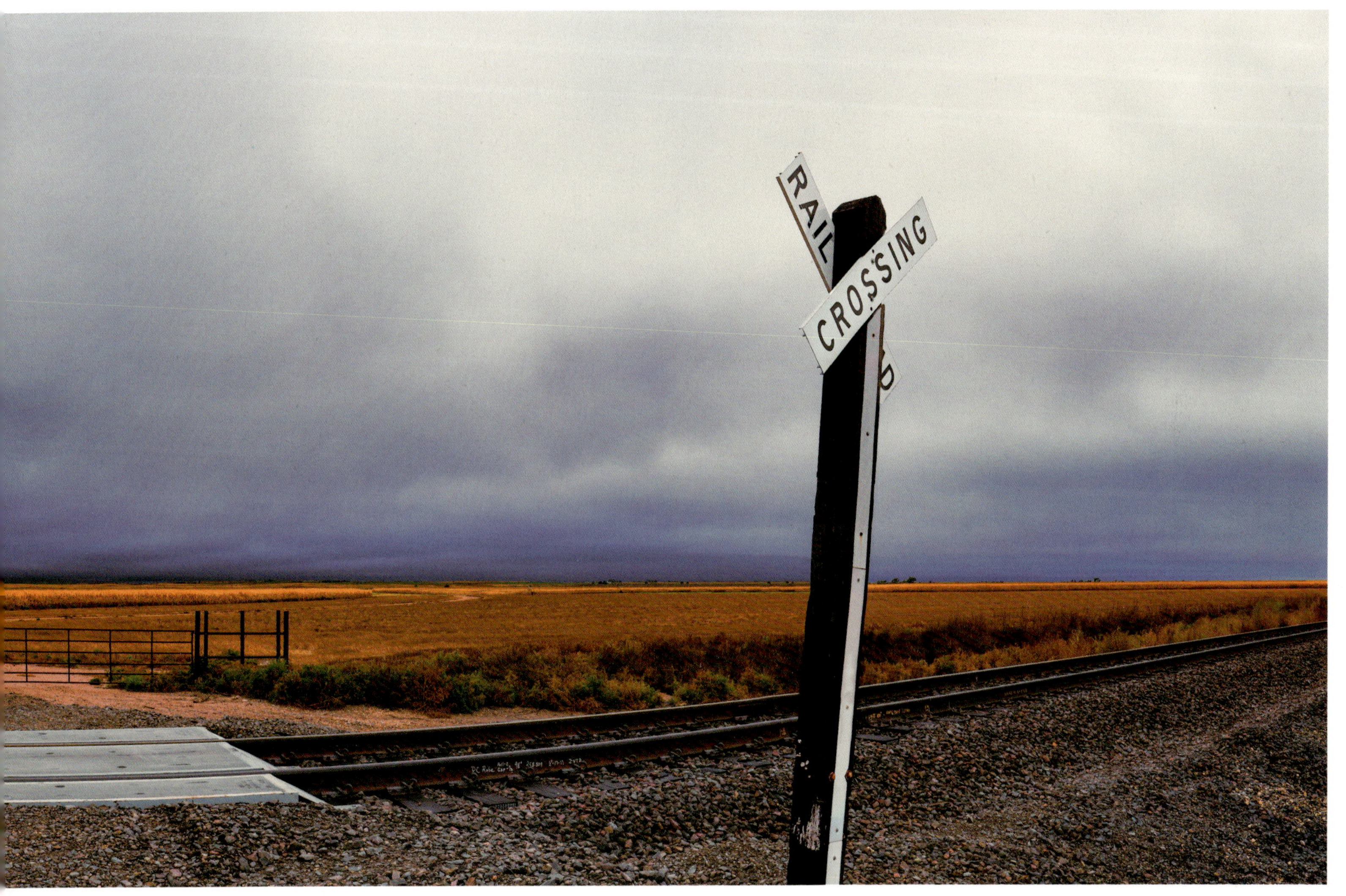
RAIL
CROSSING

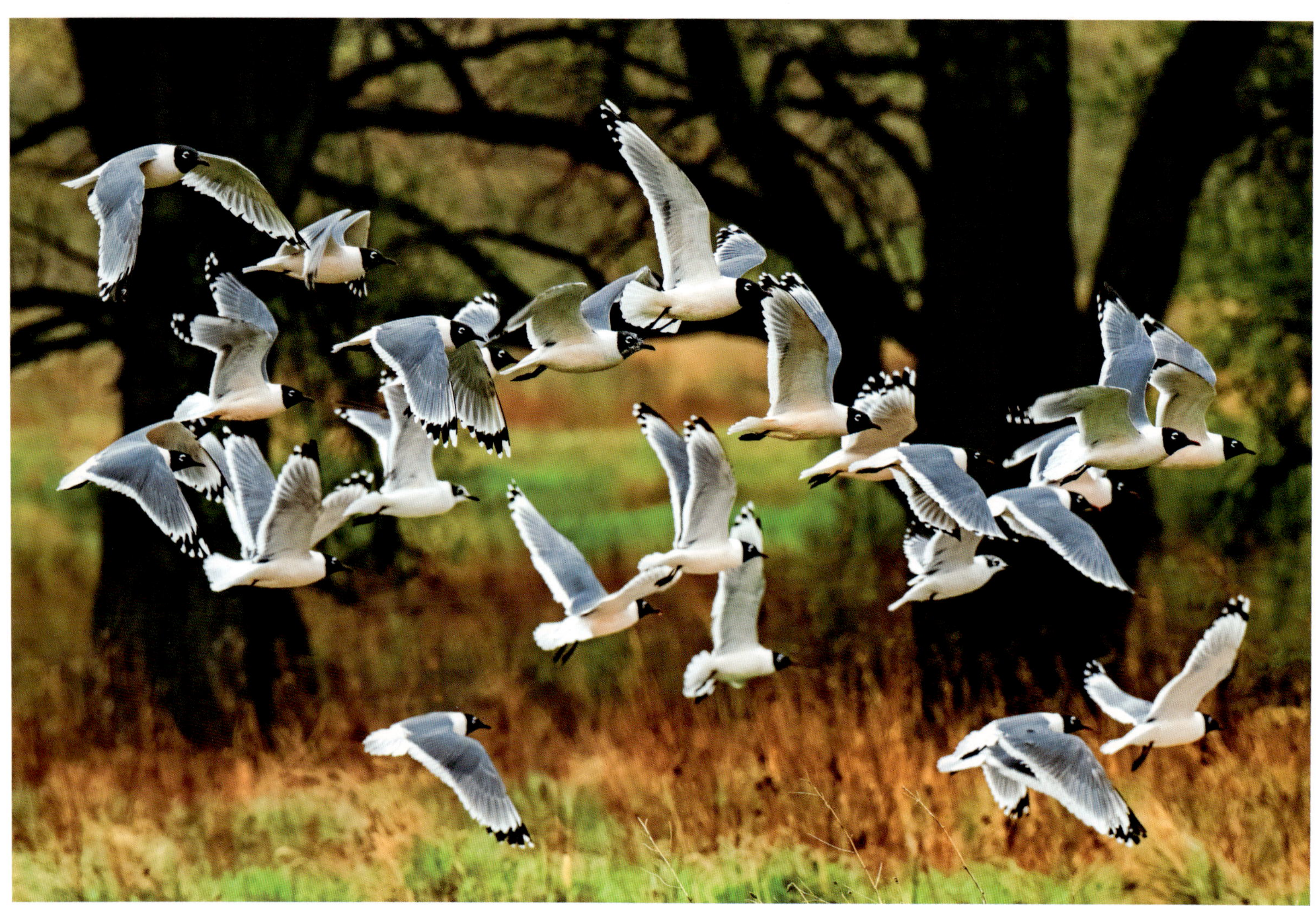

Franklin's gulls or prairie doves, Kansas

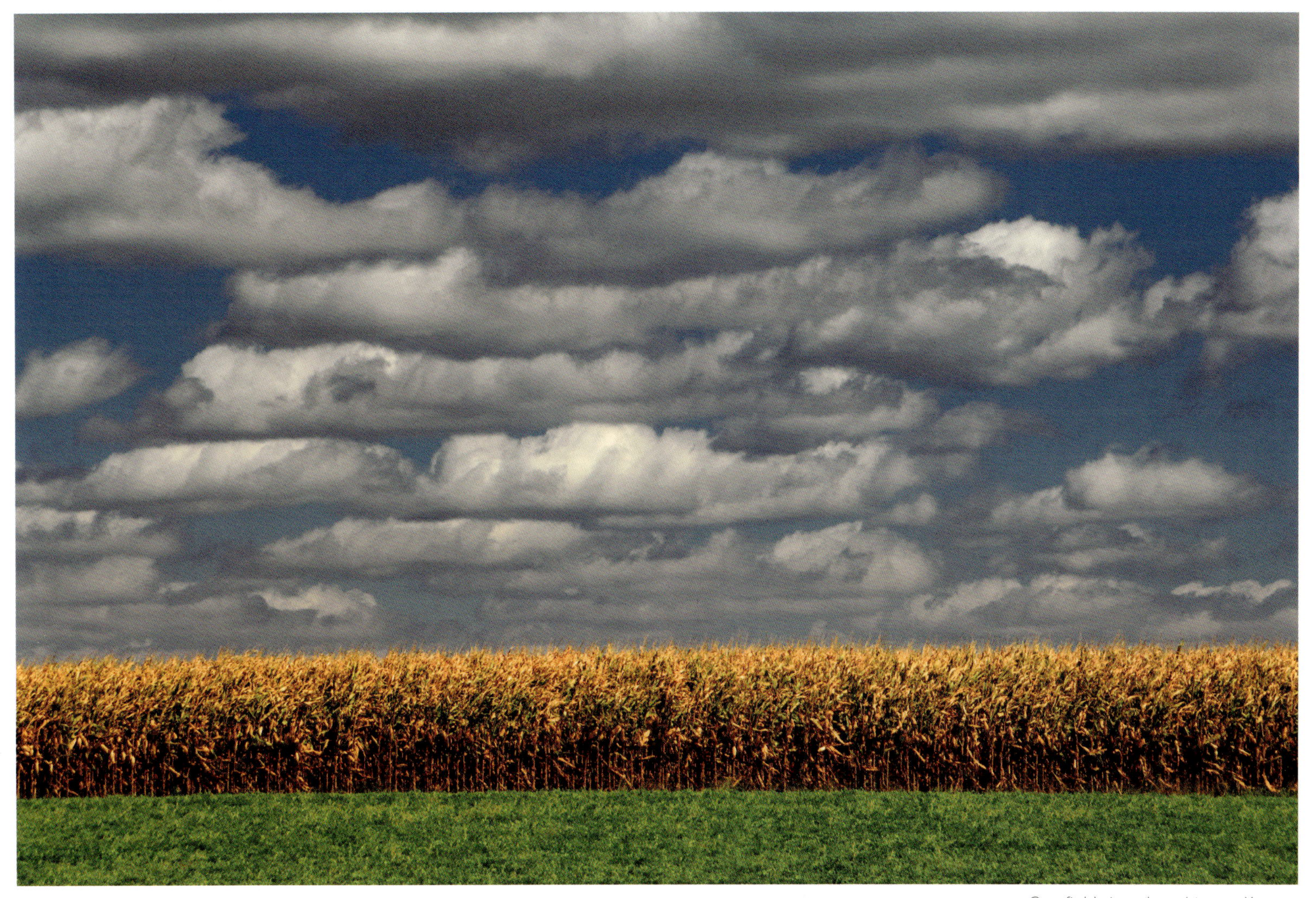

Cornfields in a drought year, Kansas

Train near Holcomb, Kansas

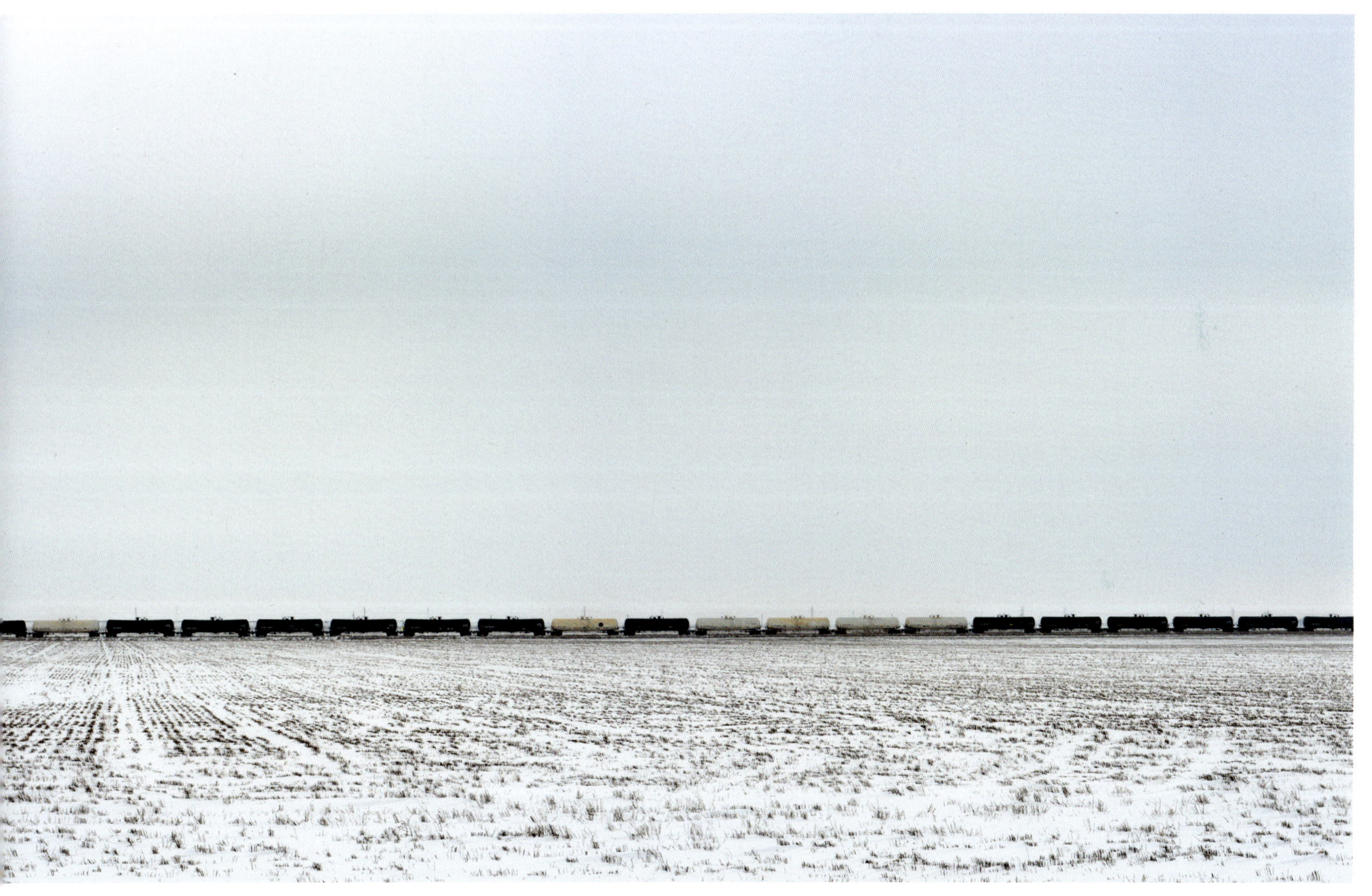

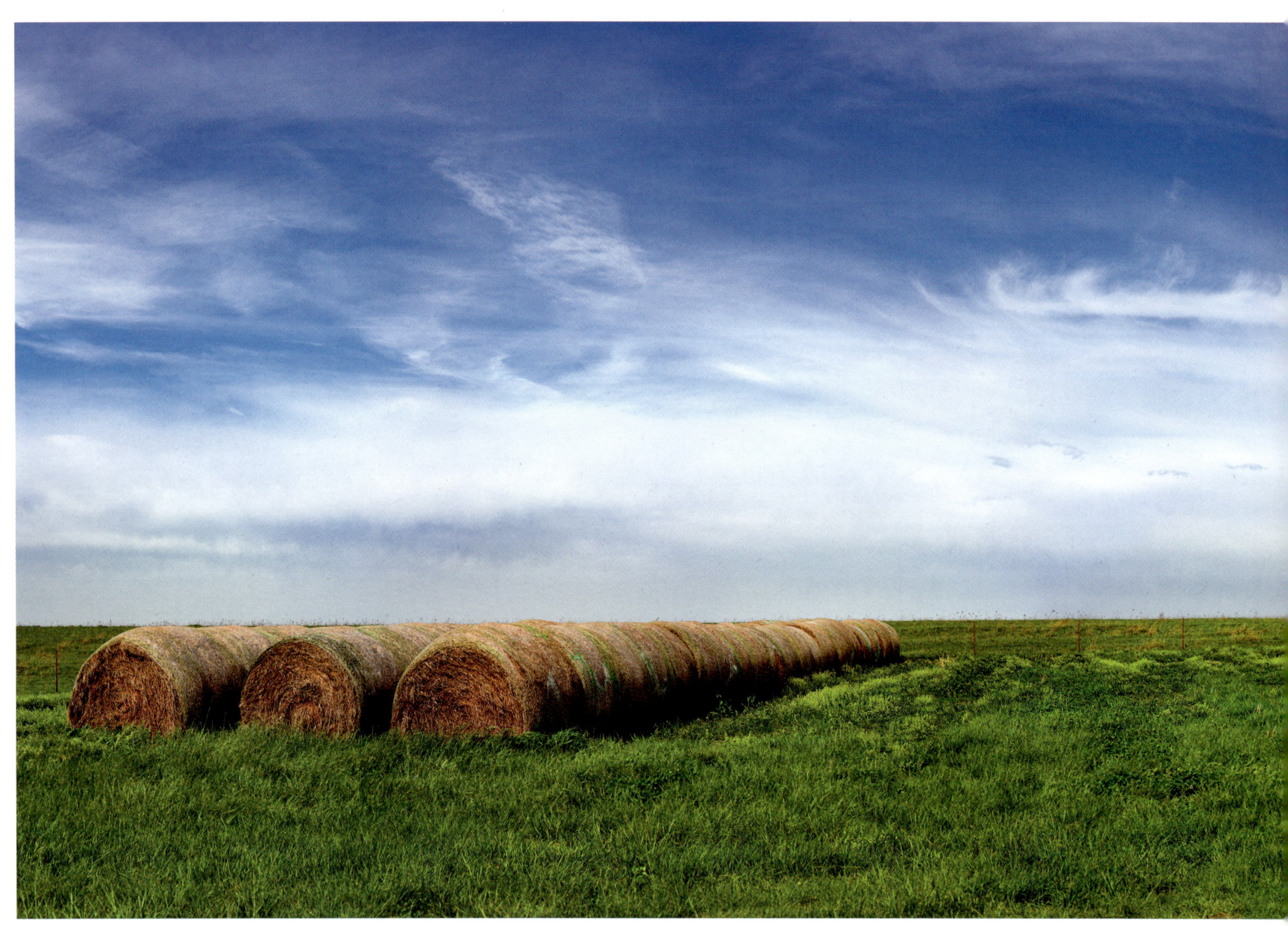

Brick barn on Angus Road, Kansas

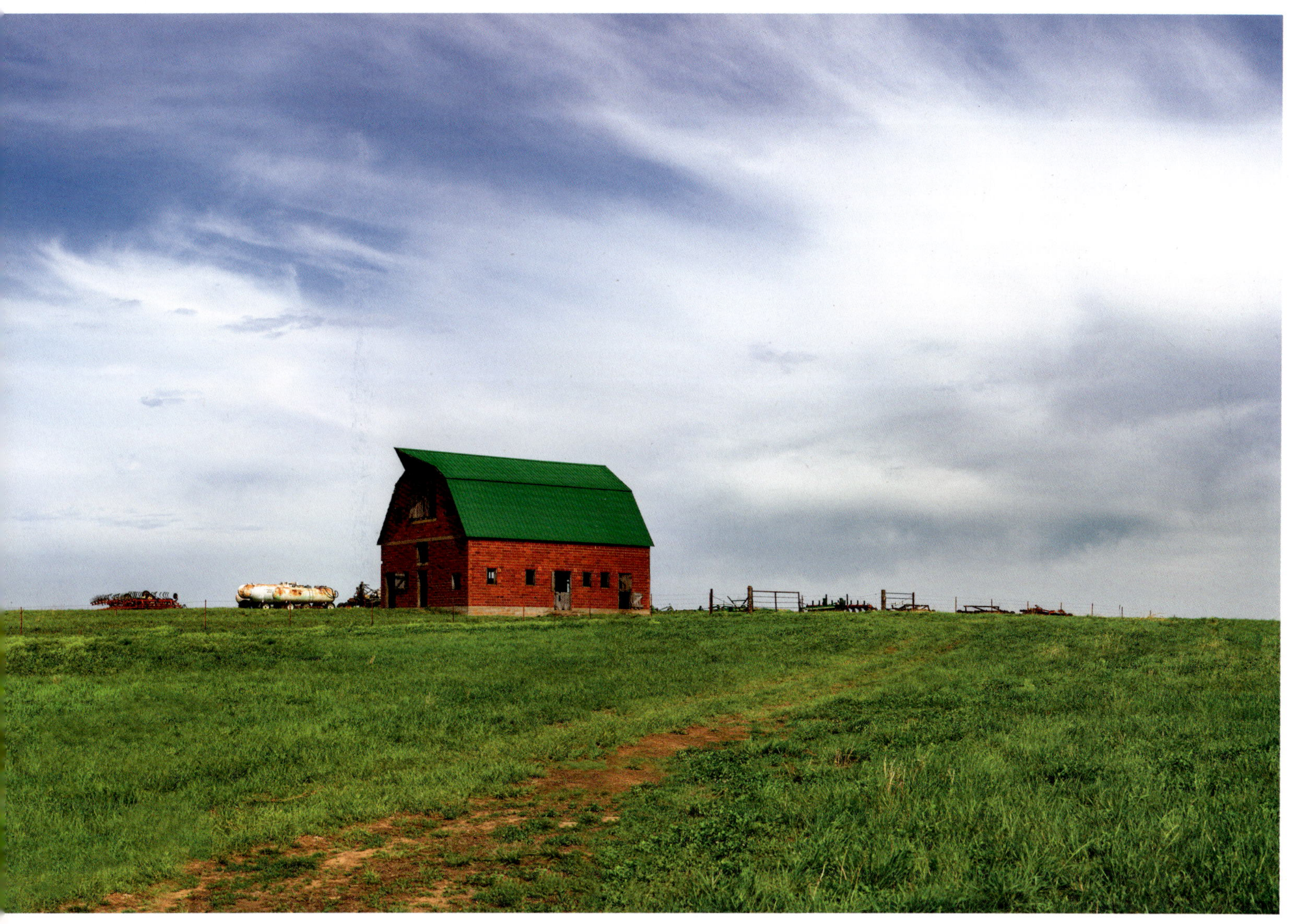

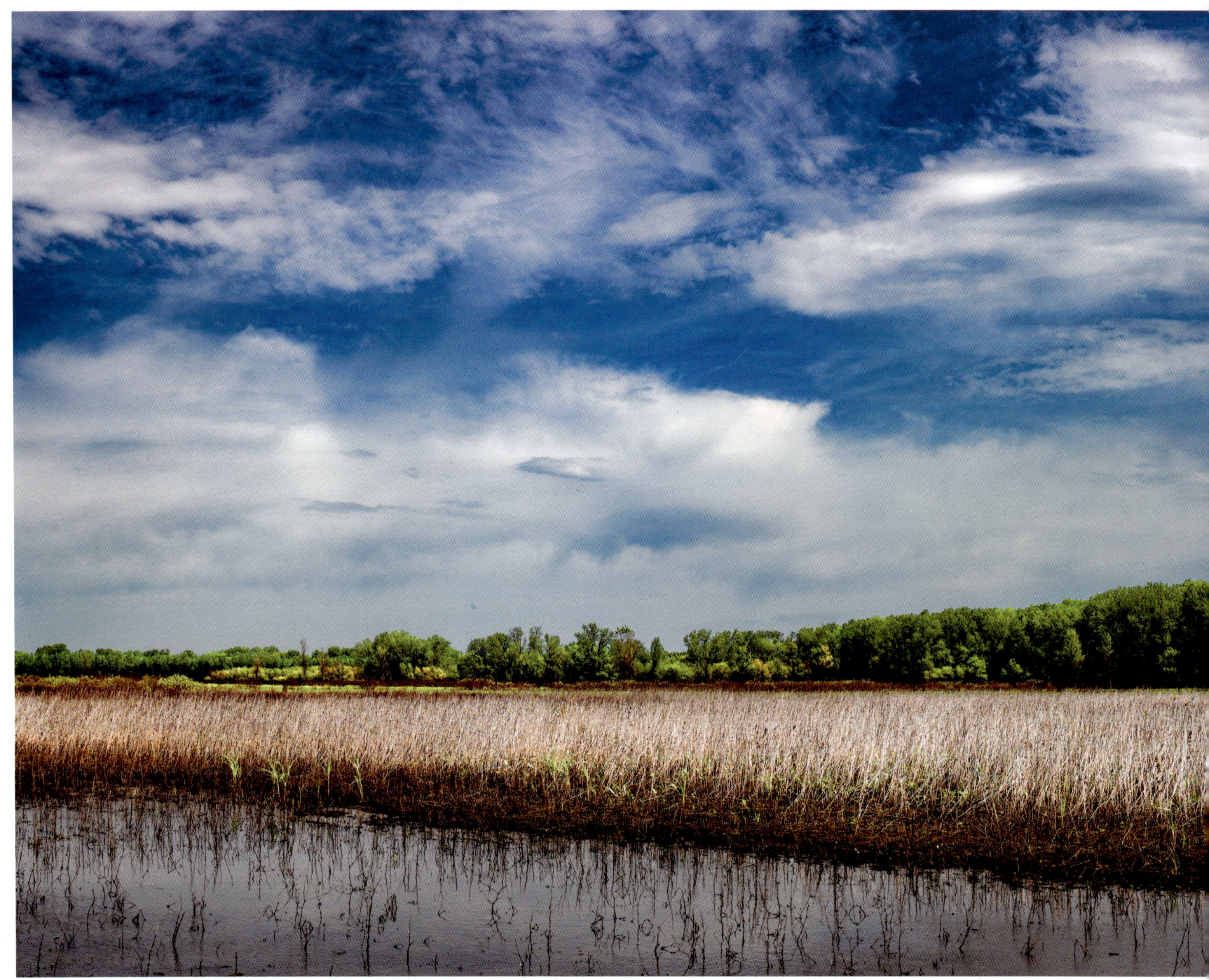

Neosho River, Flint Hills National Wildlife Refuge, Indian Hill, Kansas

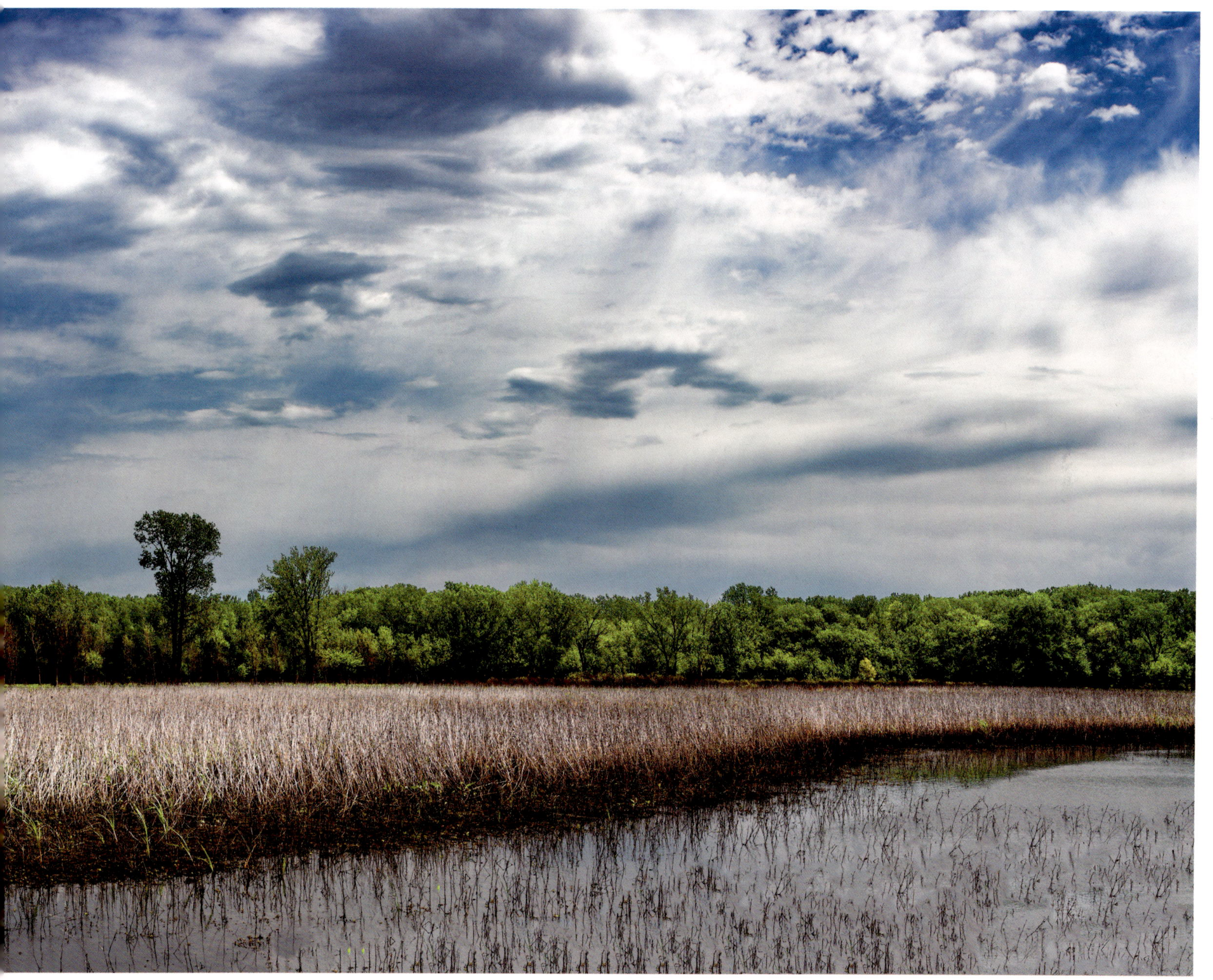

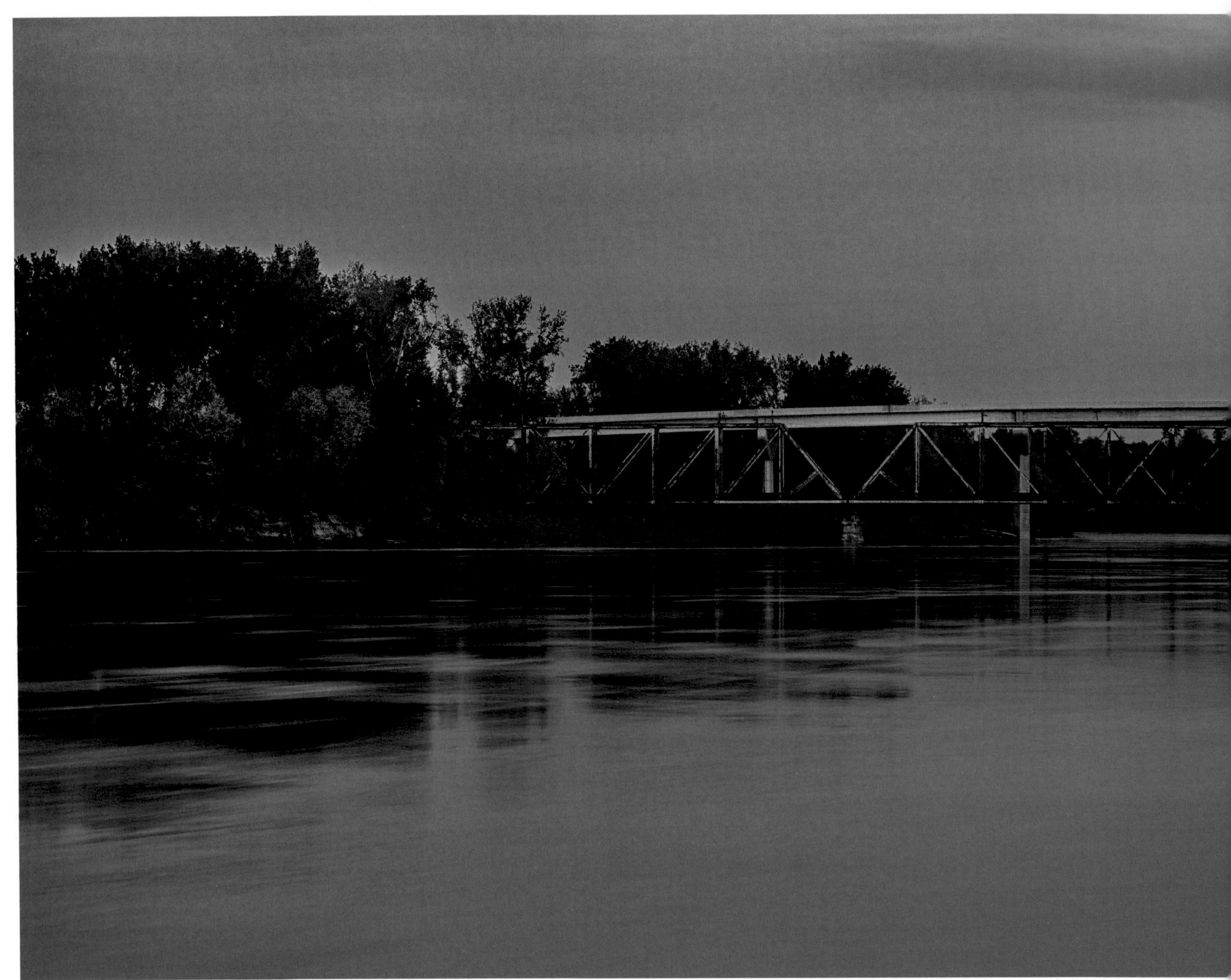

Amelia Earhart Bridge over the Missouri River, Atchison, Kansas

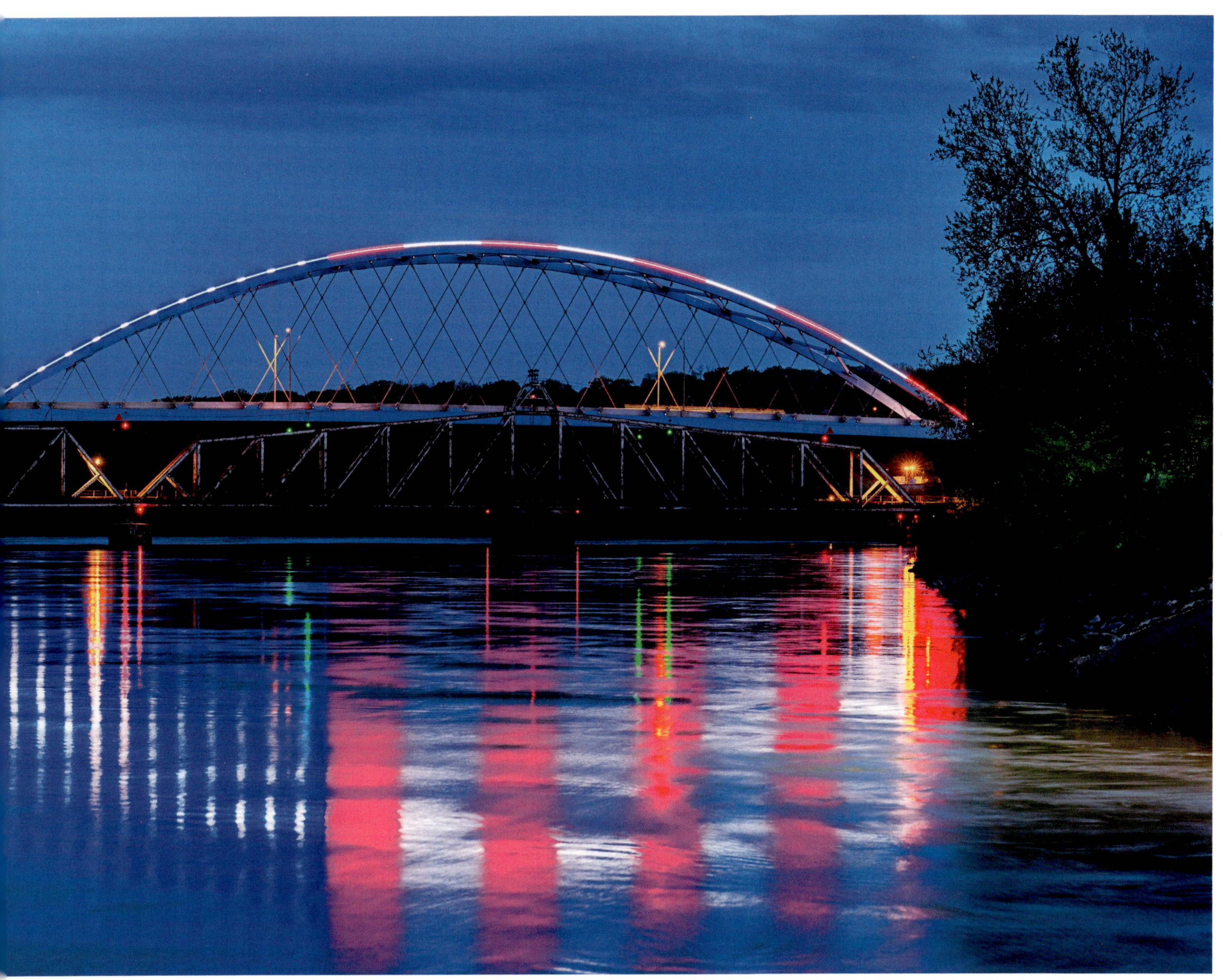

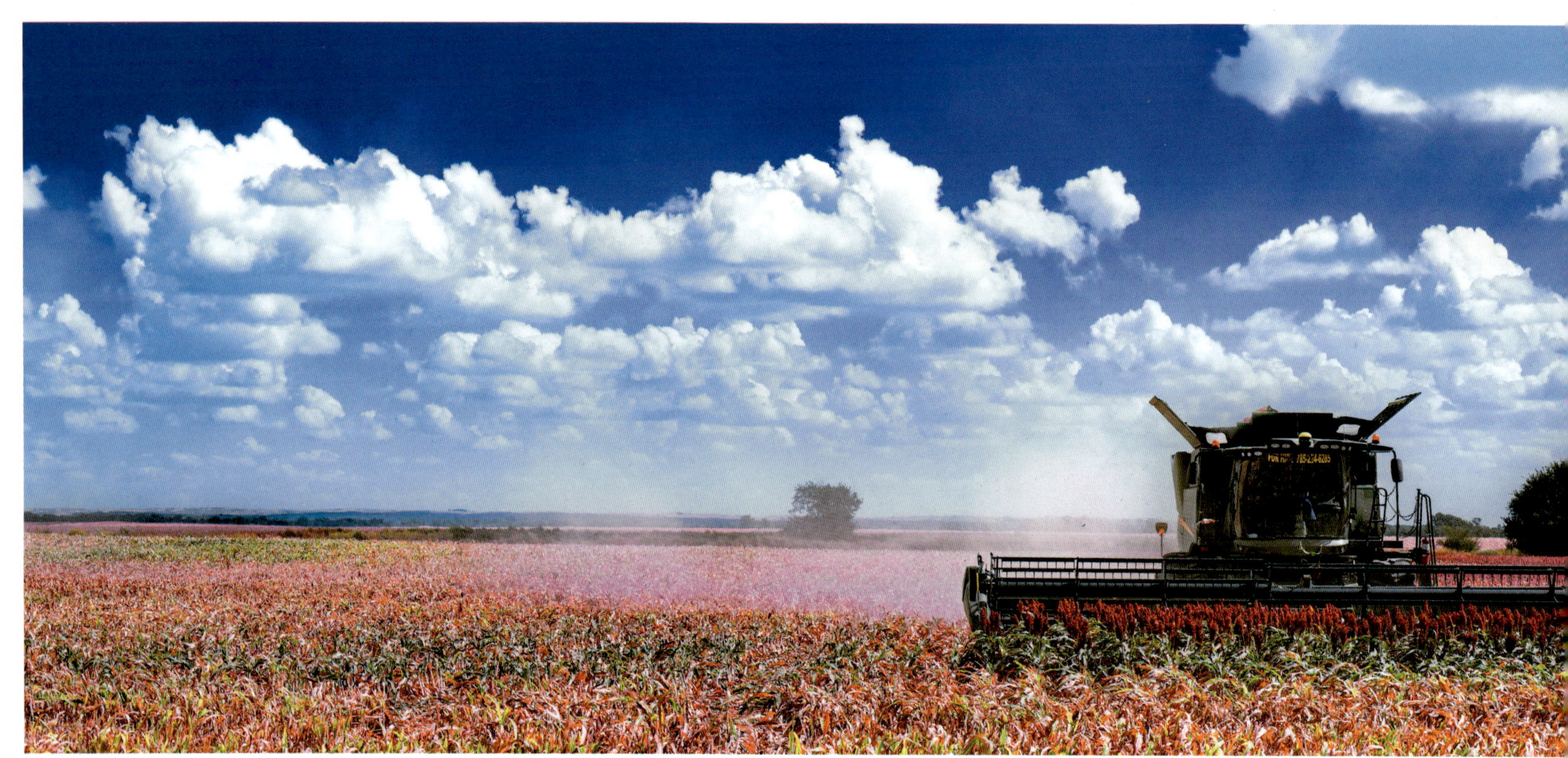

Sorghum harvest, Mitch's Farm, near Protection, Kansas

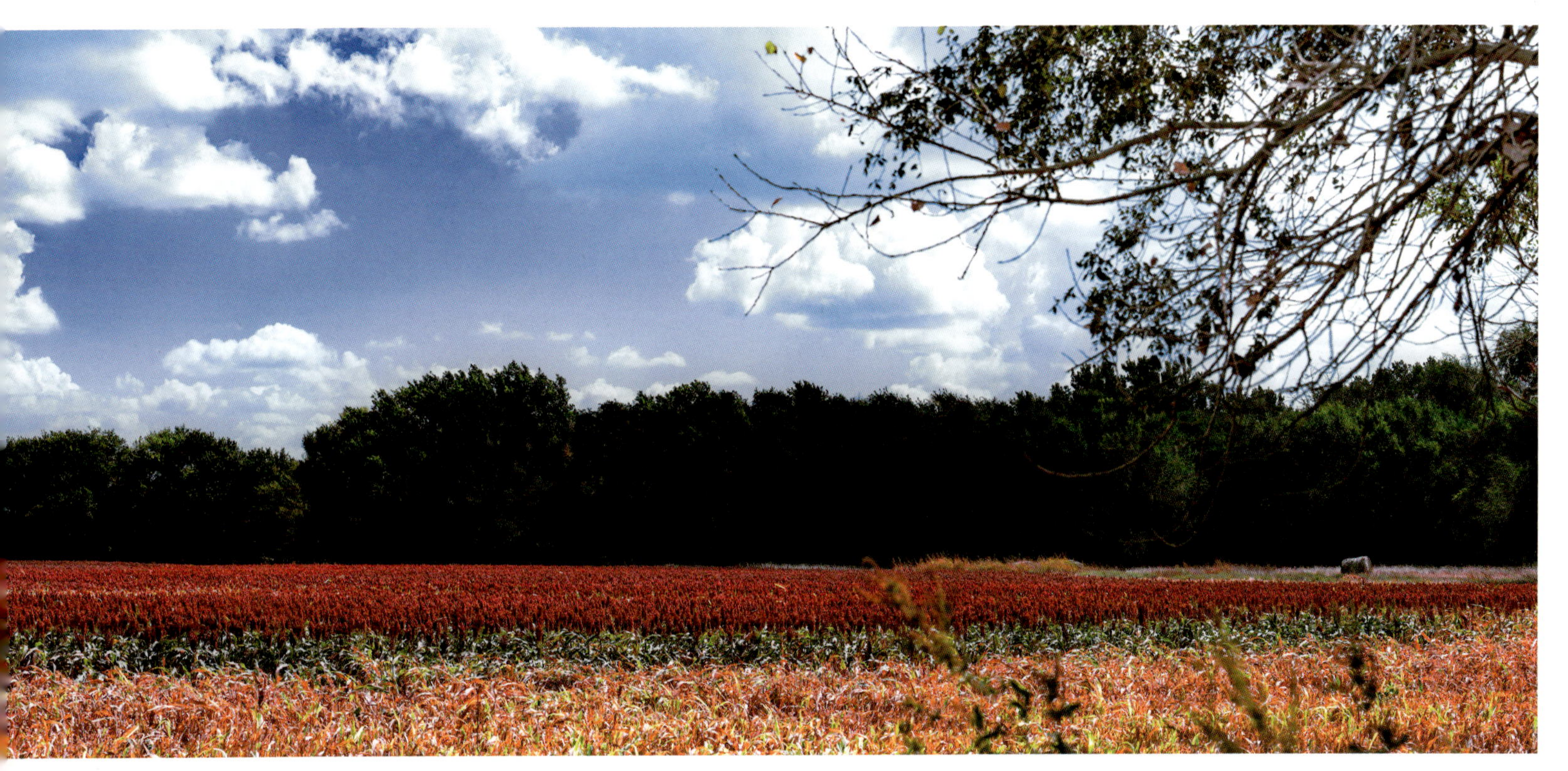

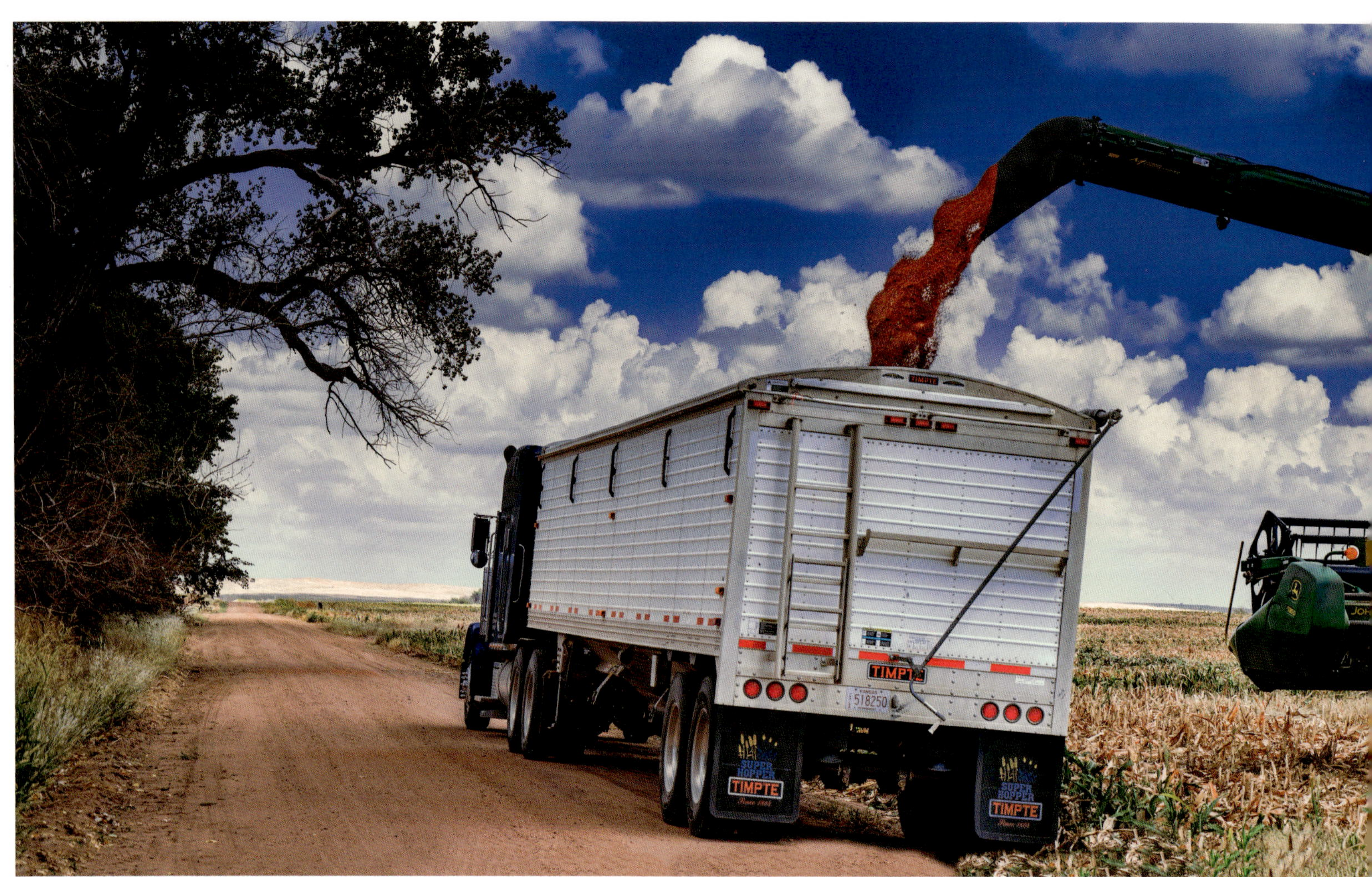

Loading sorghum, Mitch's Farm, near Protection, Kansas

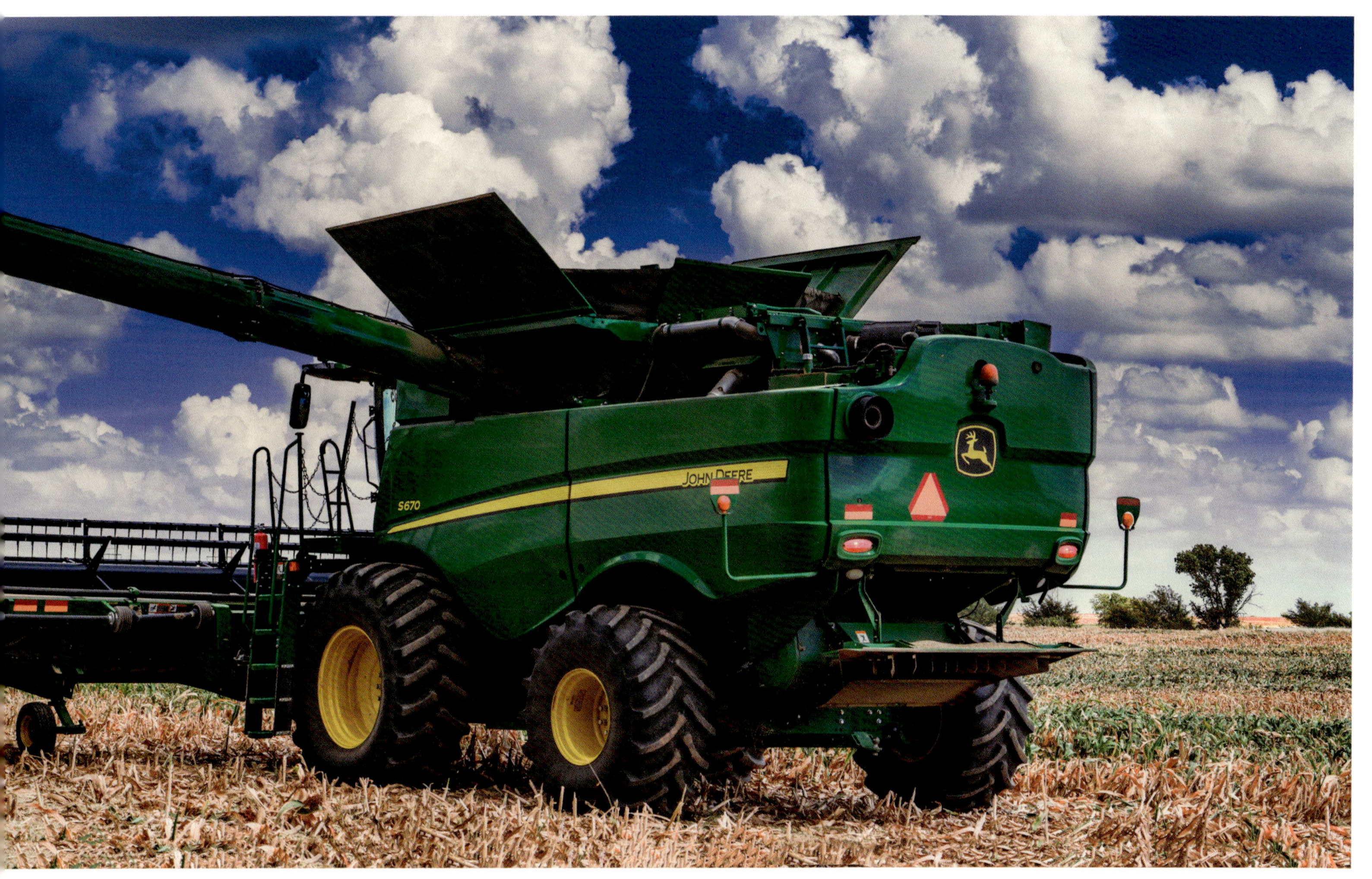
JOHN DEERE
S670

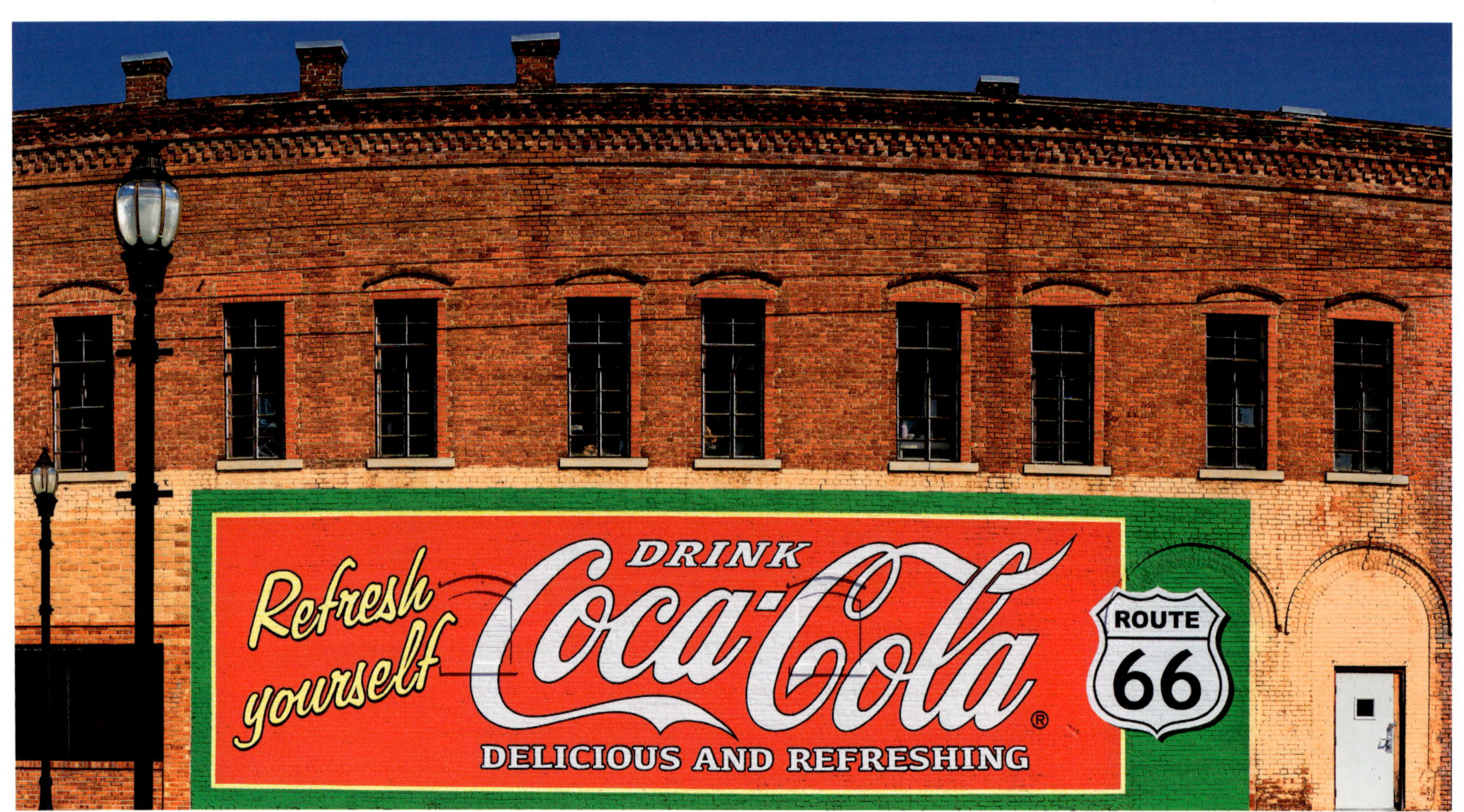

7th and Main, Route 66, Galena, Kansas

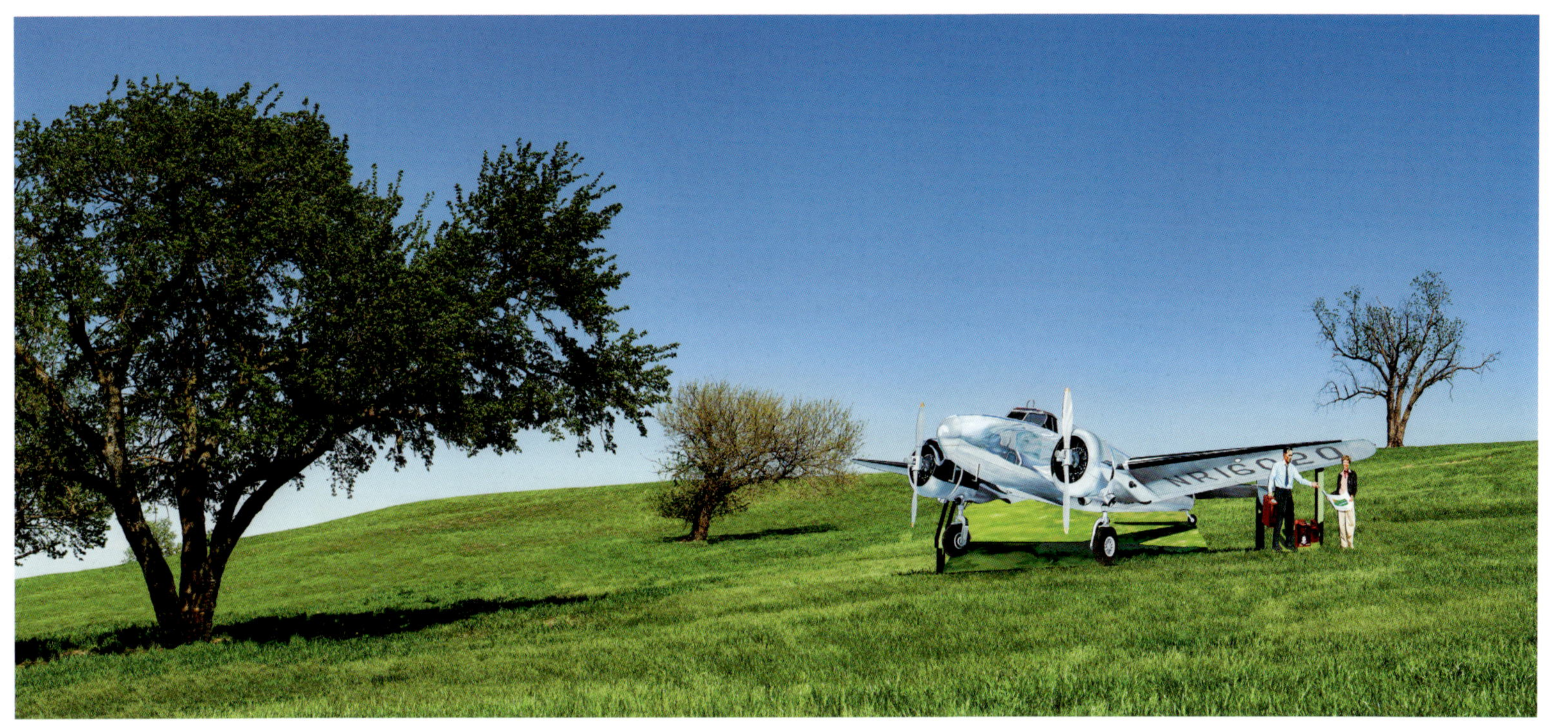

John Cerney's public art can be found all over the back roads of America.

Amelia Comes Home, by John Cerney, Atchison, Kansas

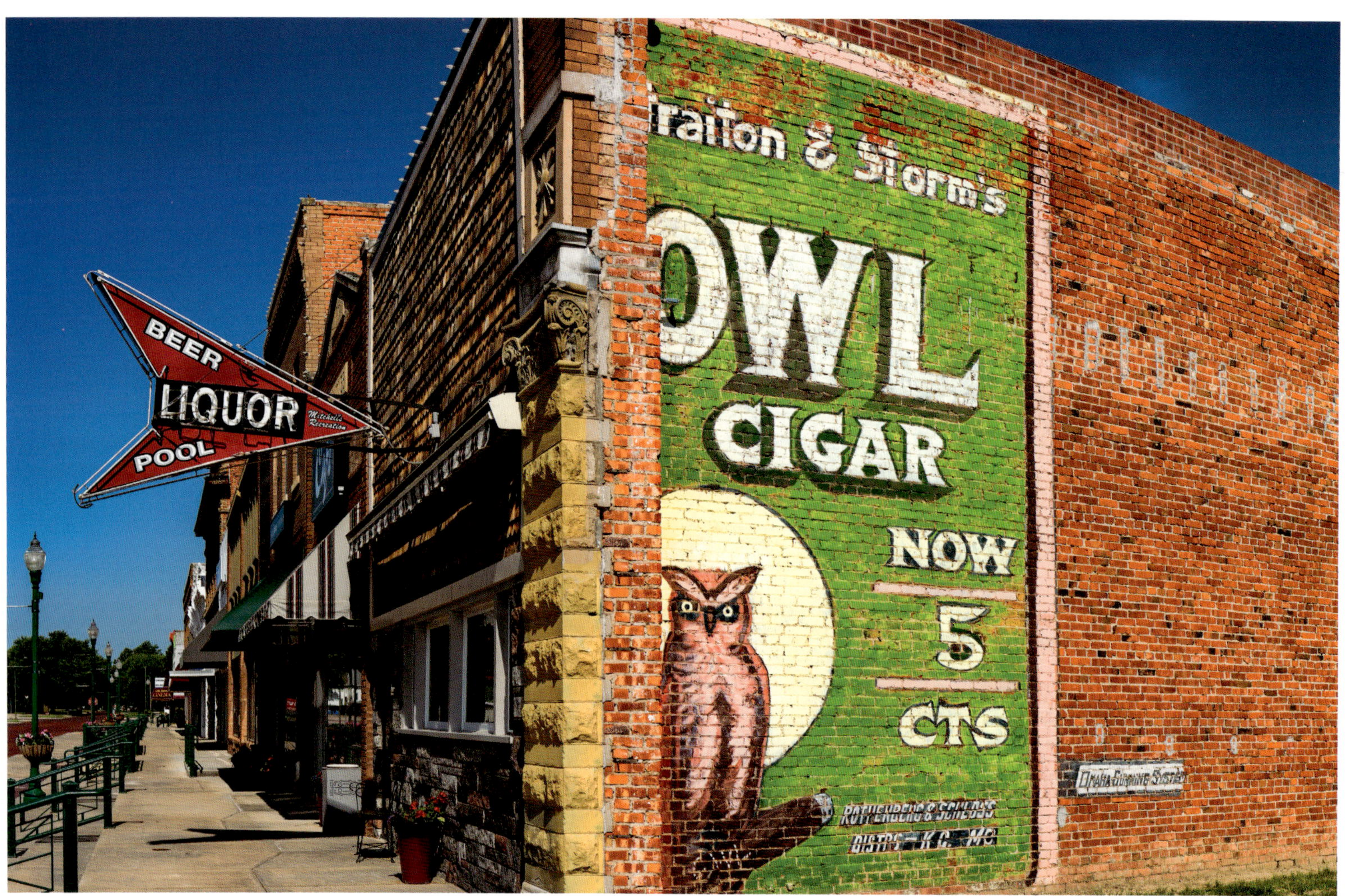

Aurora, Nebraska

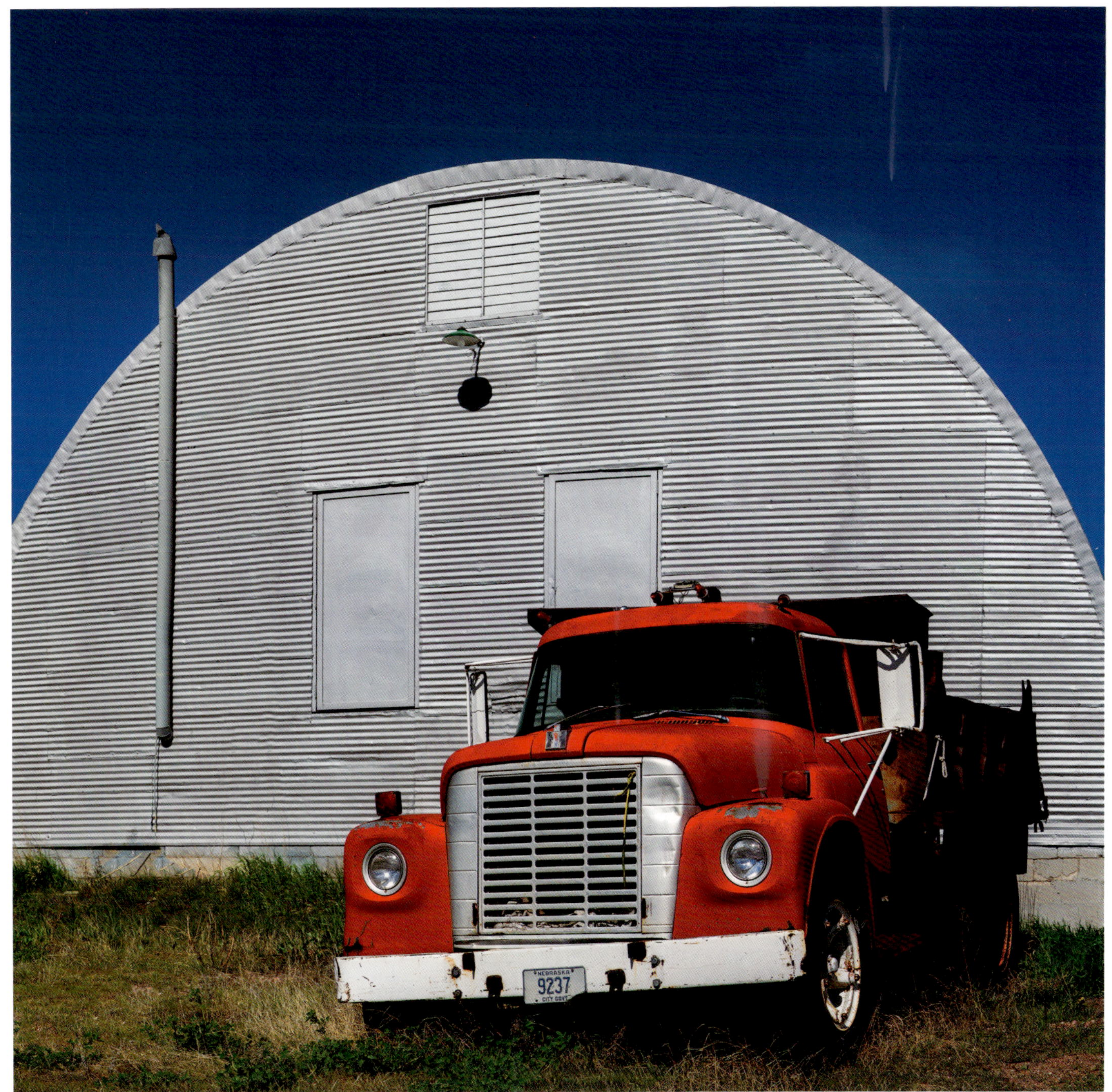

Truck and shed, Hyannis, Nebraska

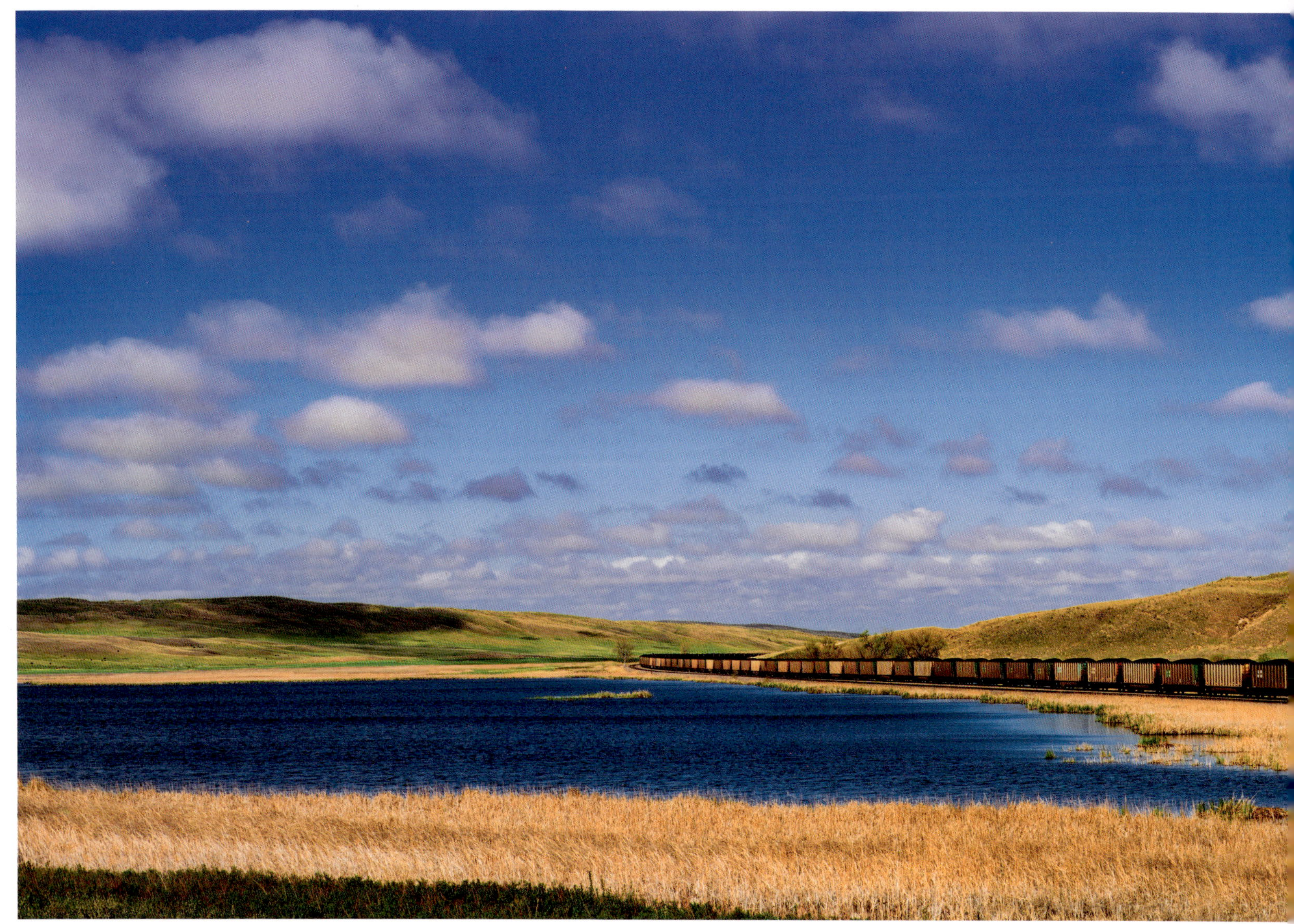

Freight train, Doc Lake, Nebraska

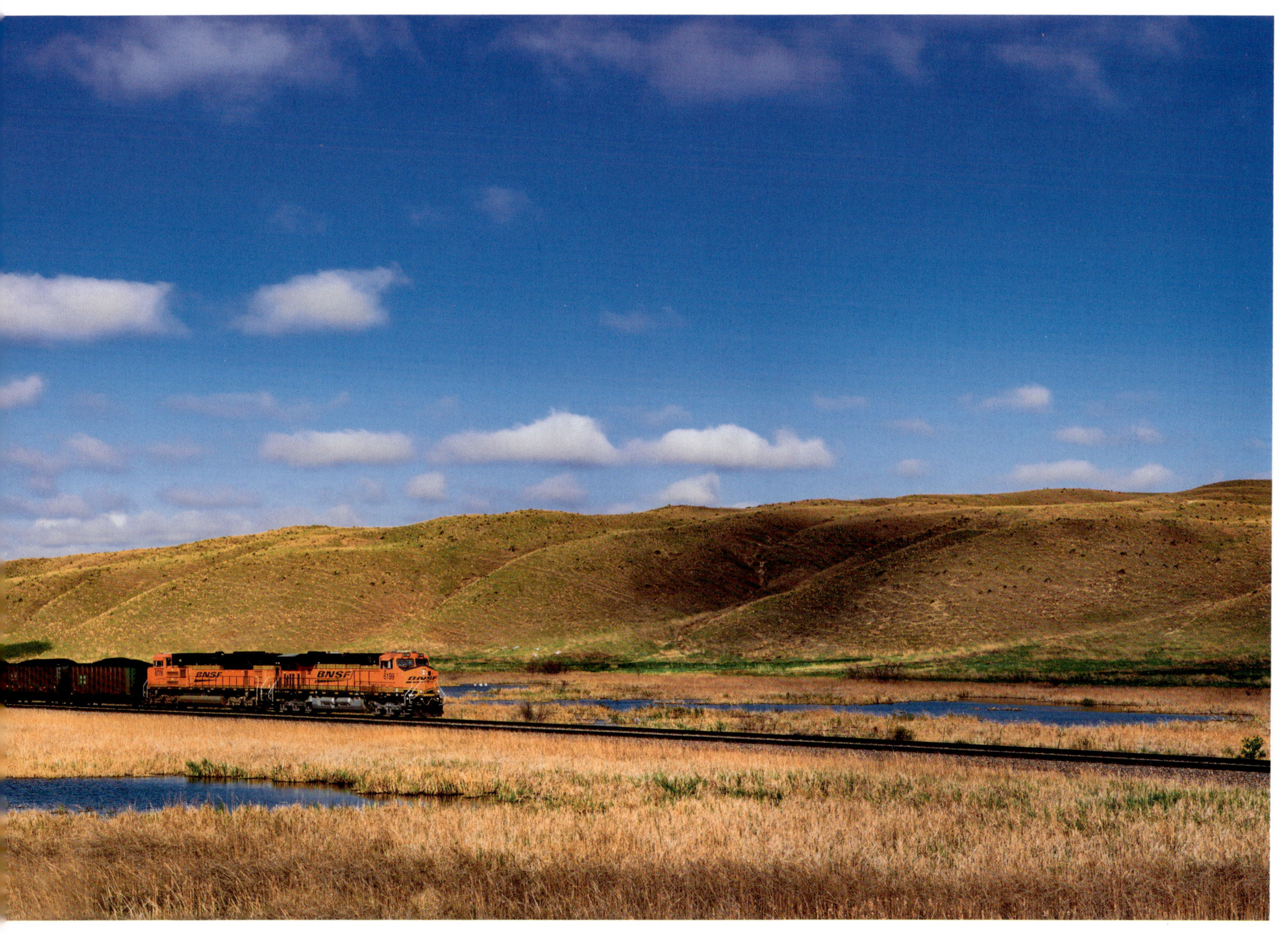
BNSF
BNSF

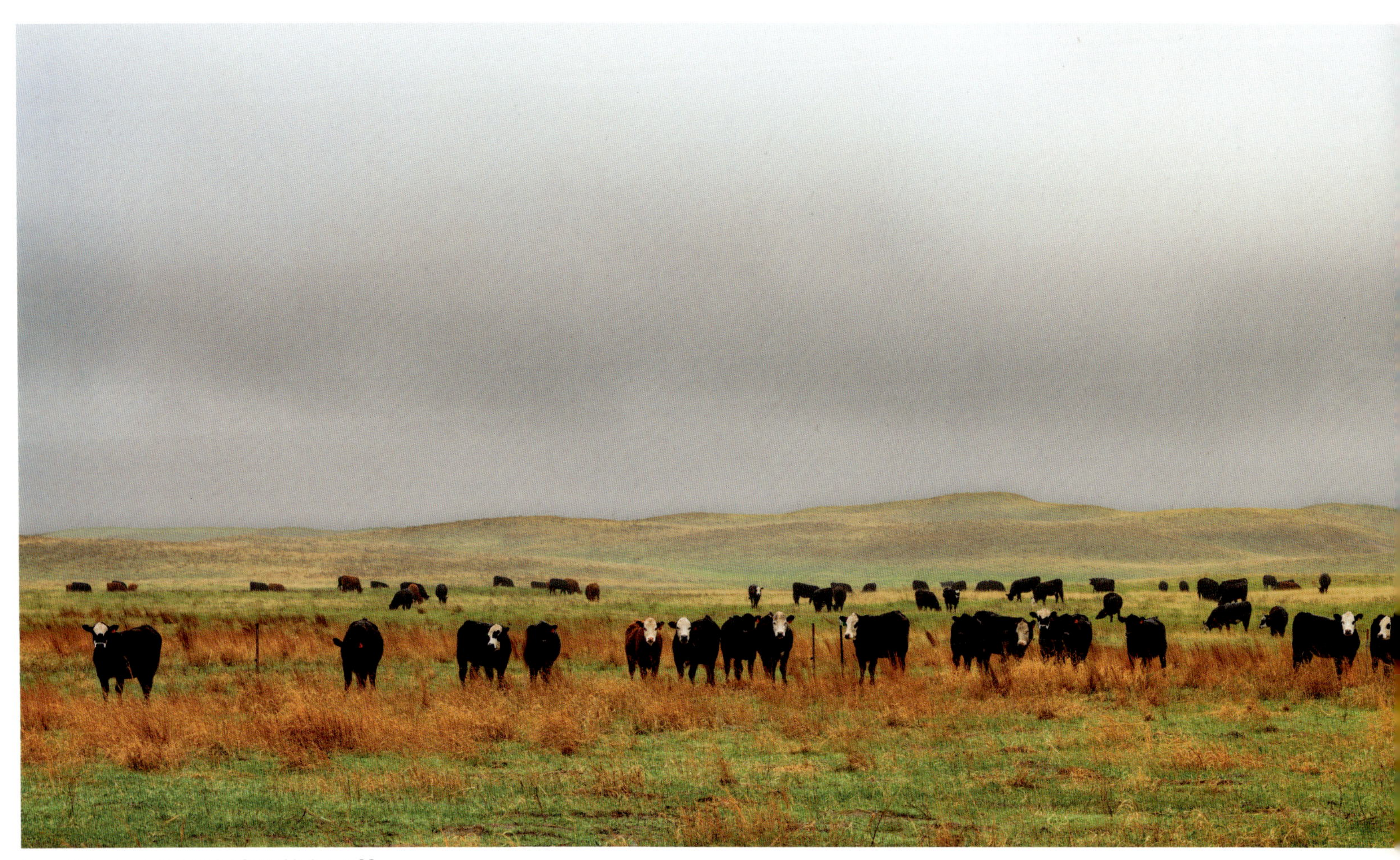

Cows in the mist, Nebraska State Highway 83

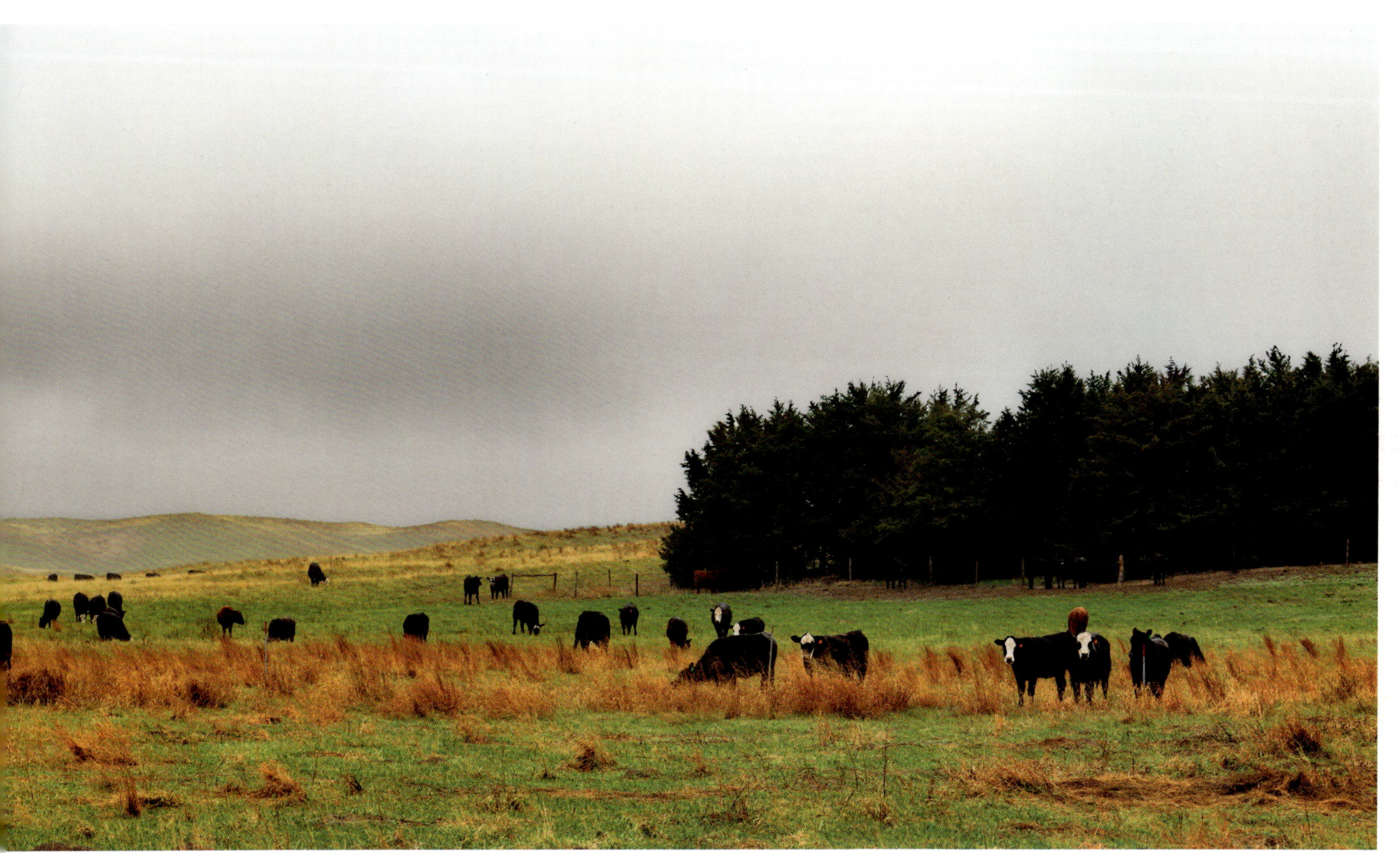

If you sing to cows, they look at you. Try it!

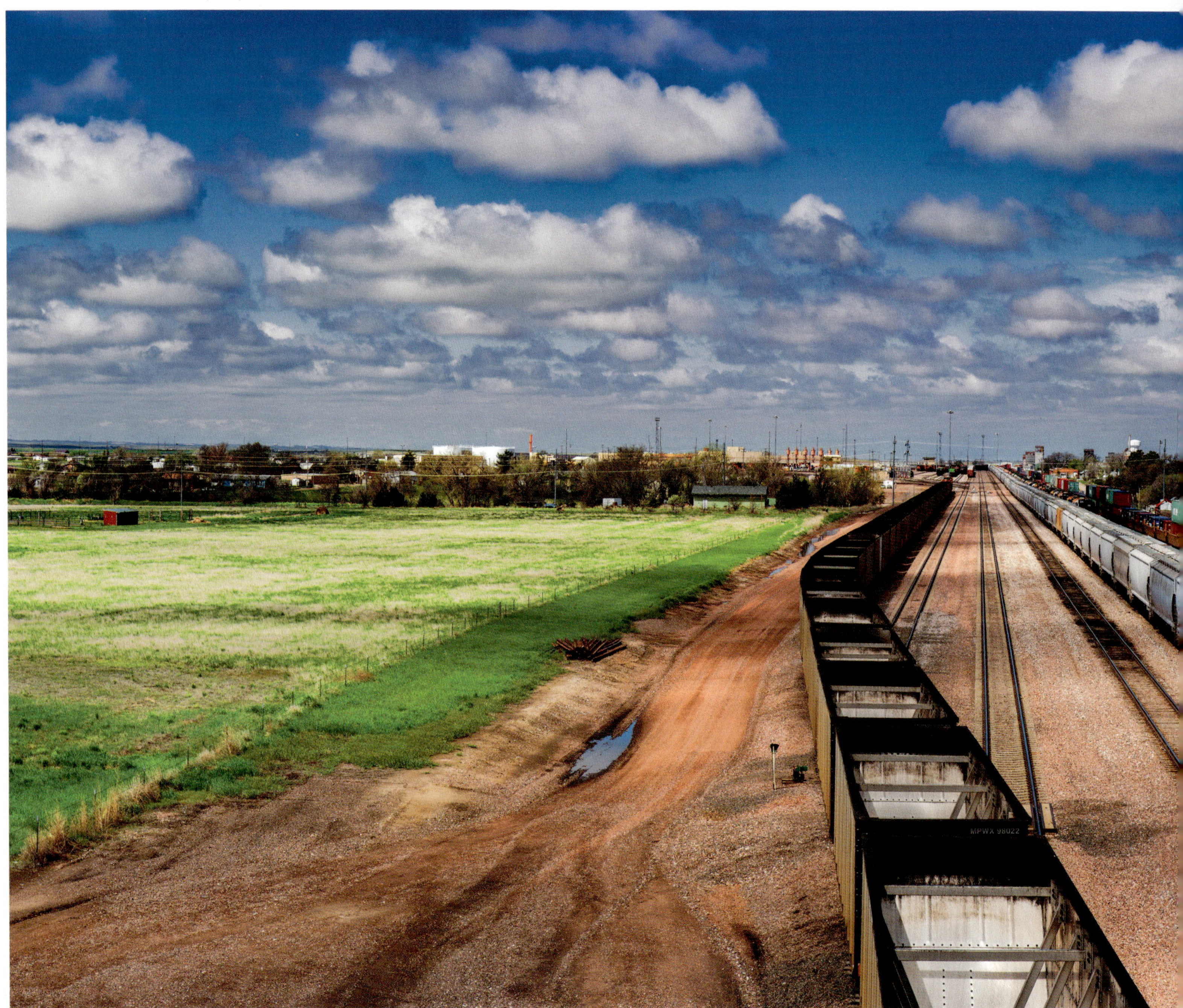

Rail yard, Alliance, Nebraska

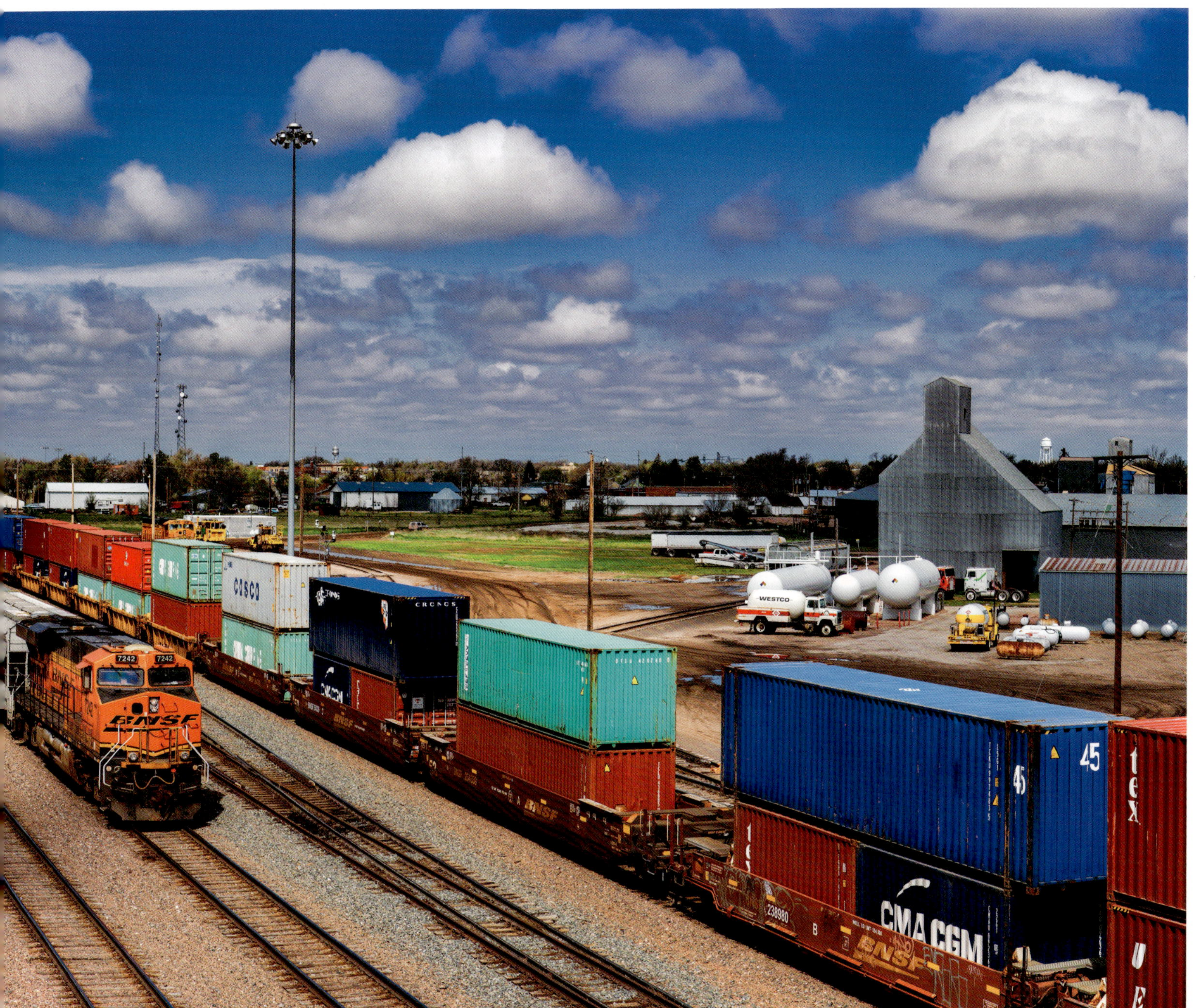
7242
BNSF
COSCO
CRONOS
WESTCO
45
CMA CGM
BNSF

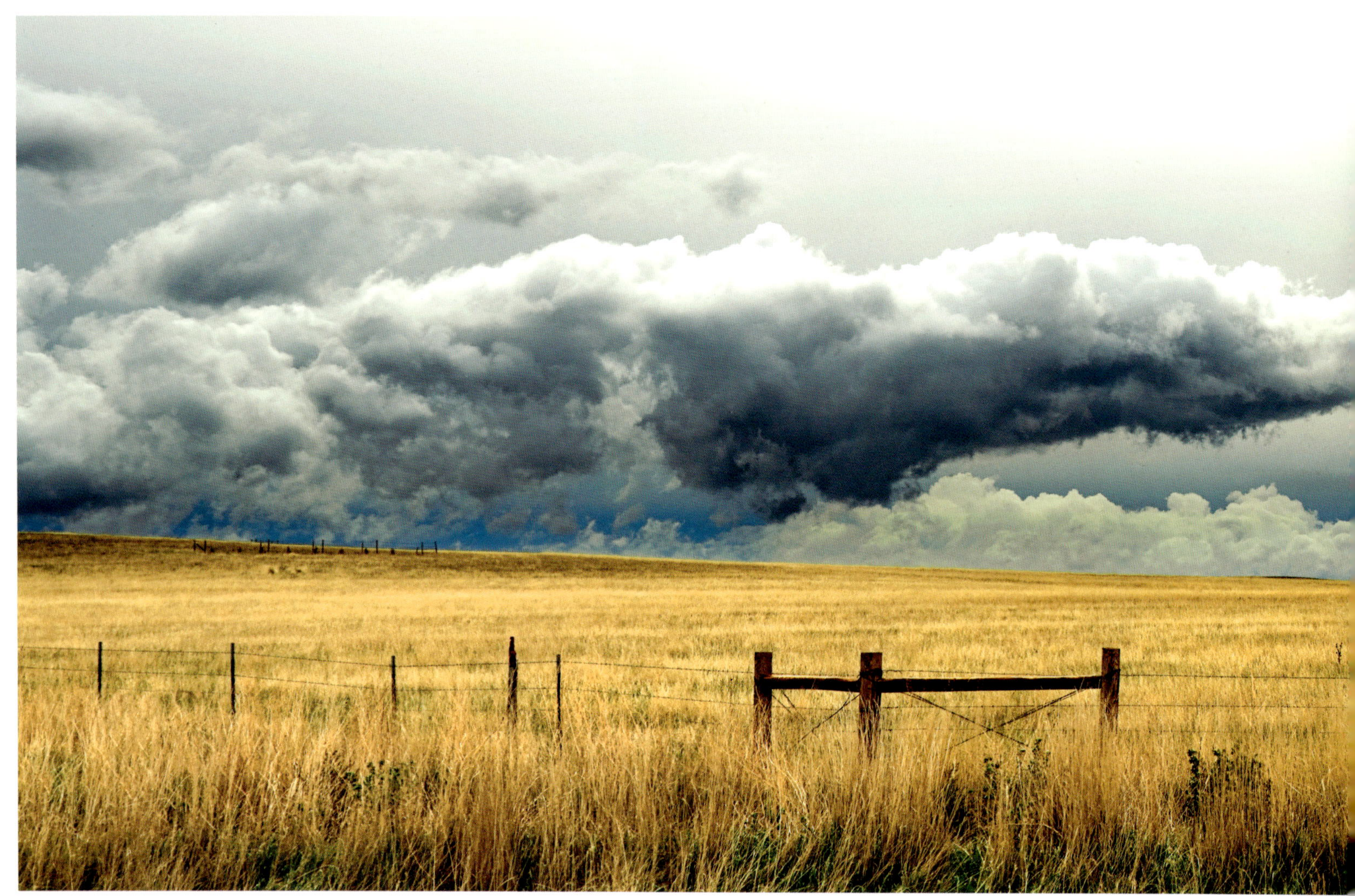

Fields and clouds along Nebraska State Highway 61

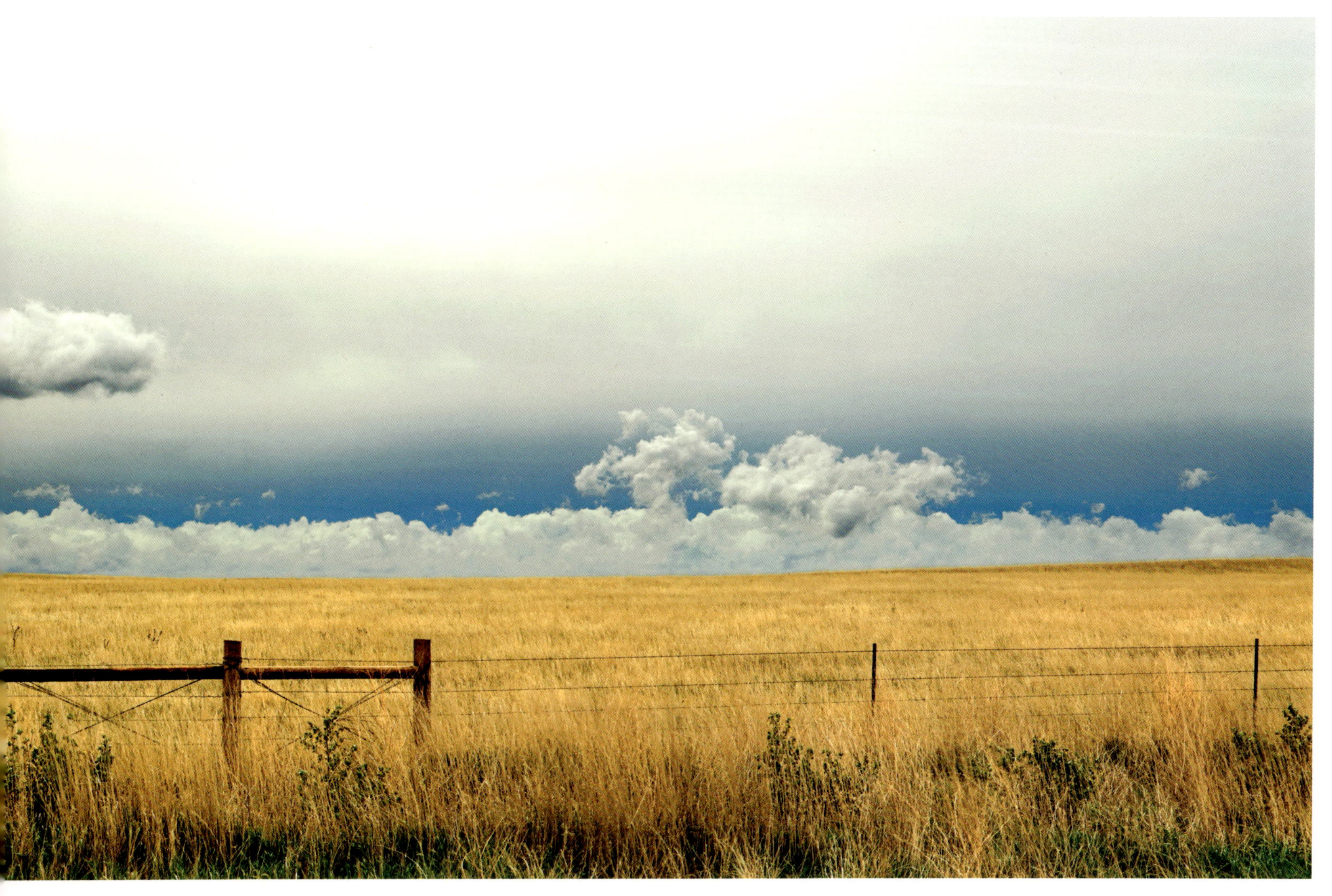

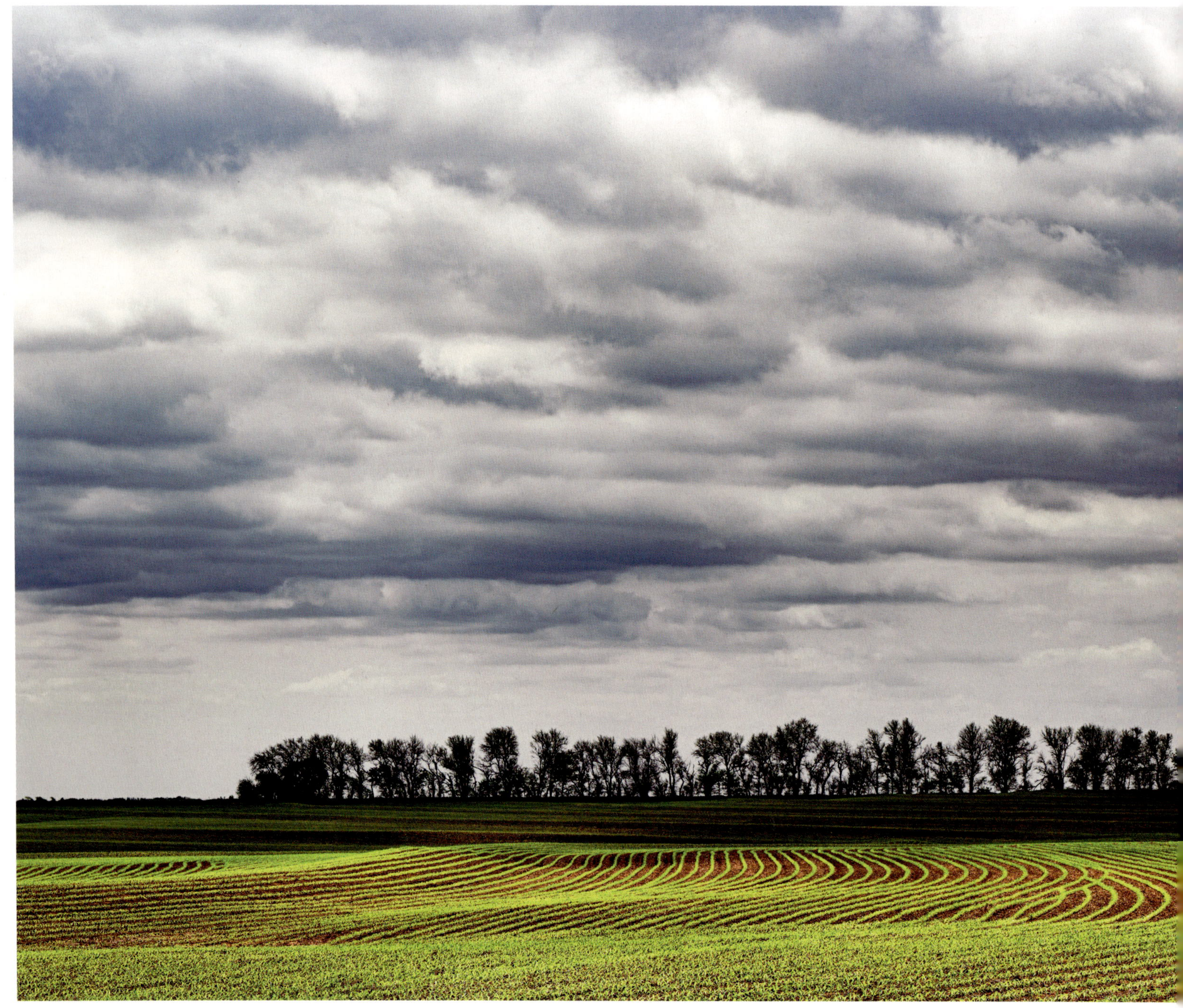

Planted fields, Nebraska State Highway 73

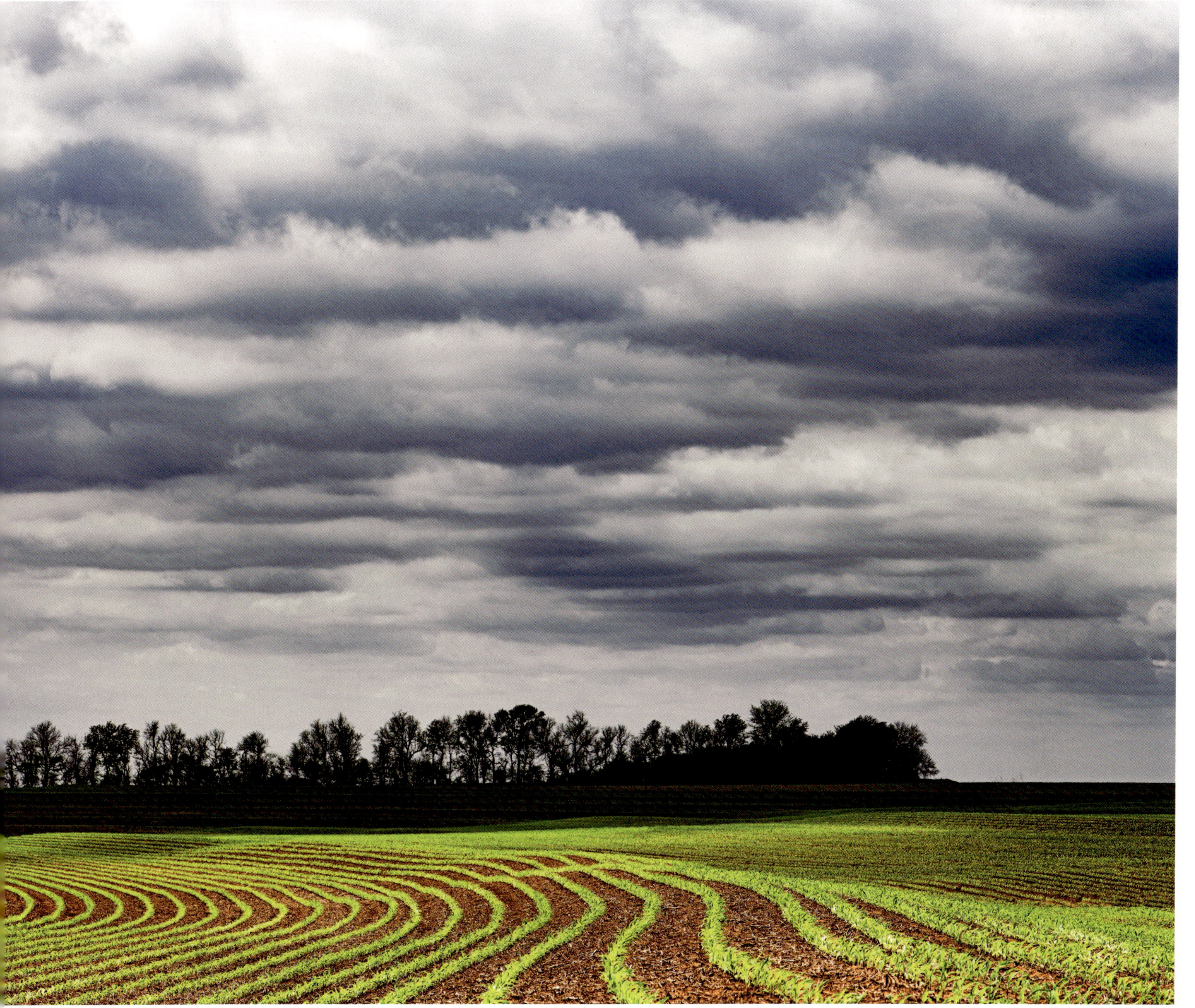

The light was dancing around. It took several attempts and a lot of patience to do justice to this scene.

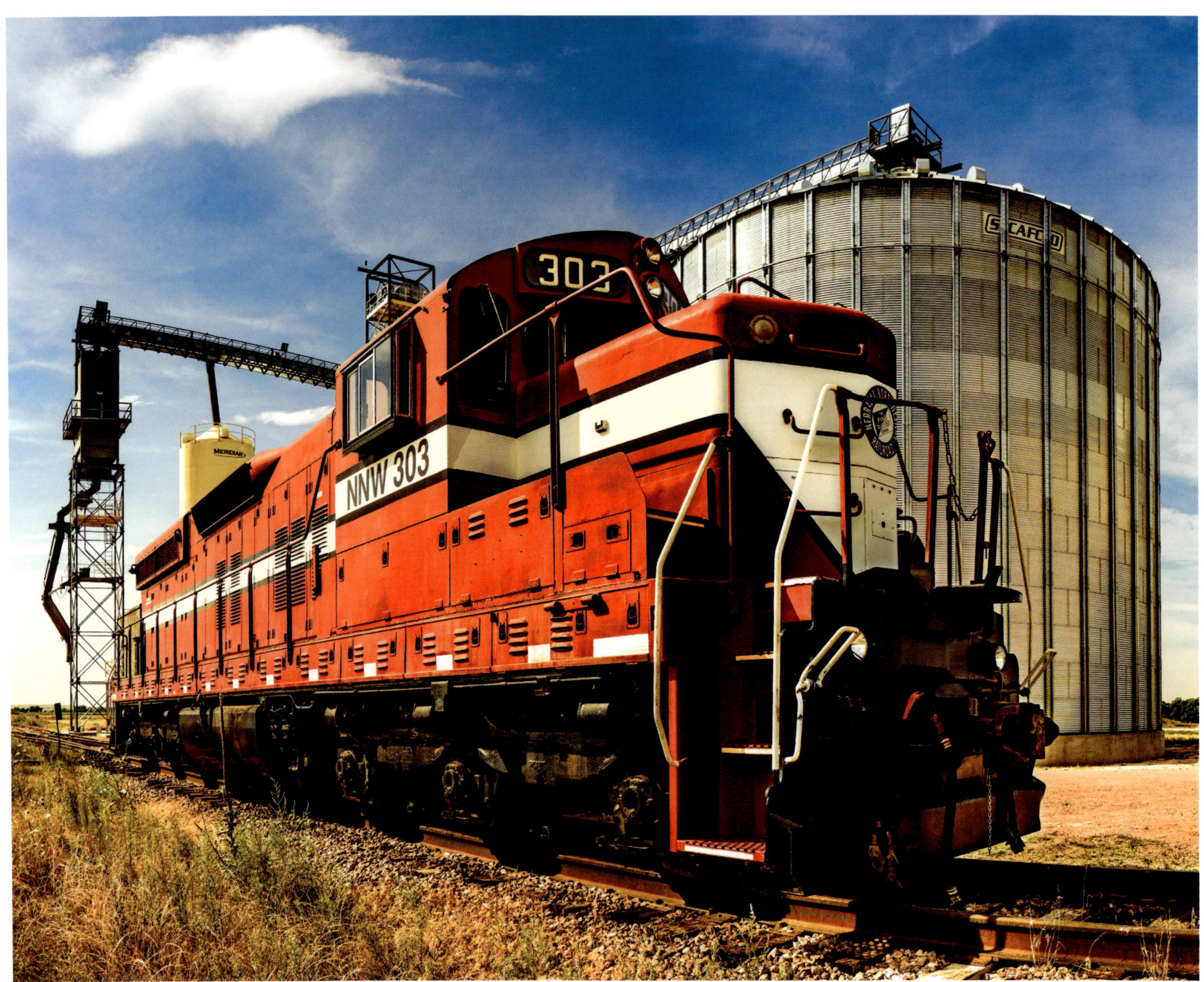

Nebraska Northwest Railroad

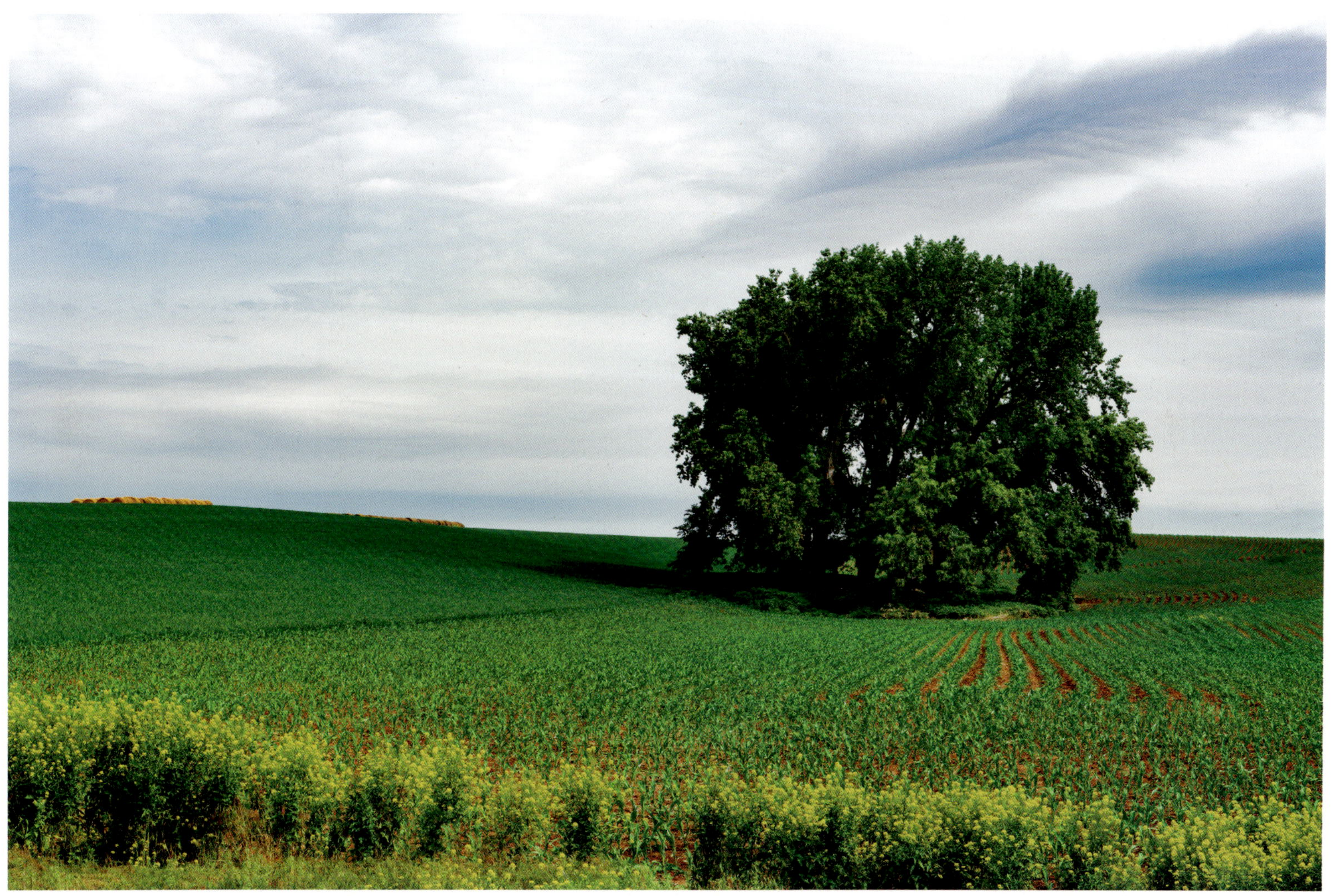

Doernemann Farm, Colfax County, Nebraska

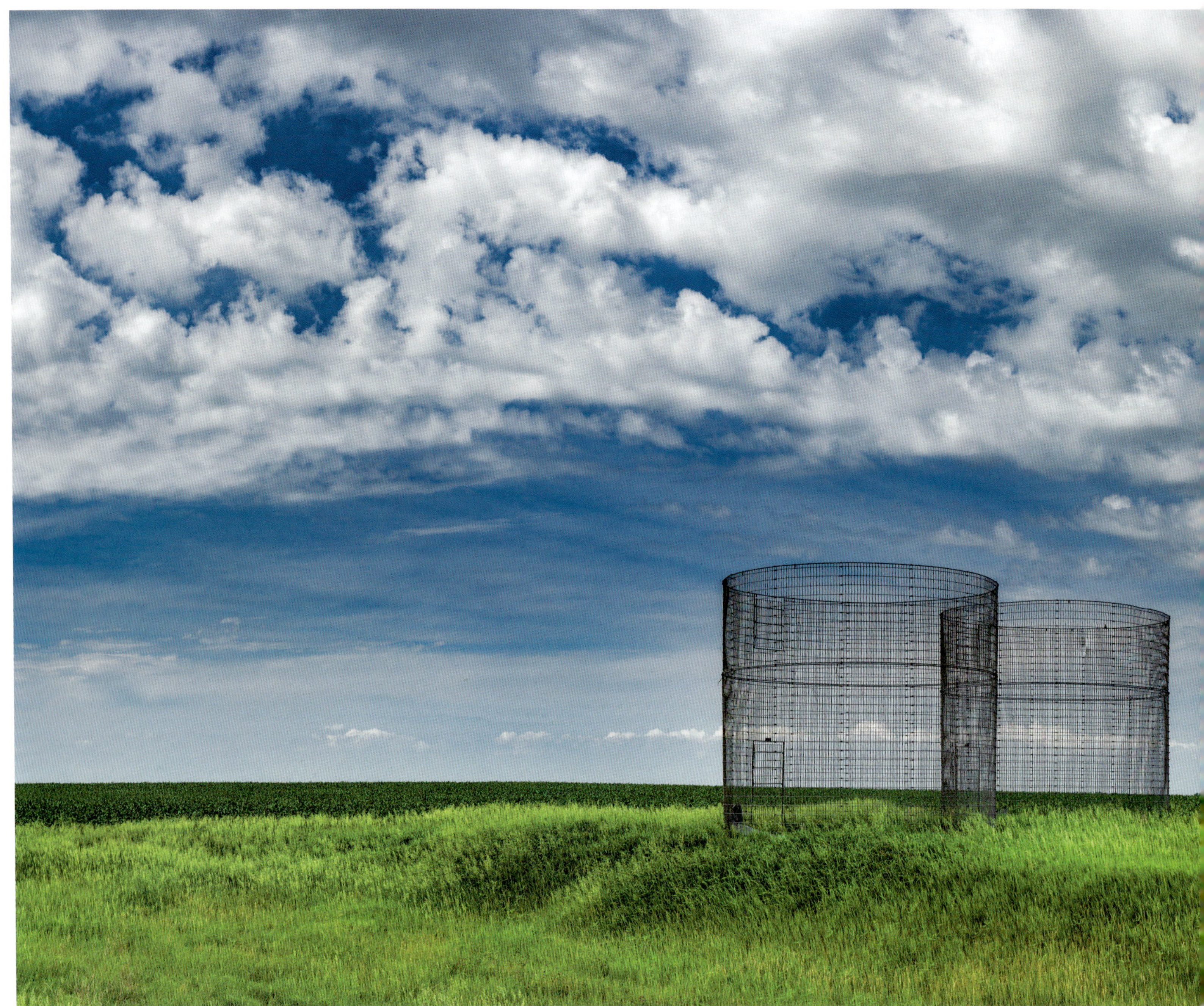

Empty corn cribs along Nebraska State Highway 79

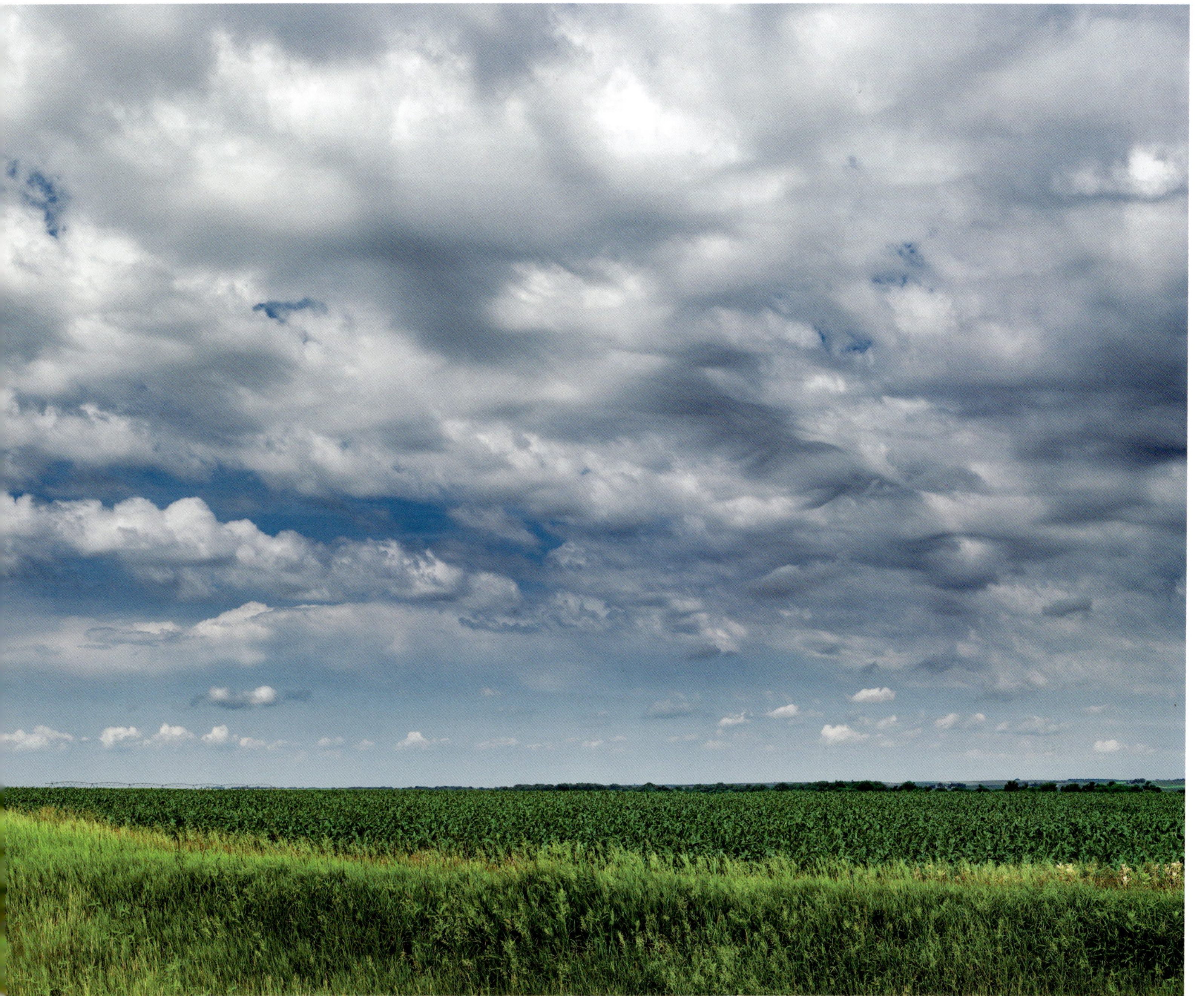

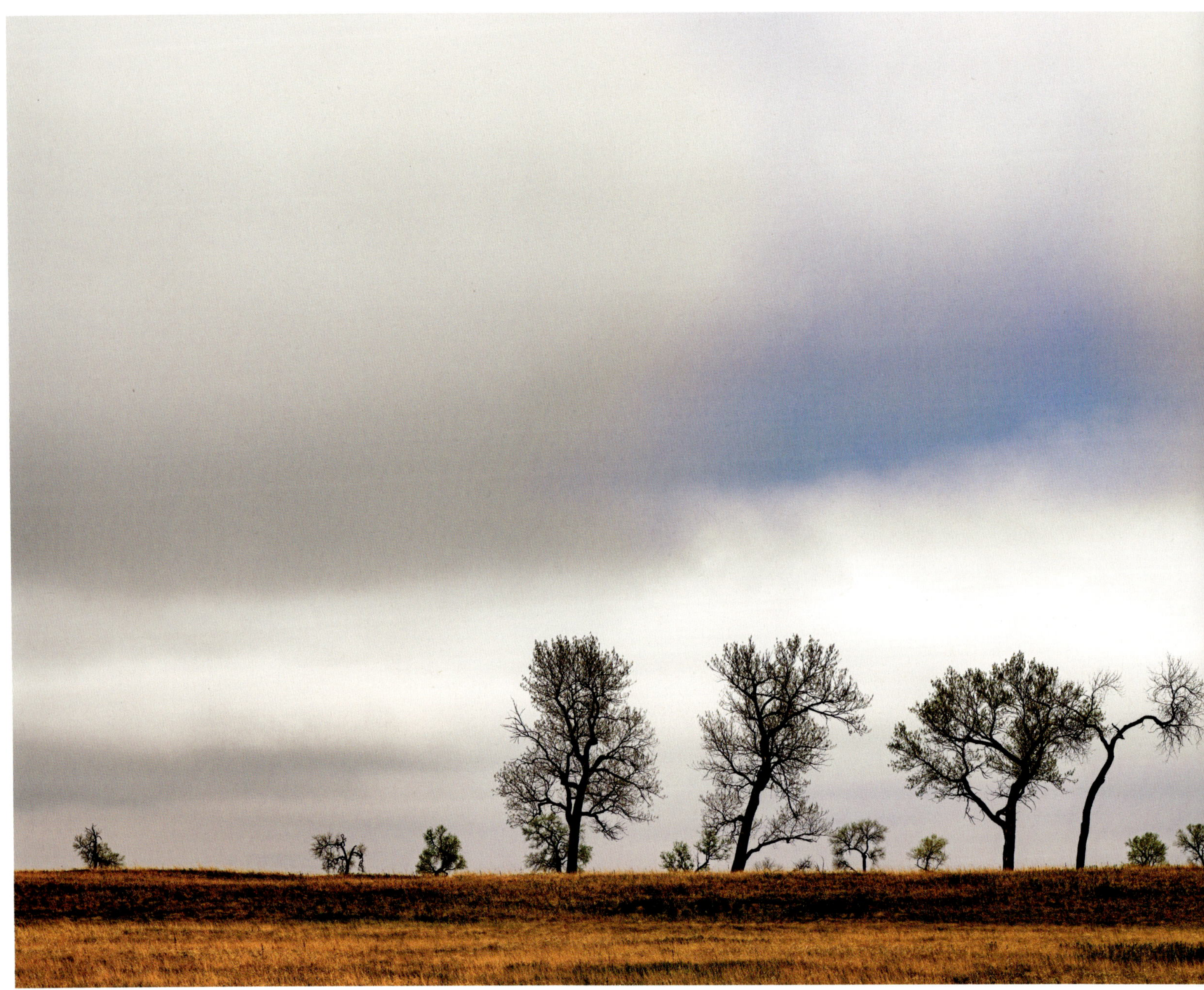

Trees along Nebraska State Highway 12

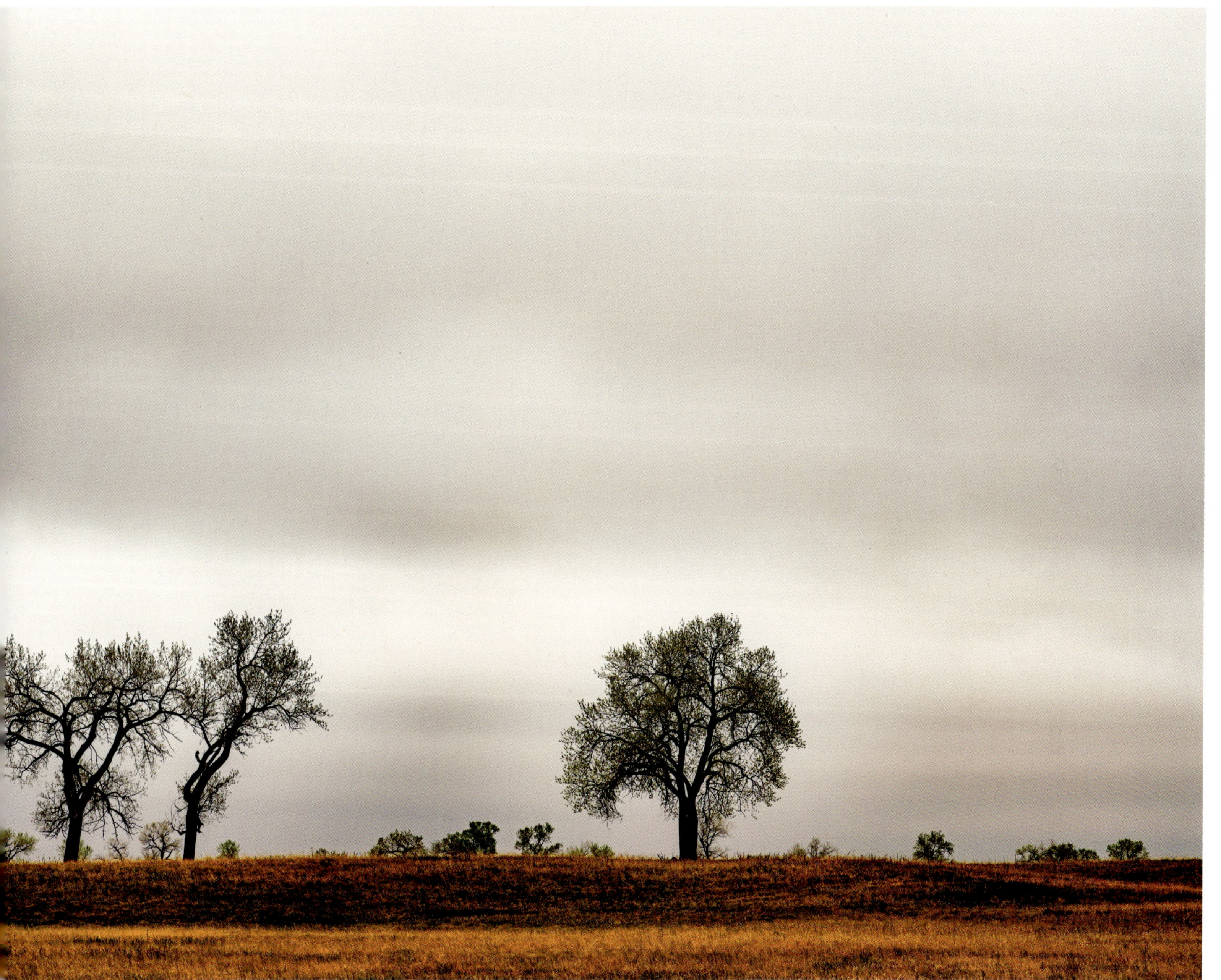

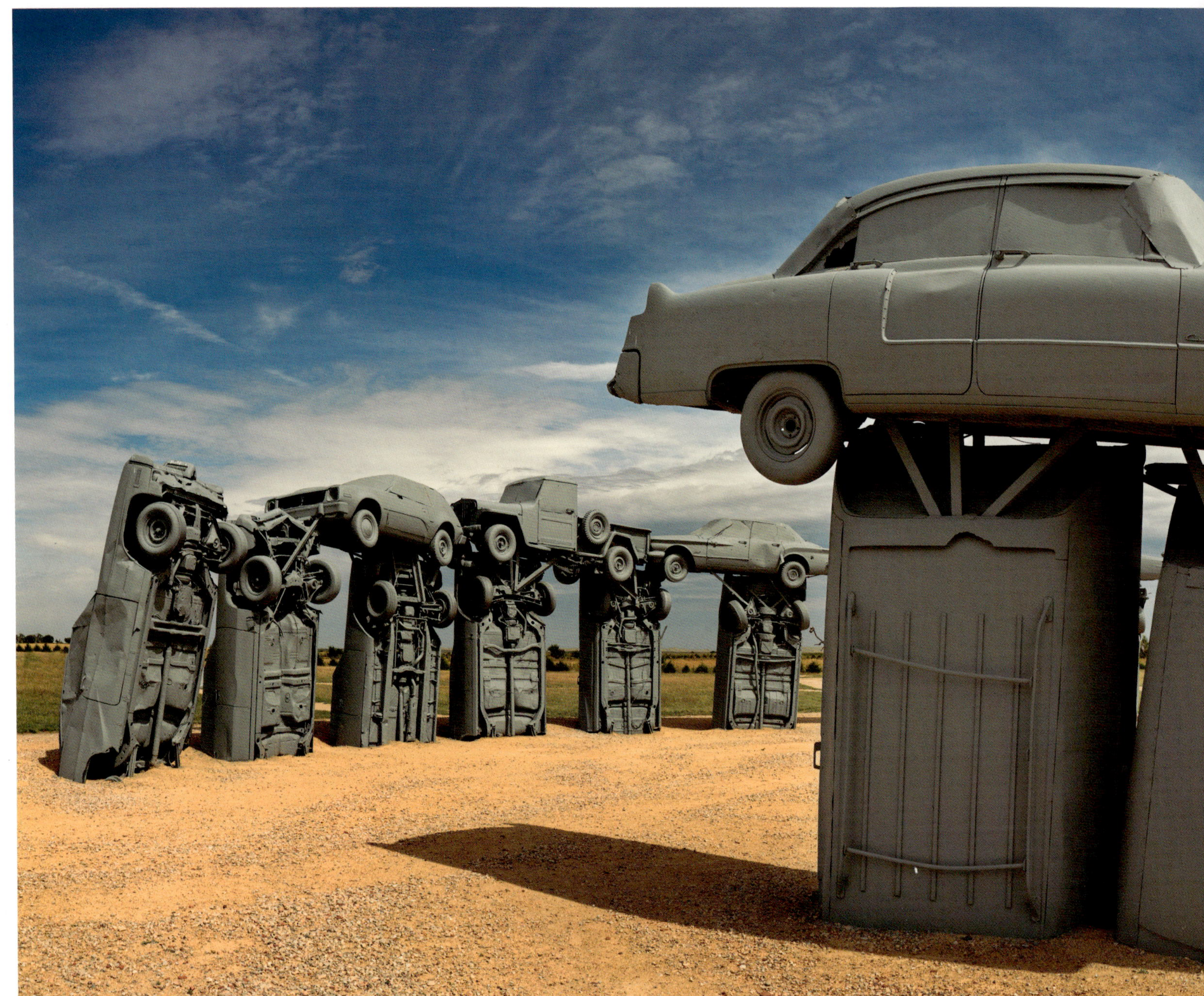

Carhenge, by Jim Reinders, Alliance, Nebraska

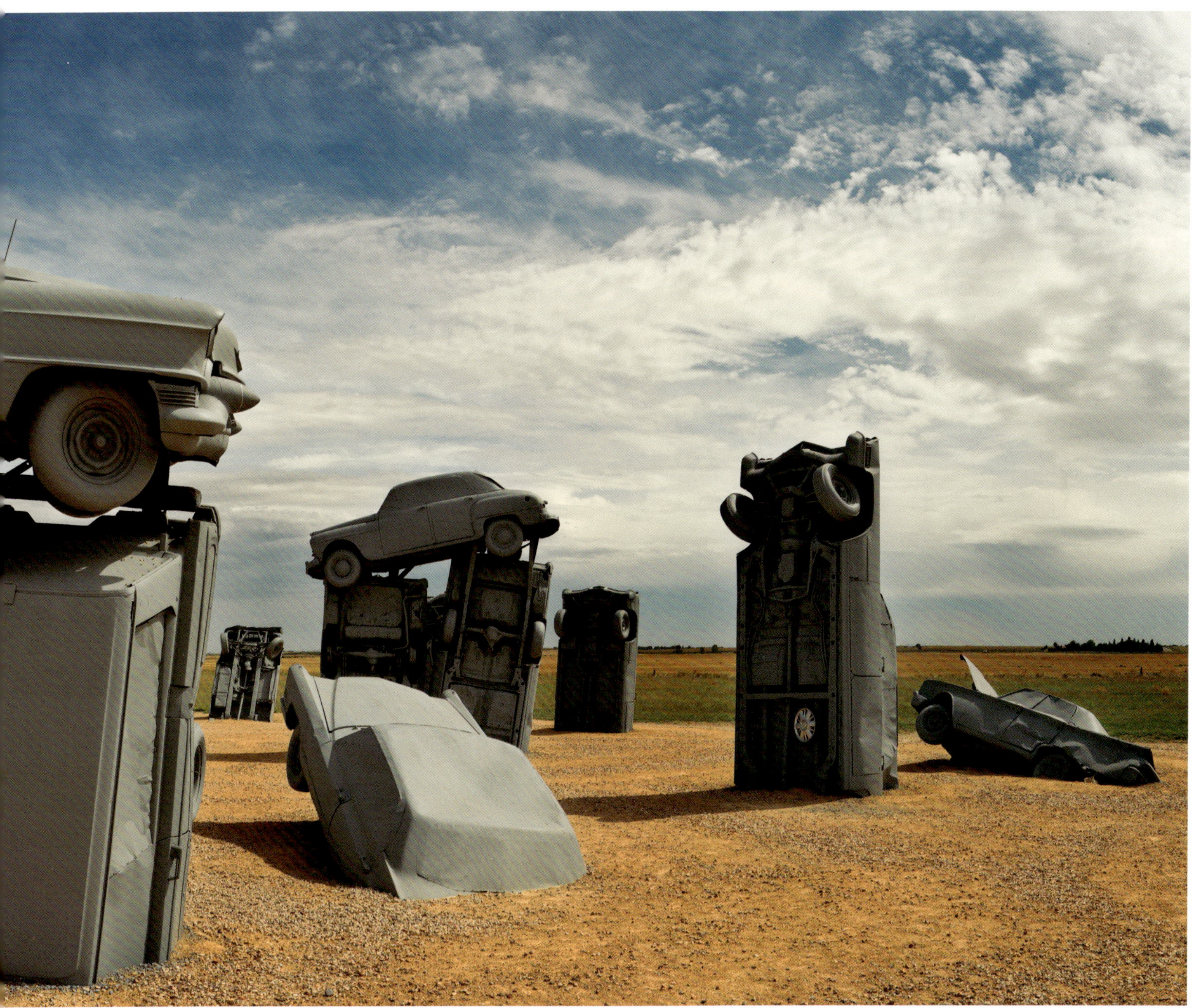

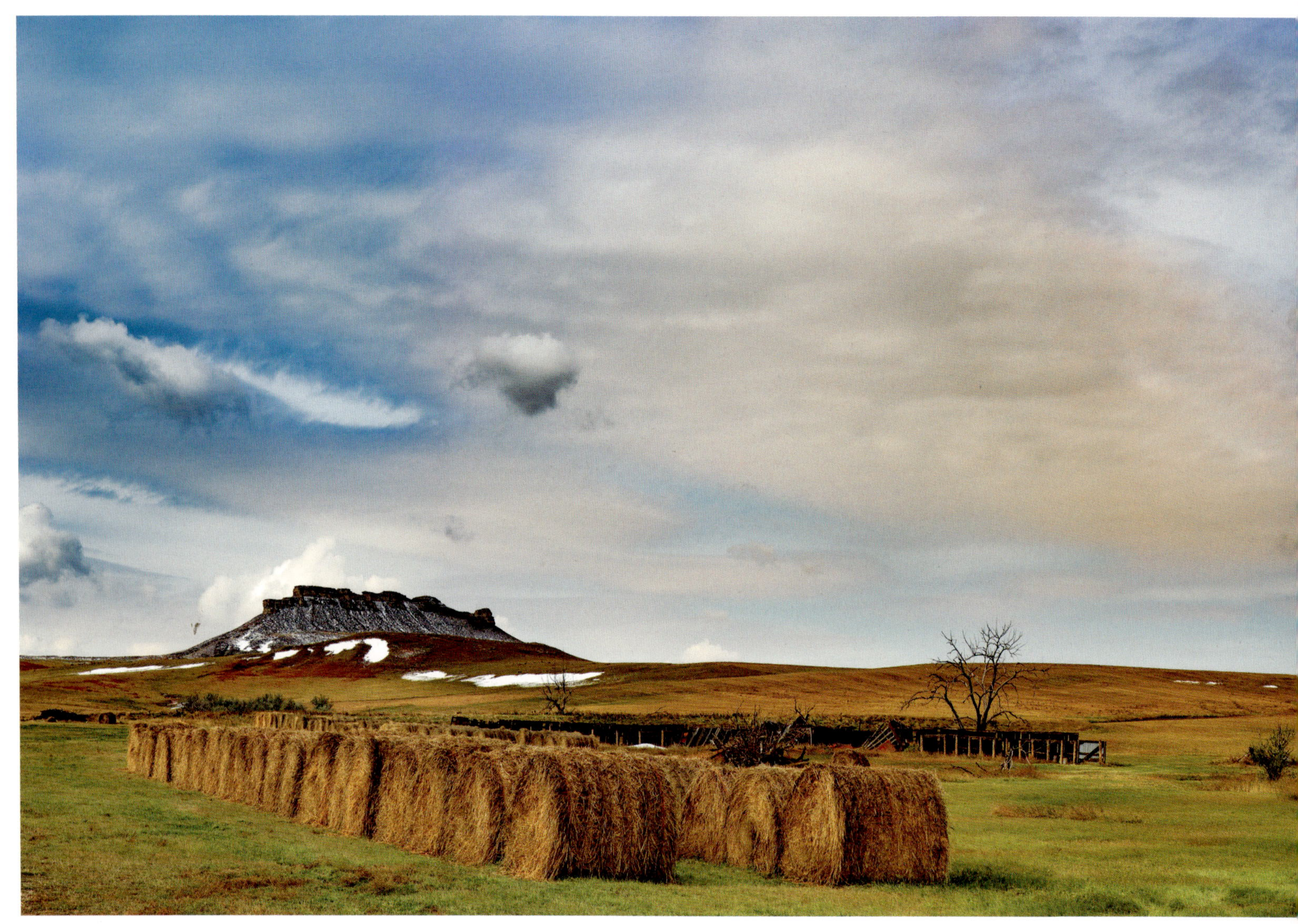

Castle Rock Ranch, South Dakota

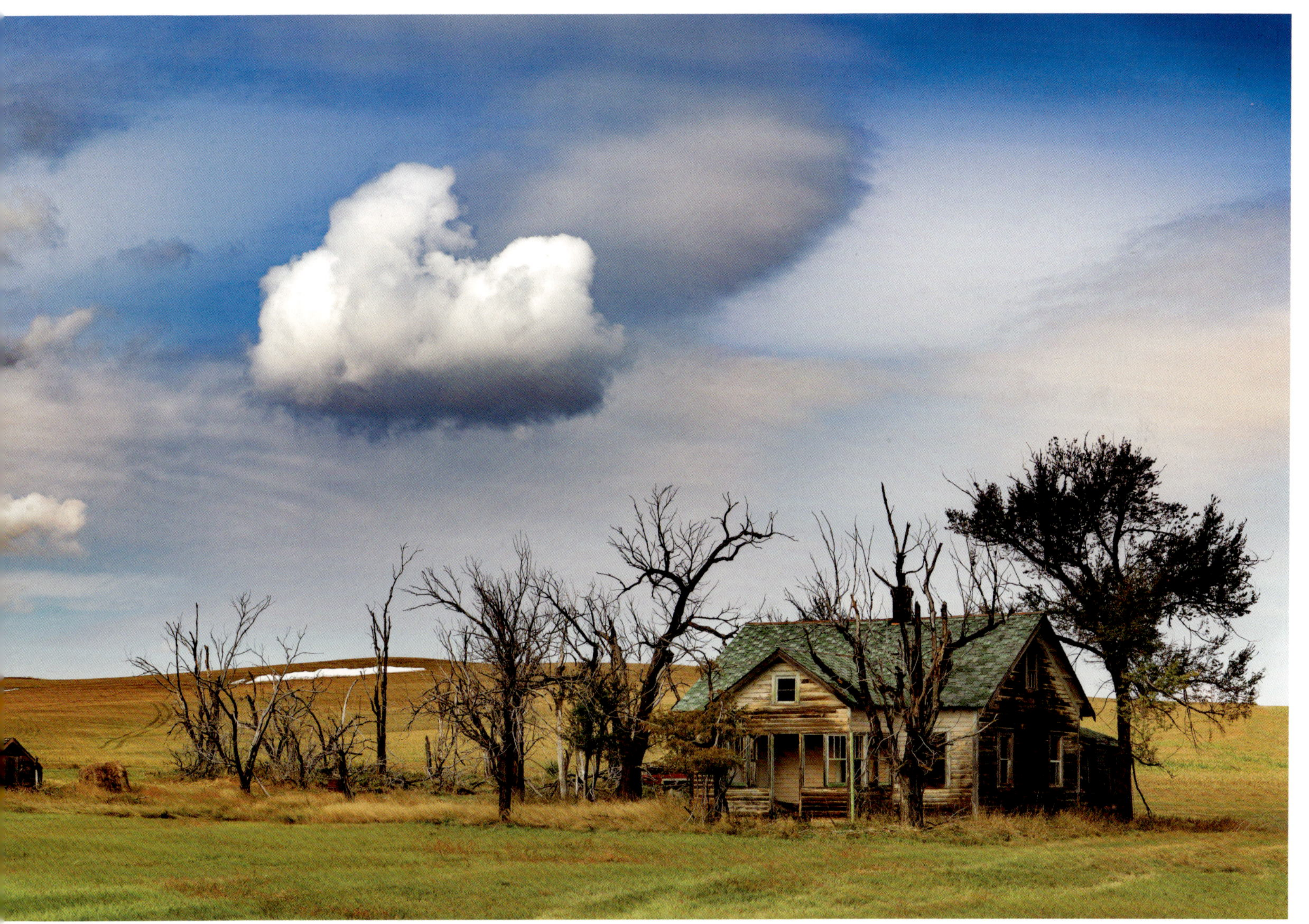

I couldn't figure out what my subject should be in this shot, so I included everything.

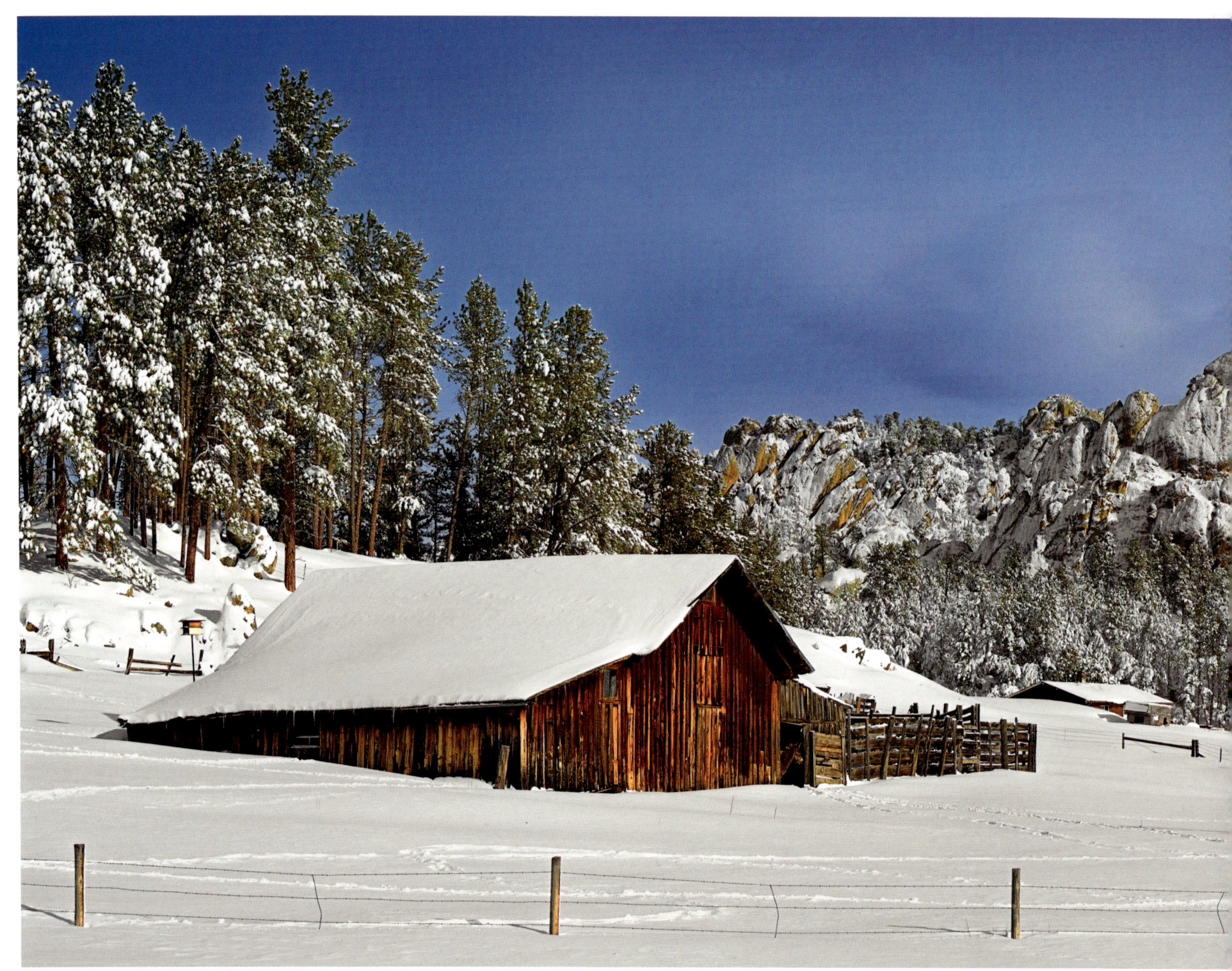

South Dakota ranch after winter storm Atlas, State Highway 16A

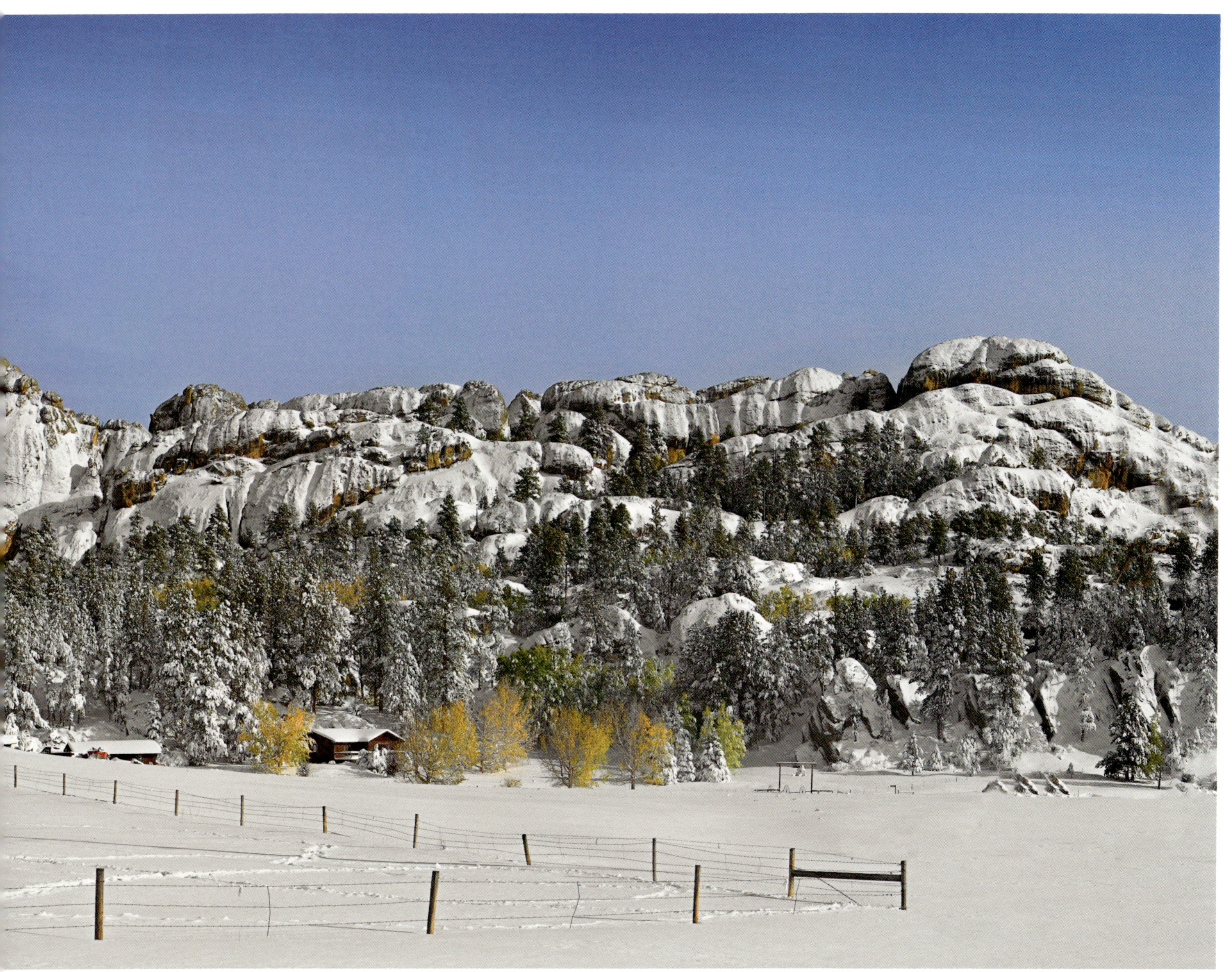

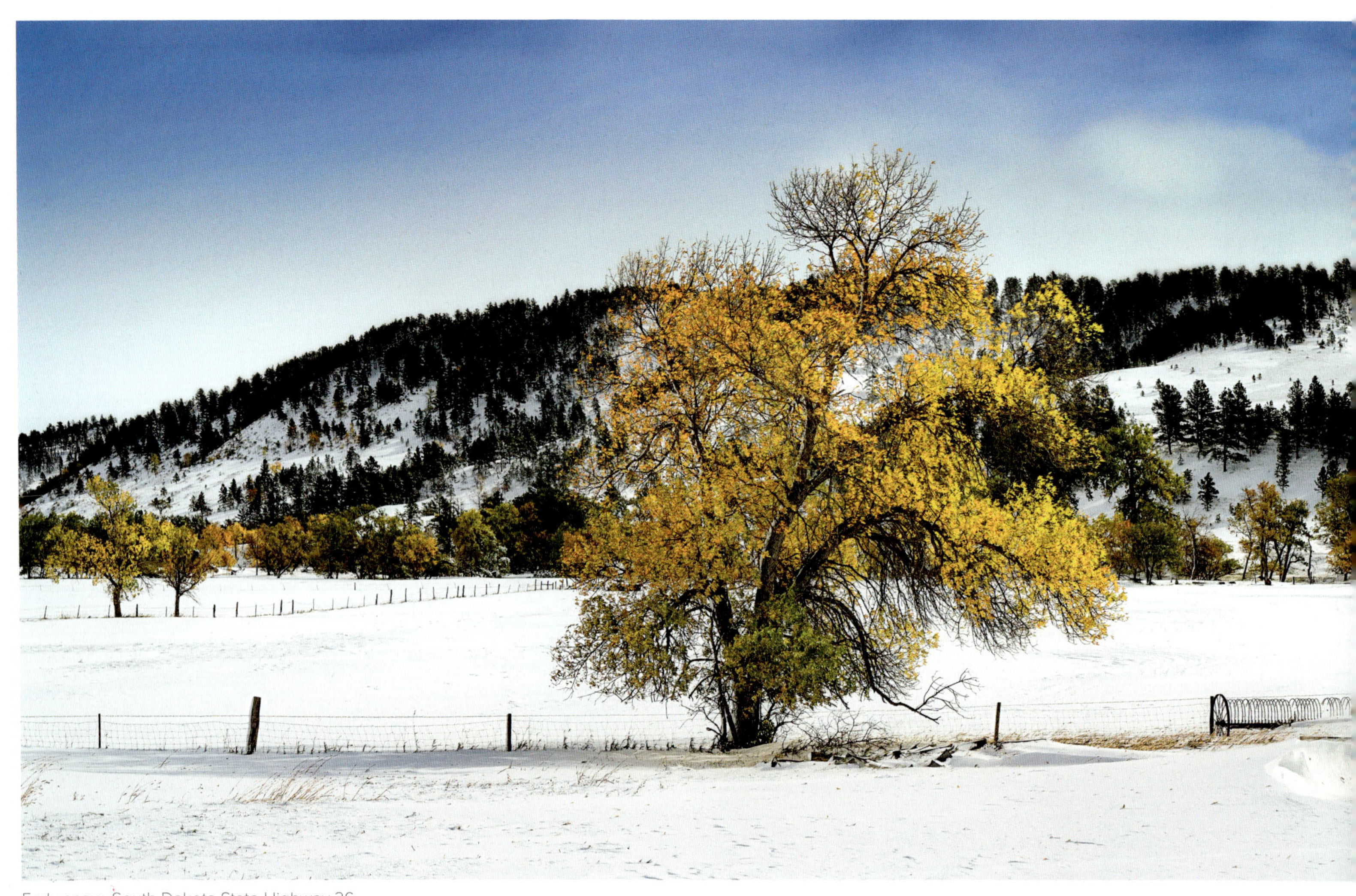

Early snow, South Dakota State Highway 36

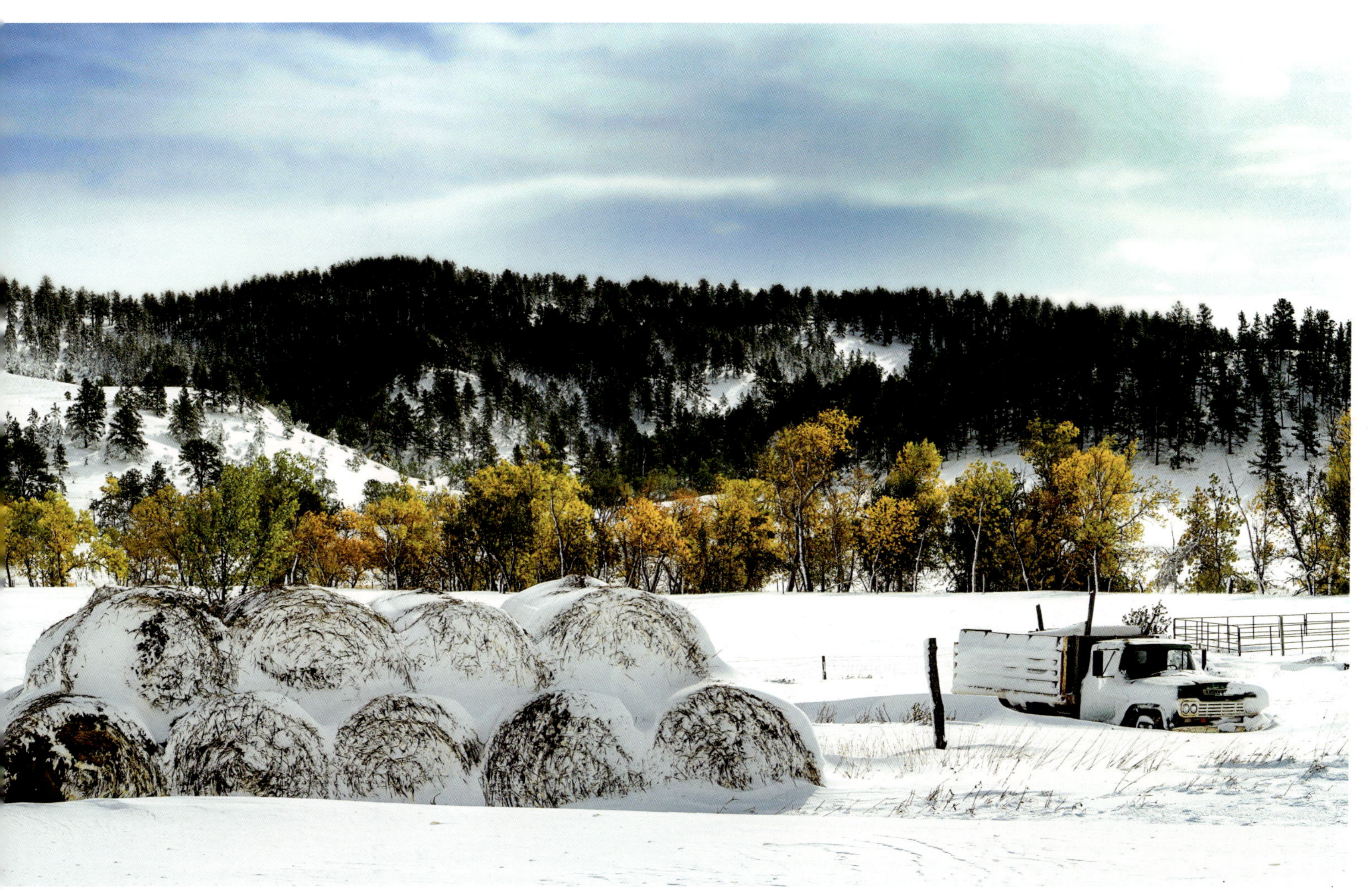

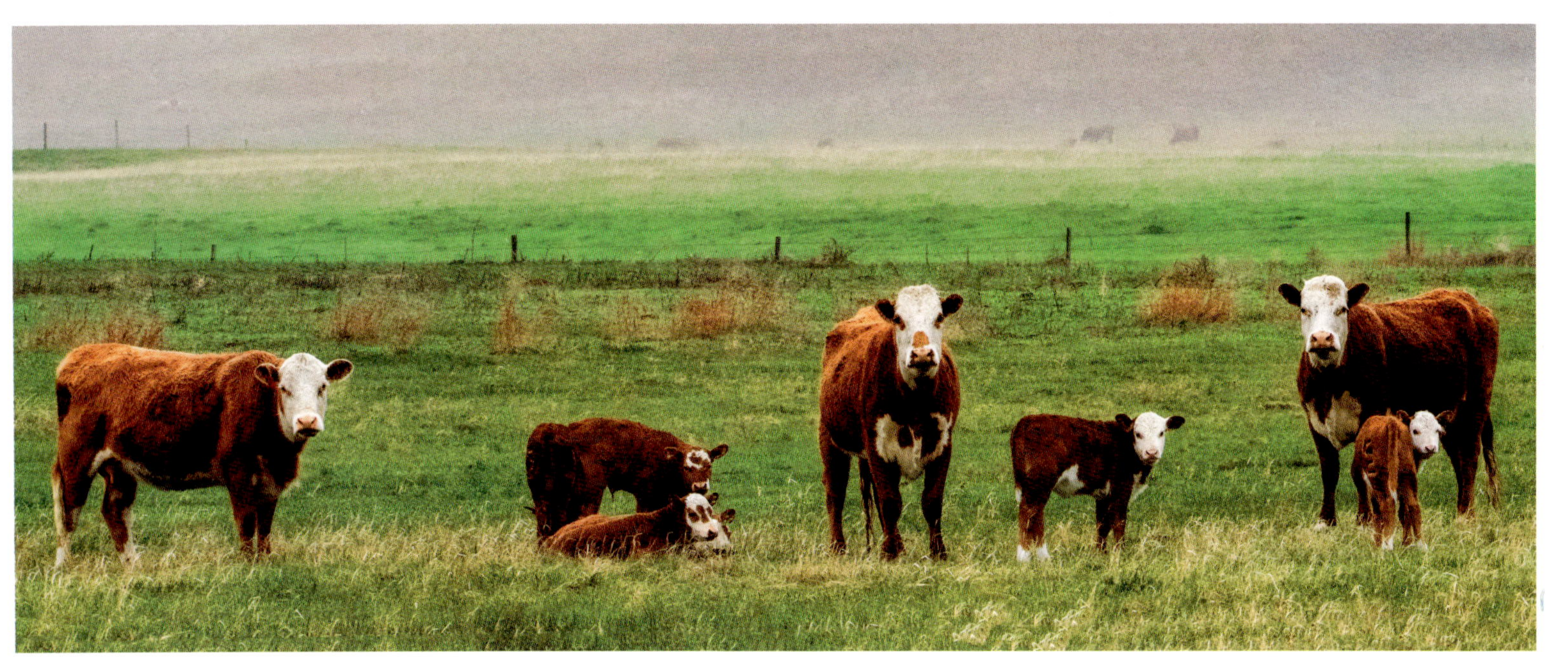

Hereford cattle, South Dakota

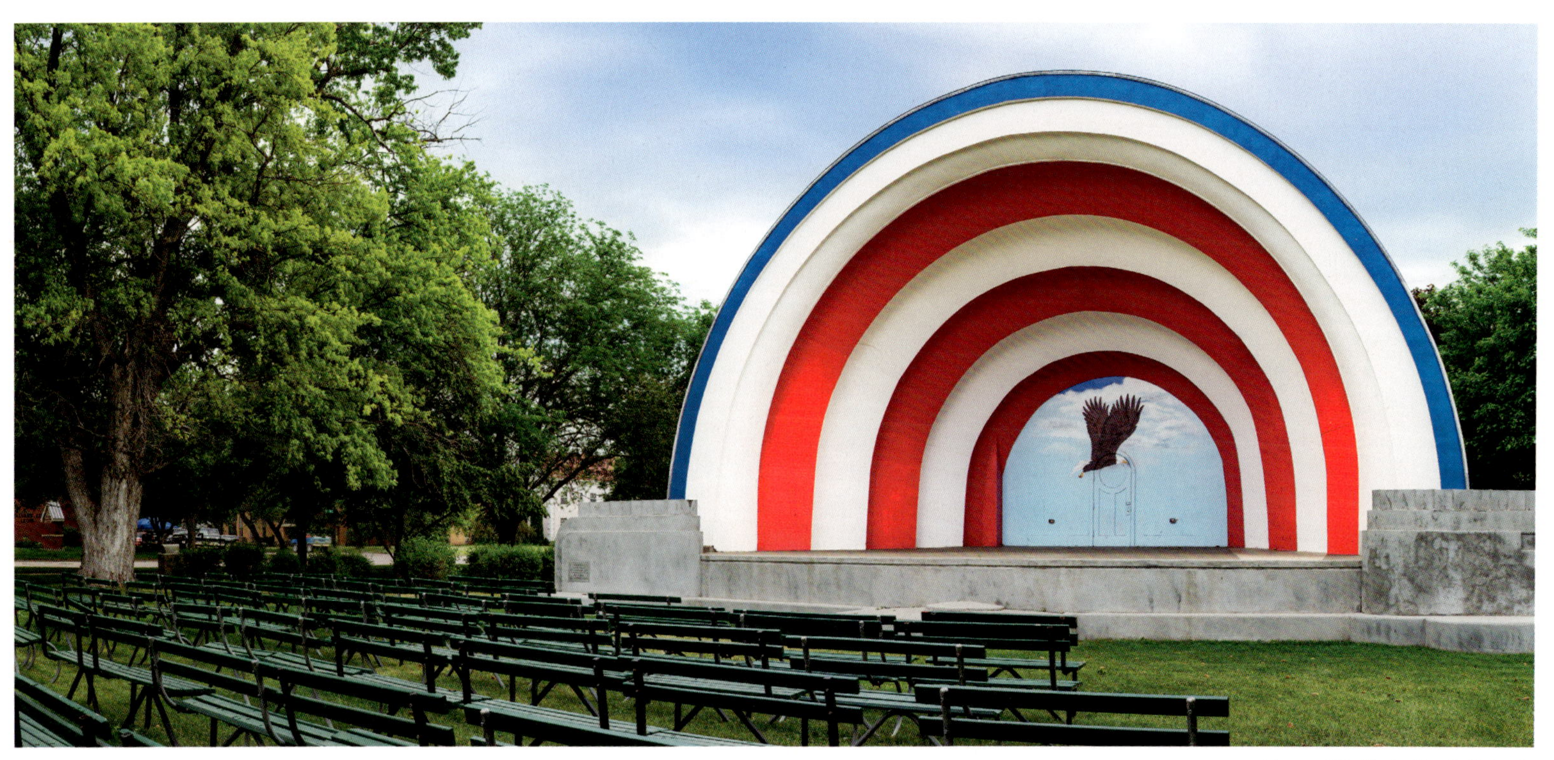

Huron City Park, South Dakota

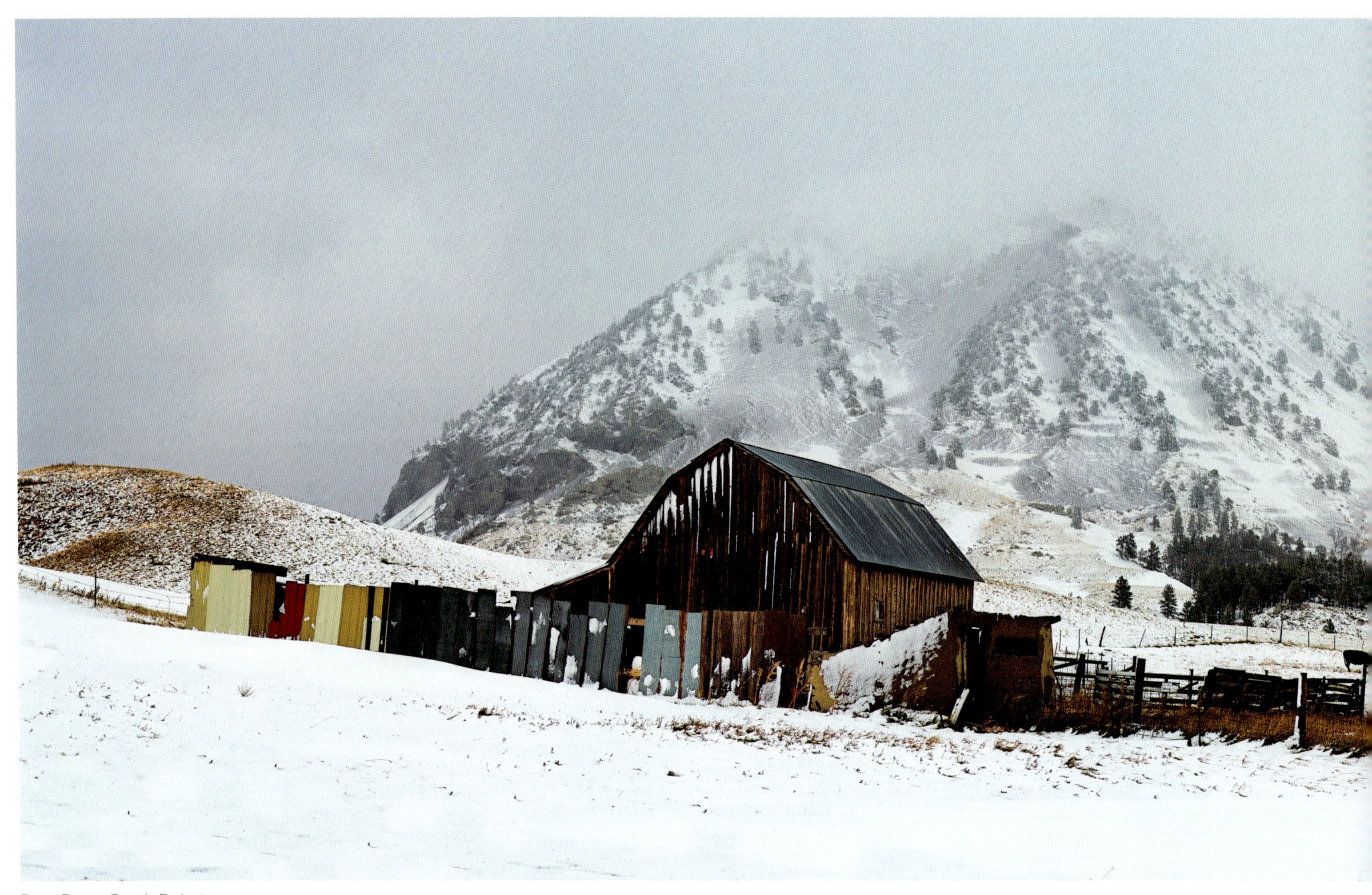

Bear Butte, South Dakota

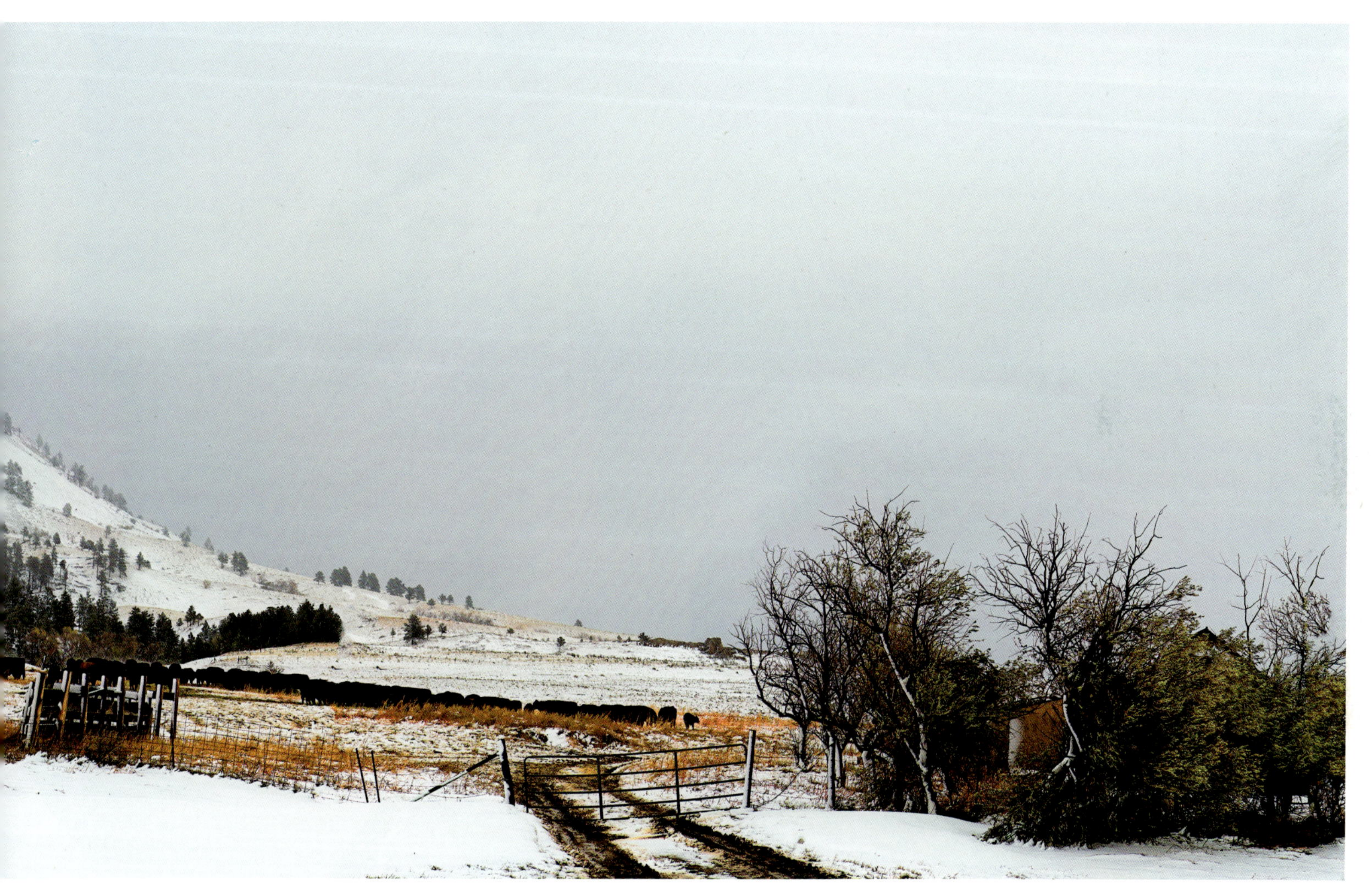

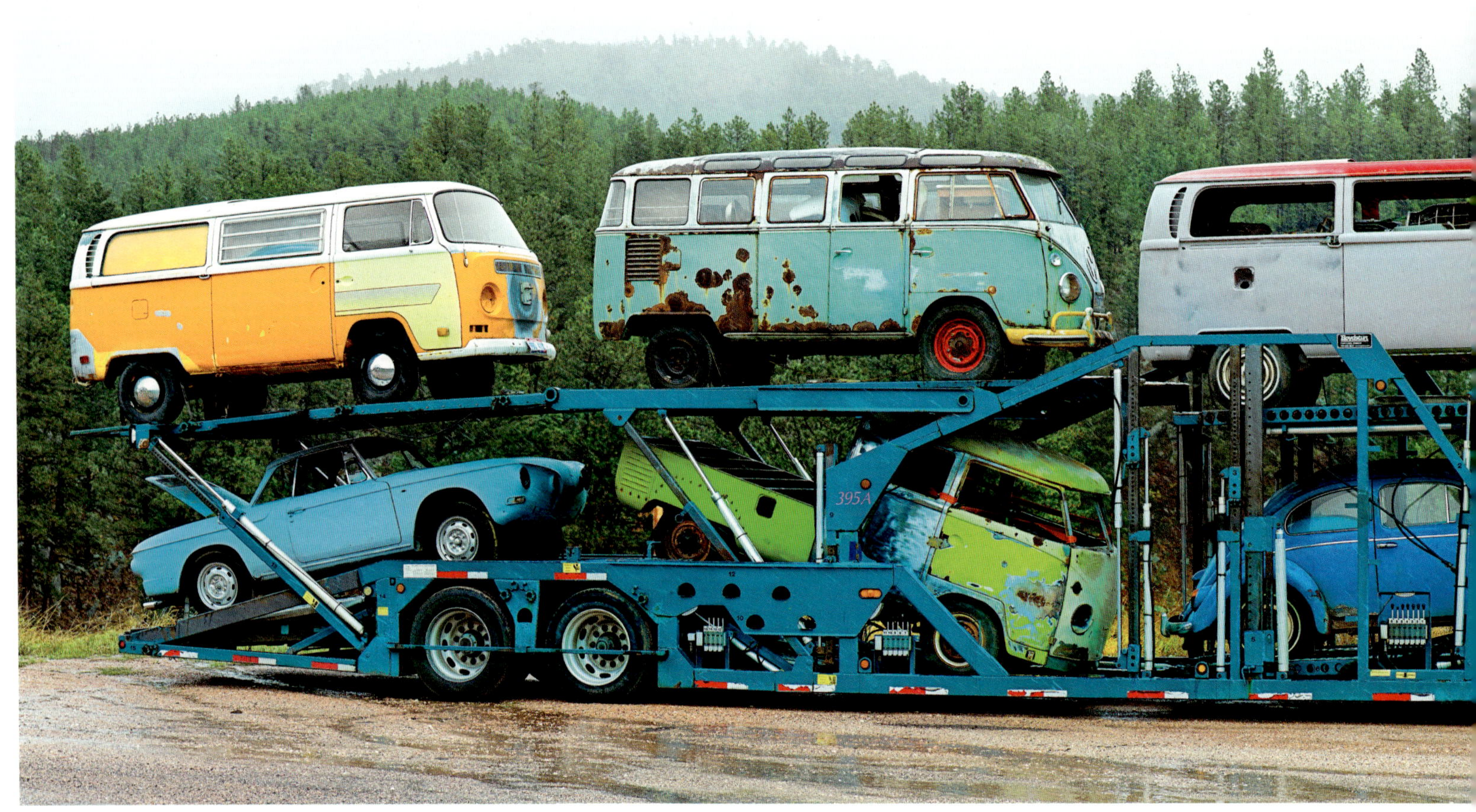

Car carrier along South Dakota State Highway 385

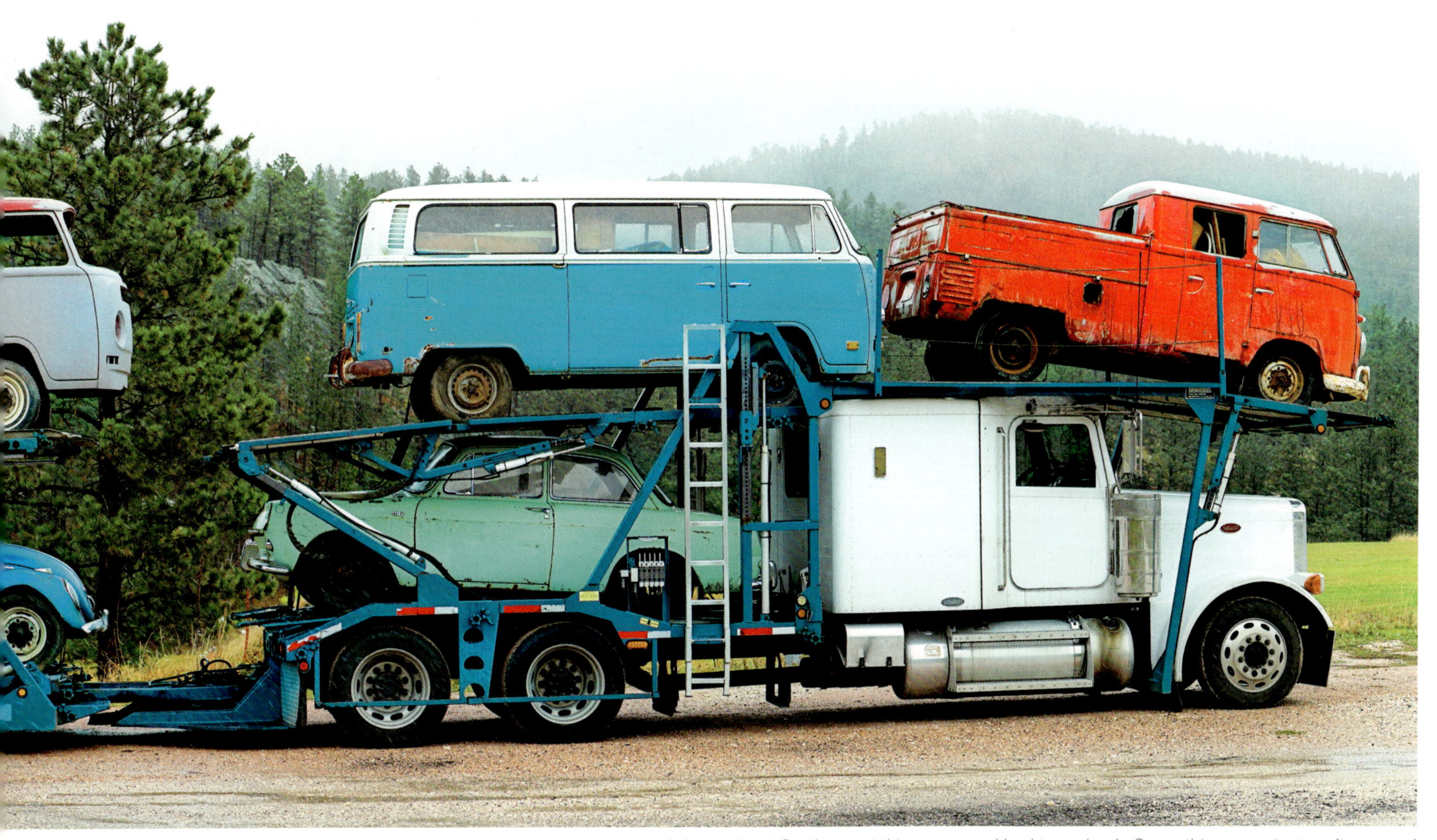

I drove about 2 miles past this scene and had to go back. Some things you just can't pass up!

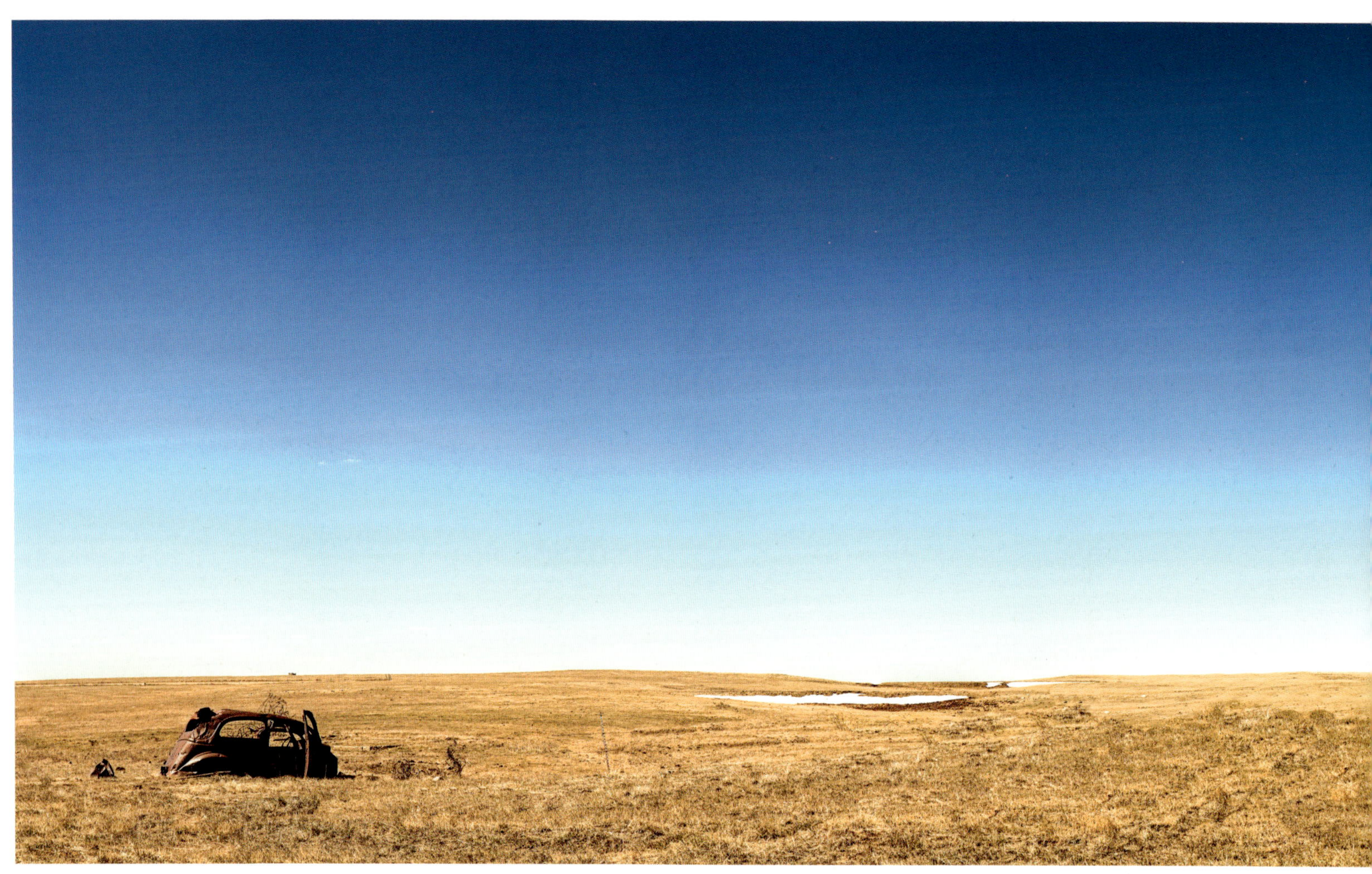

Abandoned homestead, South Dakota State Highway 34

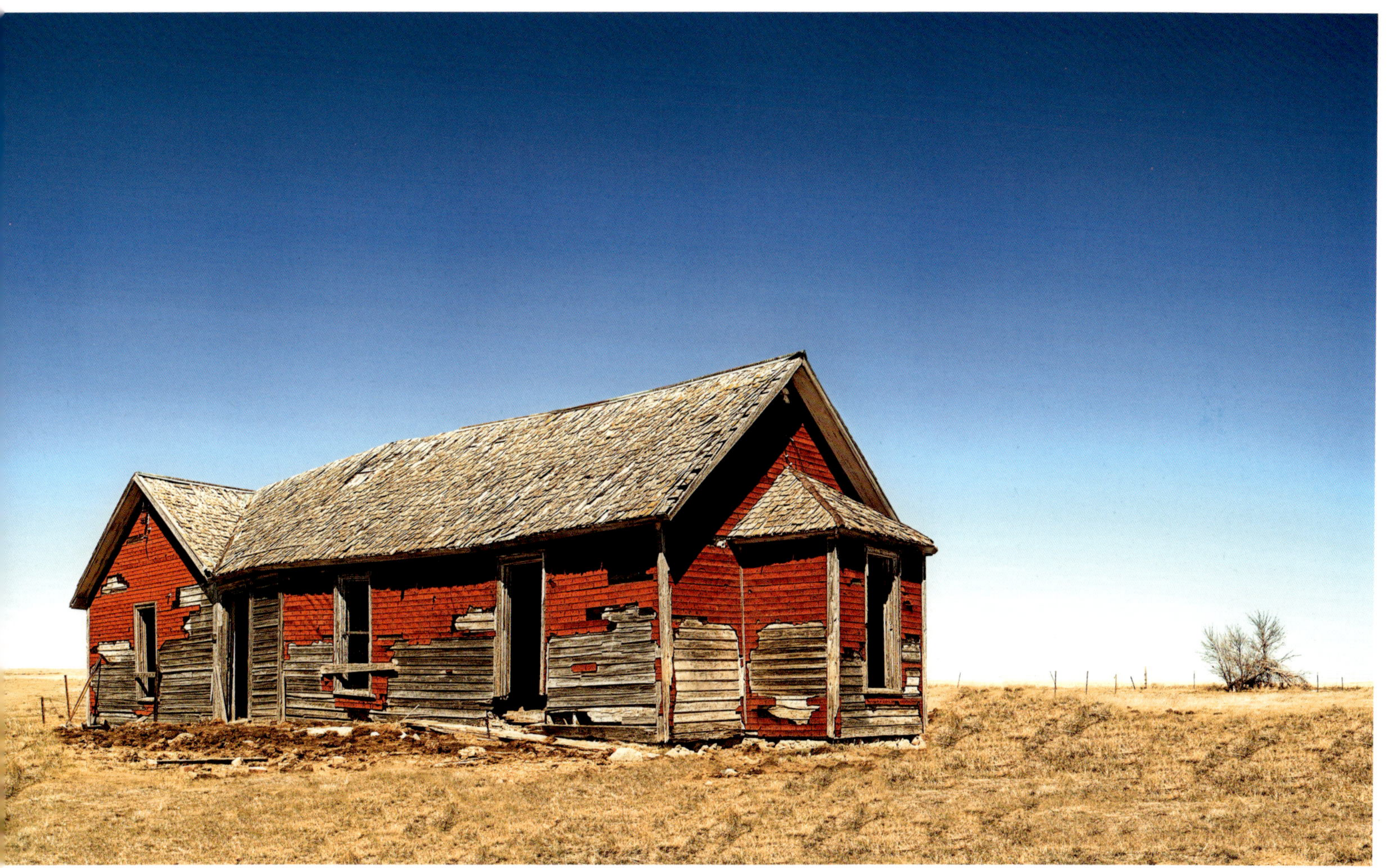

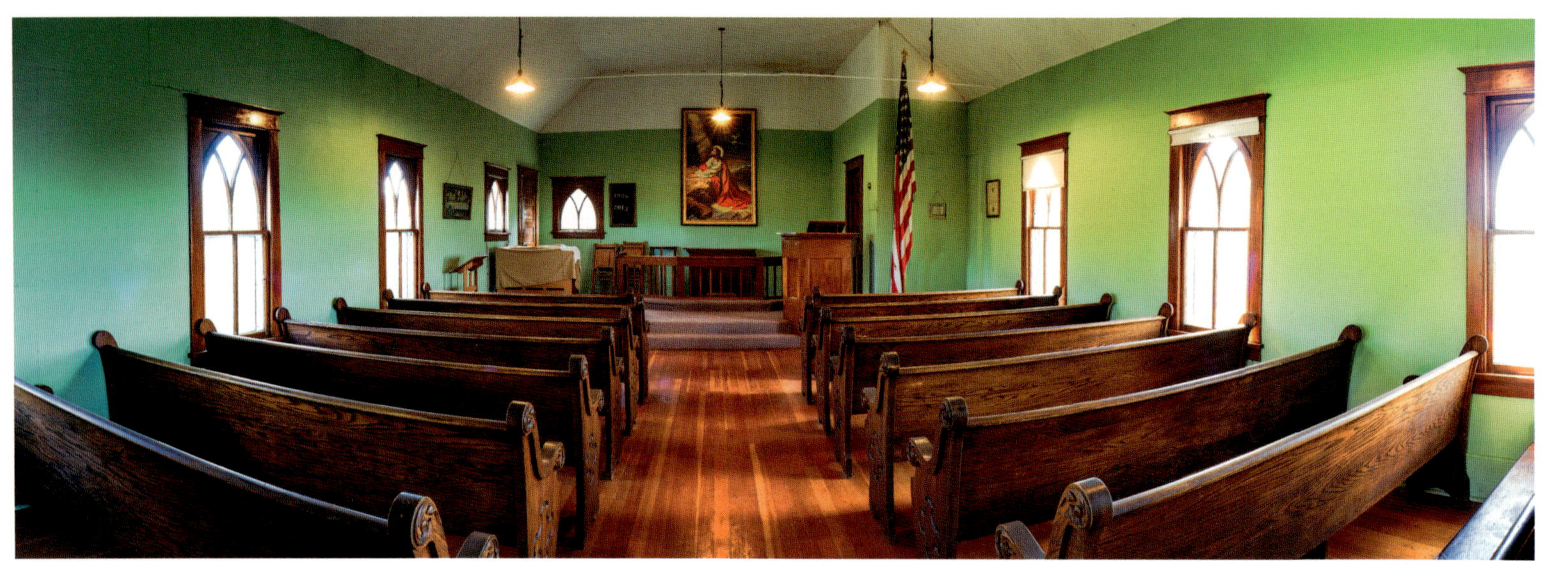

Cave Hills Lutheran Church, 1928, South Dakota

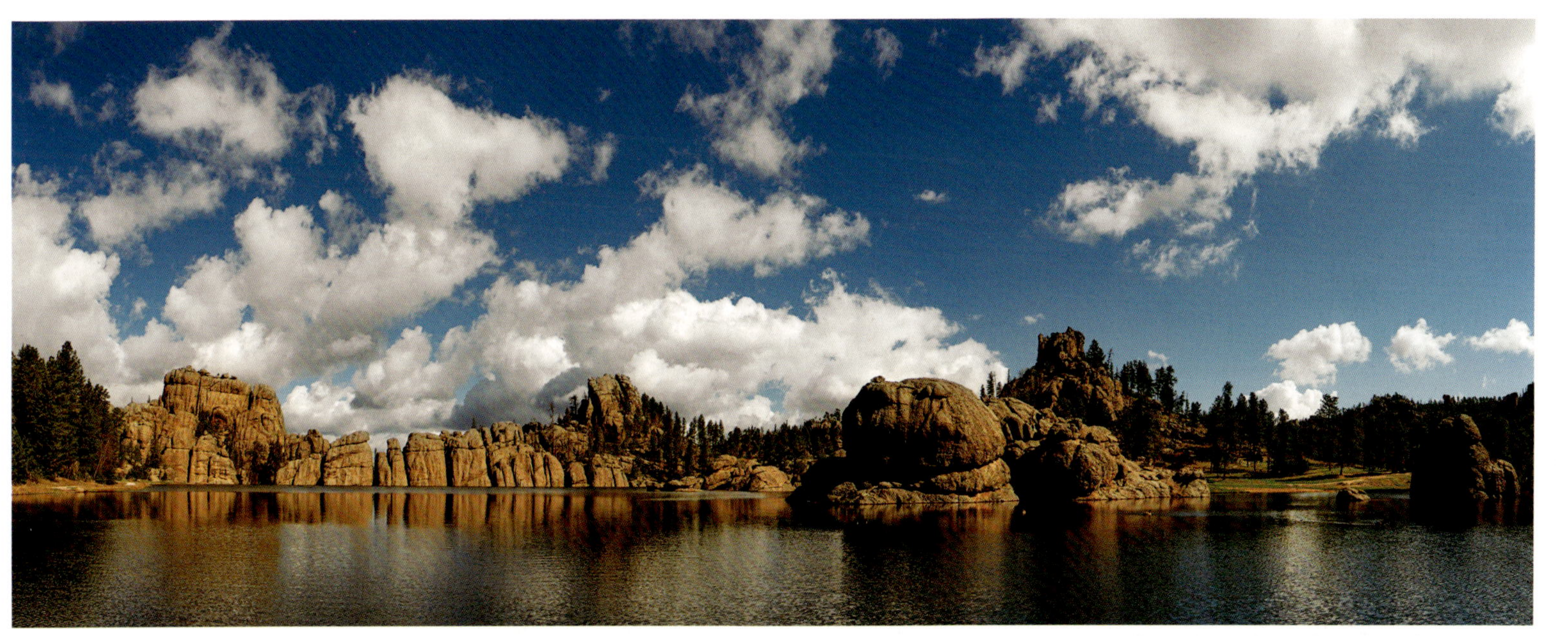

Sylvan Lake, Custer State Park, South Dakota

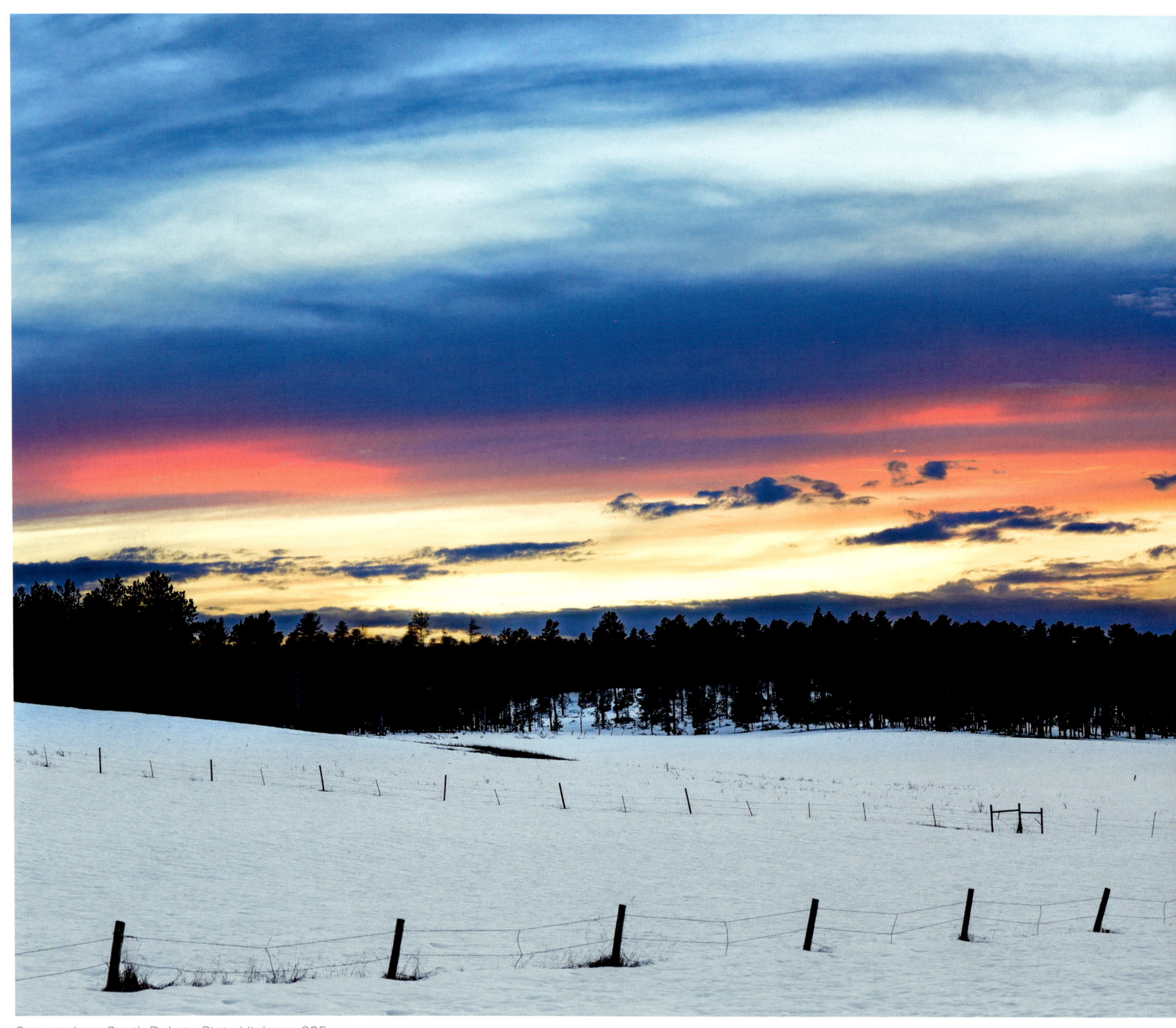

Sunset along South Dakota State Highway 385

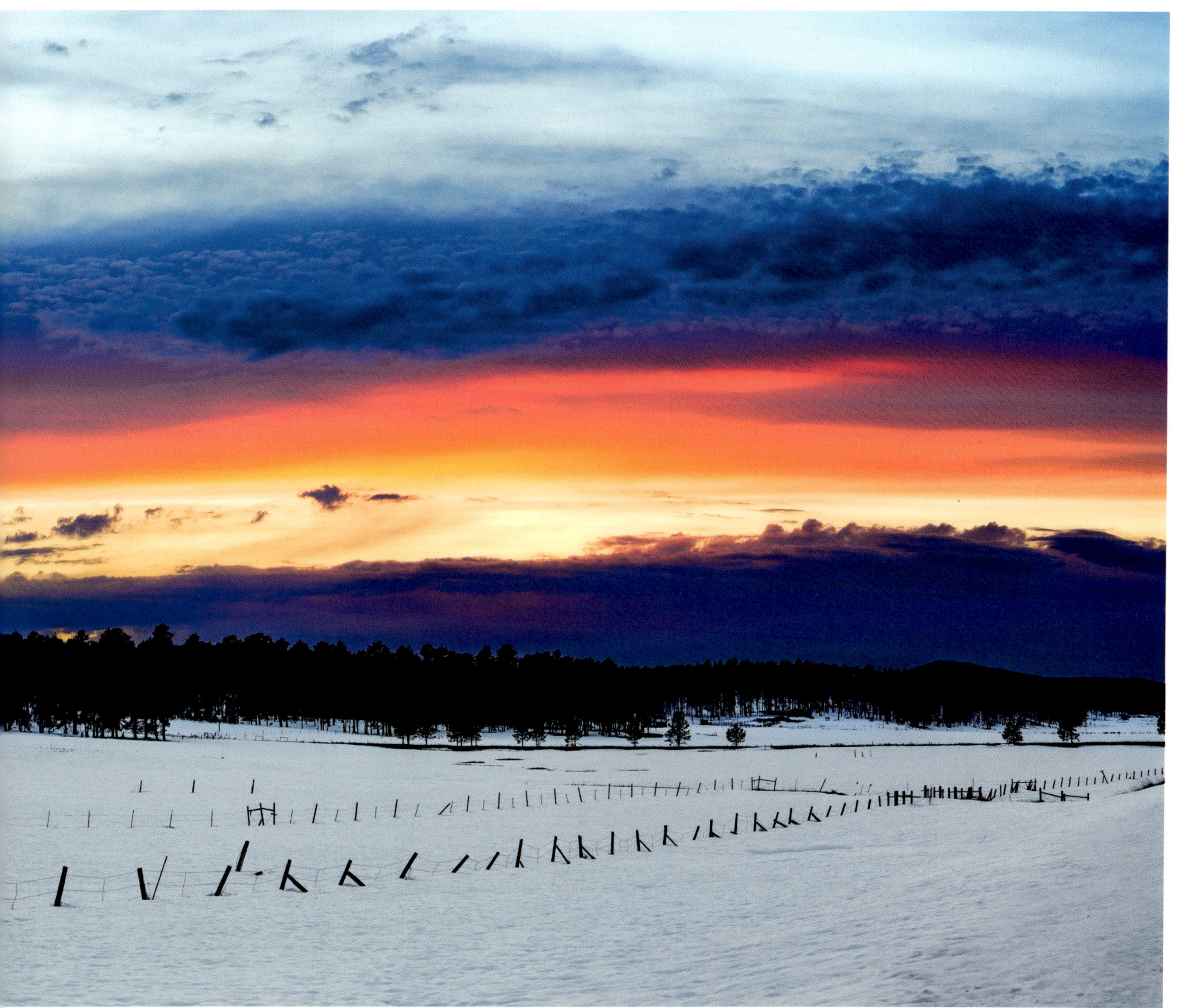

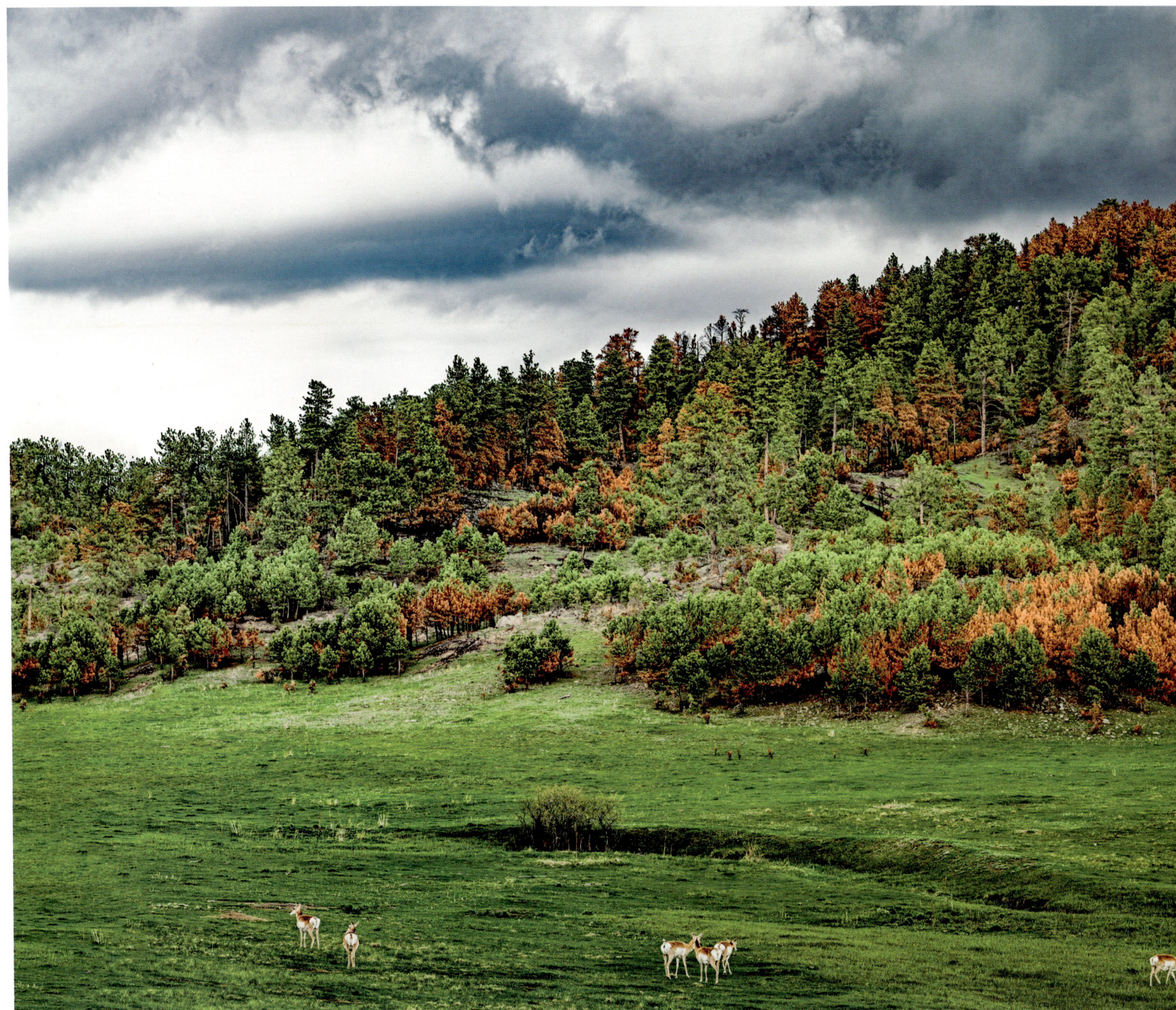

Pronghorn antelope in the Black Hills, South Dakota

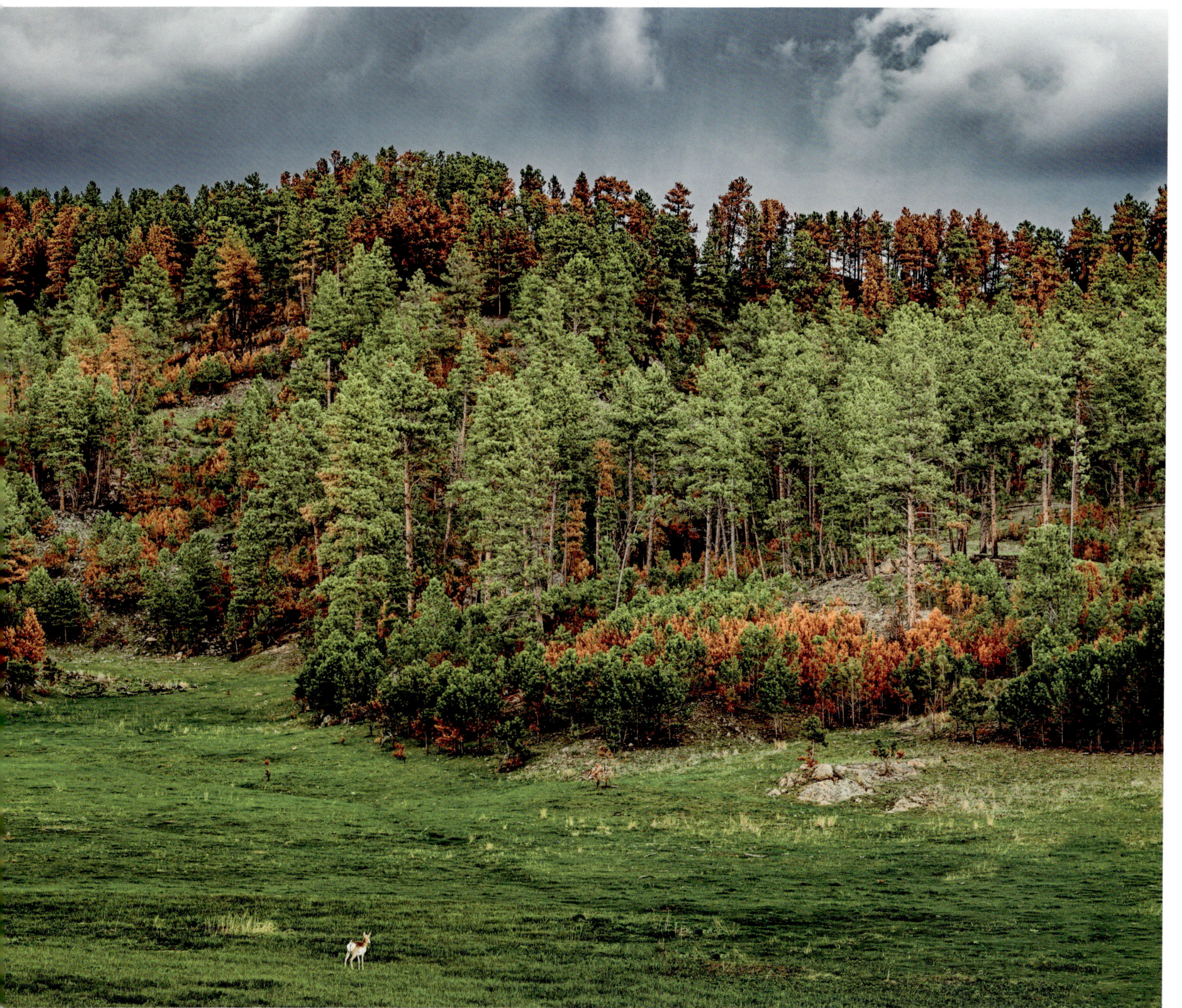

The color in the trees was caused by a combination of fire damage and beetle infestation.

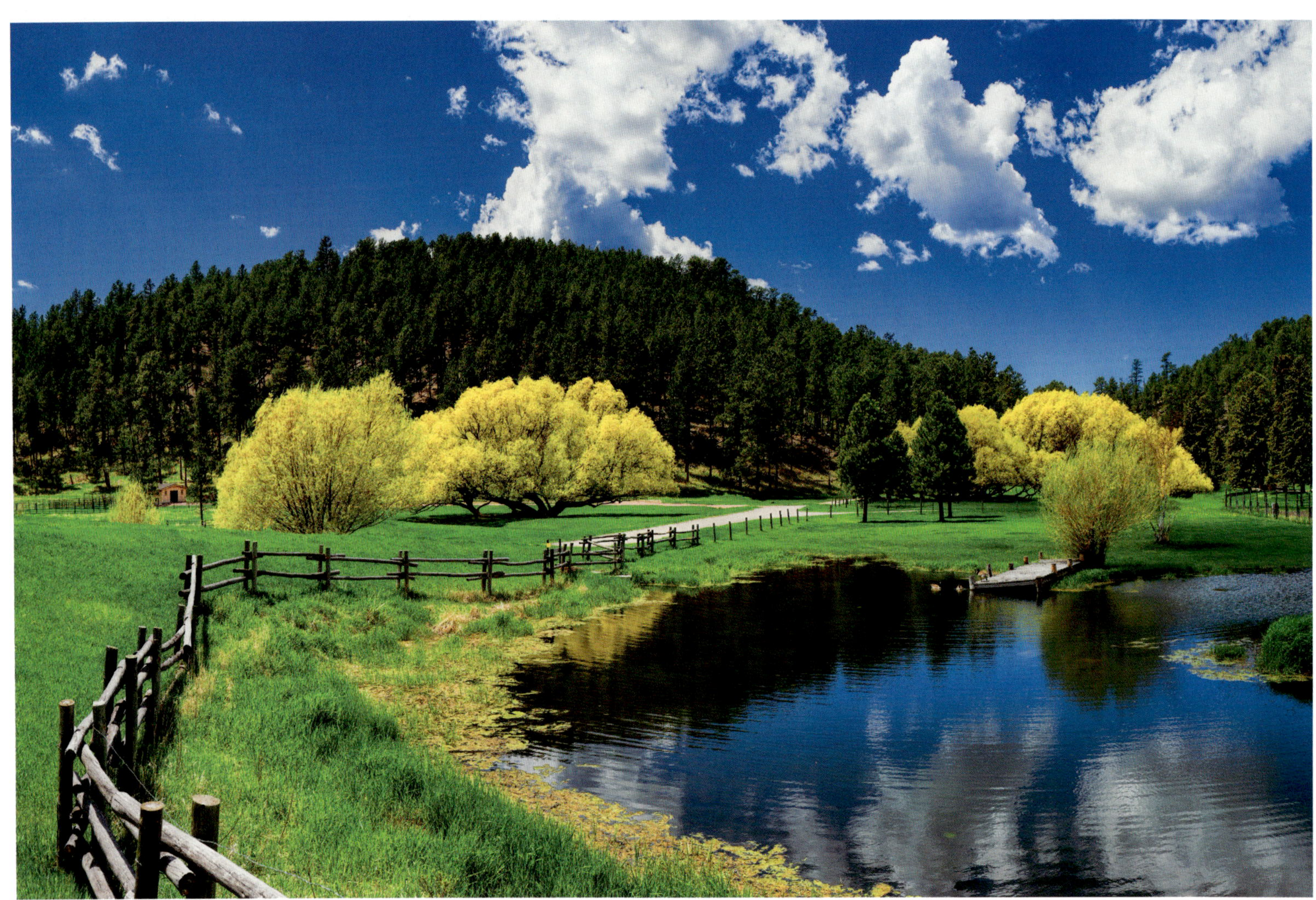

Pond near Pringle, South Dakota

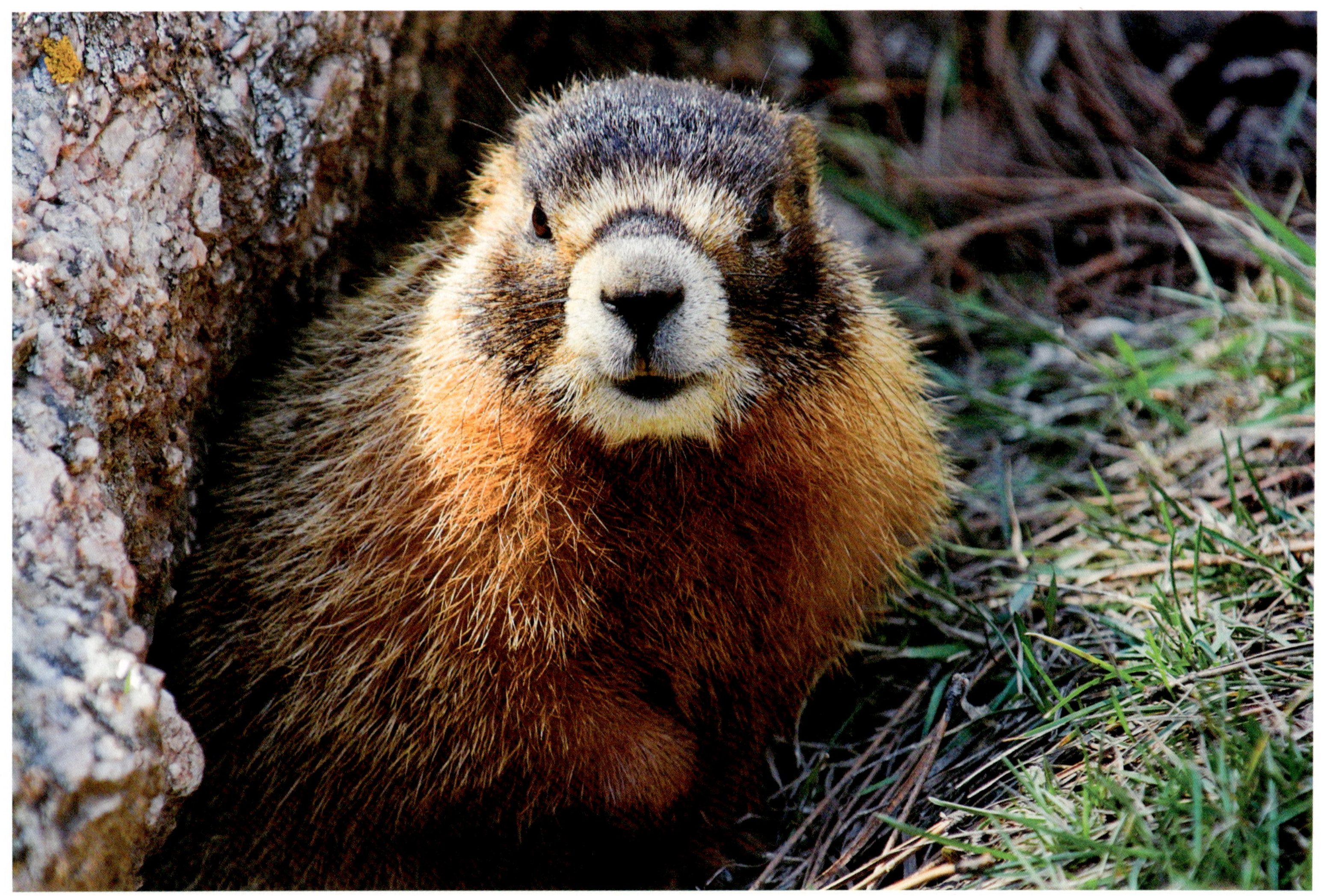

Yellow-bellied marmot, Black Hills National Forest, South Dakota

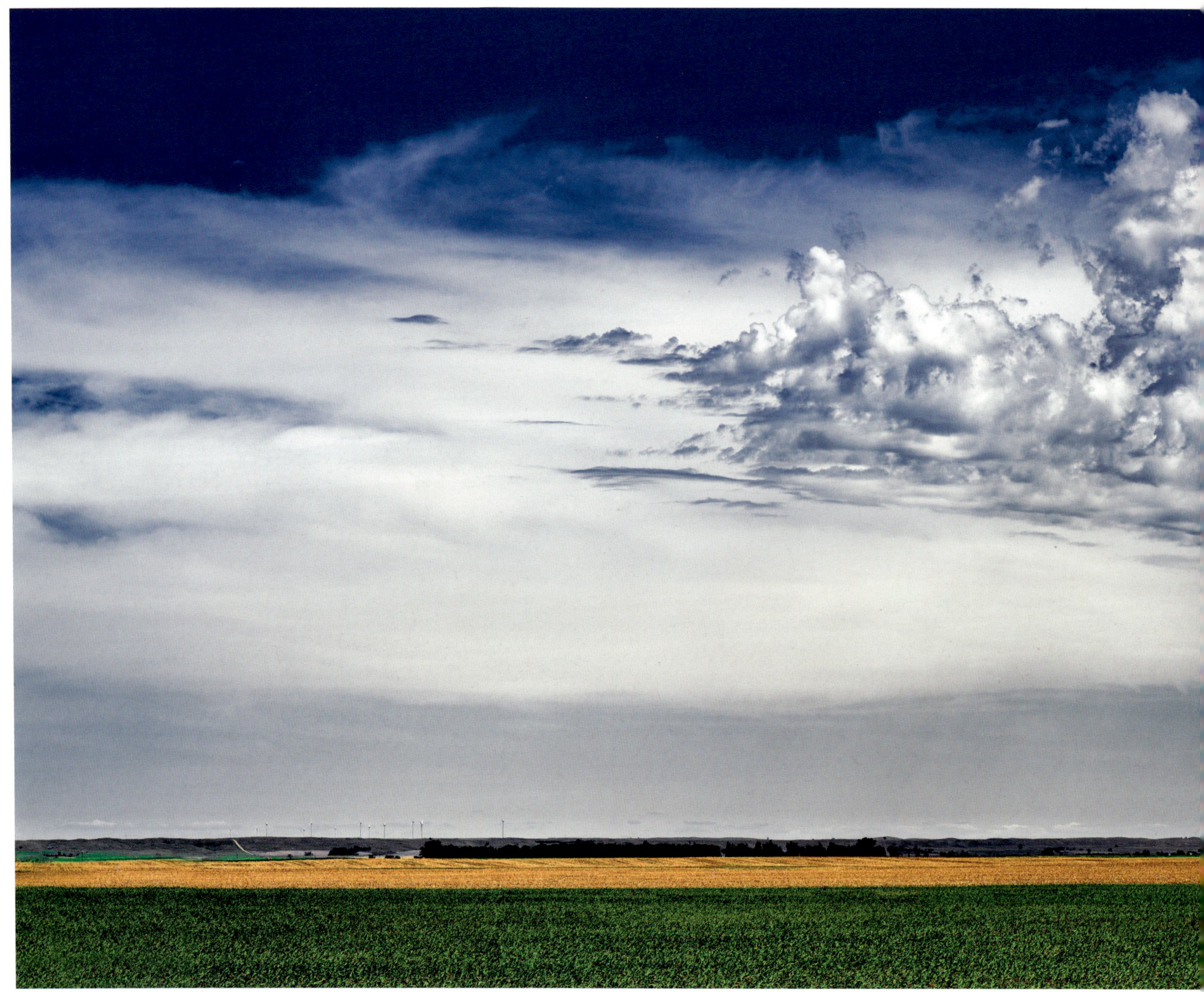

Cloud formation along South Dakota State Highway 37

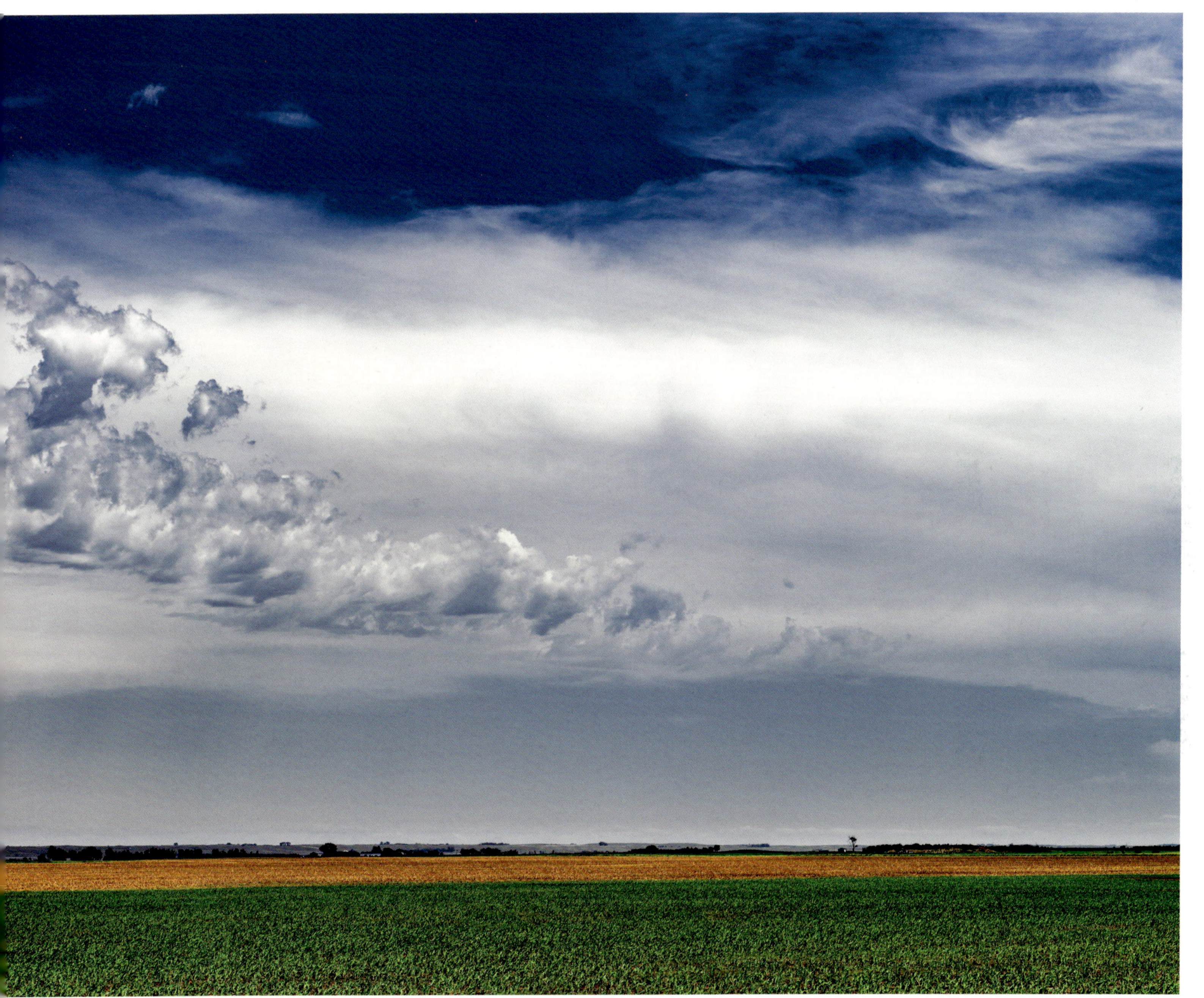

I chased this cloud for about 15 miles, looking for a foreground I liked.

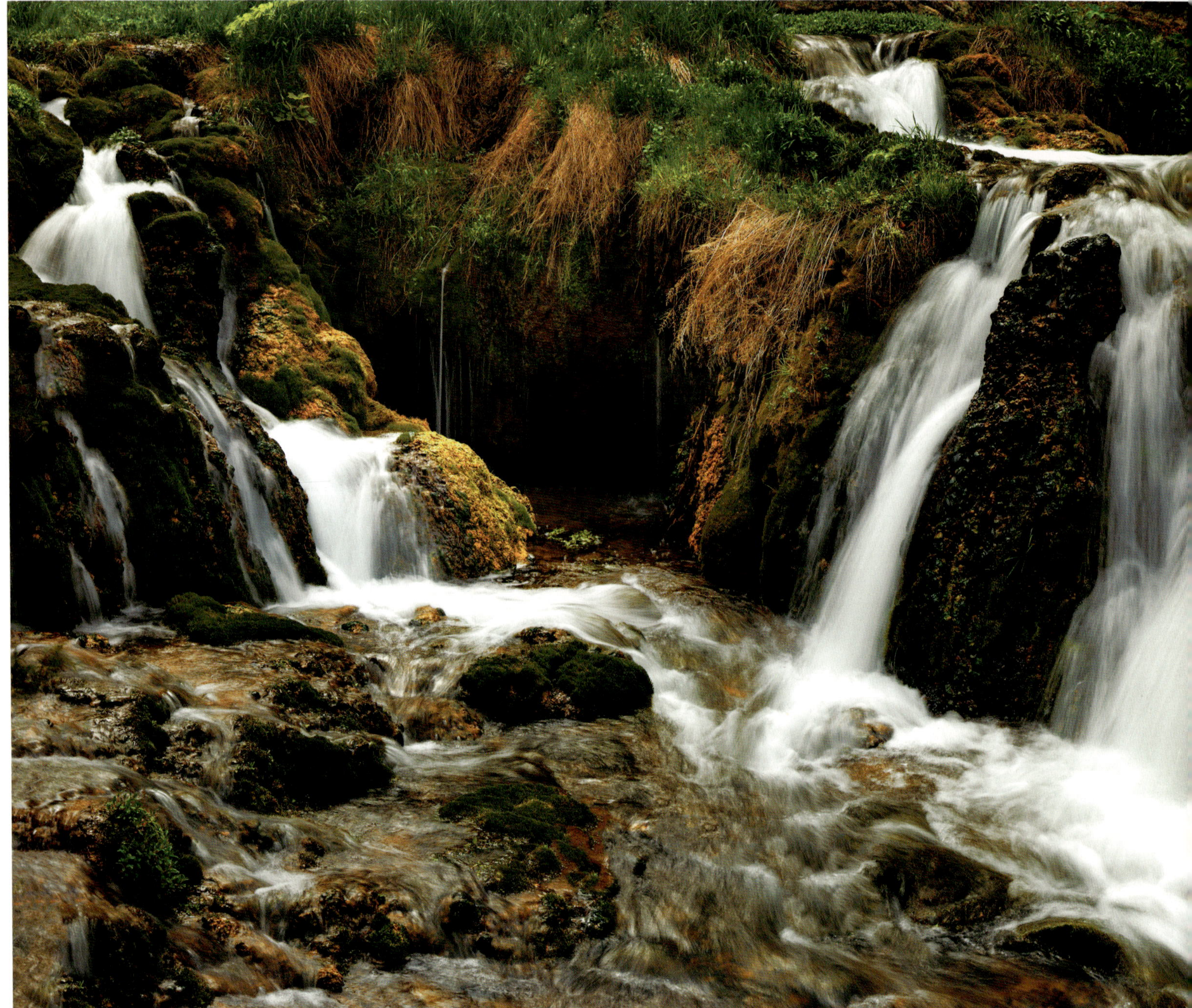

Roughlock Falls, Spearfish Canyon, South Dakota

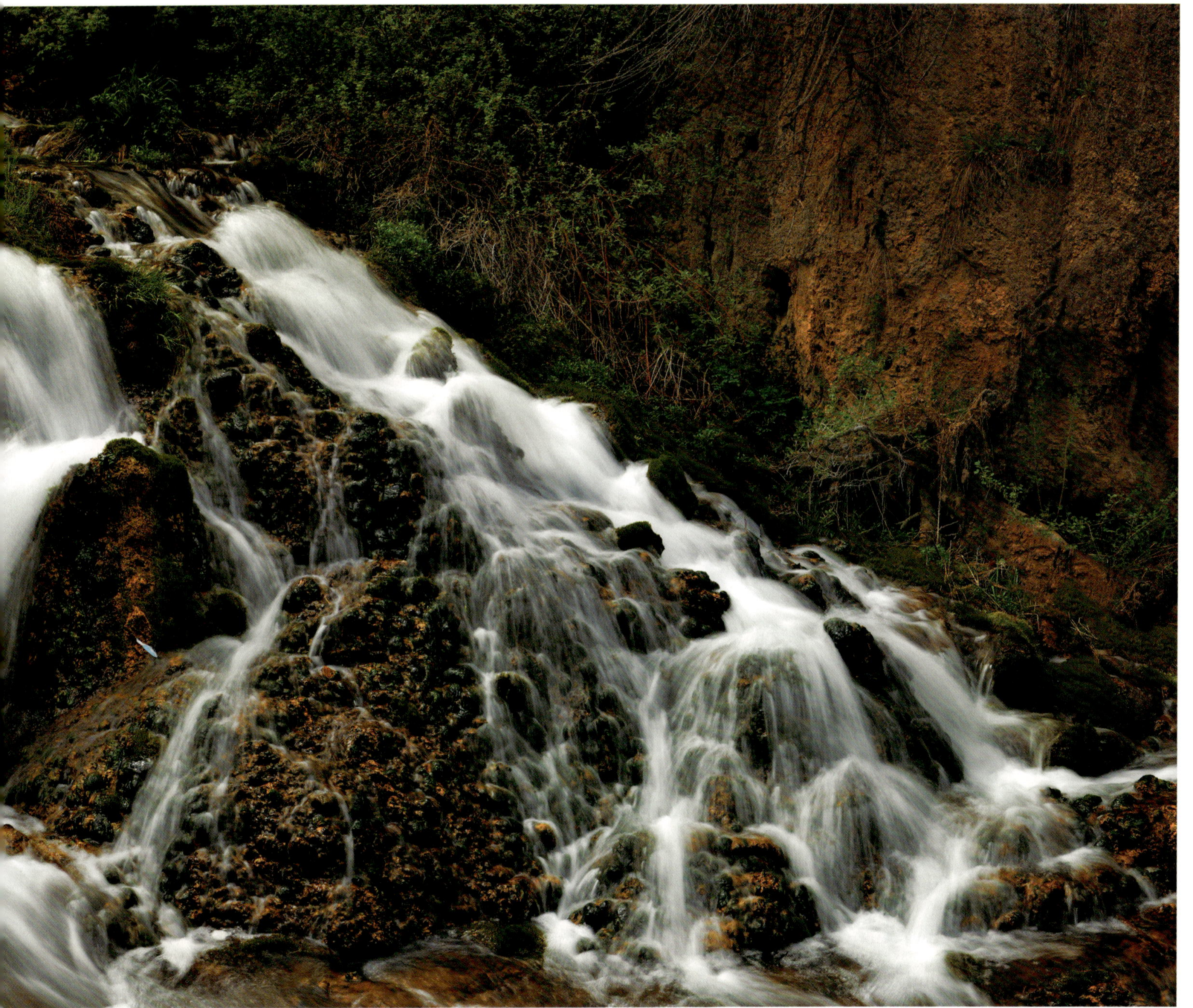

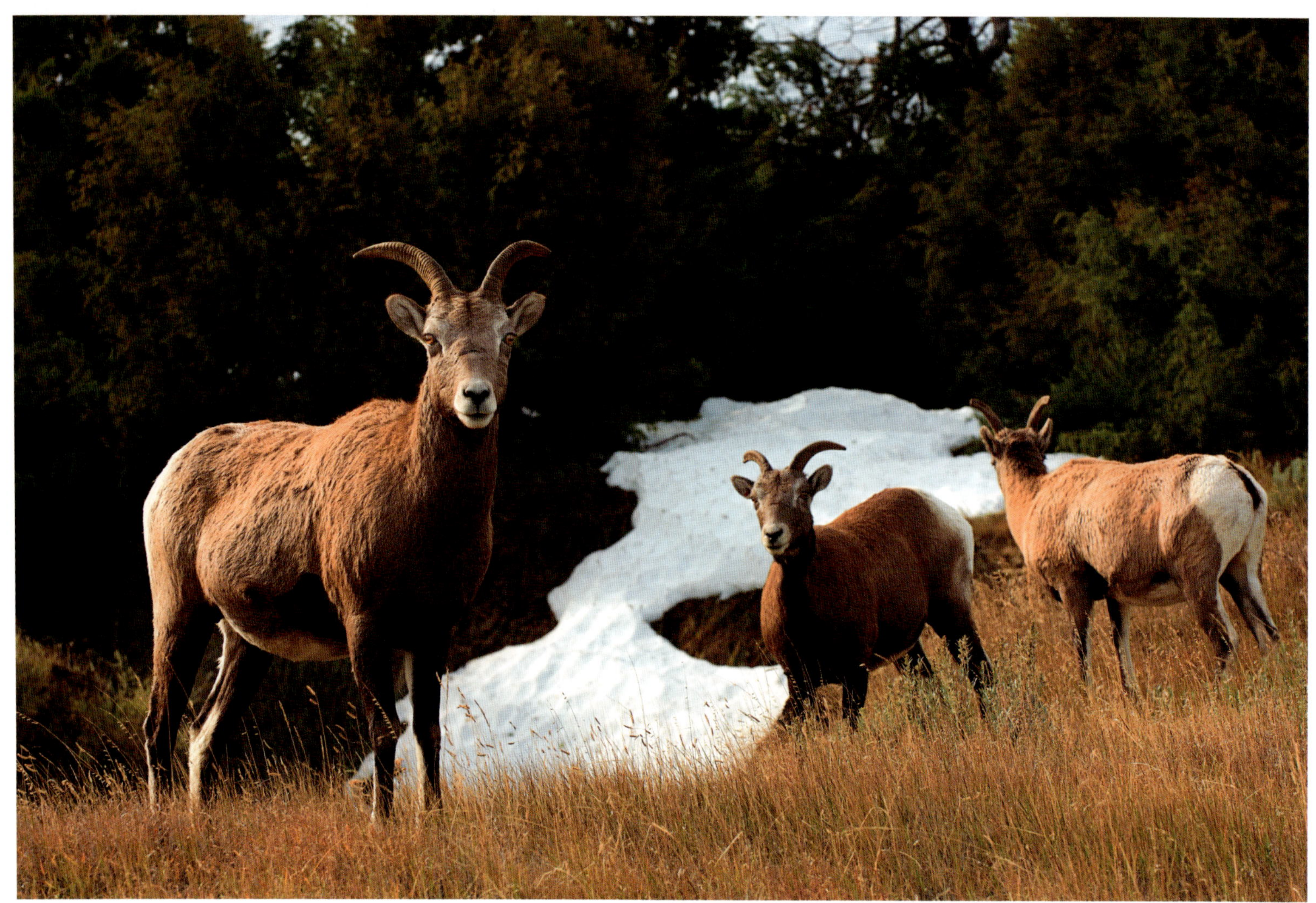

Female bighorn sheep, Badlands National Park, South Dakota

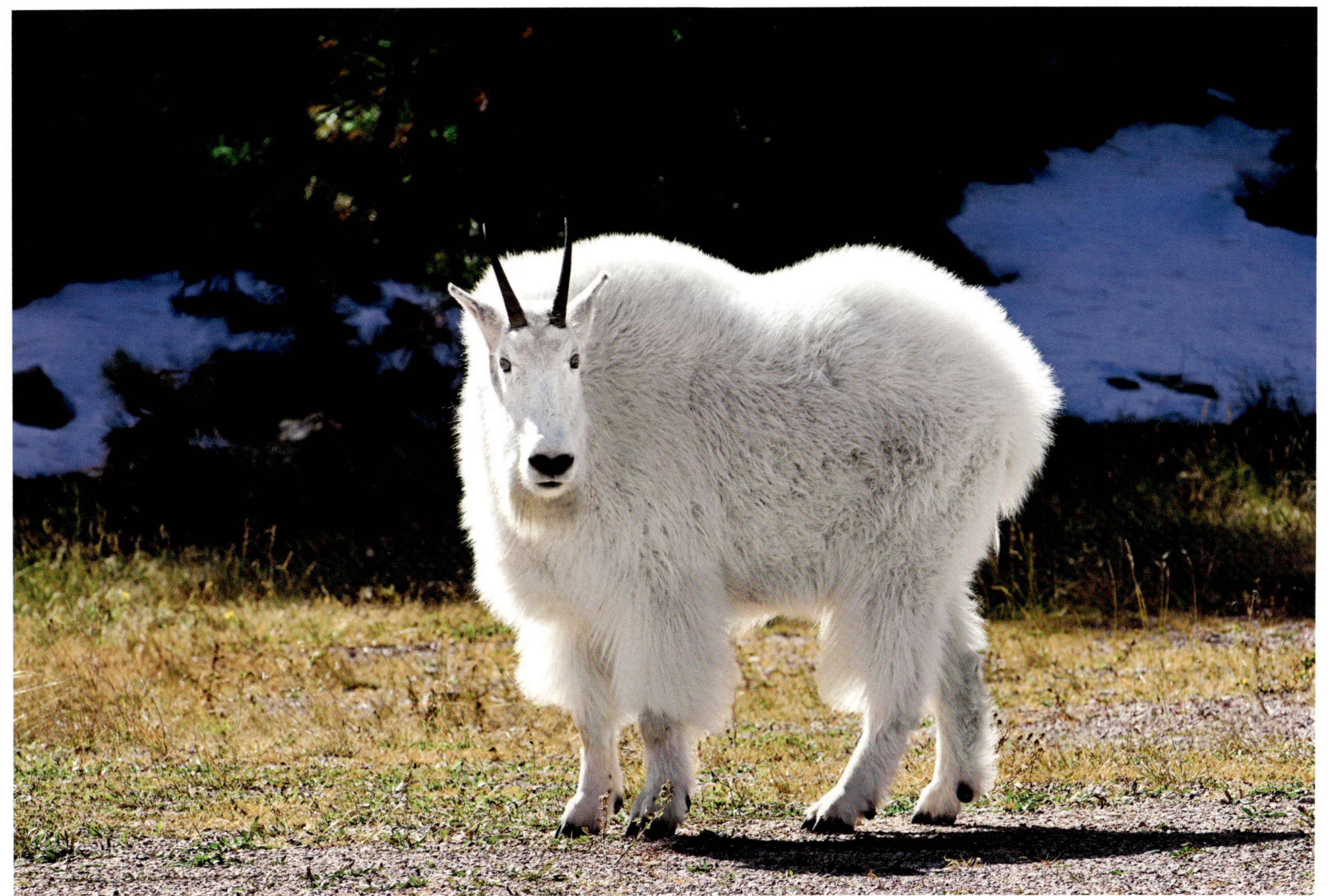

Rocky Mountain goat, Harney Peak, South Dakota

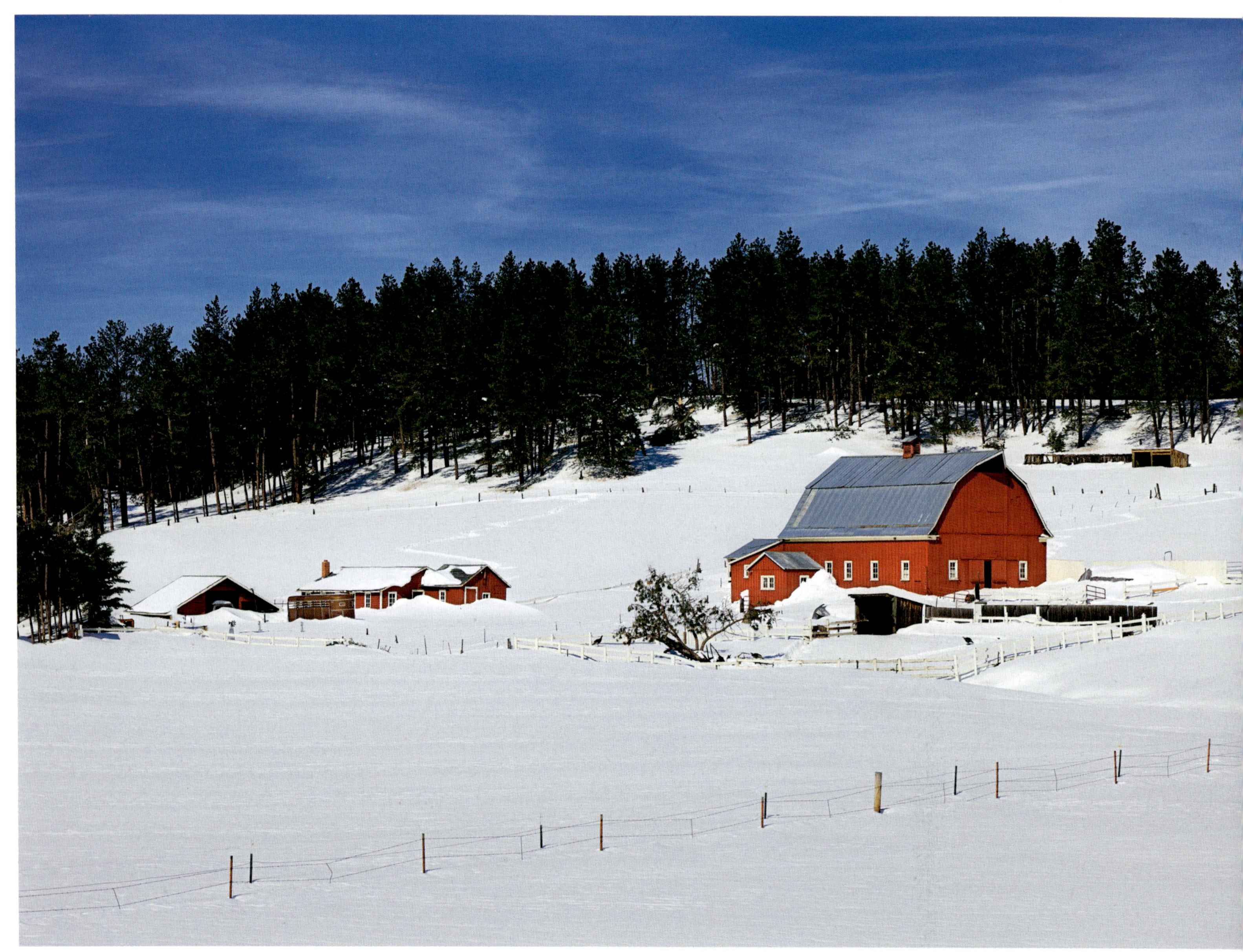

Farm on Vanoker Road, South Dakota

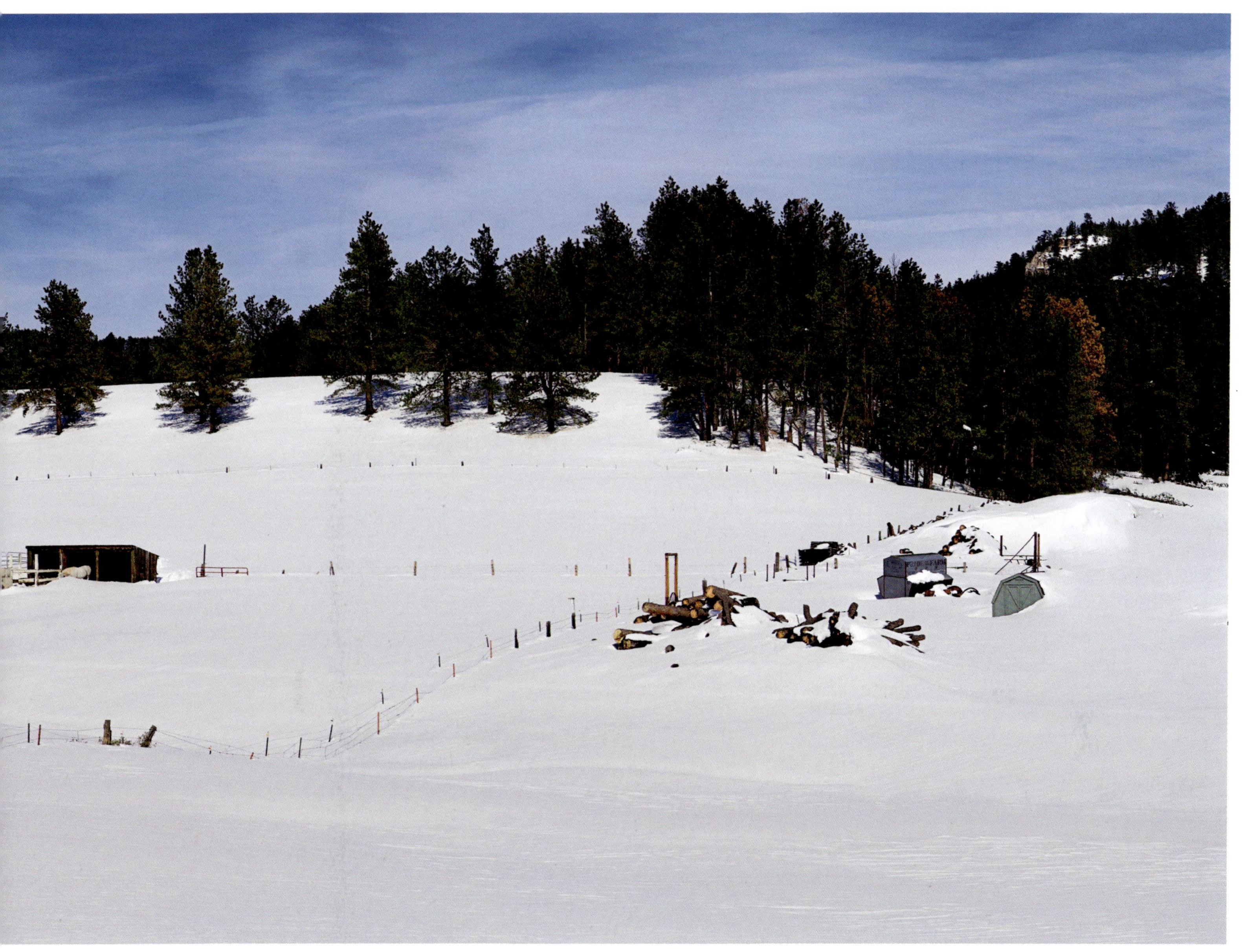

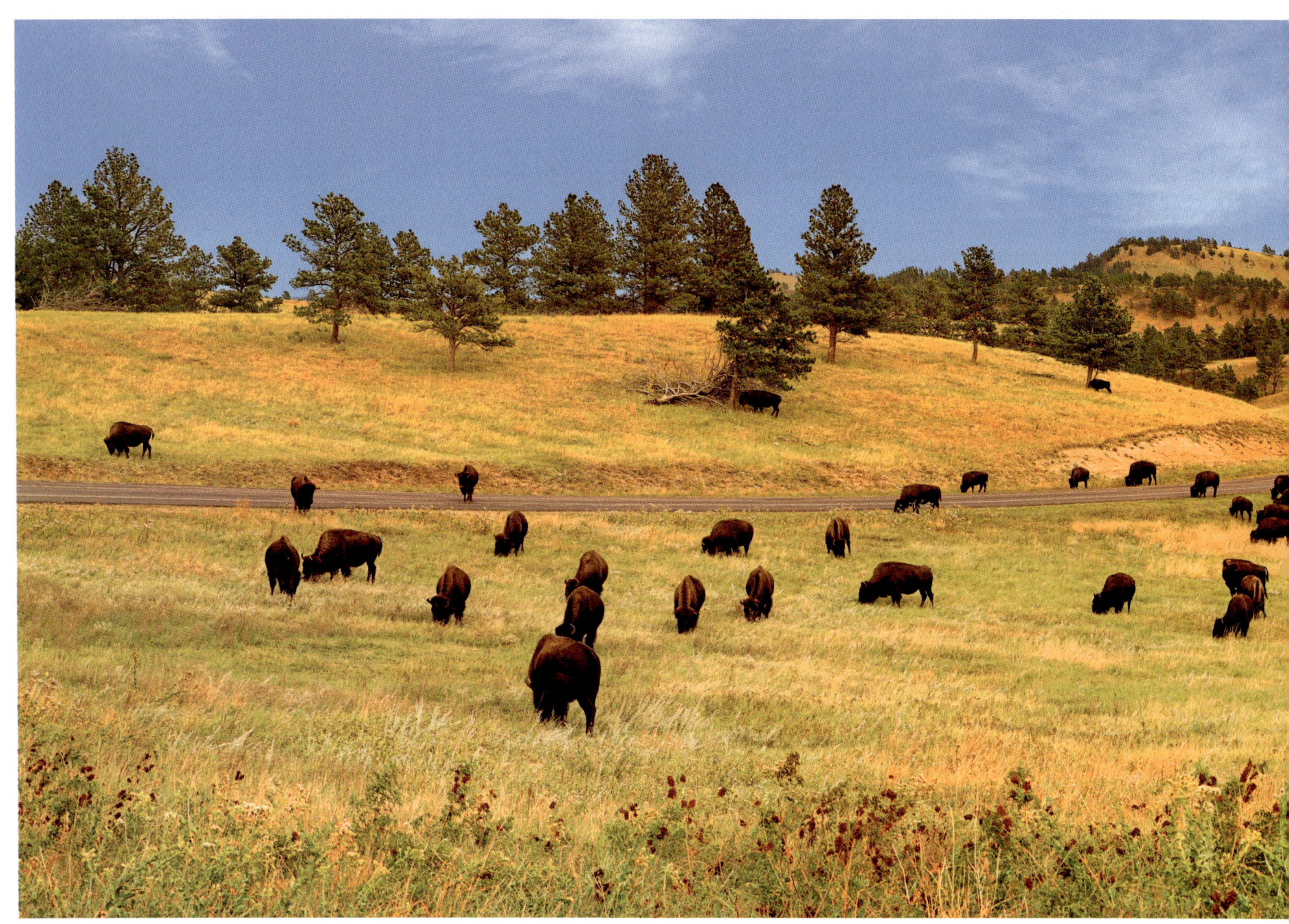

American bison, Custer State Park, South Dakota

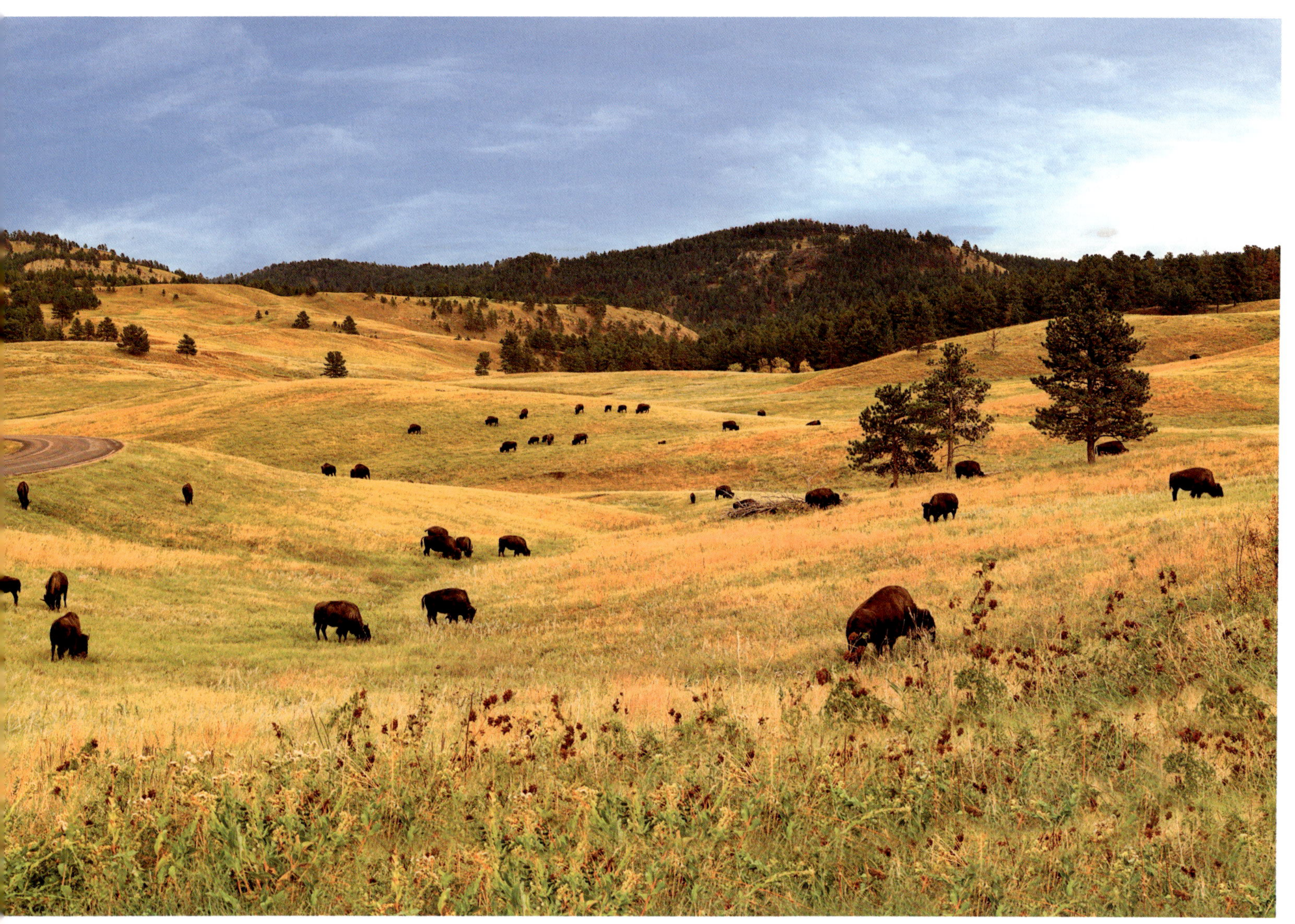

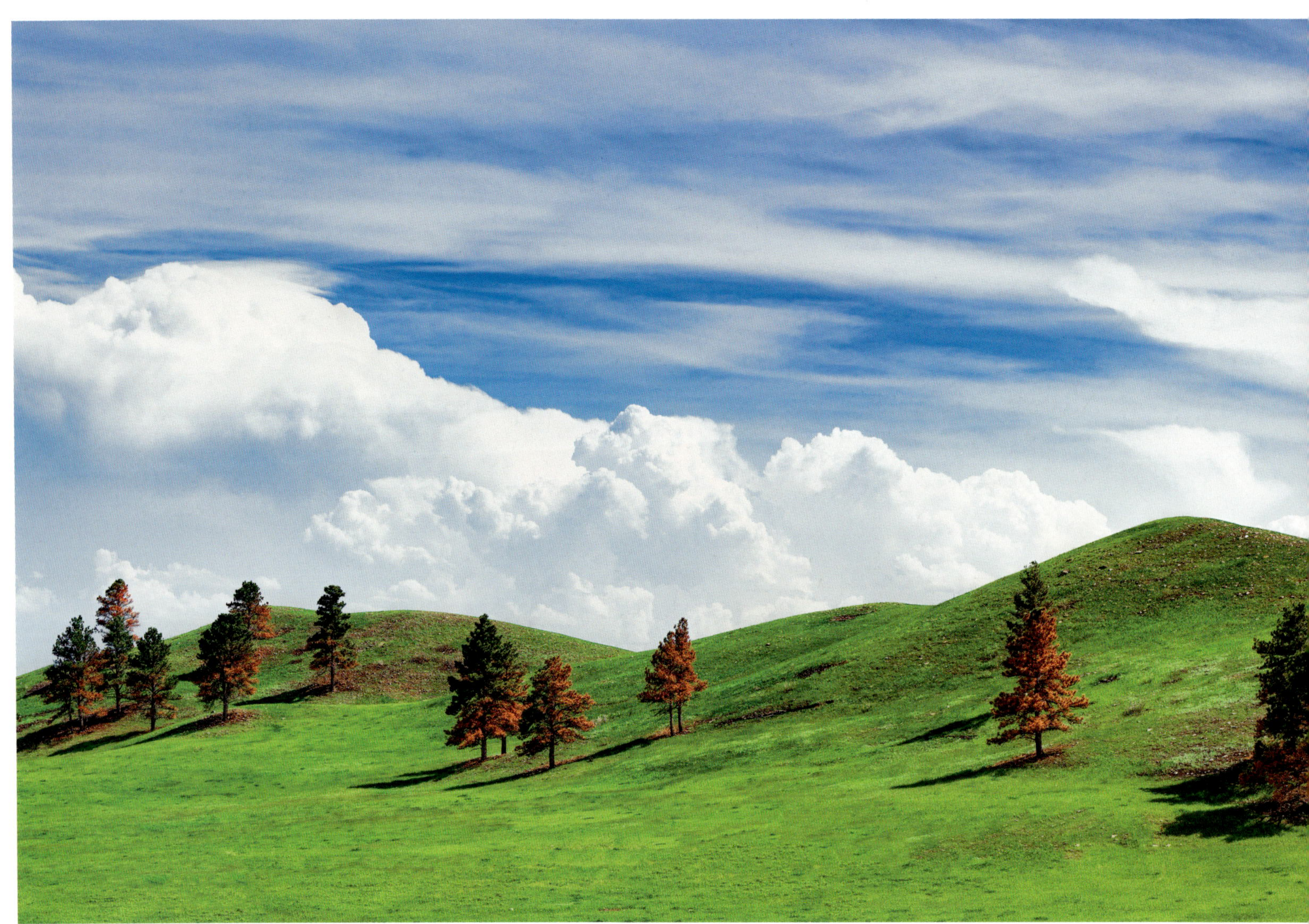

Trees and hills along the Wildlife Loop, Custer State Park, South Dakota

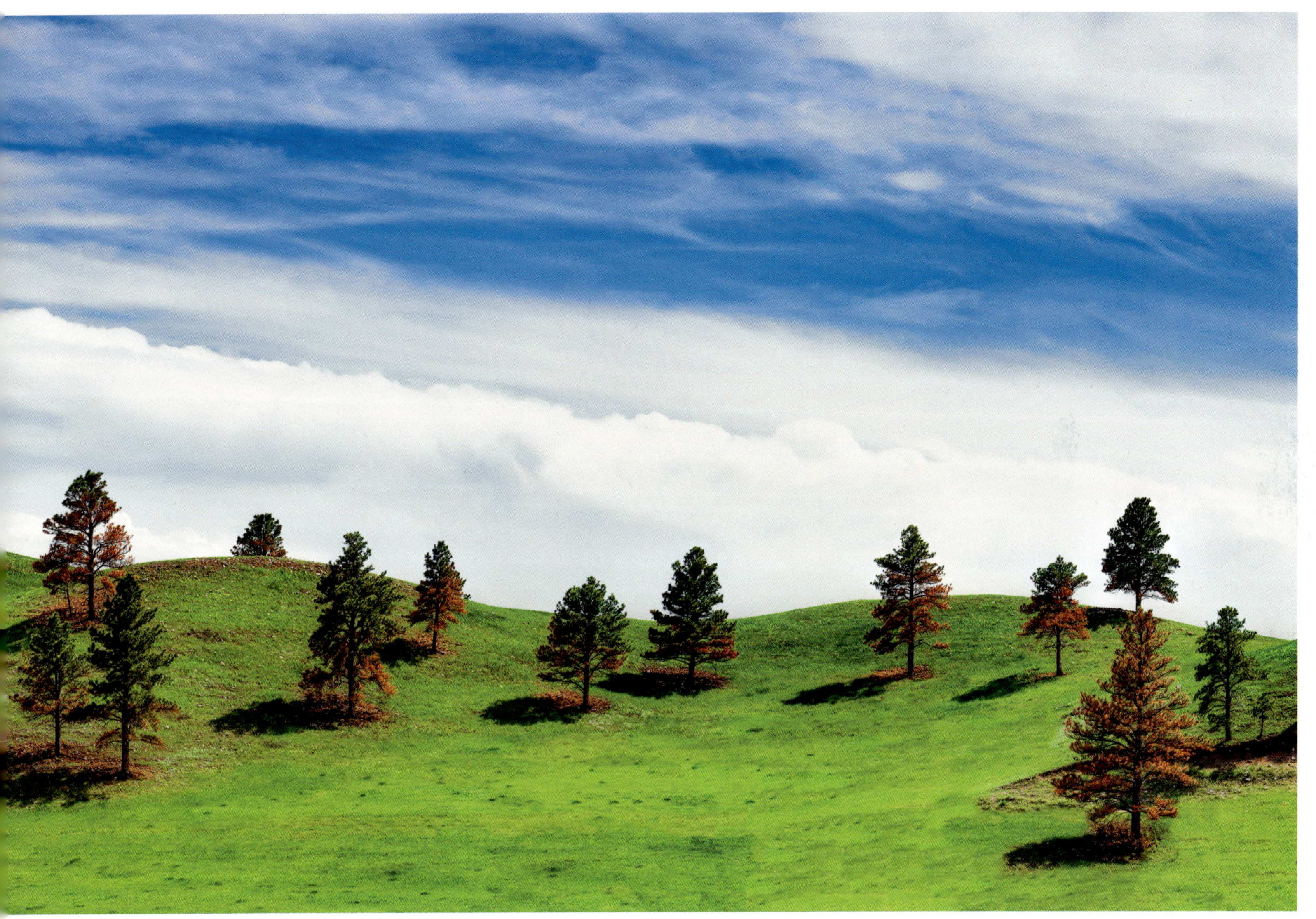

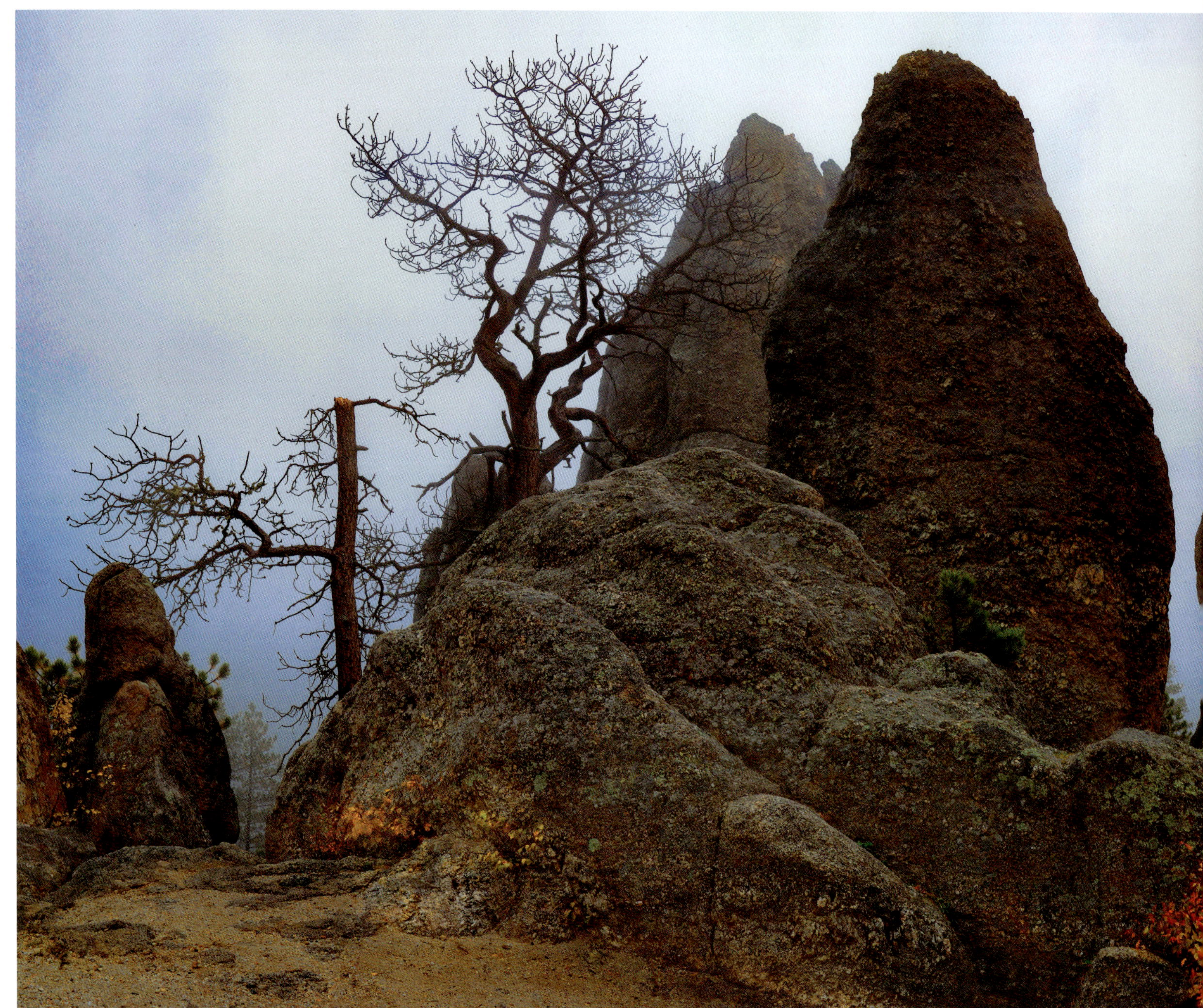

The Needles, Black Hills, South Dakota

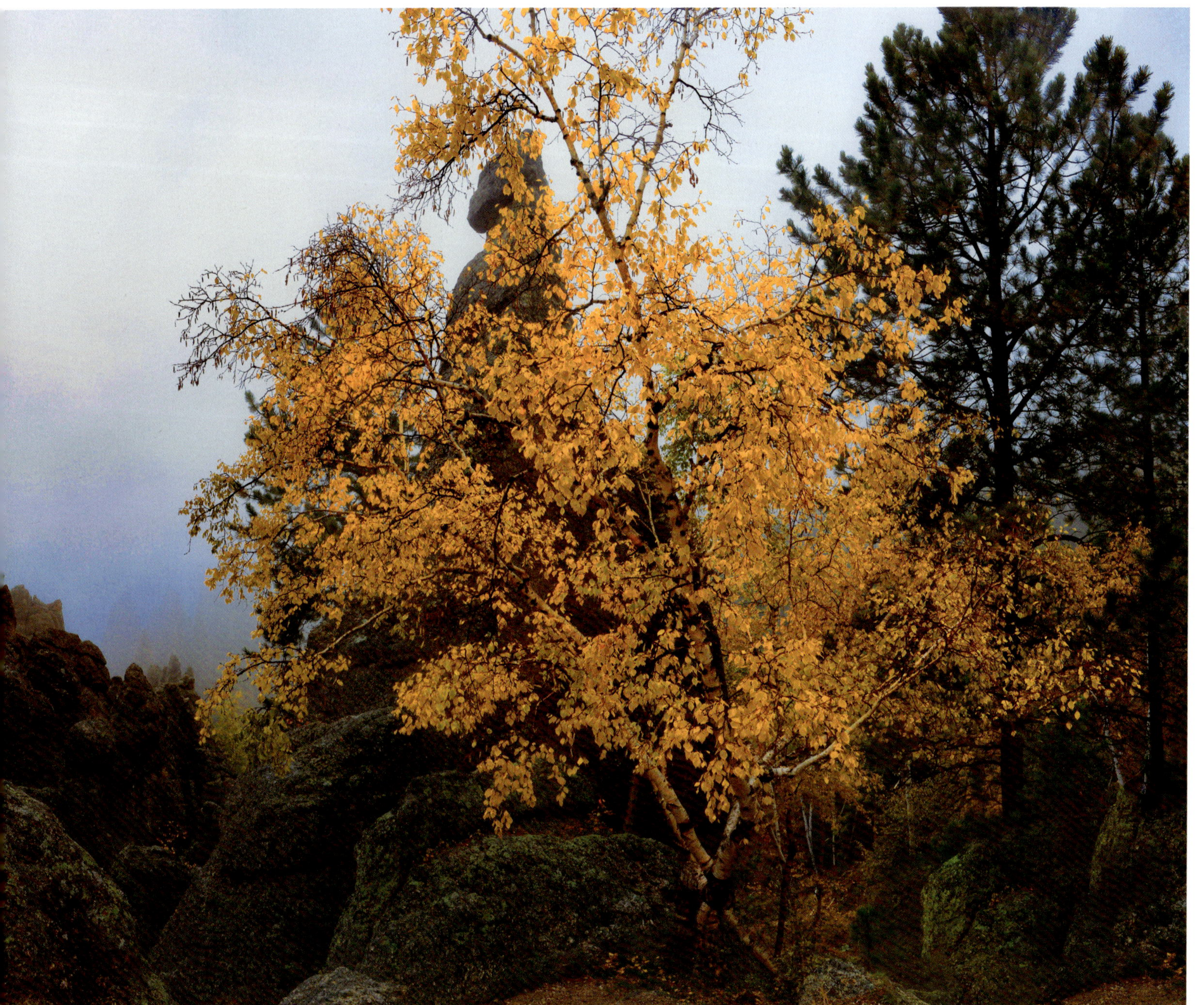

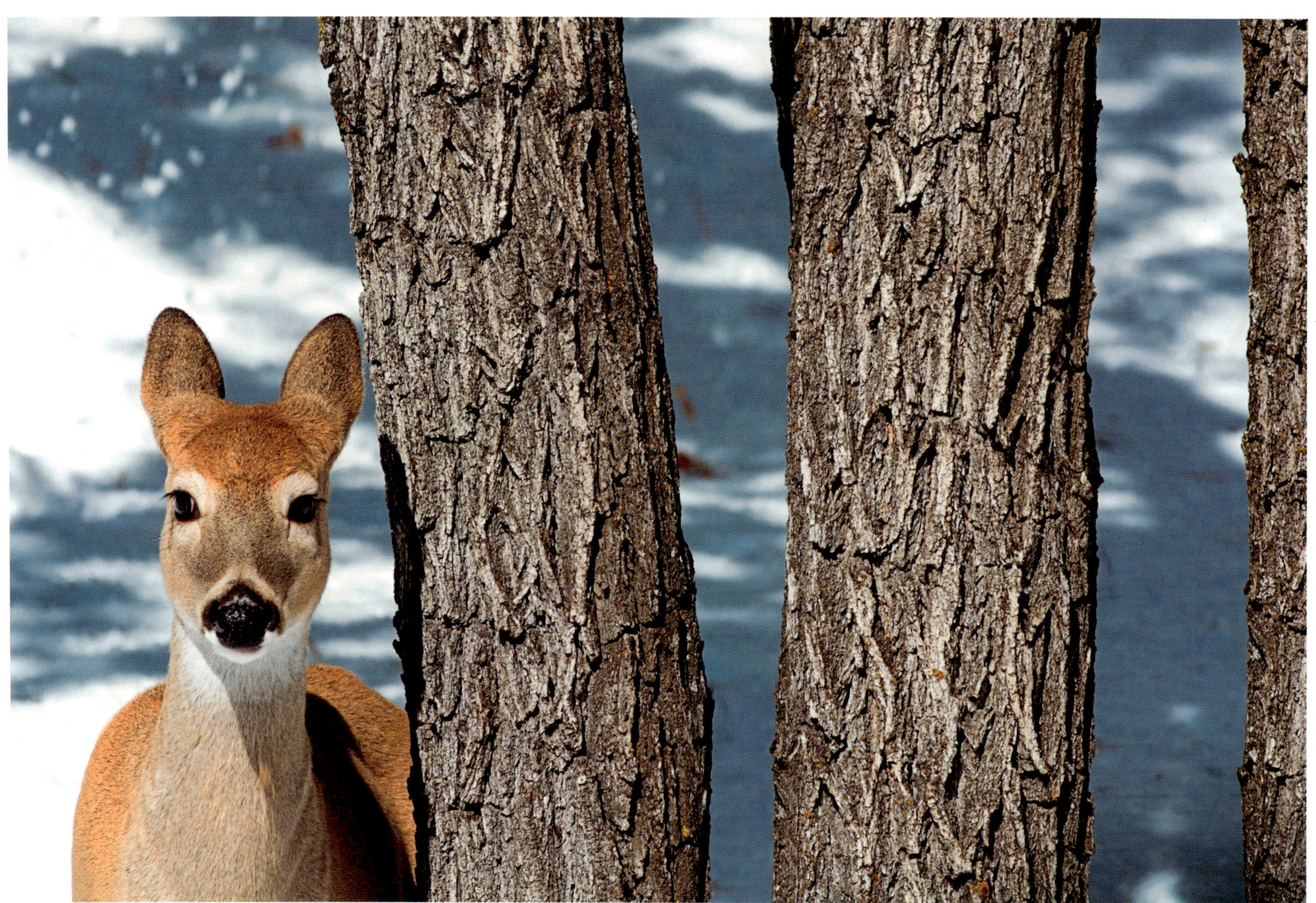

White-tailed deer, Custer State Park, South Dakota

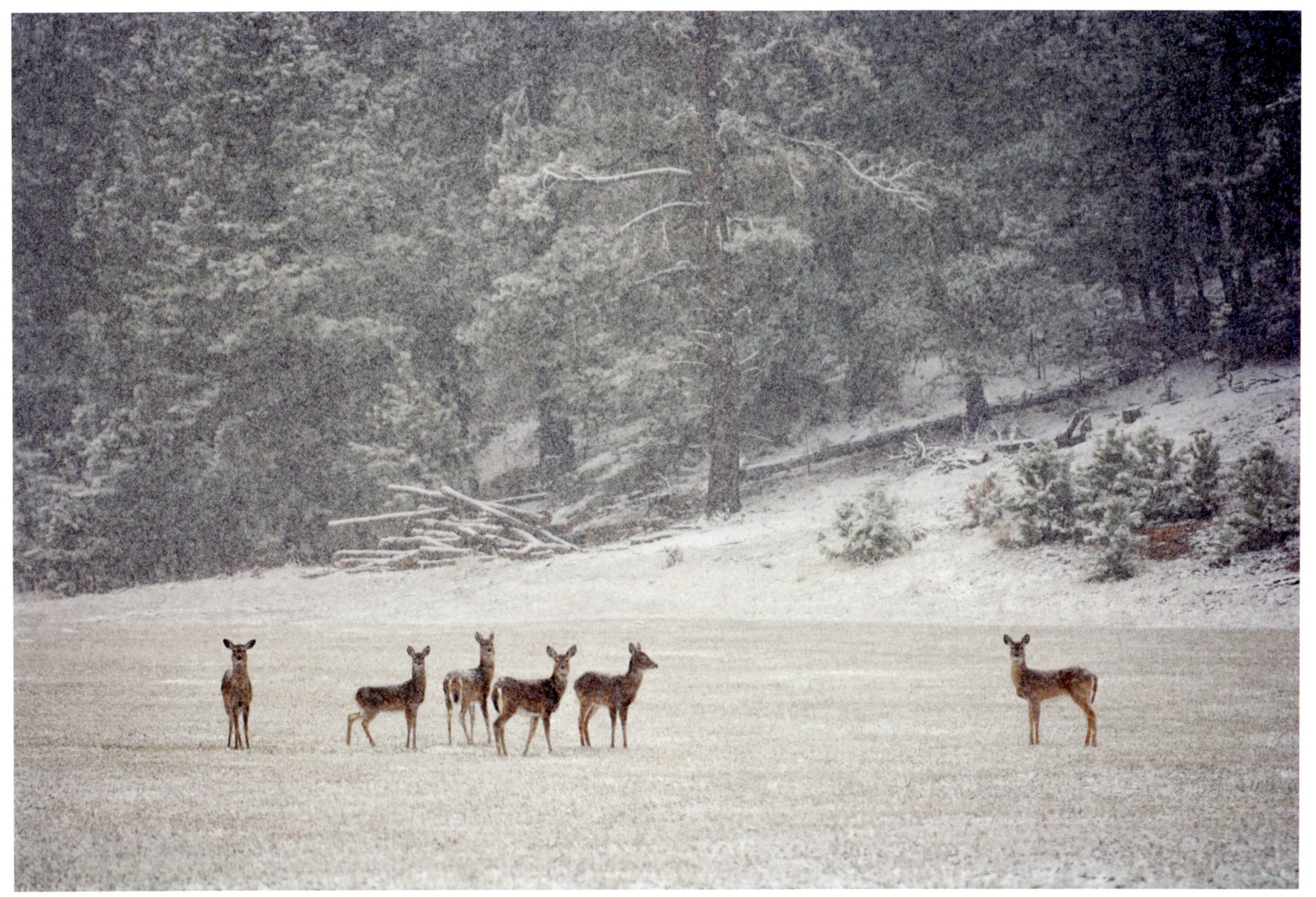

Deer caught in early snowfall, South Dakota

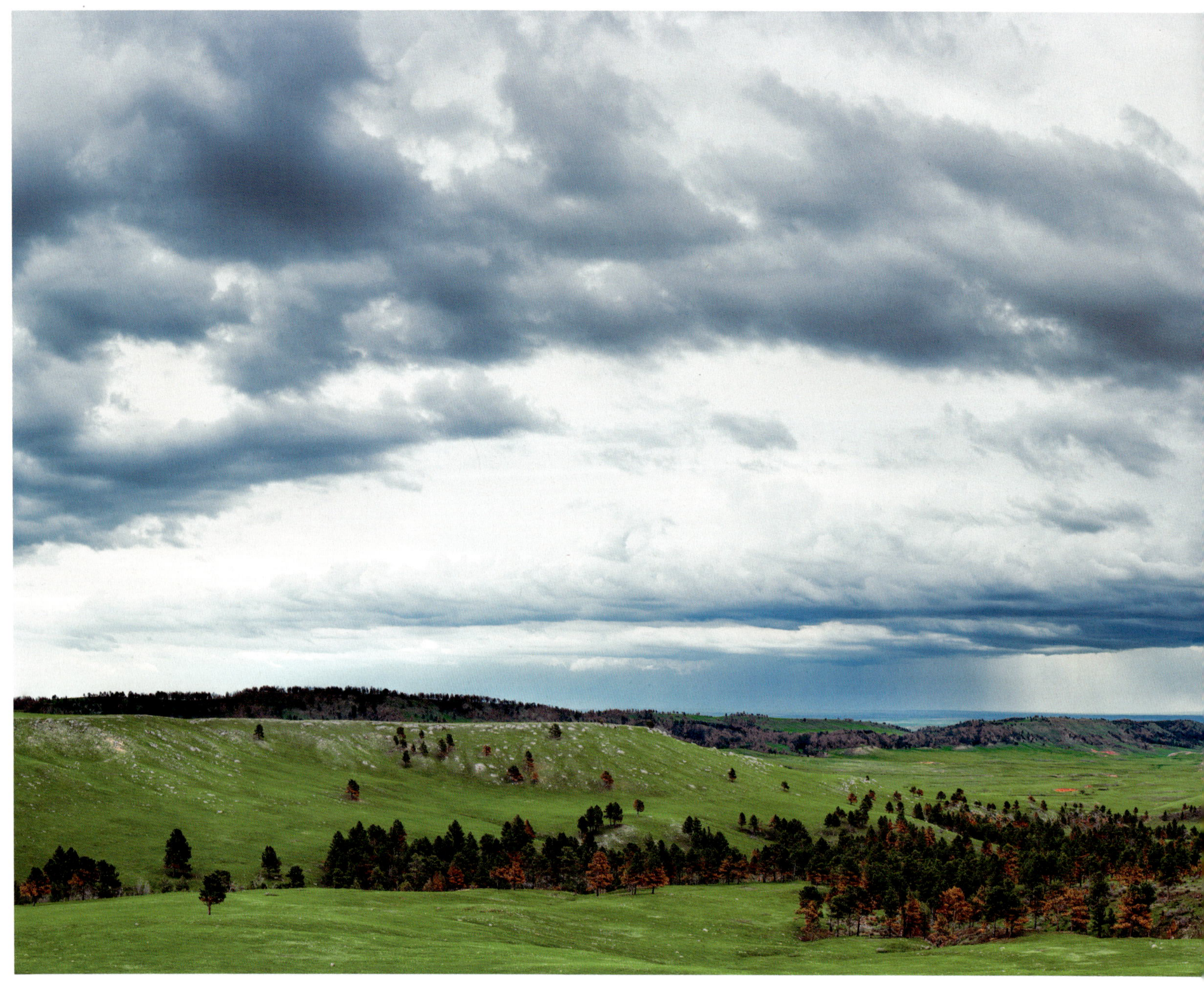

Storm, Highland Ridge, South Dakota

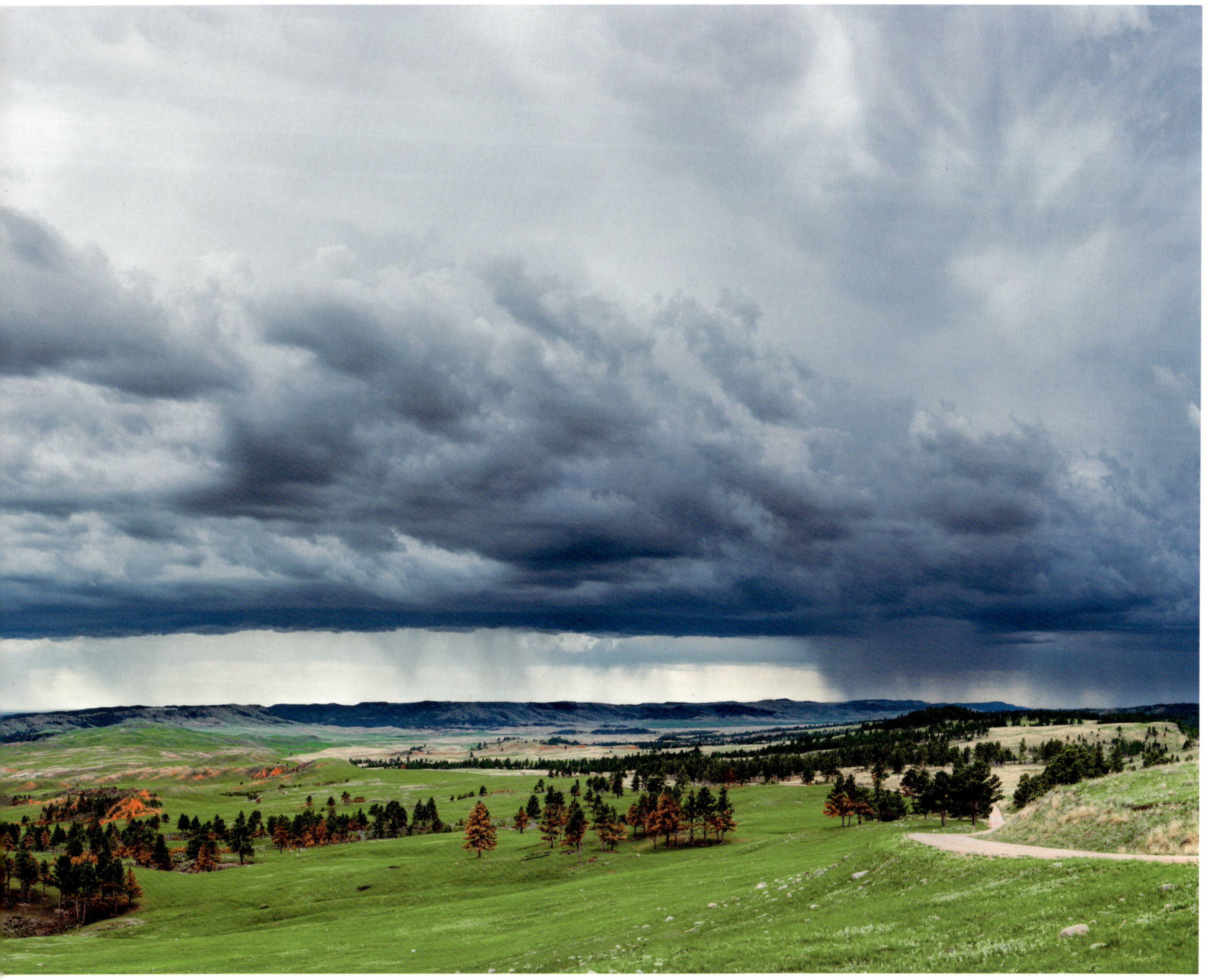

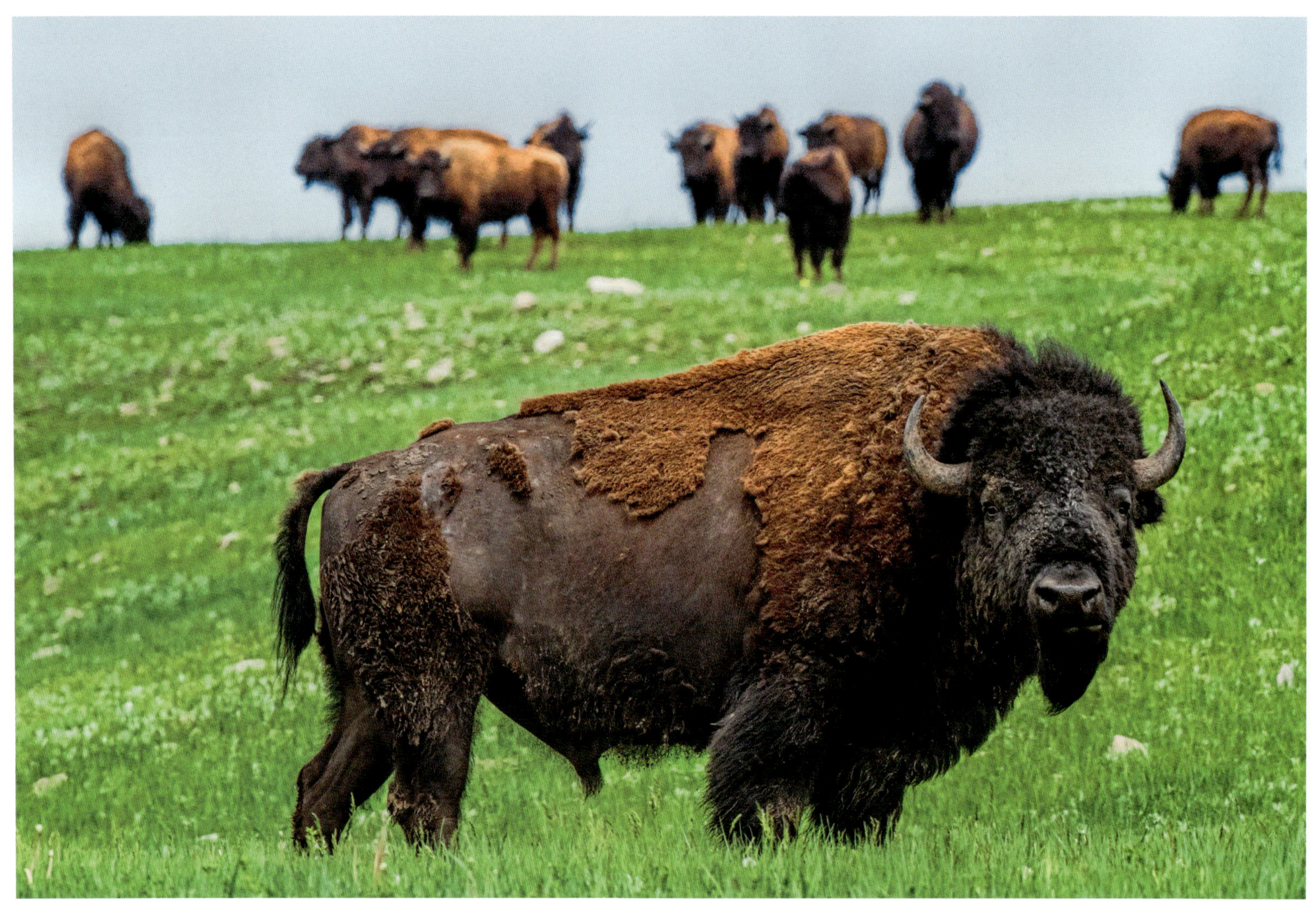

Bison bull, Custer State Park, South Dakota

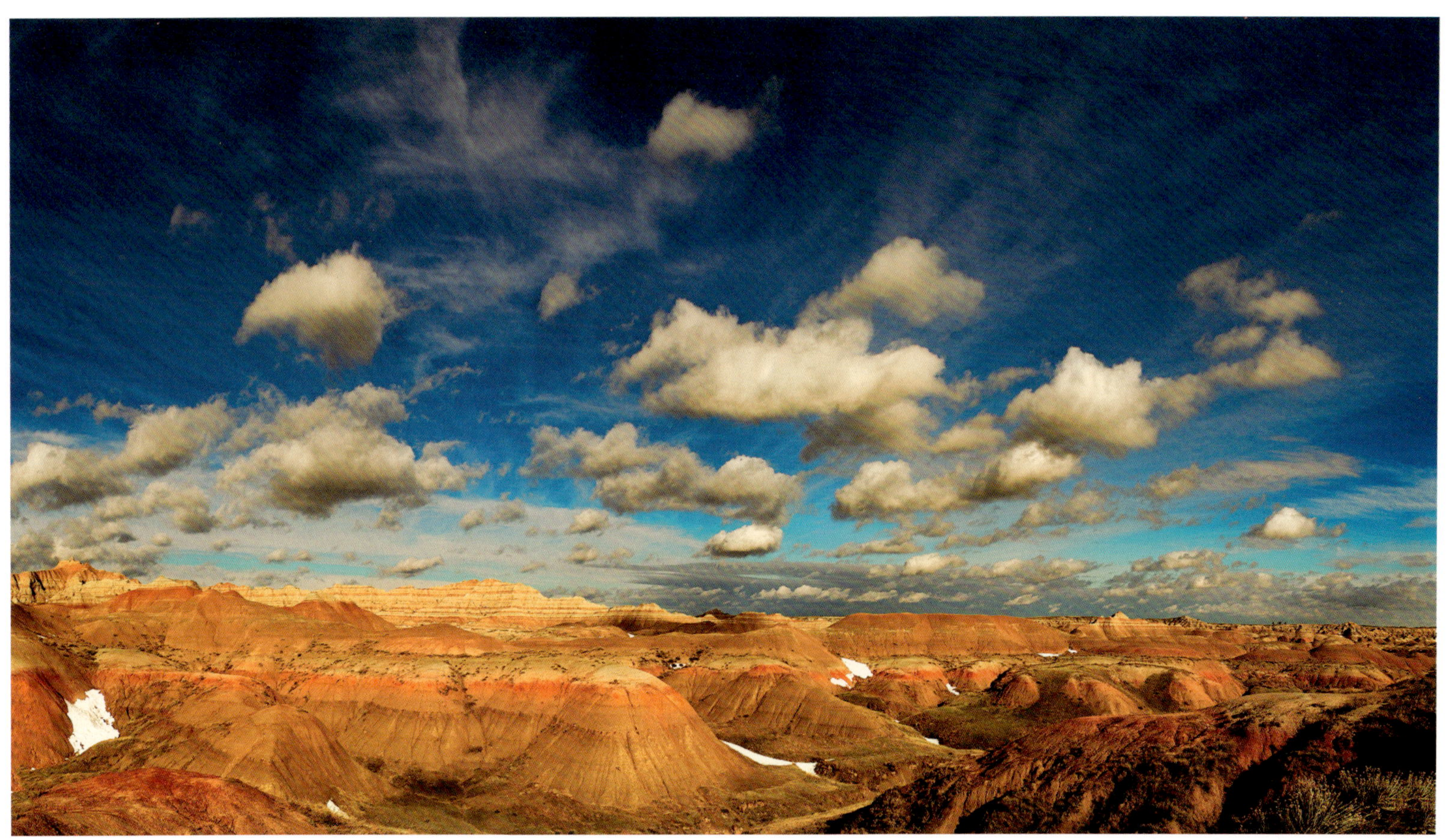

Yellow mounds, Badlands National Park, South Dakota

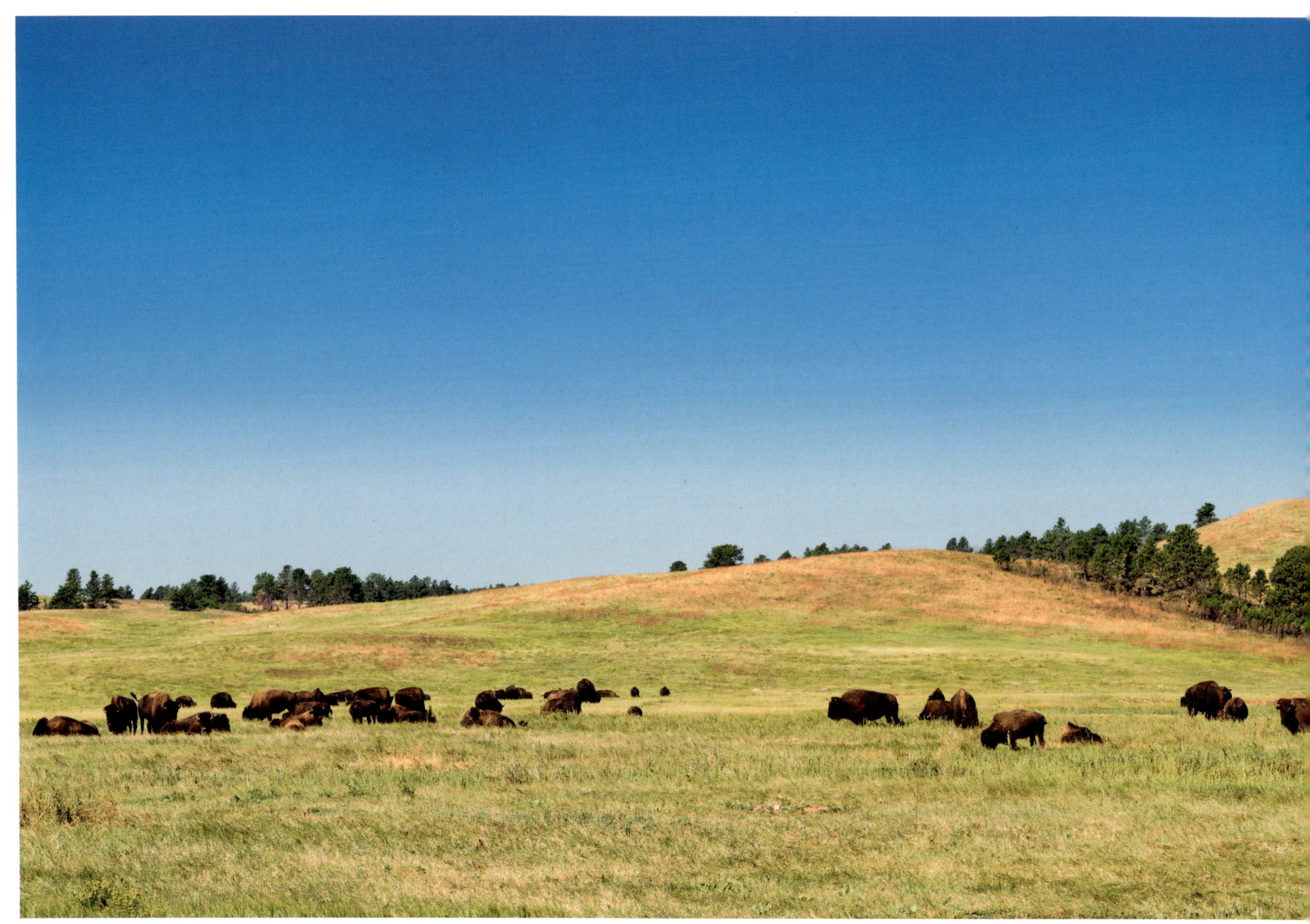

Bison and moon, Wind Cave National Park, South Dakota

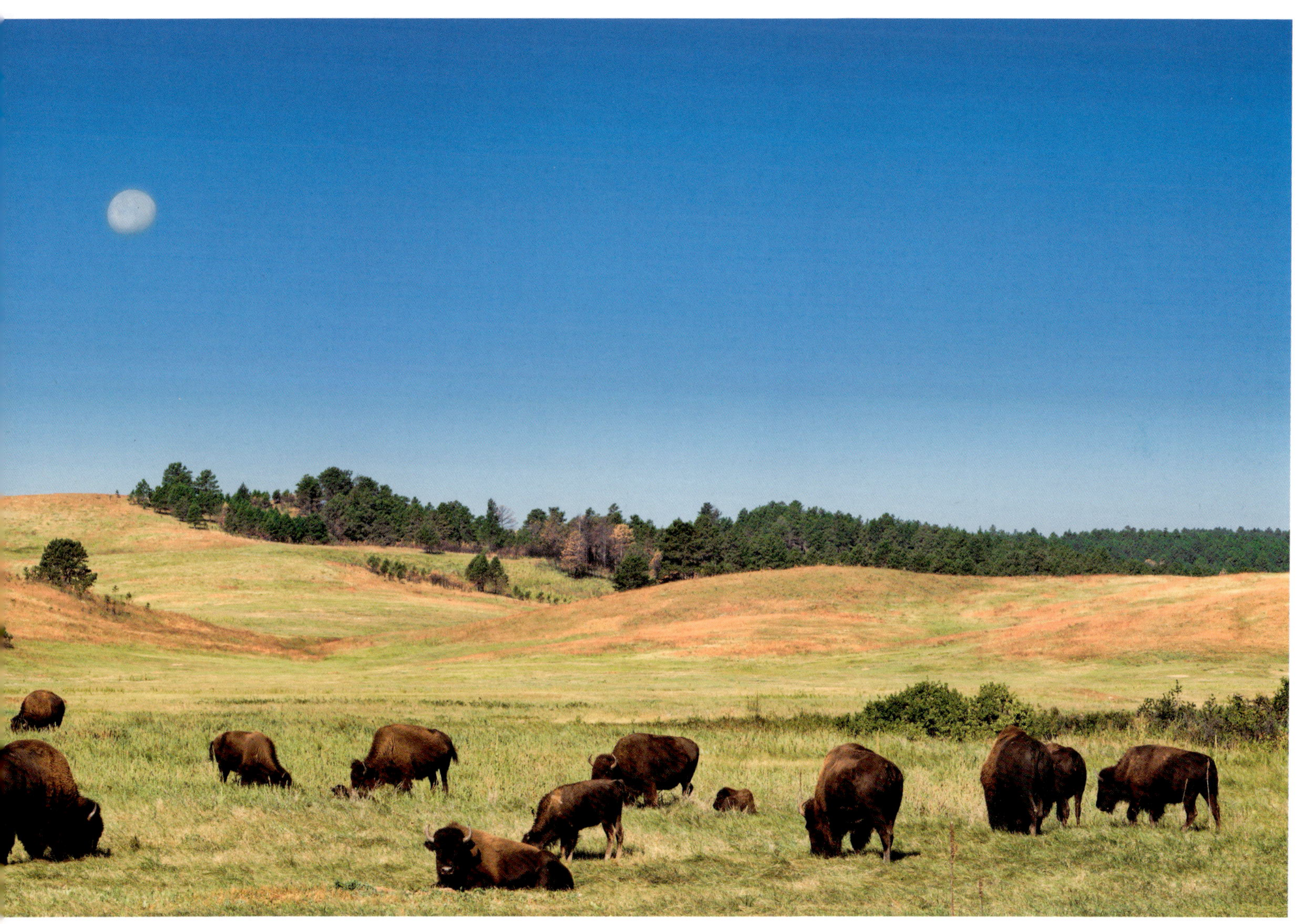

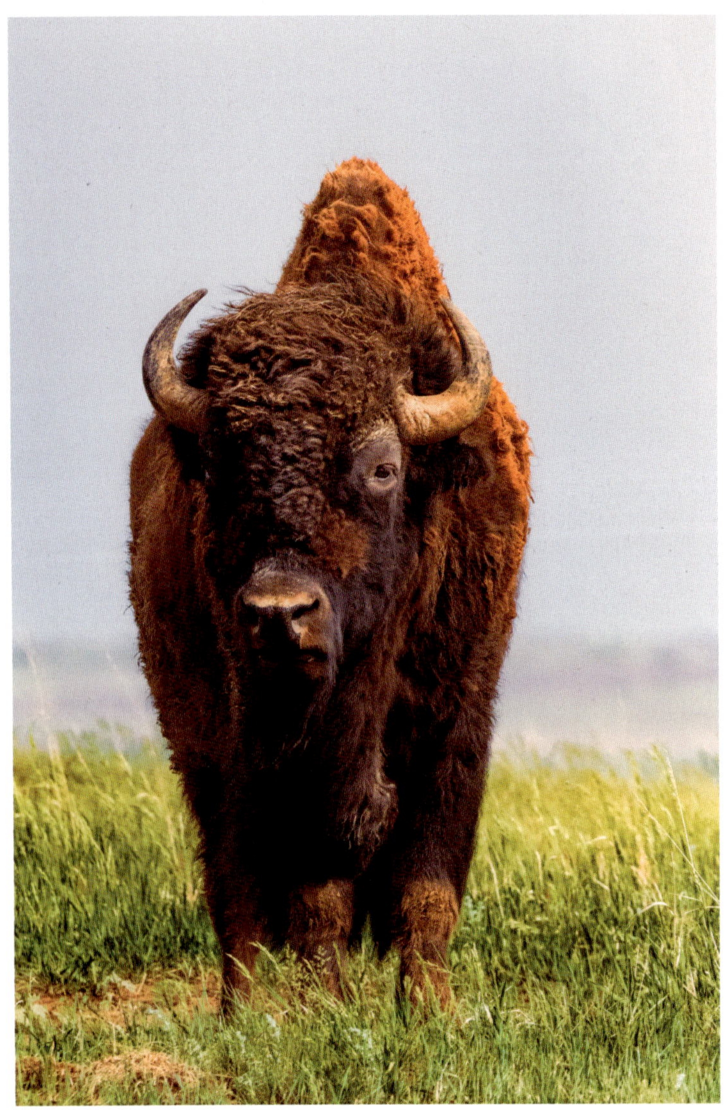

Bison, Black Hills, South Dakota

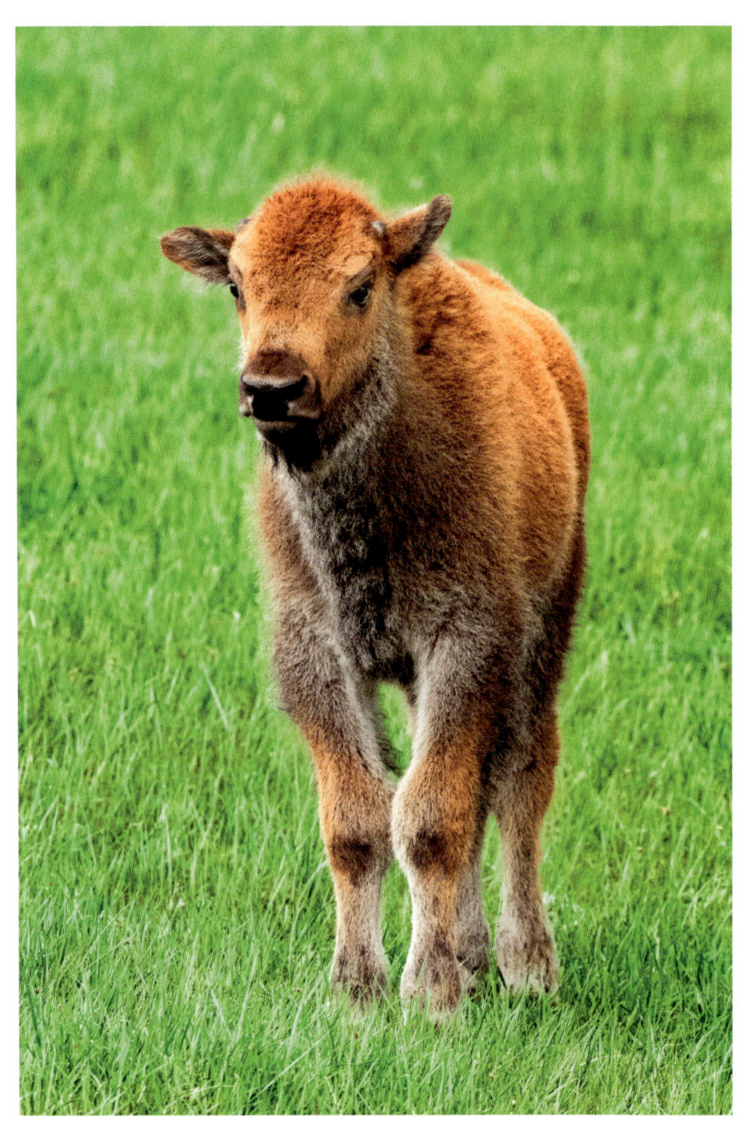

Bison calf, Black Hills, South Dakota

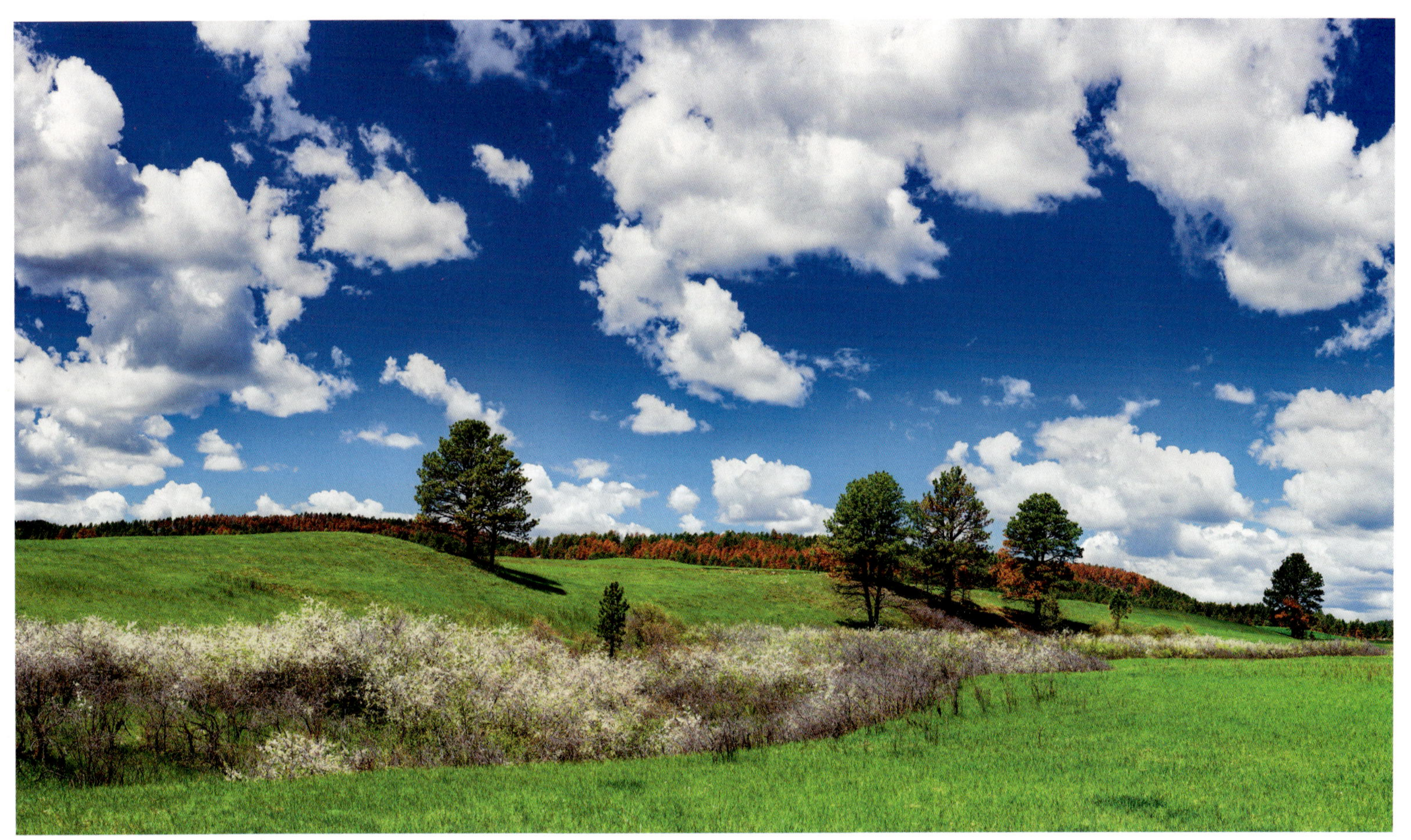

Grand Lodgepole River National Grassland, South Dakota

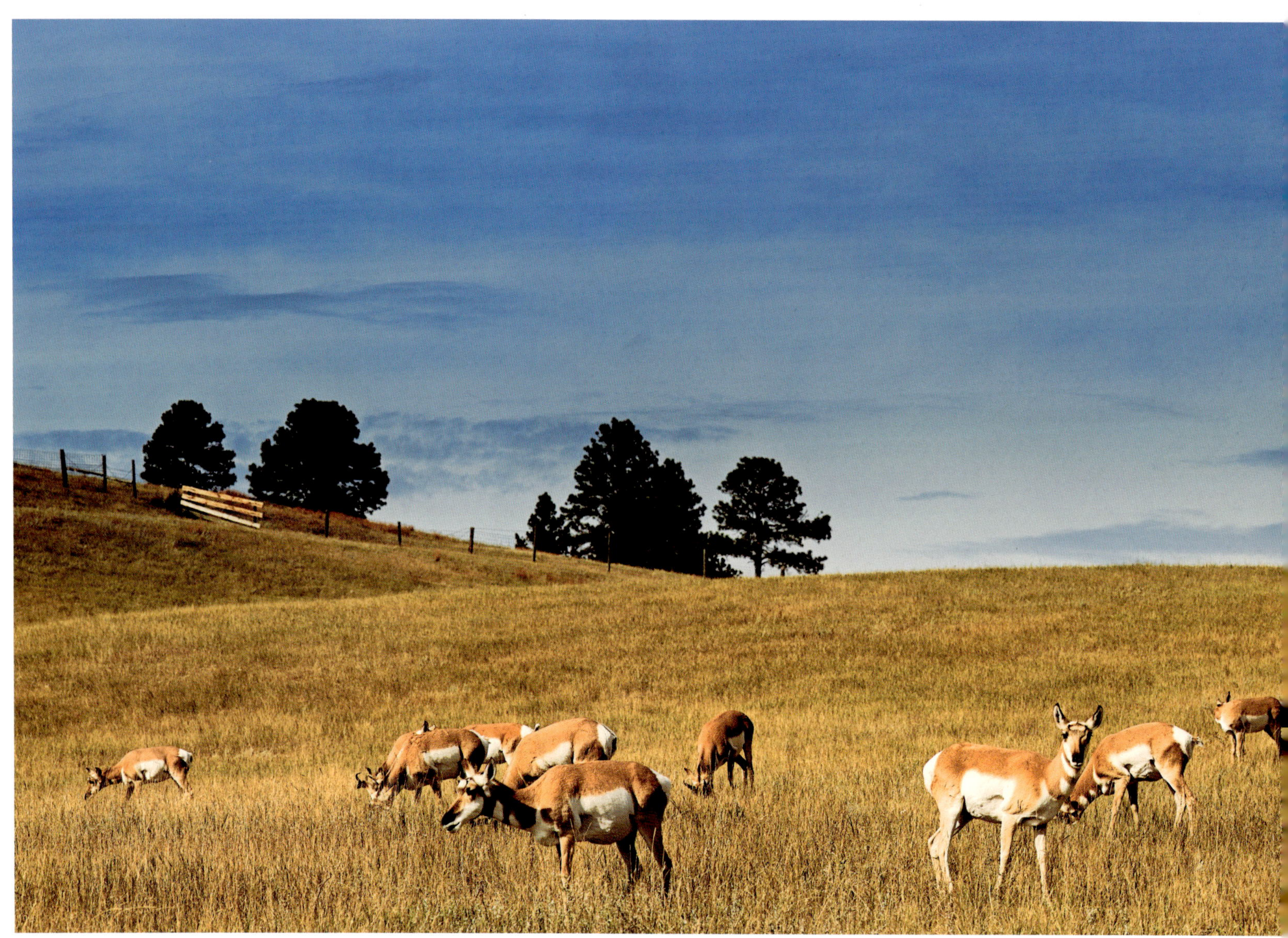

Pronghorn antelope, Wildlife Loop, Custer State Park, South Dakota

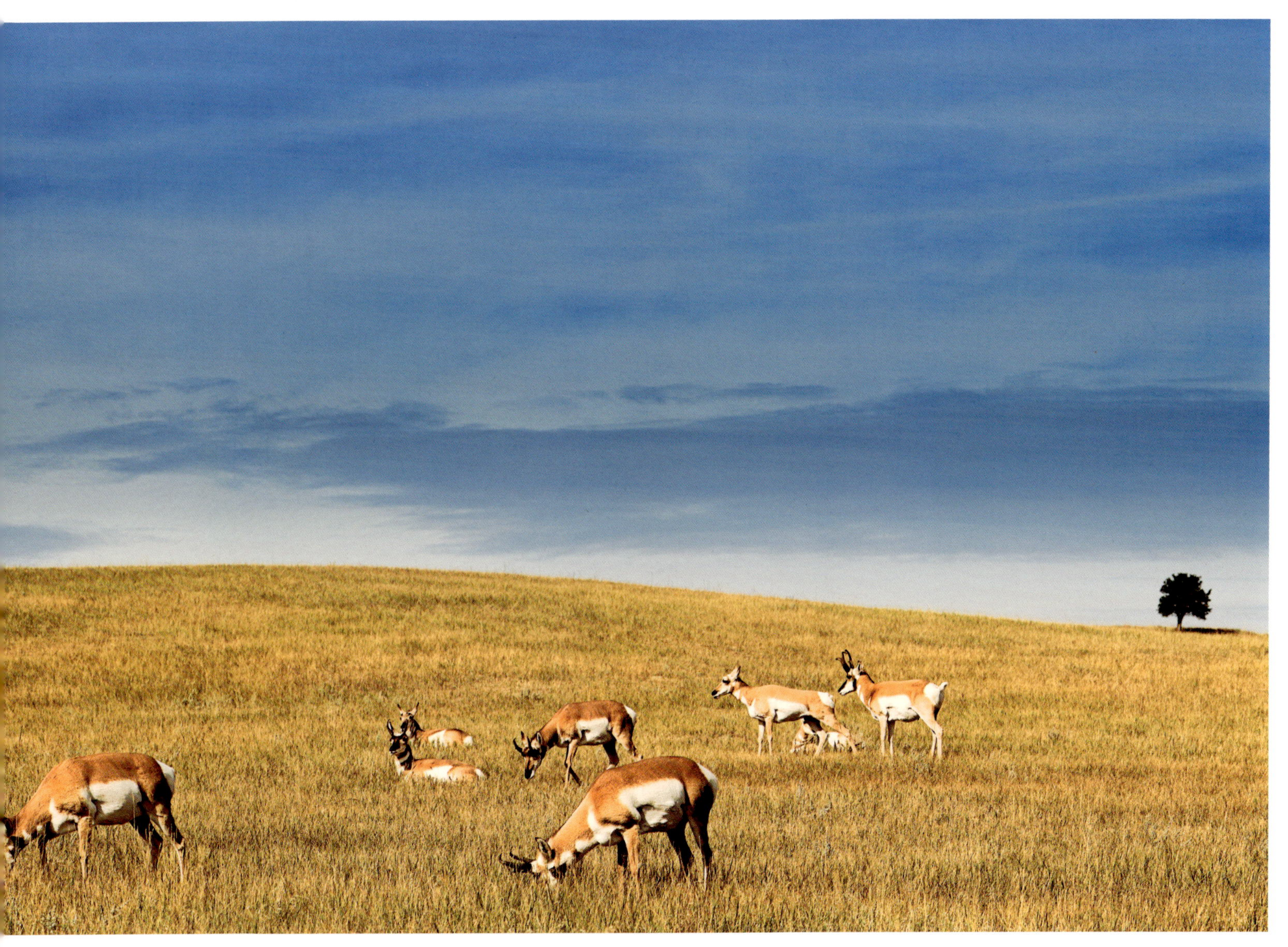

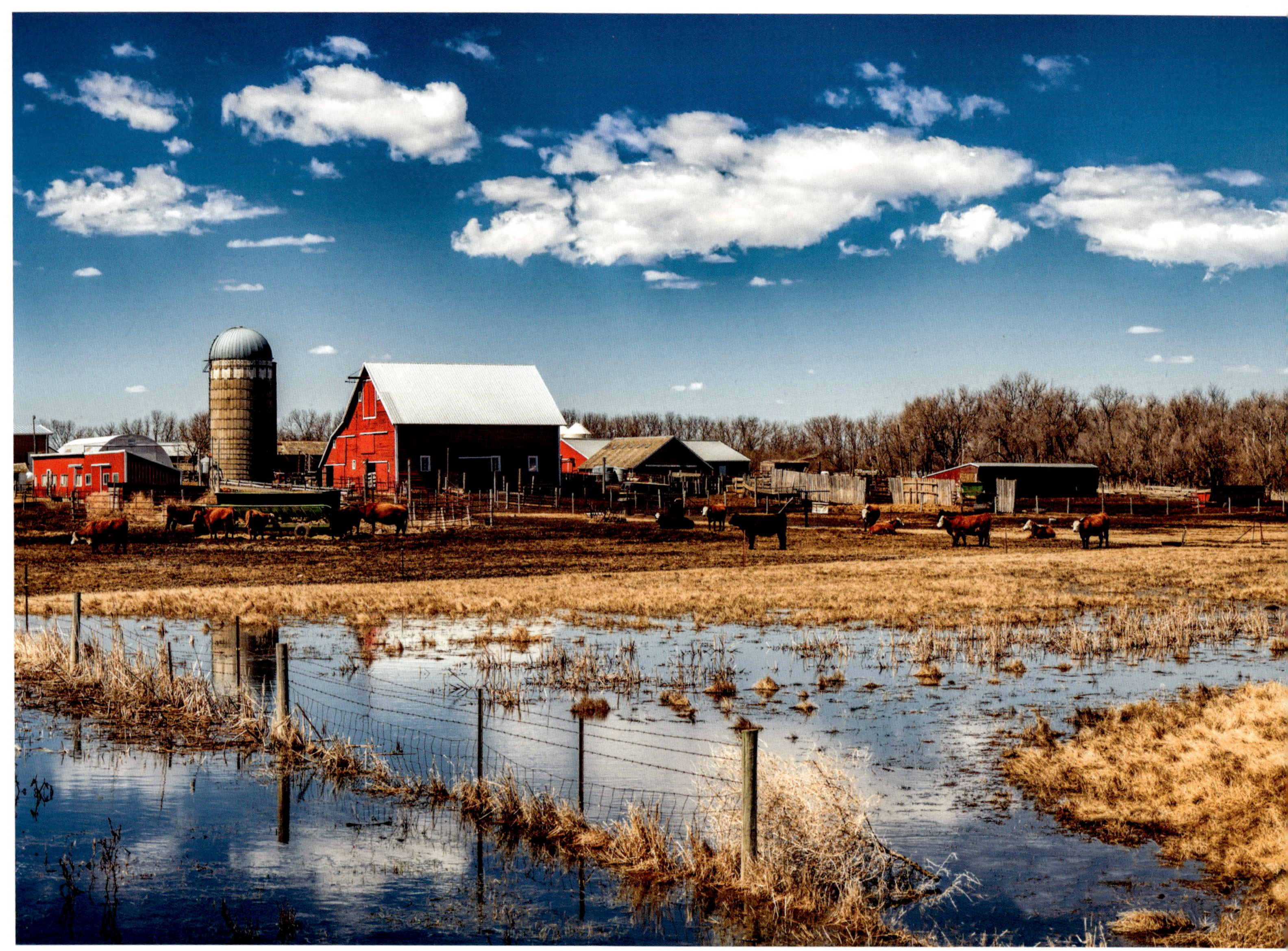

Brink's Farm, South Dakota

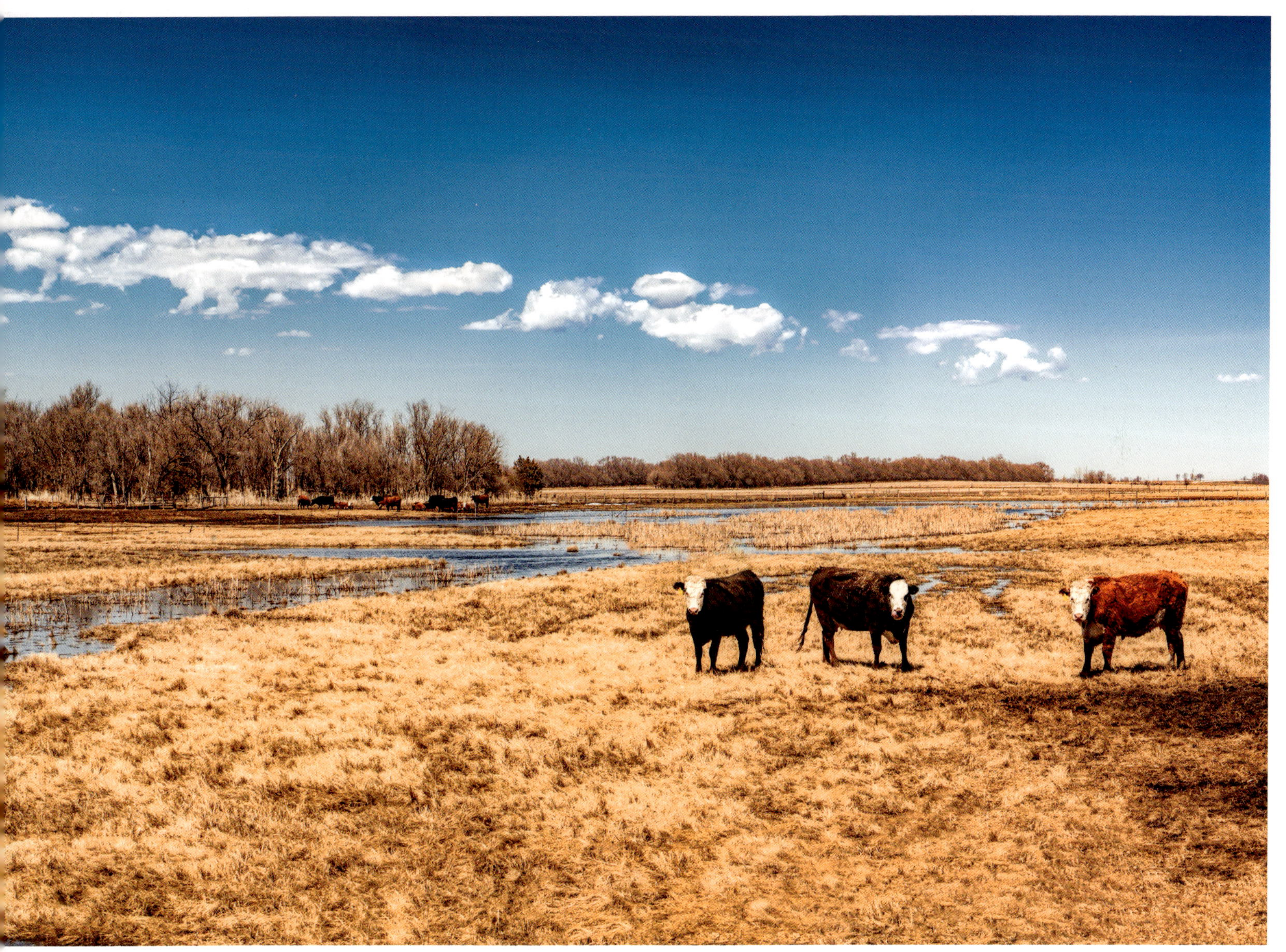

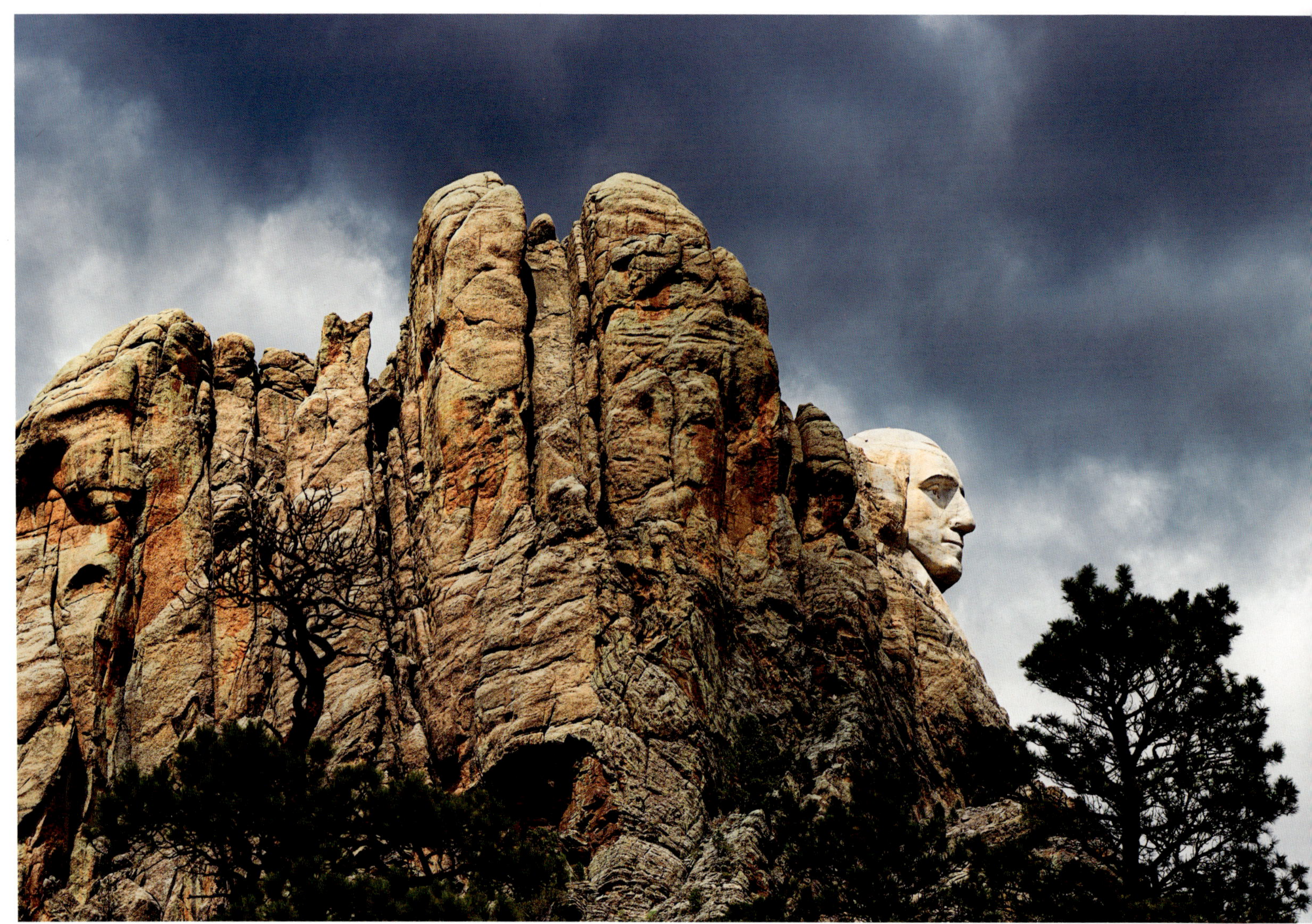

Profile, Mount Rushmore National Memorial, South Dakota

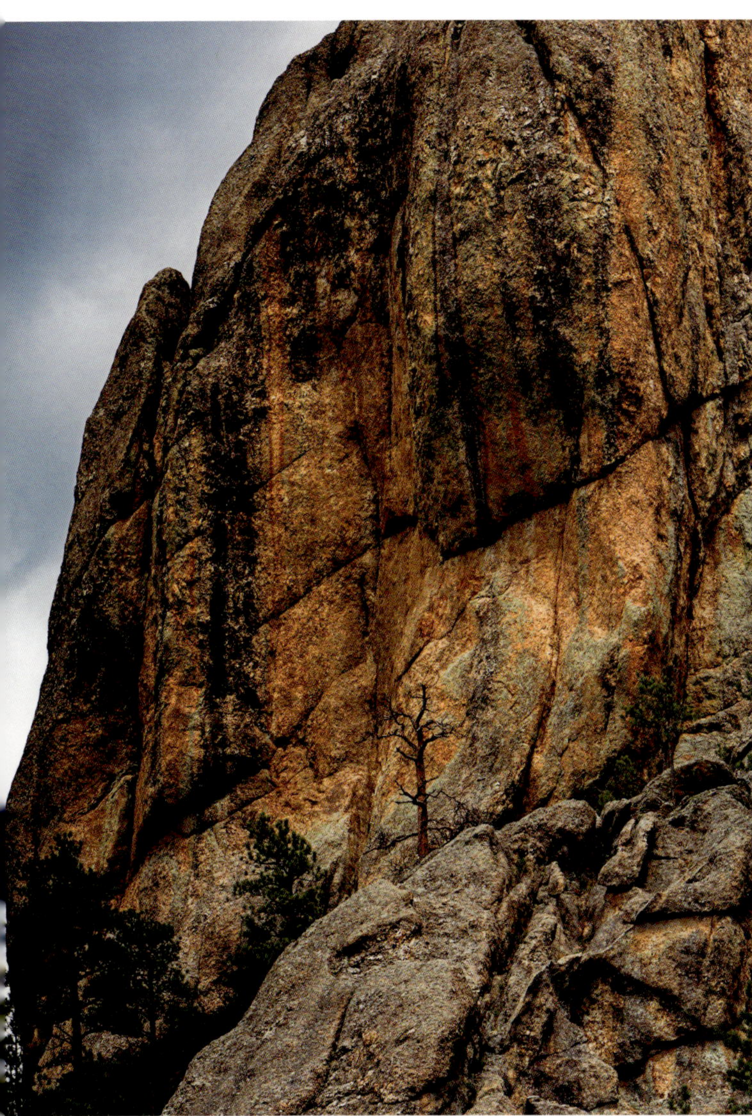

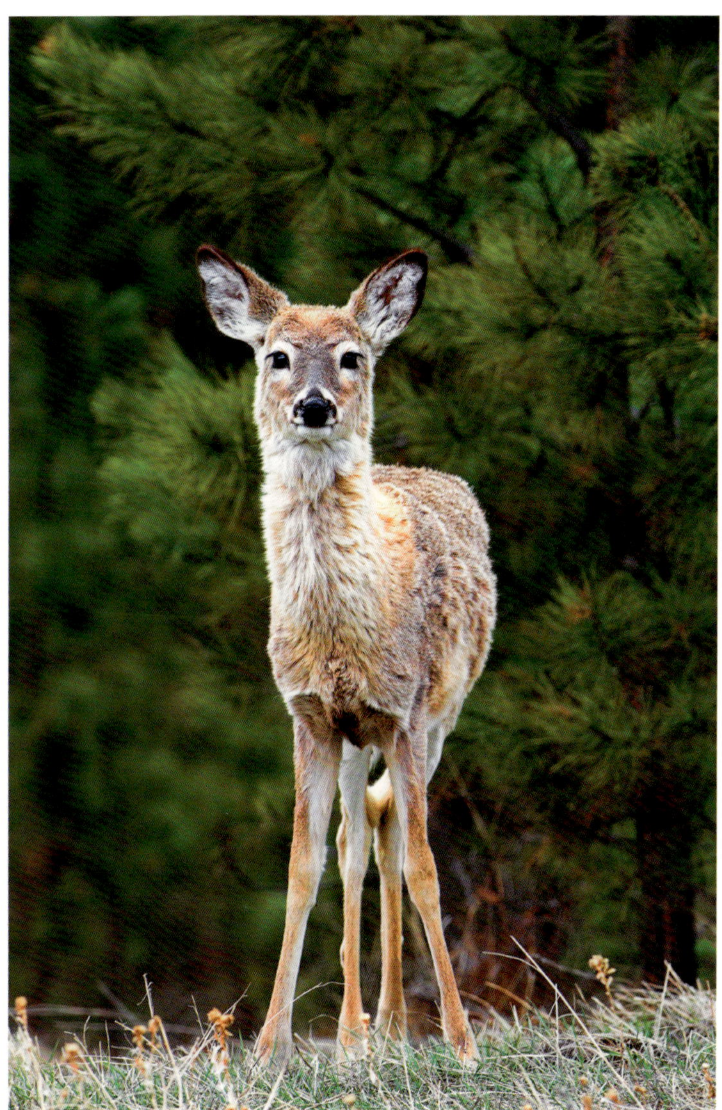

Deer, Black Hills National Forest, South Dakota

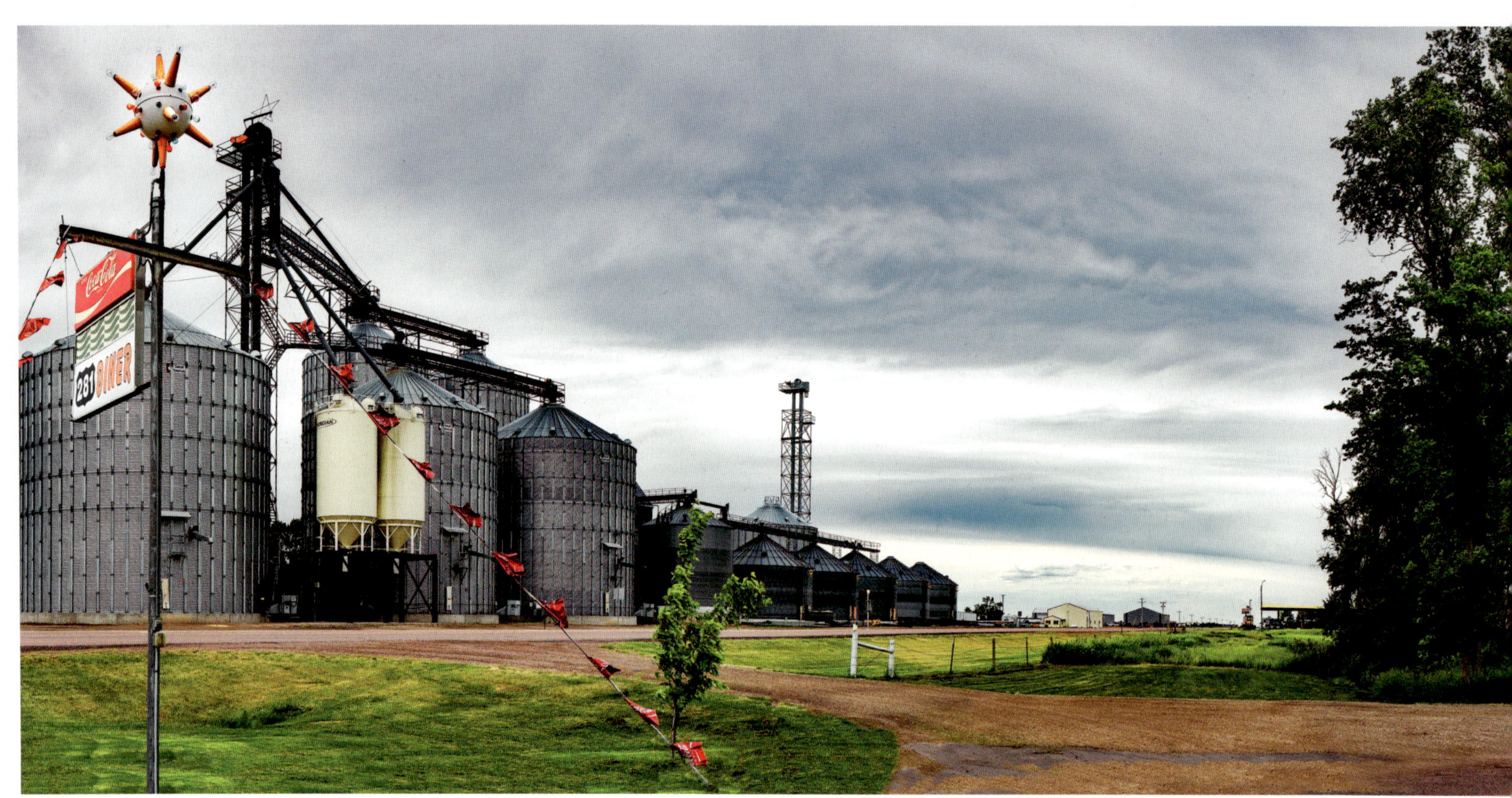

281 Diner, Stickney, South Dakota

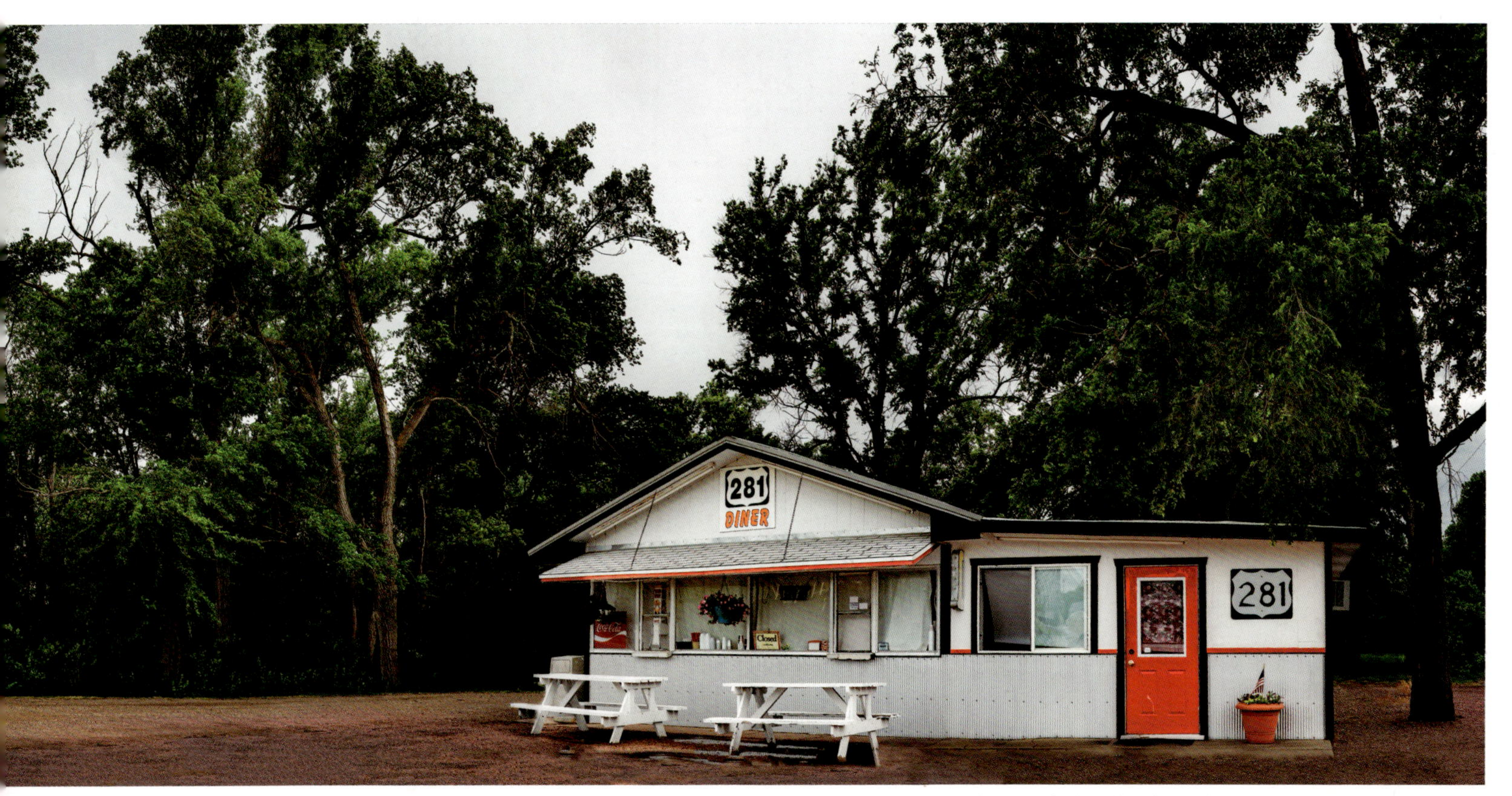

I wish this place had been open. I have a feeling the cheeseburgers would have been terrific.

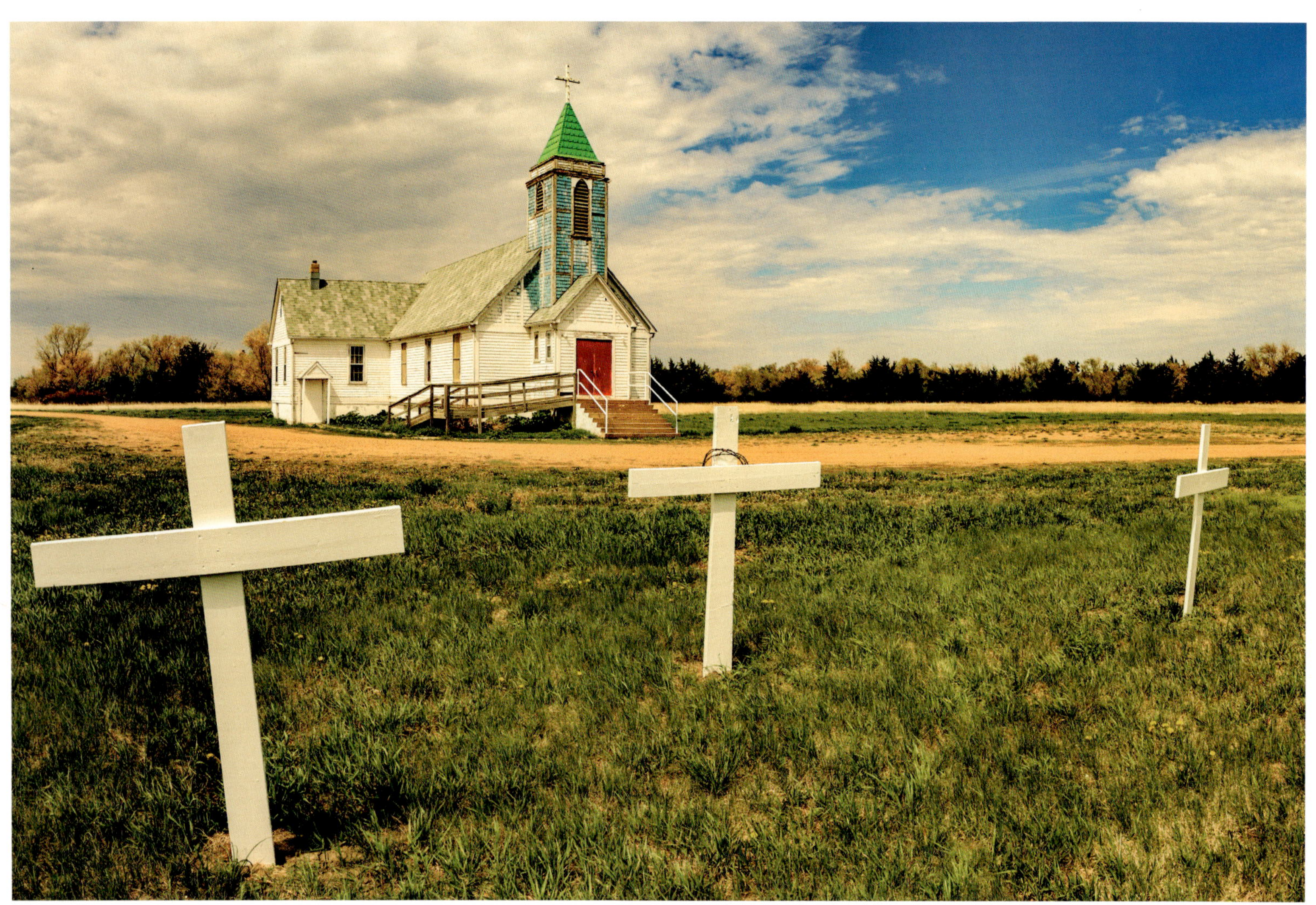

Church along South Dakota State Highway 34

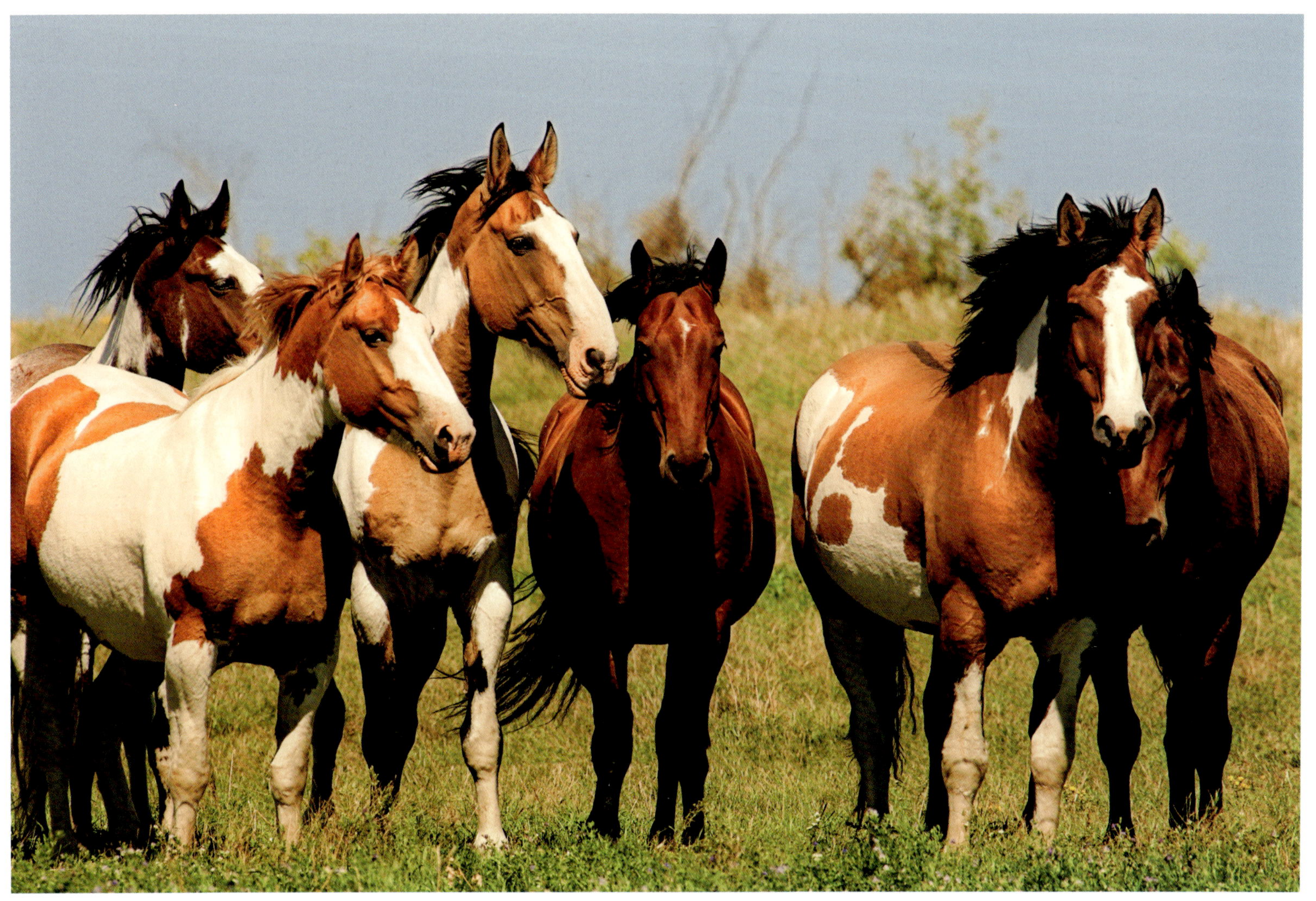

Friendly horses off North Dakota State Highway 22

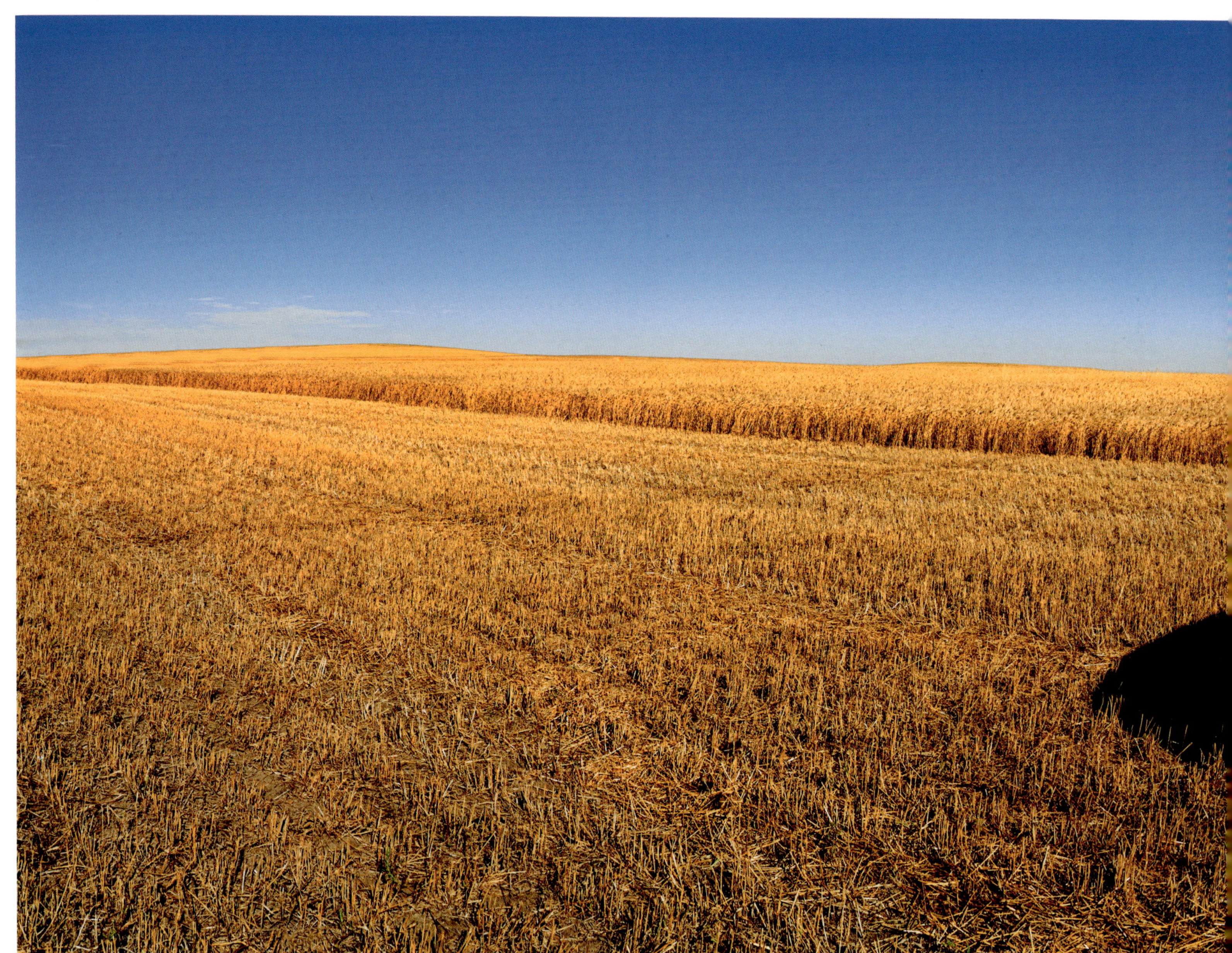

Giant hay roll along North Dakota County Road 4531, the Enchanted Highway

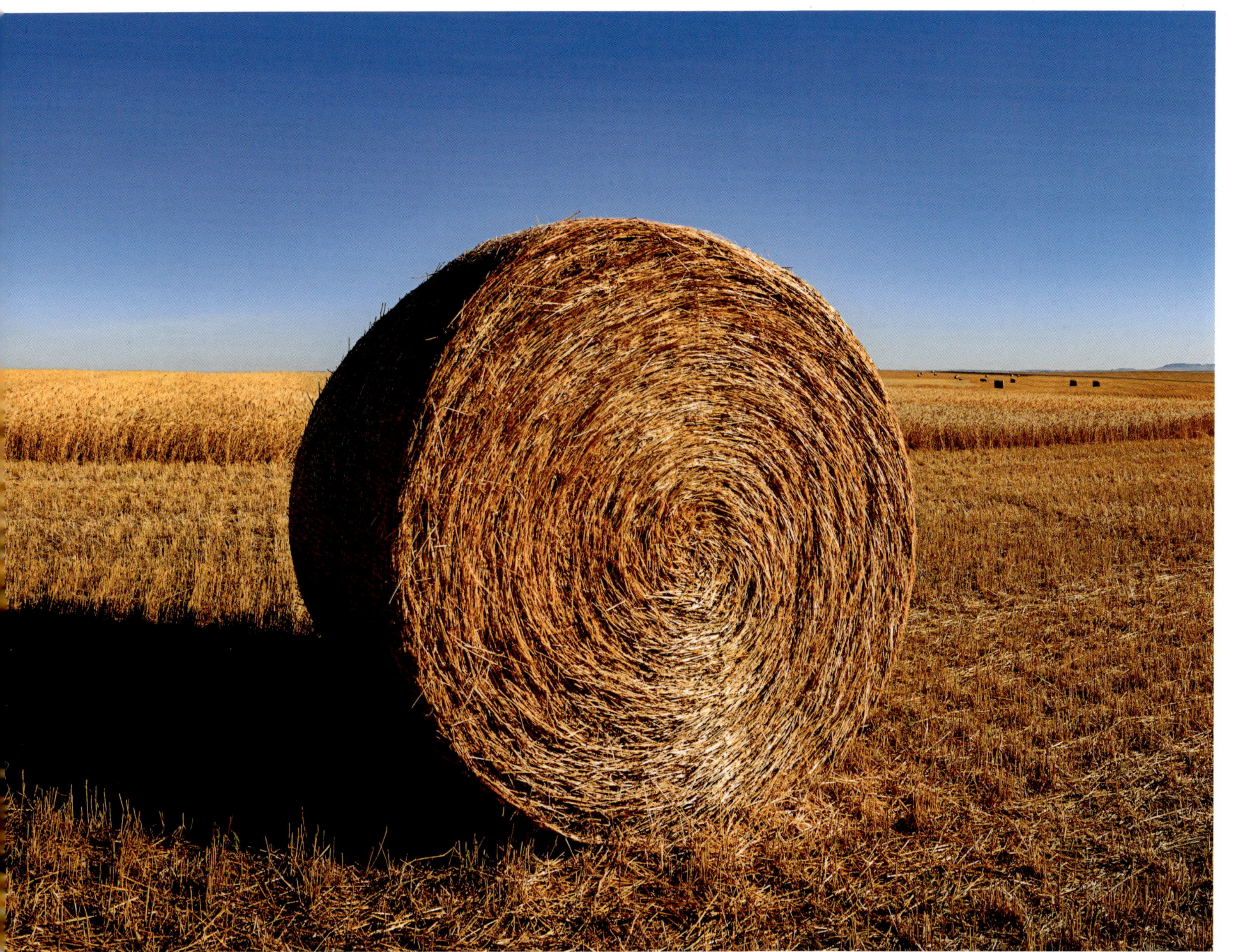

This thing was about a foot taller than me.

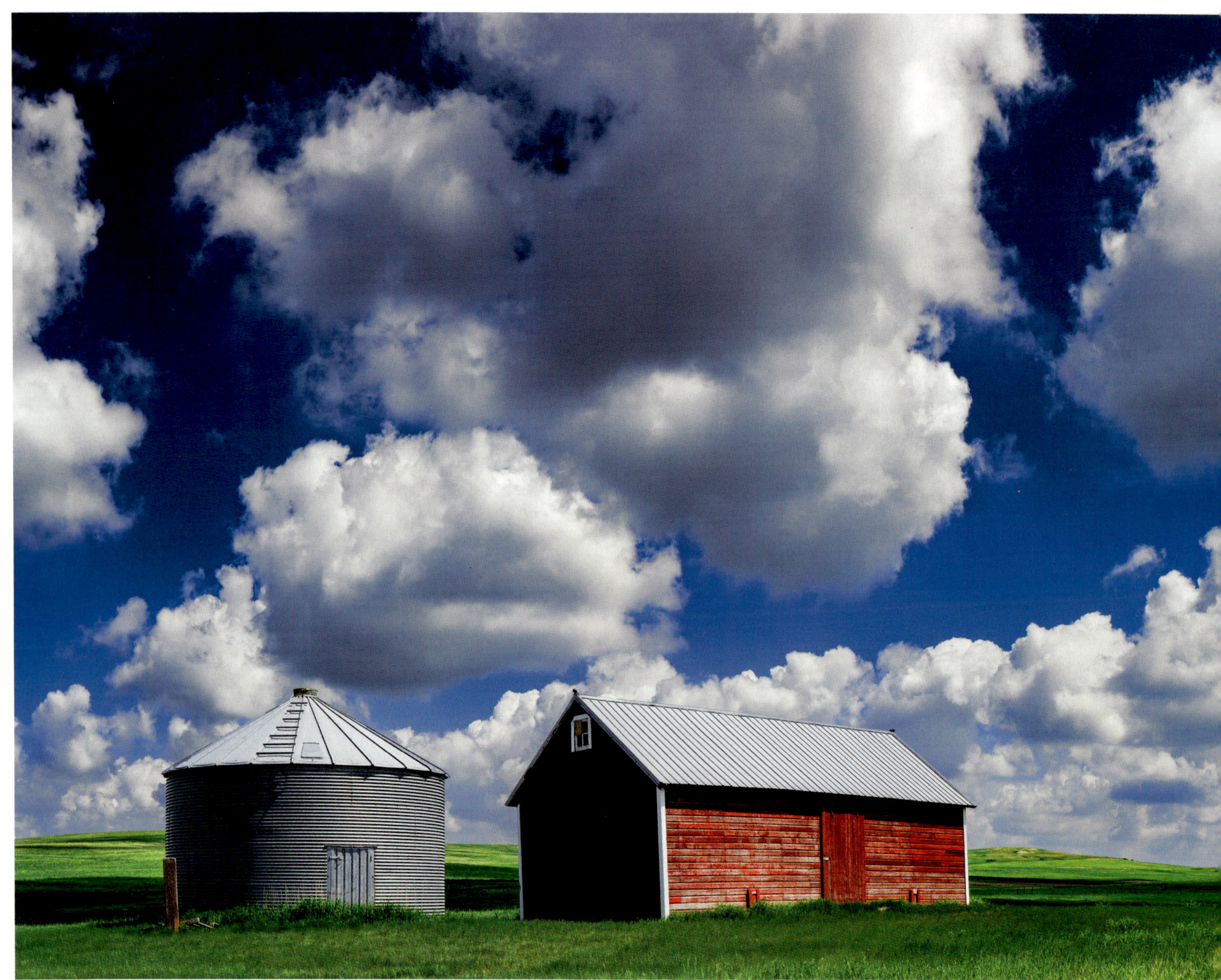

Silos, barn, and clouds along North Dakota State Highway 16

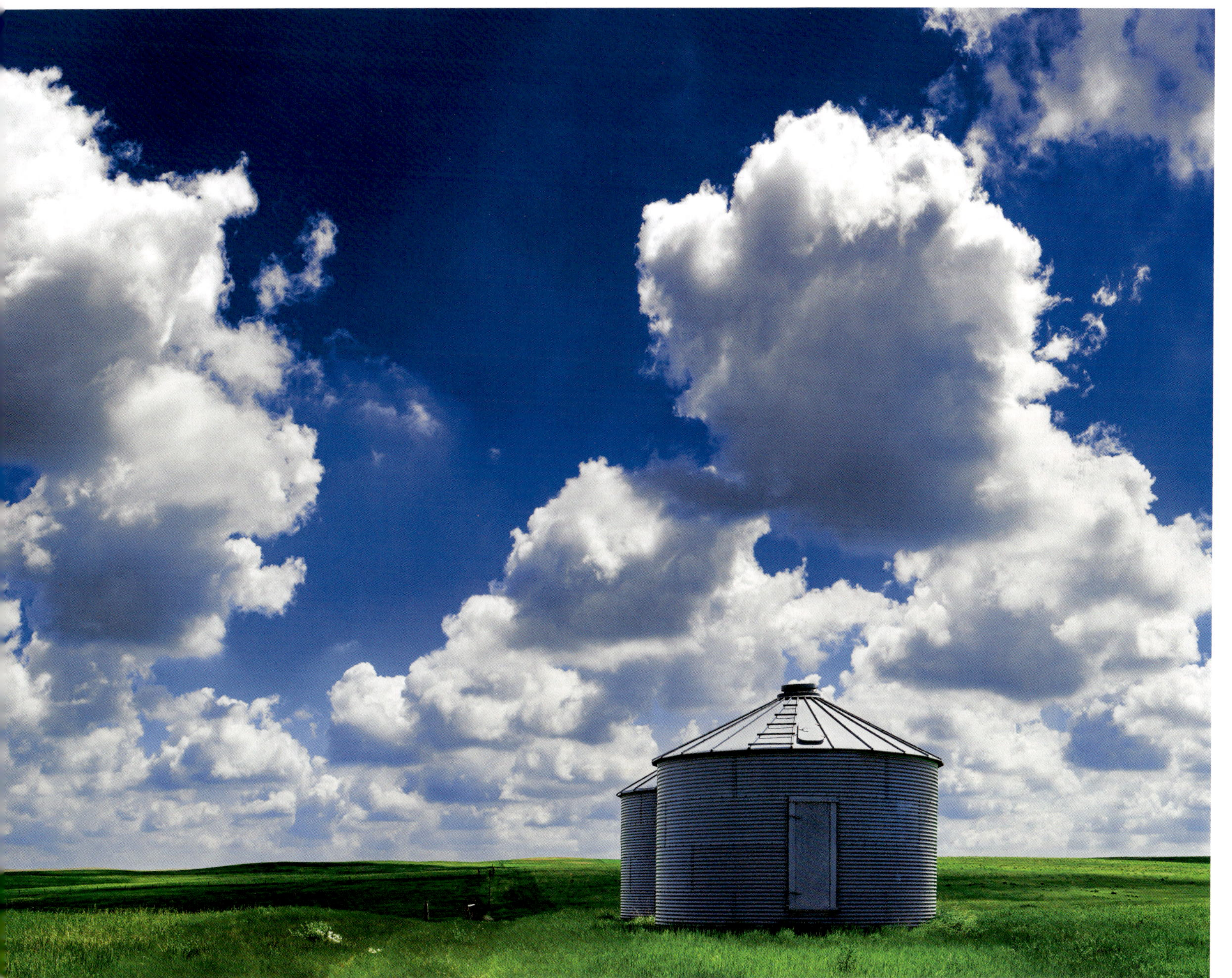

I felt like I could reach up and touch those clouds.

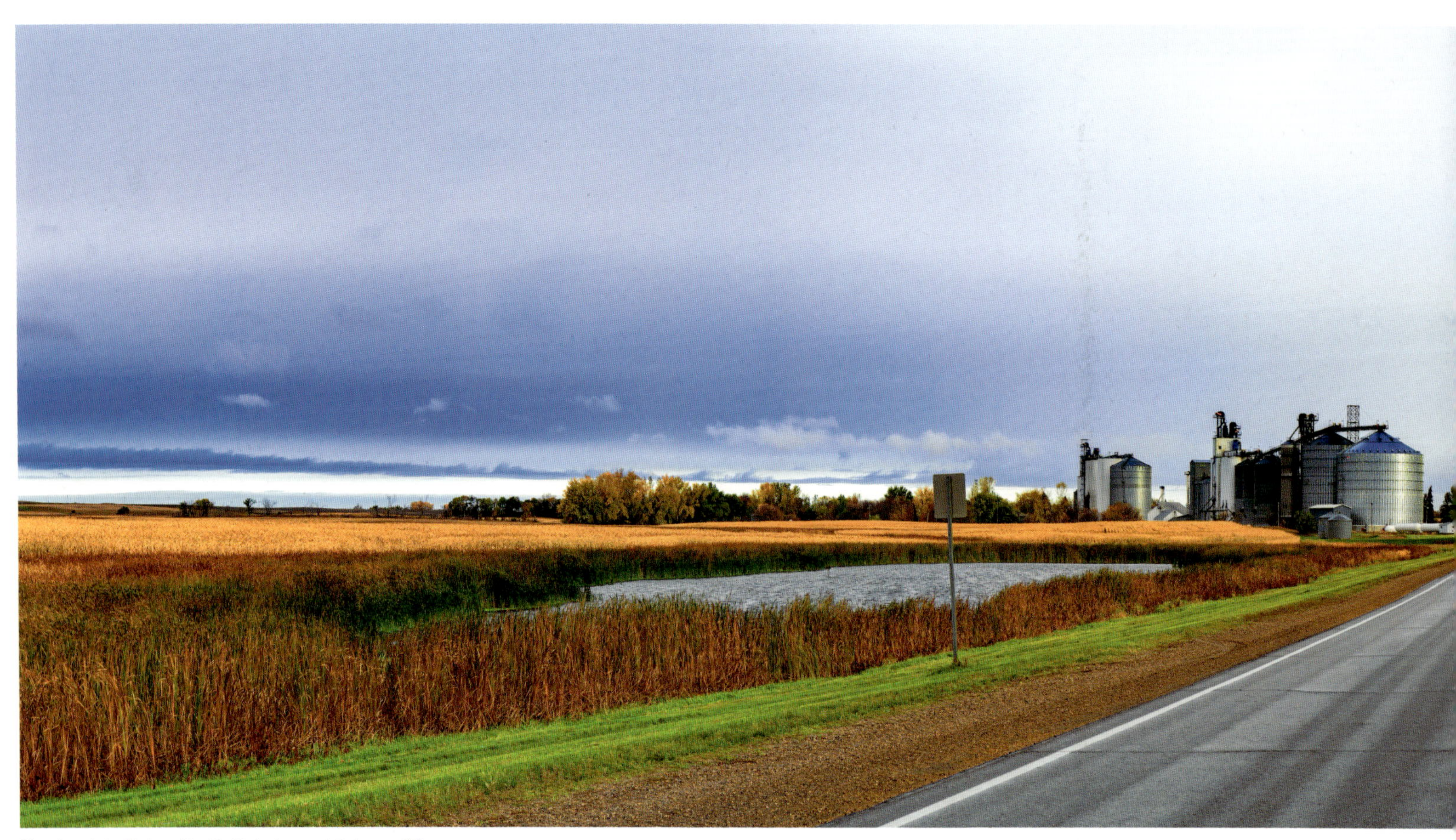

Coming into Finley, North Dakota, on Highway 32

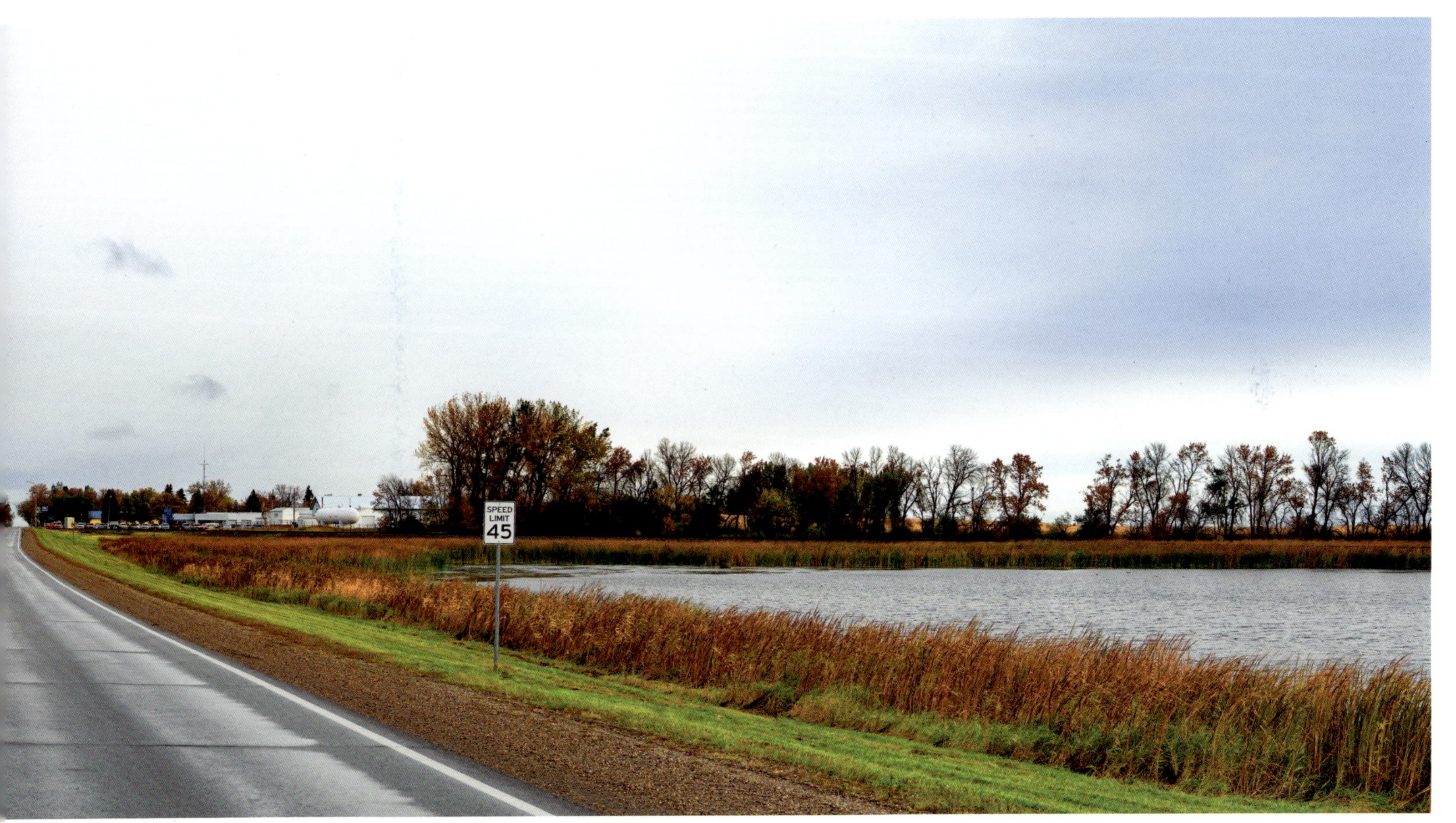
SPEED
LIMIT
45

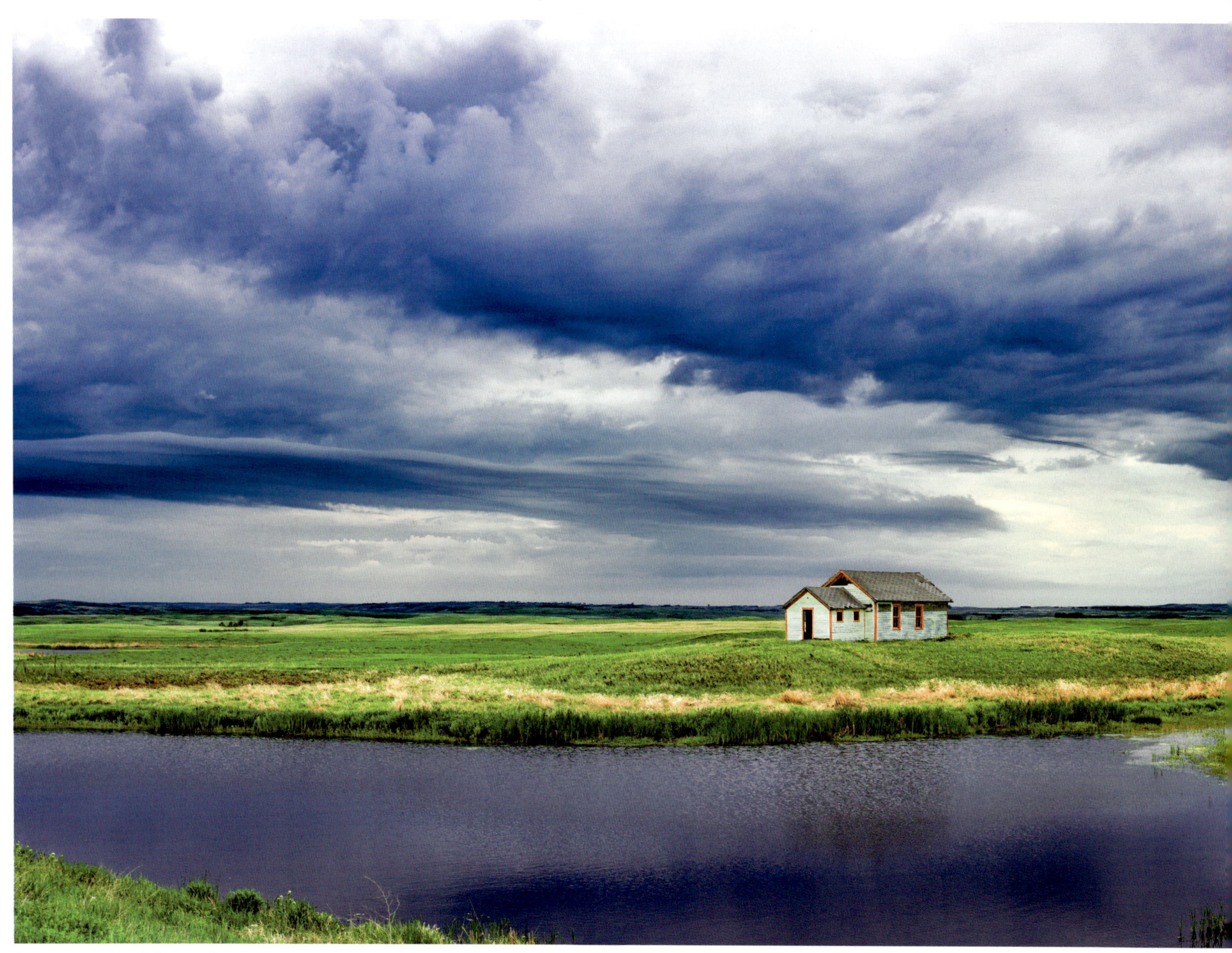

Old house on North Dakota State Highway 8

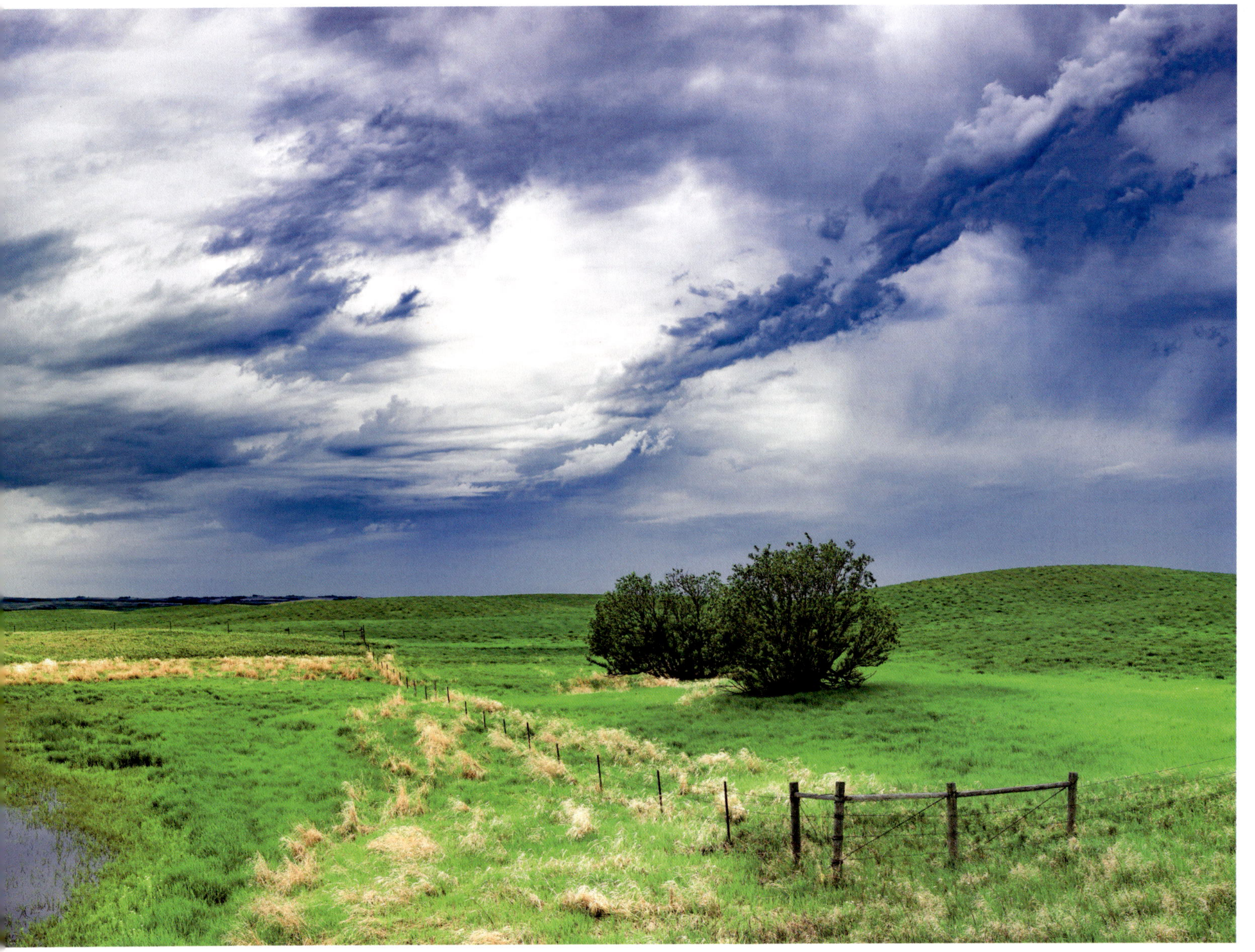

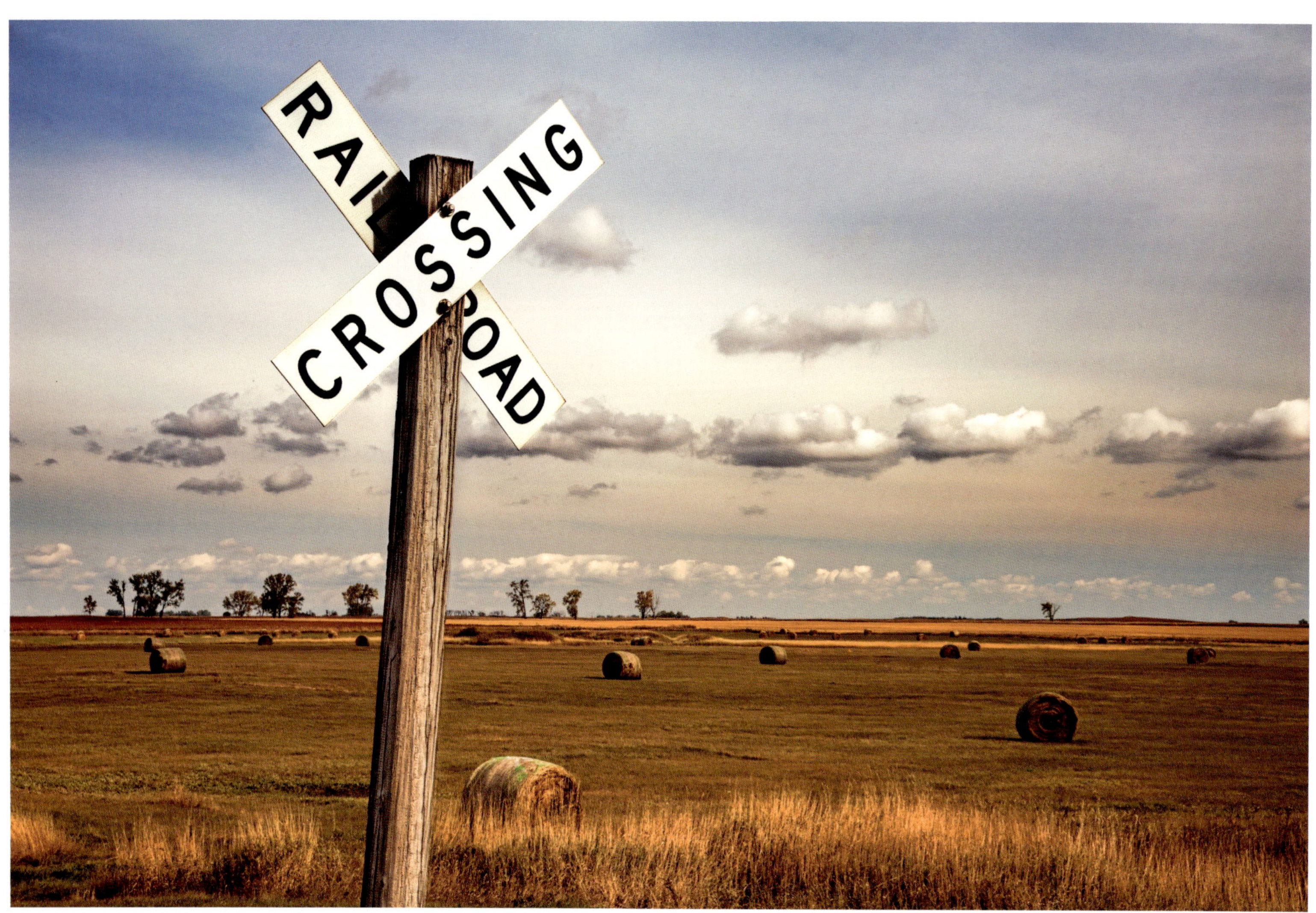

Railroad crossing near Chaseley, North Dakota

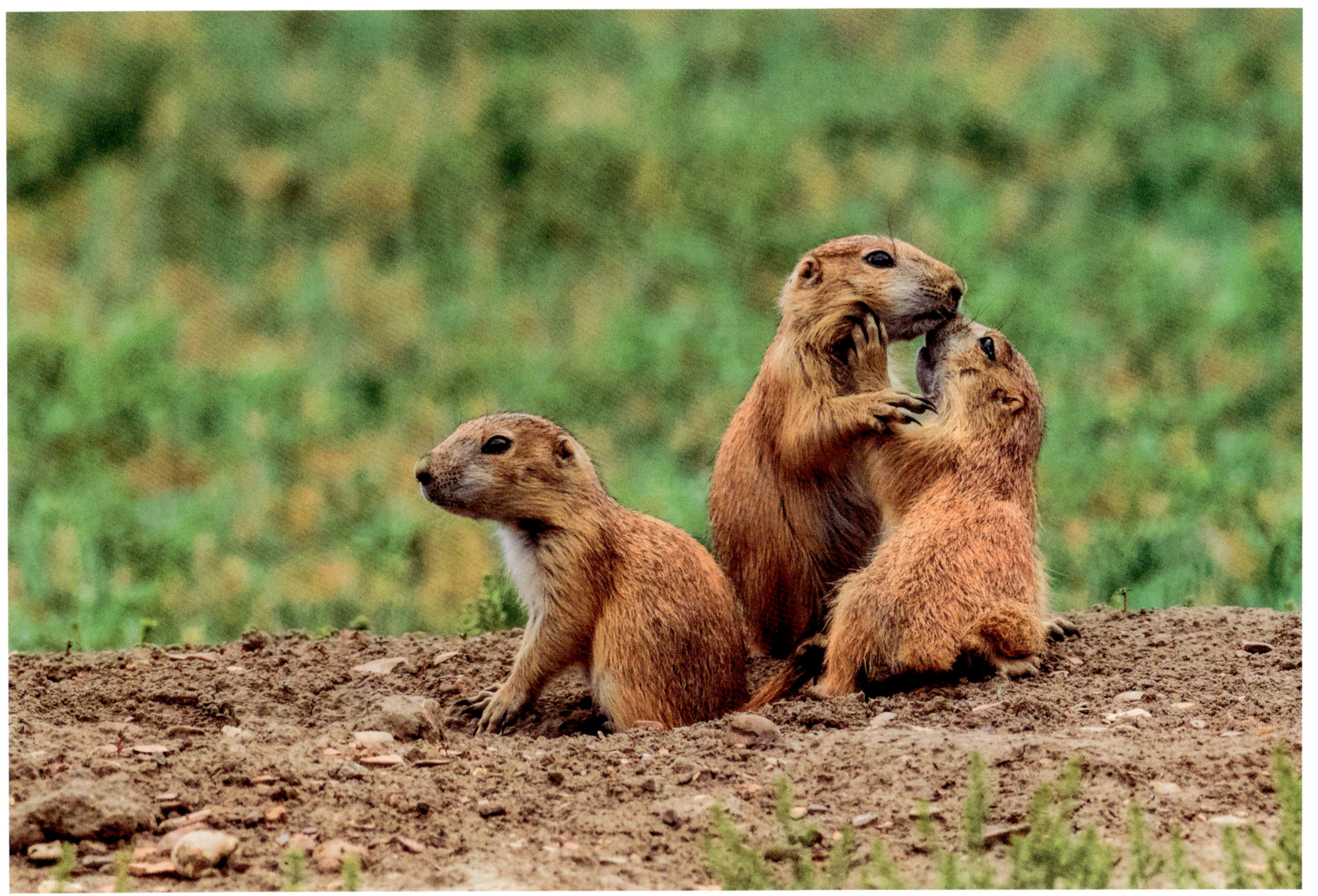

Prairie dog pups, Half-Way Lake National Wildlife Refuge, North Dakota

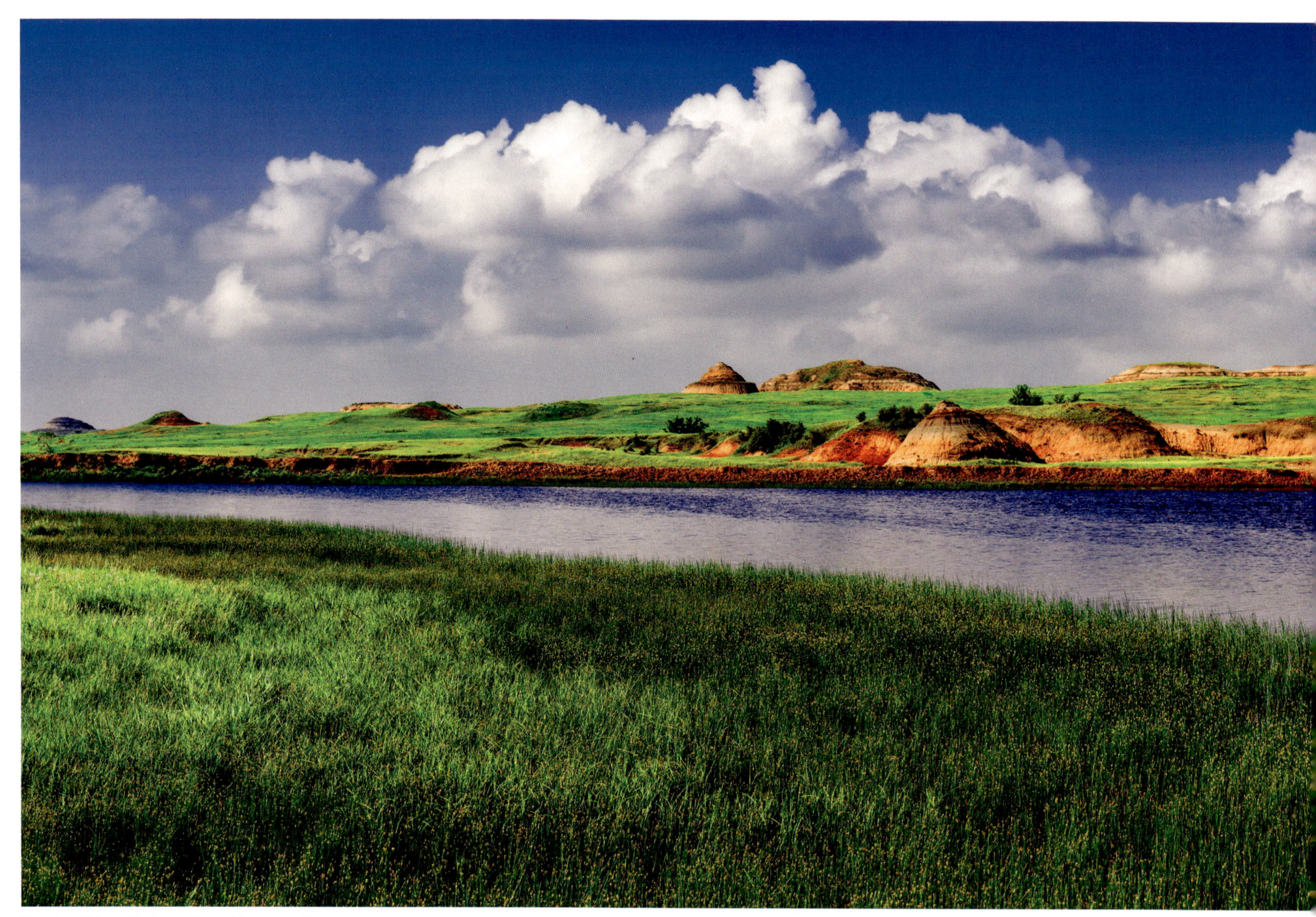

Pond off North Dakota State Highway 16

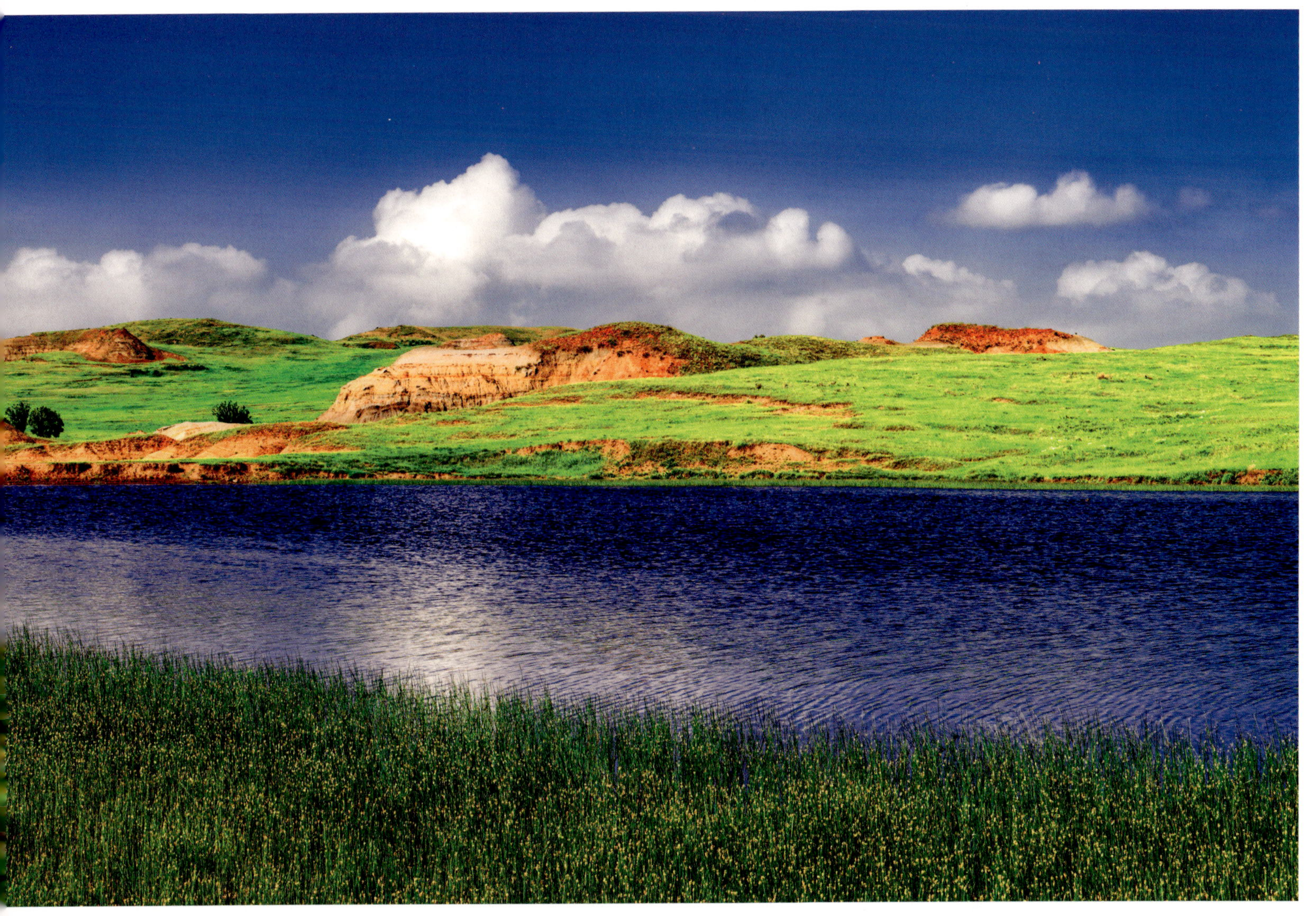

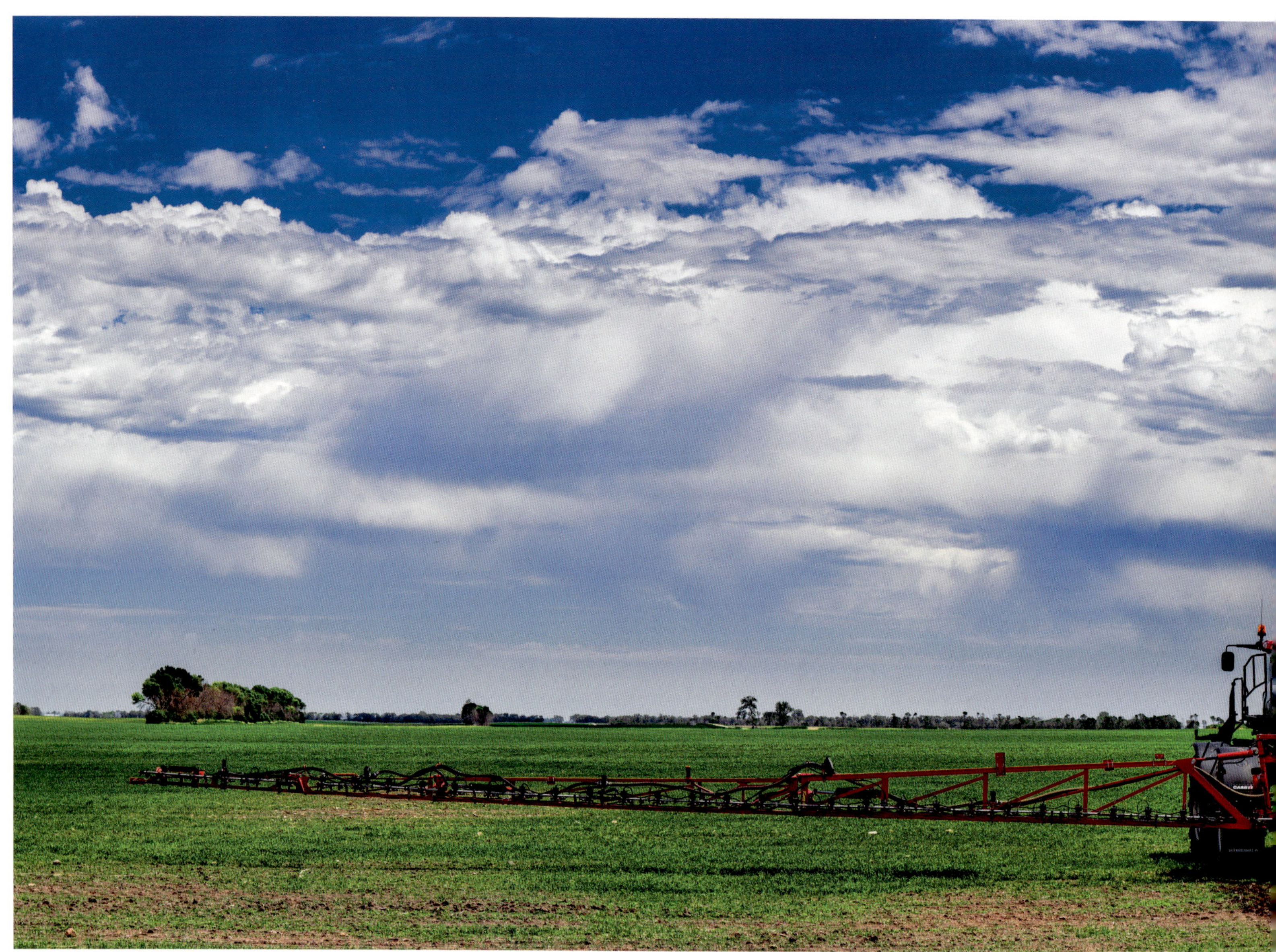

Jim Olsen's sprayer along County Road 4805, North Dakota

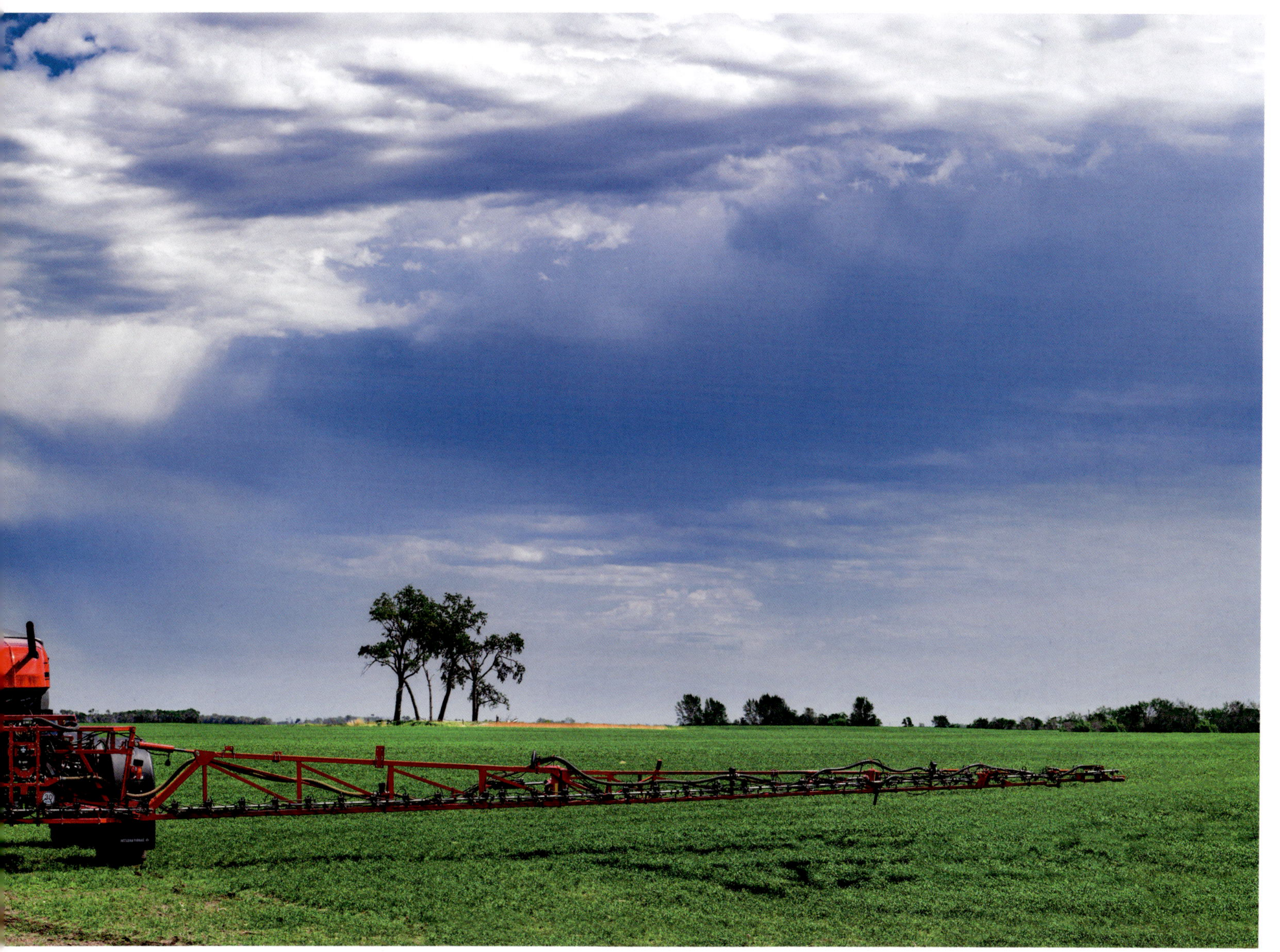

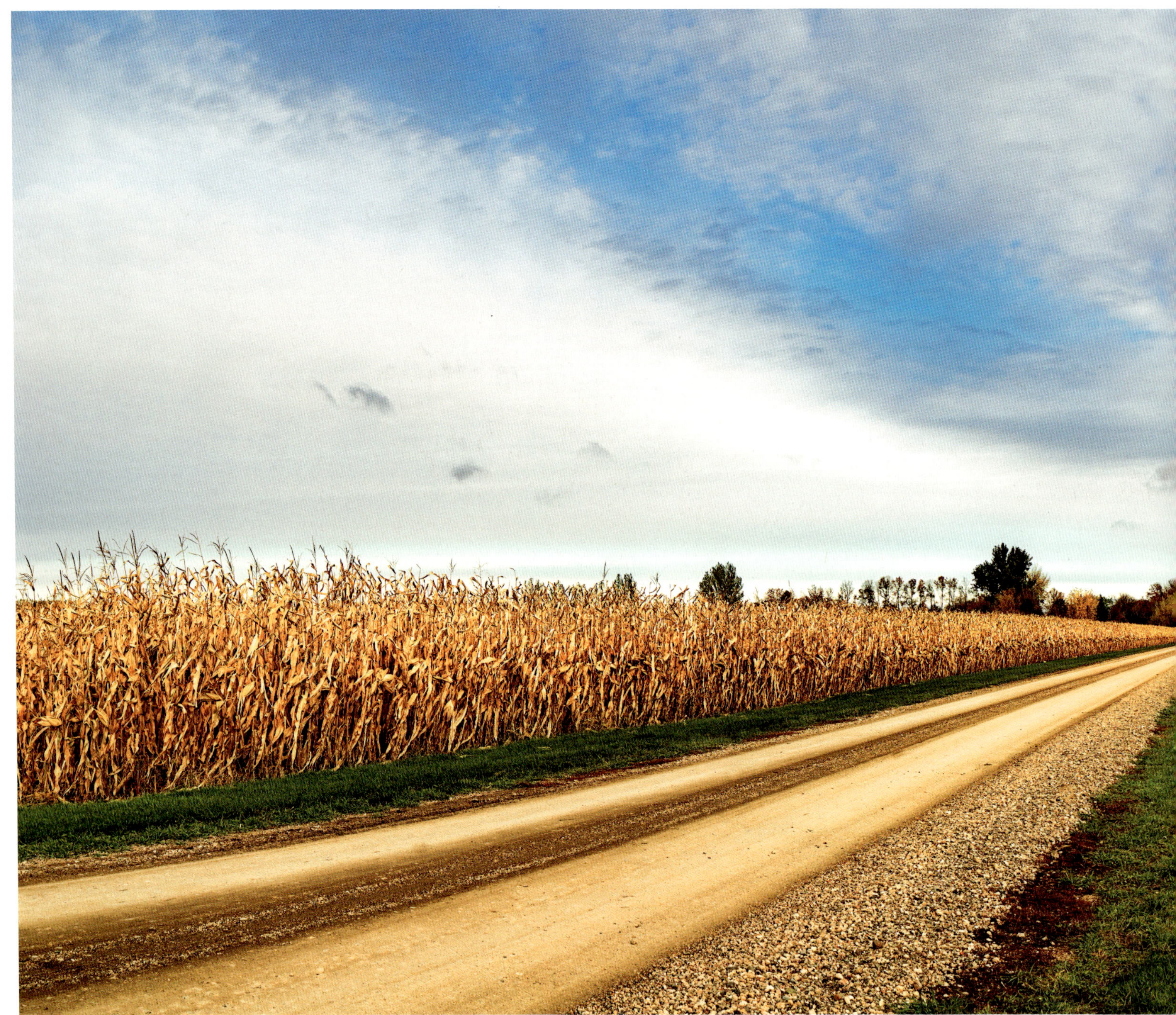

Ash Road, North Dakota

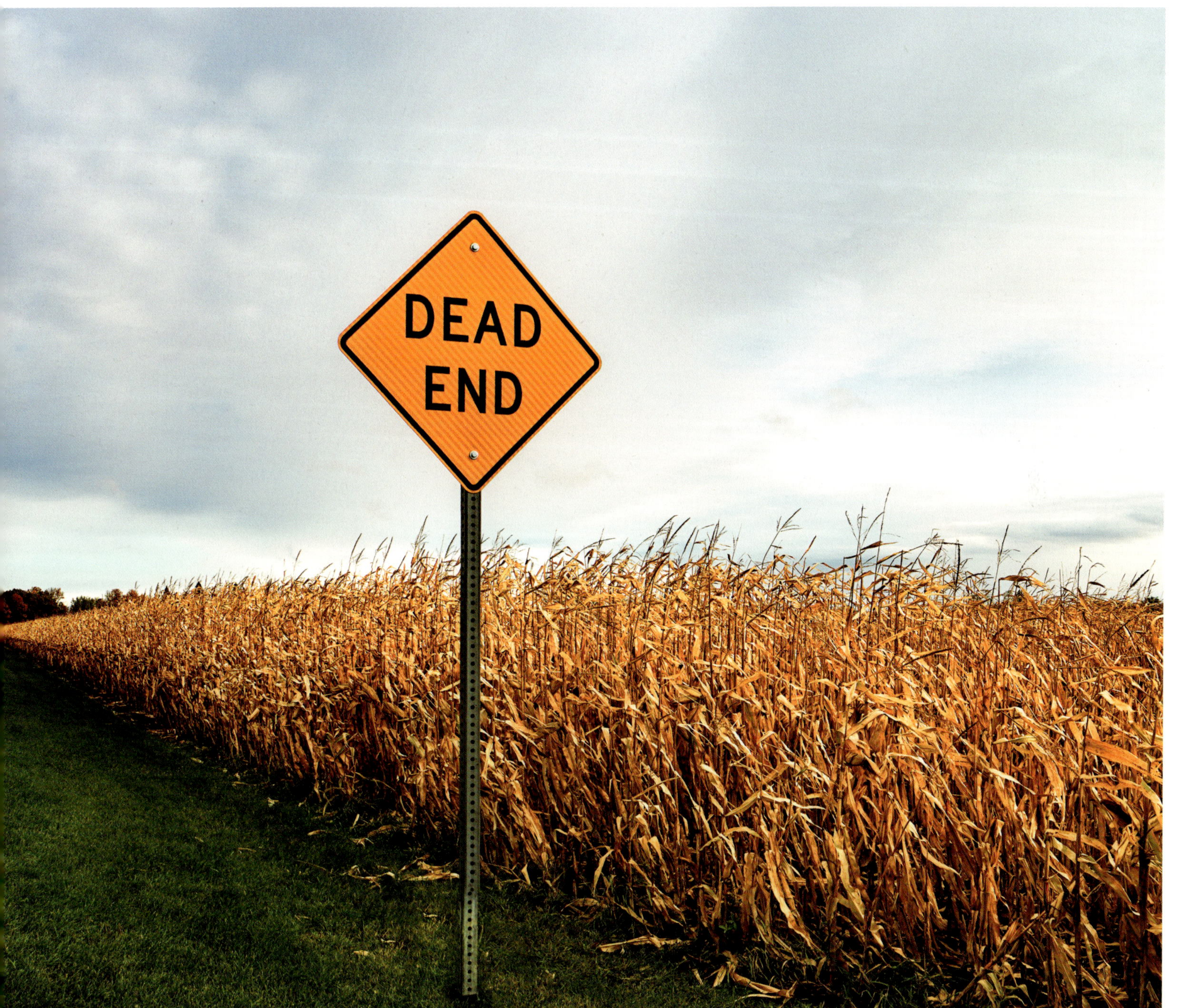
DEAD
END

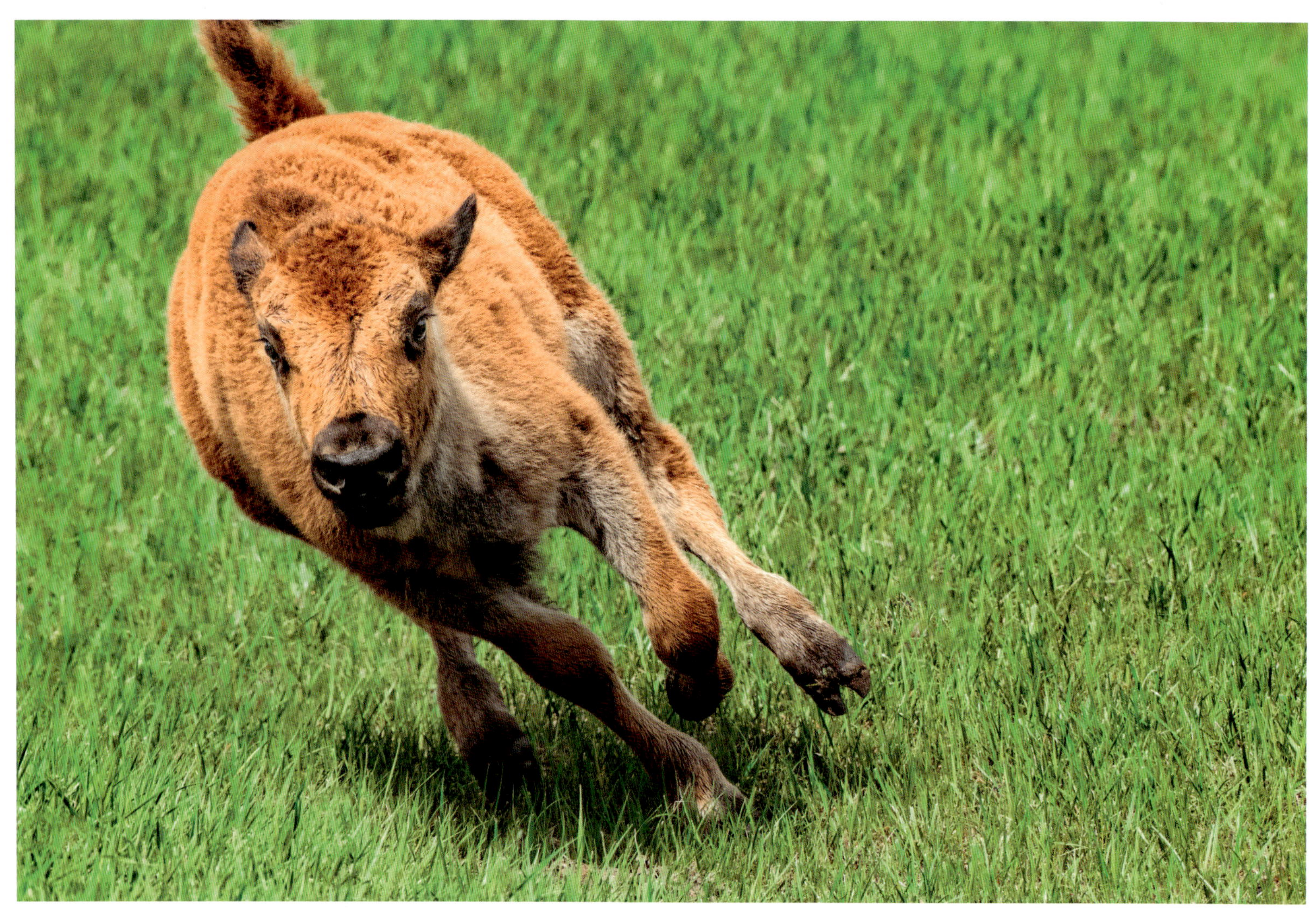

American bison calf, Little Missouri National Grassland, North Dakota

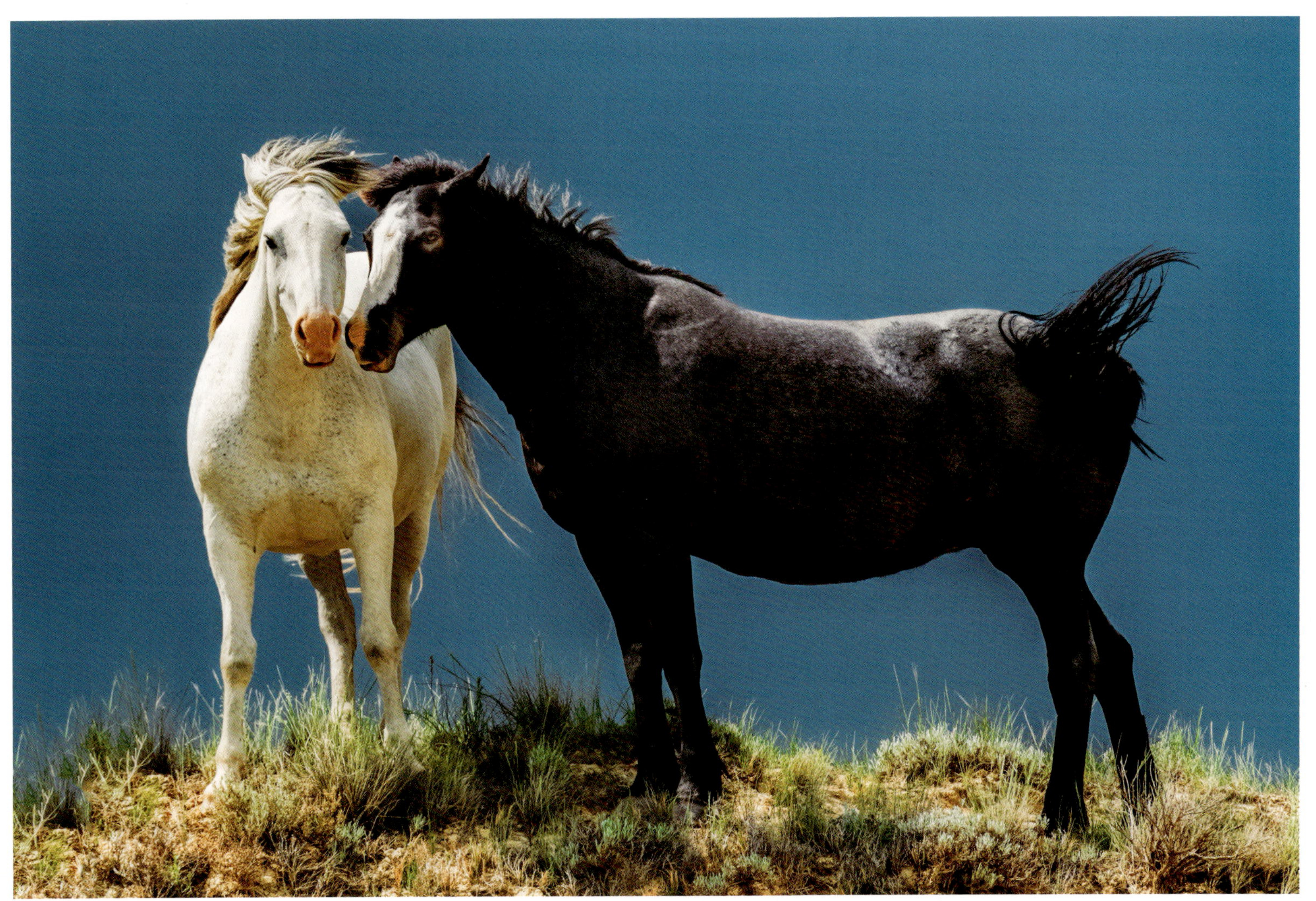

Wild horses, Theodore Roosevelt National Park, North Dakota

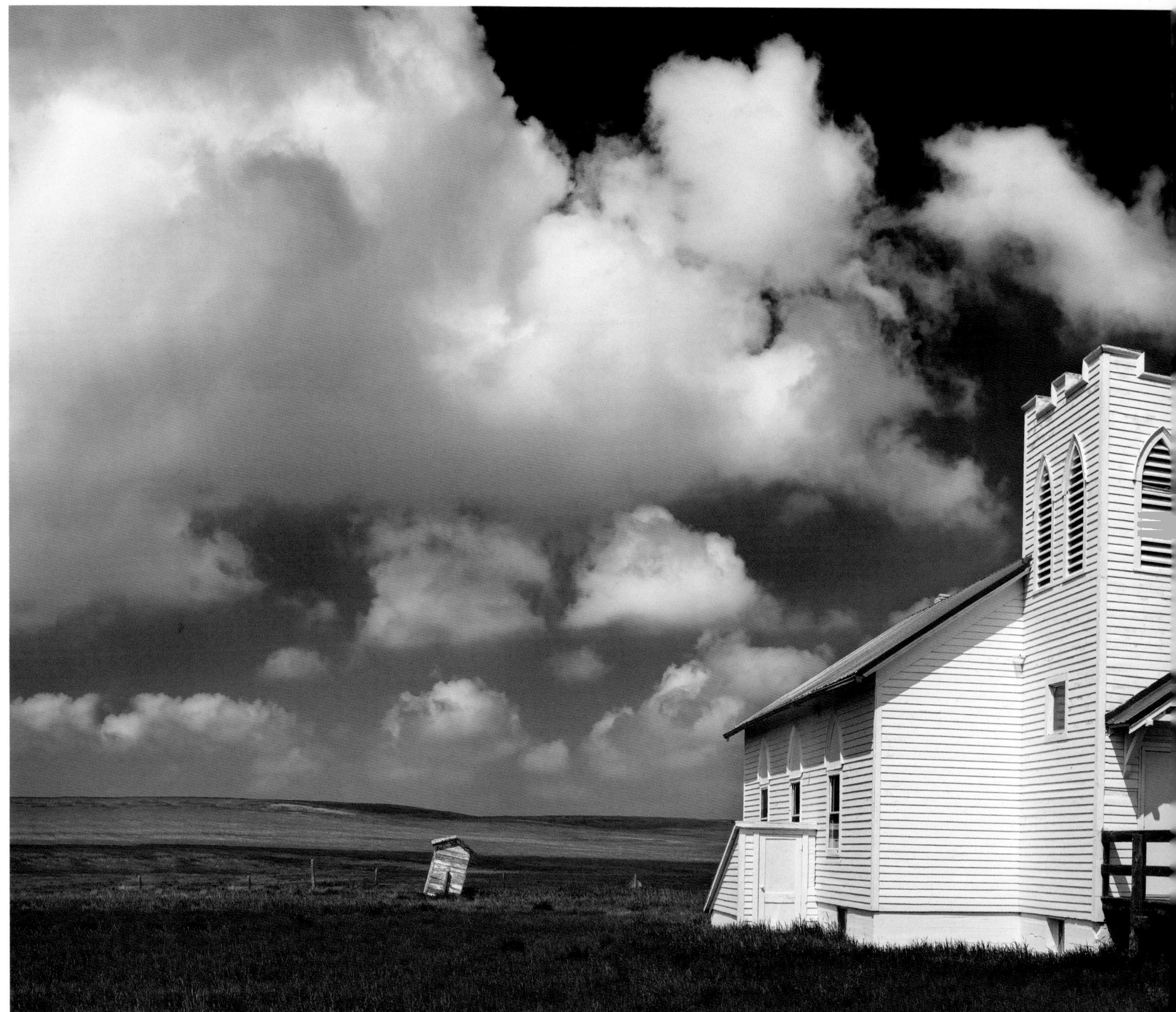

Trotters Church, North Dakota

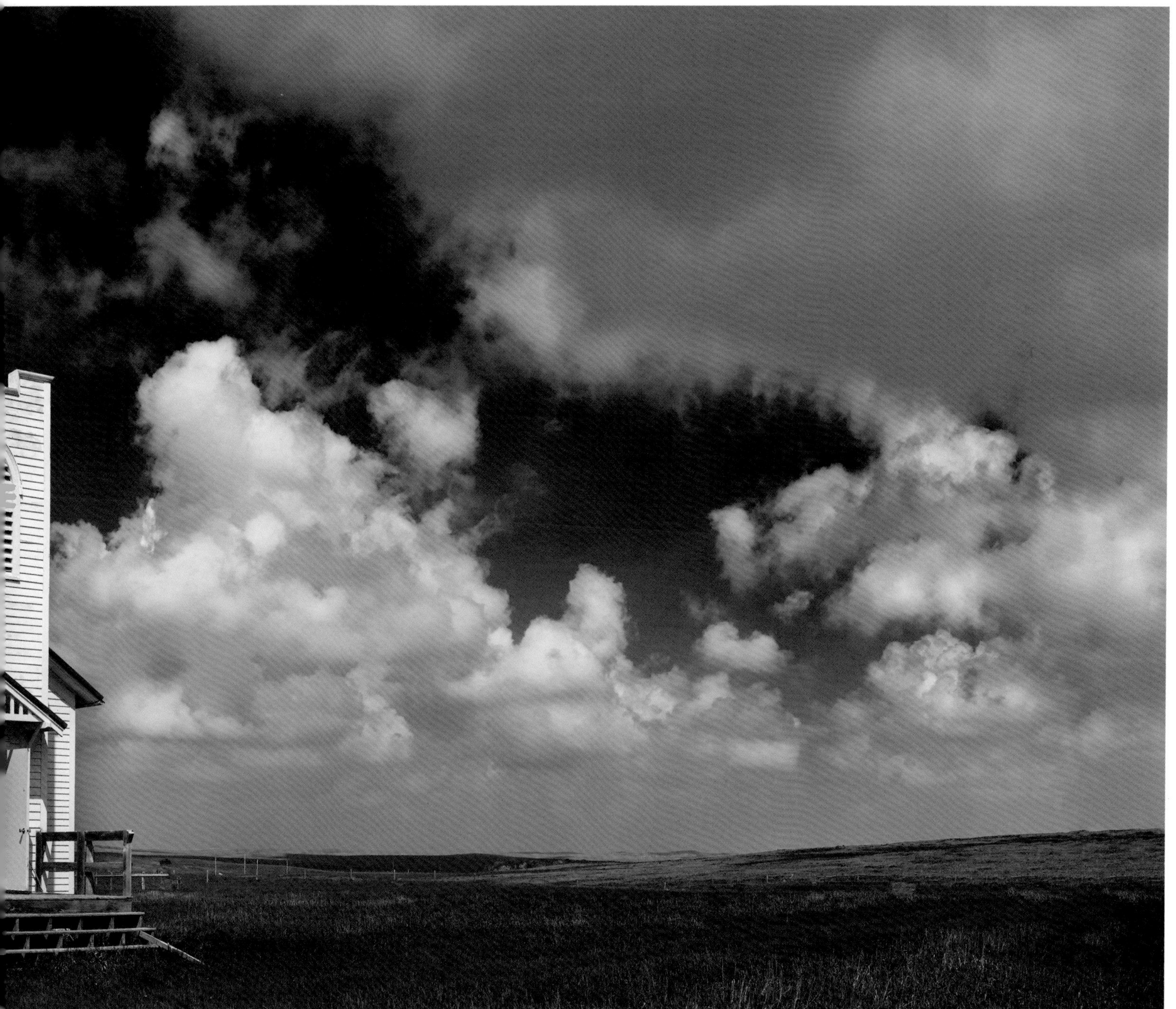

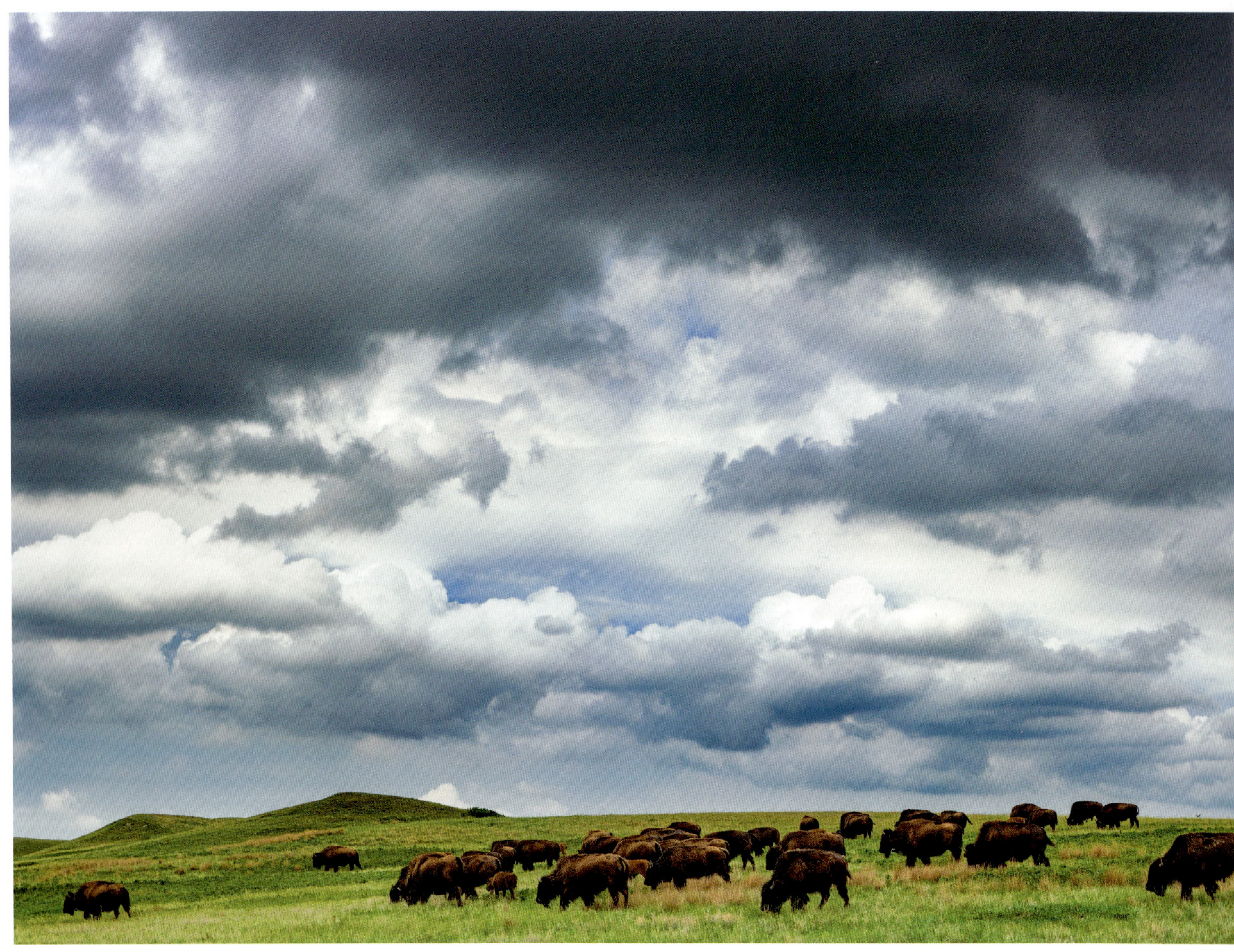

American bison herd in the grasslands, North Dakota

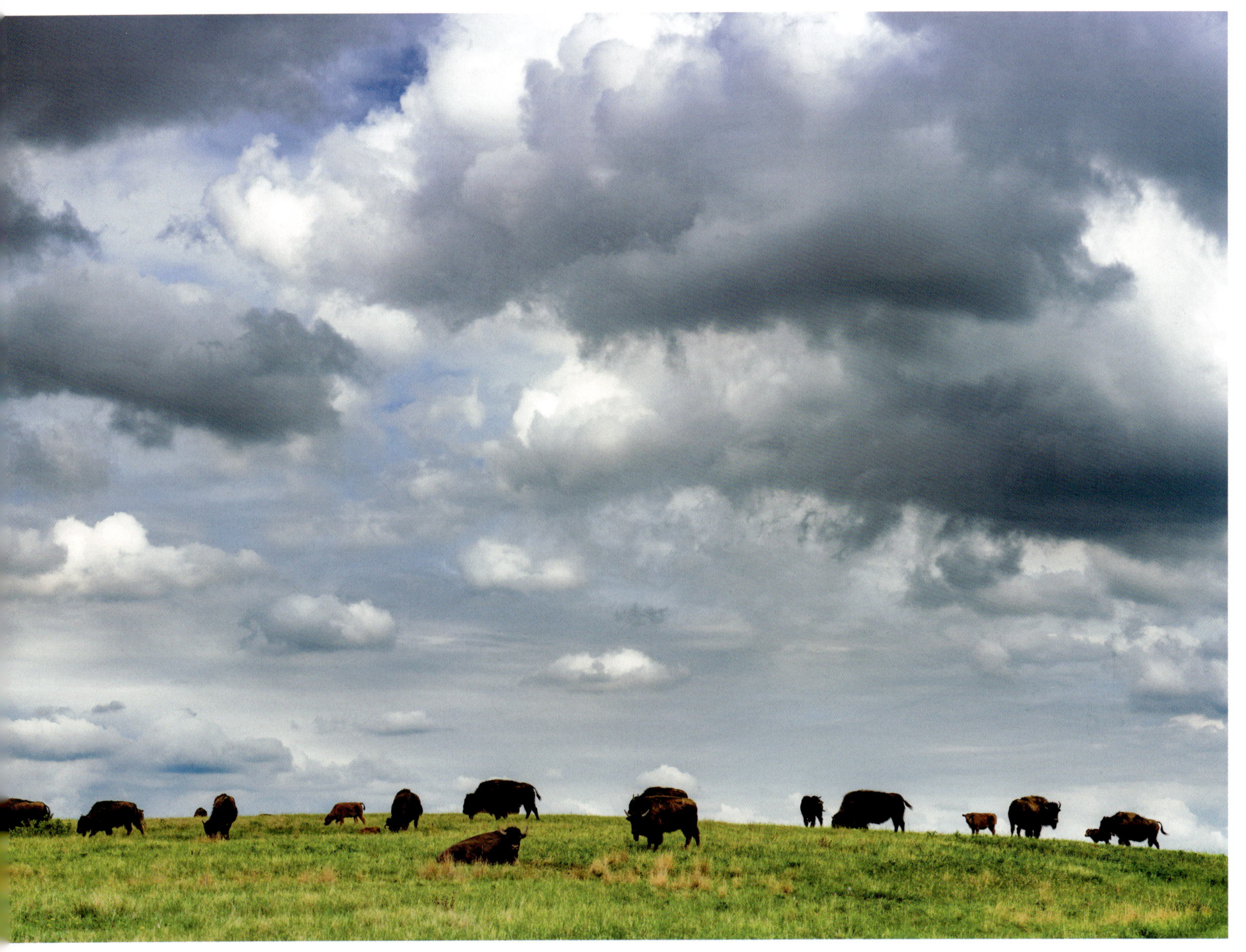

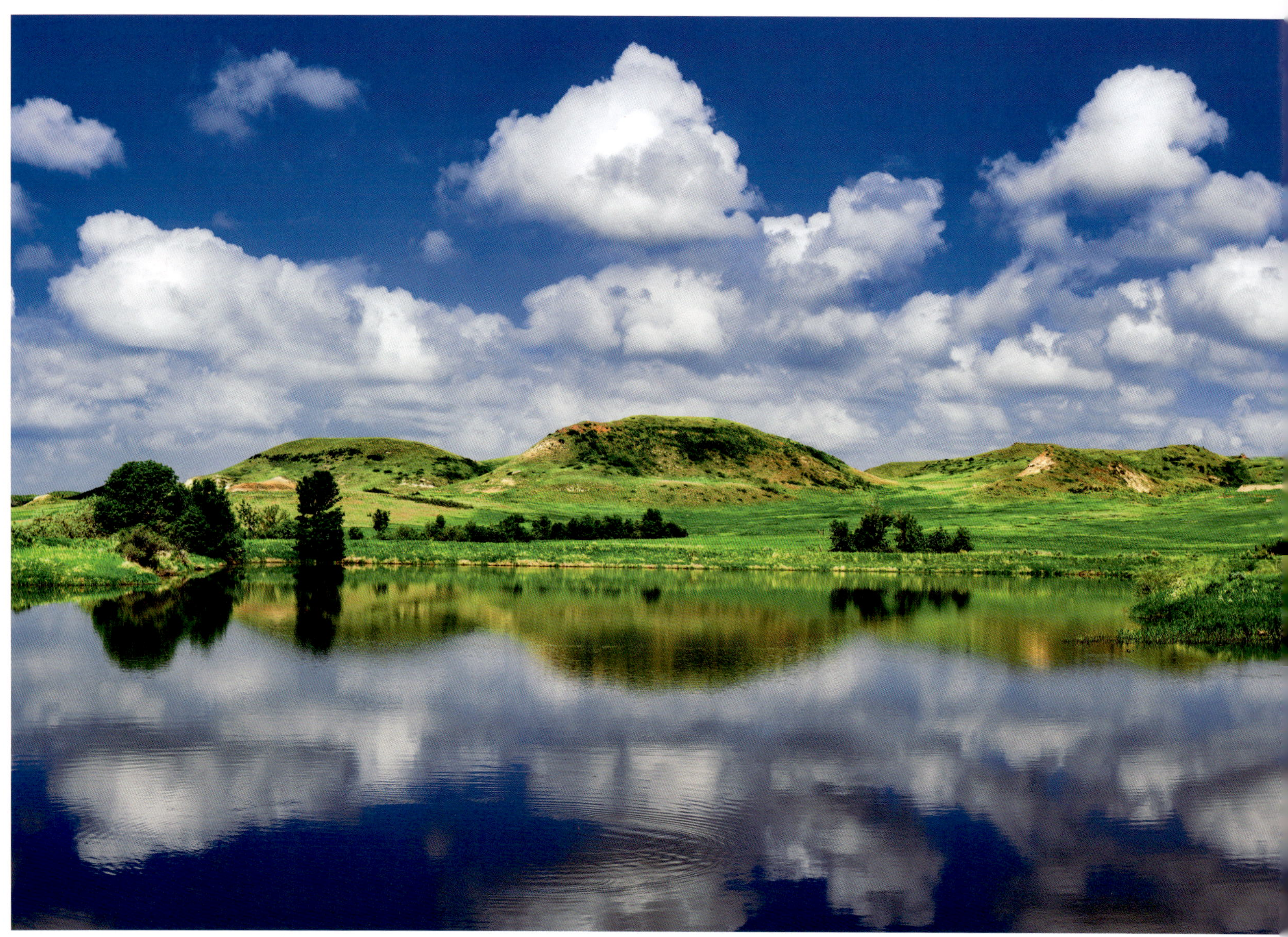

Leland Dam, North Dakota

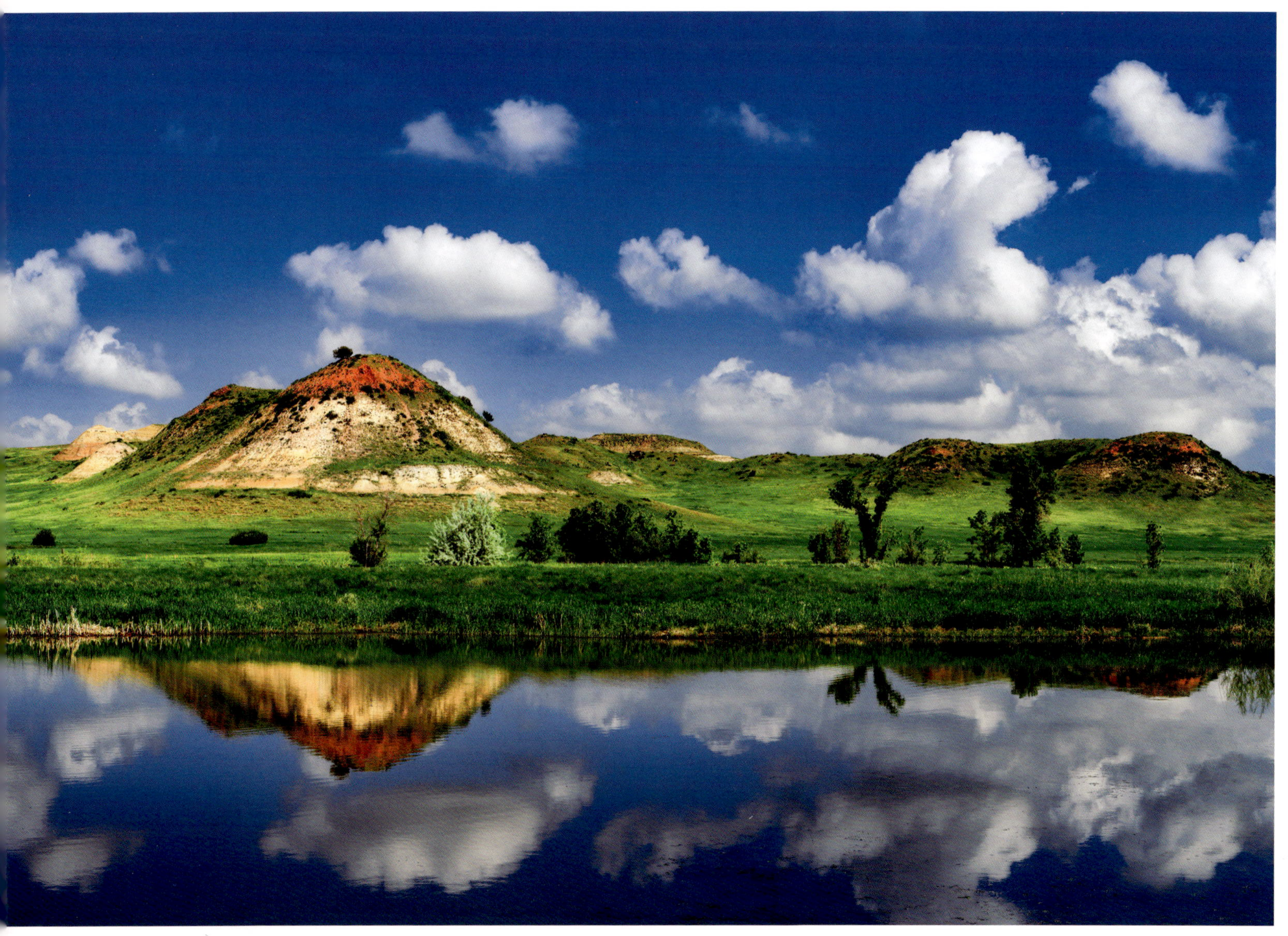

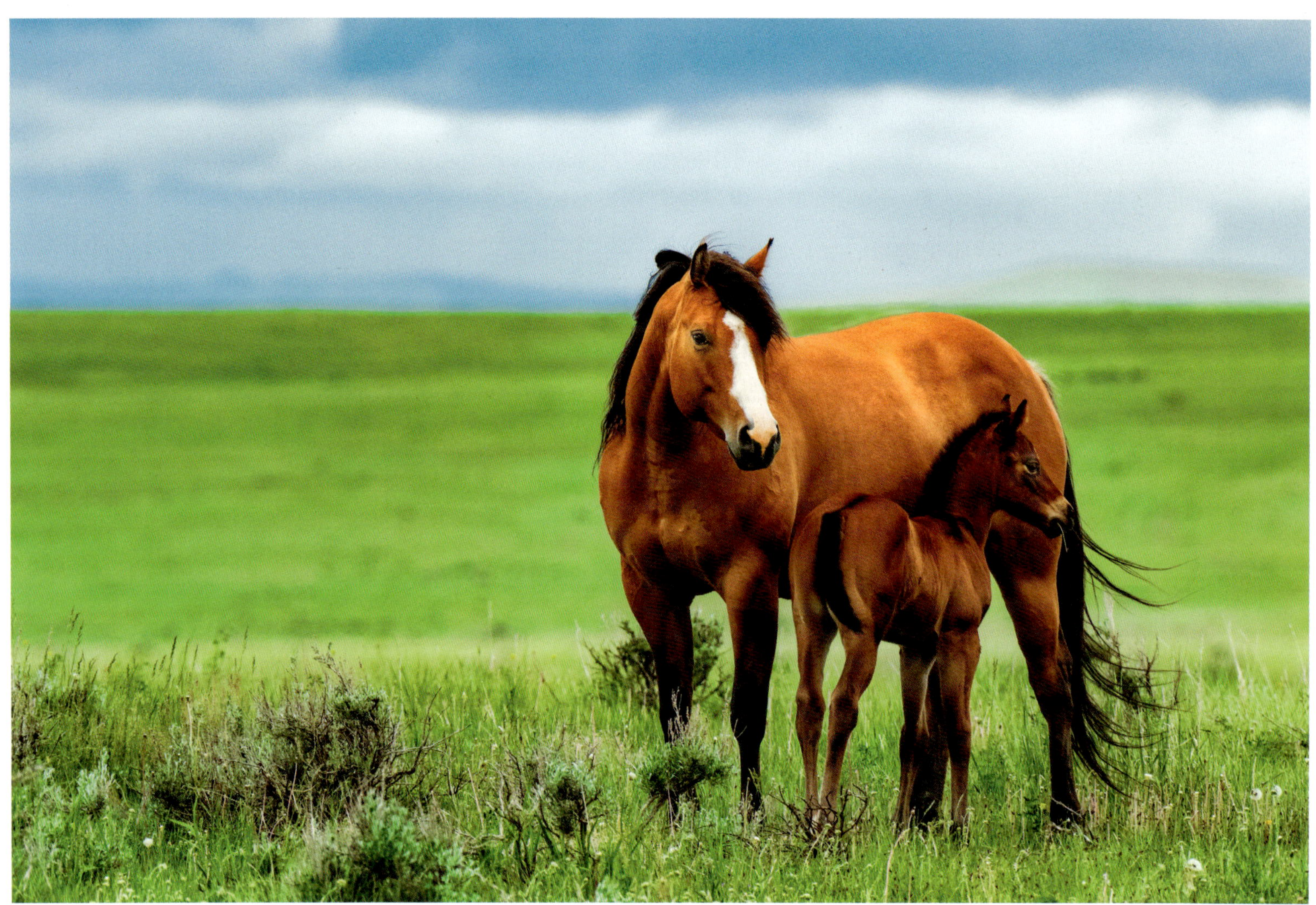

Wild horses, Little Missouri National Grasslands, North Dakota

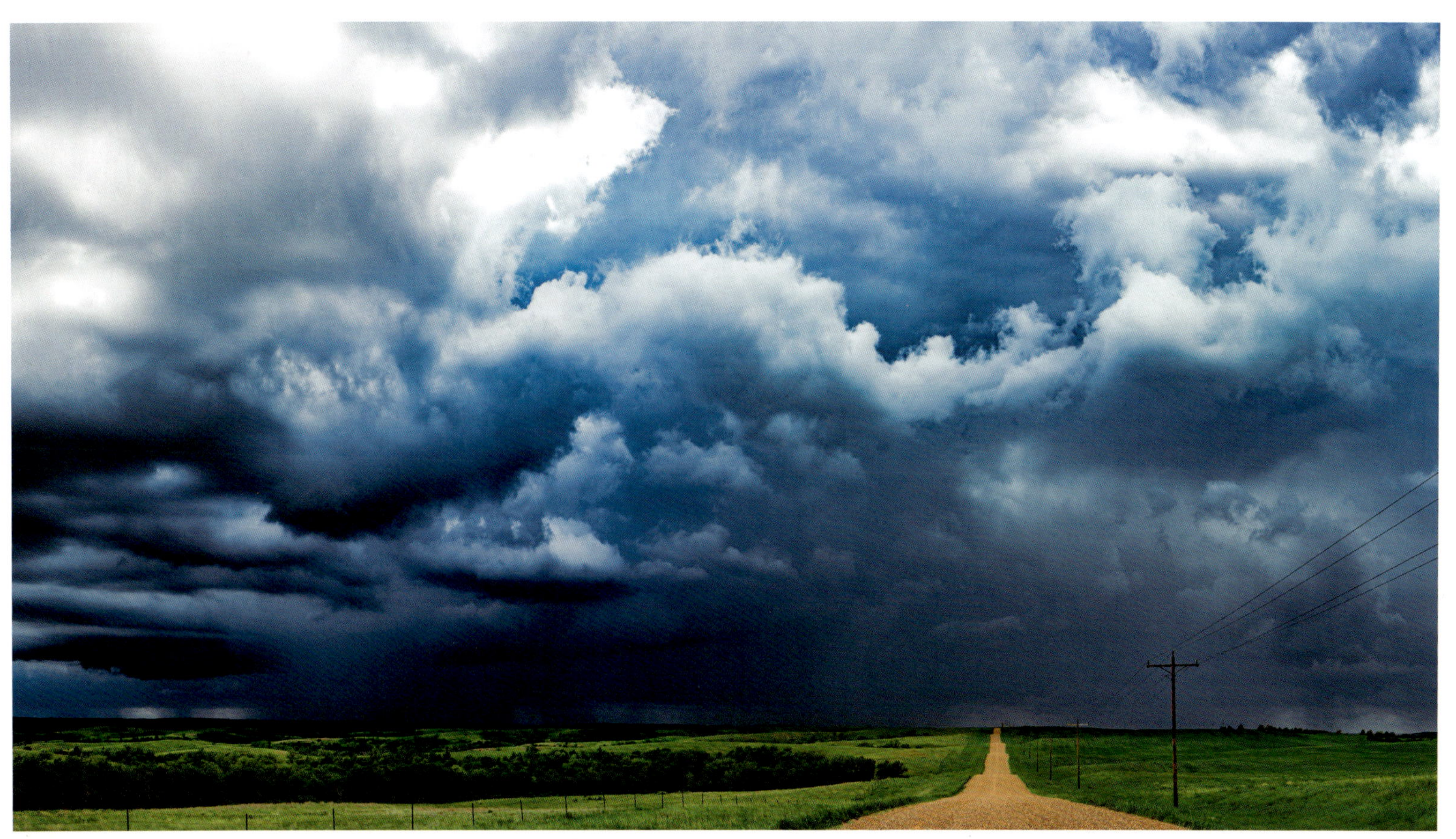

Storm over Forest Road 2, Little Missouri National Grasslands, North Dakota

APPENDIX

Page	Image Name	Camera	Lens	F/Stop	Shutter Speed	ISO	Pano Image Count	Pano Levels	Dimensions in Inches
7	Tiny Conoco, on Route 66, Commerce, Oklahoma	Nikon D810	Nikkor 85mm f/1.8	f/11	1/250	64	7	1	63 × 31
8	Homestead off Oklahoma State Highway 171	Nikon D810	Nikkor 85mm f/1.8	f/9.0	1/160	64	16	2	52 × 29
9	Brahman cattle, Oklahoma	Nikon D500	Nikkor 200–500mm f/5.6	f/11	1/500	500	n/a	n/a	24 × 14
10	Sooner Market, Porum, Oklahoma	Nikon D810	Nikkor 85mm f/1.8	f/13	1/60	64	8	1	47 × 20
12	Old house in Salt Plains National Wildlife Refuge, Oklahoma	Nikon D810	Nikkor 85mm f/1.8	f/11	1/60	31	5	1	44 × 18
14	Glossy ibis, Wichita Mountains National Wildlife Refuge, Oklahoma	Nikon D500	Nikkor 200–500mm f/5.6	f/7.1	1/1600	560	n/a	n/a	24 × 16
15	Red-winged blackbird, pond on Harris Road, Oklahoma	Nikon D500	Nikkor 200–500mm f/5.6	f/11	1/3200	2800	n/a	n/a	24 × 16
16	Belter's Auto Salvage, Route 66, Clinton, Oklahoma	Nikon D810	Nikkor 85mm f/1.8	f/11	1/320	100	18	2	67 × 28
18	Oklahoma State Highway 60	Nikon D700	Nikkor 50mm f/1.4	f/13	1/60	100	n/a	n/a	24 × 16
19	Canada goslings, Salt Plains National Wildlife Refuge, Oklahoma	Nikon D500	Nikkor 200–500mm f/5.6	f/8	1/2000	4000	n/a	n/a	24 × 16
20	Old granary, Cherokee, Oklahoma	Nikon D810	Nikkor 35mm f/1.4	f/11	1/60	31	7	1	60 × 32
21	Silos and trucks on the Great Plains	Nikon D600	Nikkor 35mm f/1.4	f/13	1/80	100	12	1	60 × 32
22	Bison cow and calf, Wichita Mountains National Wildlife Refuge, Oklahoma	Nikon D500	Nikkor 200–500mm f/5.6	f/6.3	1/2000	4000	n/a	n/a	24 × 24
23	Longhorn cattle, Wichita Mountains National Wildlife Refuge, Oklahoma	Nikon D500	Nikkor 200–500mm f/5.6	f/8	1/2000	2800	n/a	n/a	24 × 16
24	Blue whale of Catoosa, Route 66, Oklahoma	Nikon D810	Nikkor 35mm f/1.4	f/11	1/160	64	10	1	84 × 38
25	Train along Oklahoma State Highway 70	Nikon D600	Nikkor 35mm f/1.4	f/11	1/200	100	8	1	39 × 18
26	Sprinklers on a stormy day, Oklahoma	Nikon D7100	Nikkor 105mm Macro f/2.8	f/11	1/320	100	11	1	81 × 19
28	Sunflower field, Kansas	Nikon D700	Nikkor 105mm Macro f/2.8	f/16	1/250	640	8	1	27 × 18
30	Otter Creek, John Redmond Reservoir, Kansas	Nikon D810	Nikkor 50mm f/1.4	f/10	1/125	64	7	1	78 × 32
32	Giant haystacks, Kansas	Nikon D600	Nikkor 35mm f/1.4	f/11	1/125	100	14	1	102 × 36
34	Wild horse, Theodore Roosevelt National Park, North Dakota	Nikon D500	Nikkor 200–500mm f/5.6	f/8	1/4000	3600	n/a	n/a	16 × 24
35	Tree and fence, Kansas State Highway 23	Nikon D810	Zeiss 135mm f/2.0	f/11	1/135	320	6	1	40 × 17
36	Wheat field, 180th Street, Minneapolis, Kansas	Nikon D810	Nikkor 50mm f/1.4	f/11	1/800	200	10	1	61 × 19
38	Storm over the Great Plains	Nikon D810	Nikkor 50mm f/1.4	f/11	1/60	64	9	1	53 × 21
40	Trucks and silos, Kansas	Nikon D810	Nikkor 85mm f/1.8	f/13	1/60	64	18	2	51 × 23
41	Yellow-headed blackbird, Kansas	Nikon D500	Nikkor 200–500mm f/5.6	f/8	1/4000	2000	n/a	n/a	16 × 24
42	Frozen barn, Kansas State Highway 25	Nikon D810	Nikkor 85mm f/1.8	f/11	1/160	64	8	1	54 × 20
44	Ferruginous hawk, Kansas	Nikon D500	Nikkor 200–500mm f/5.6	f/7.1	1/2000	320	n/a	n/a	18 × 24
45	Barn and silos, White Cloud, Kansas	Nikon D810	Nikkor 85mm f/1.8	f/10	1/200	64	6	1	40 × 19
46	Hay rolls along Kansas State Highway 284	Nikon D810	Zeiss 135mm f/2.0	f/8	1/60	64	12	1	72 × 20
48	2178 Highway 50, Kansas	Nikon D810	Nikkor 85mm f/1.8	f/11	1/60	64	8	1	56 × 18
50	Johnson grass along Kansas State Highway 1	Nikon D810	Zeiss 135mm f/2.0	f/14	1/1250	800	13	1	82 × 20
52	George Moody, Kansas	Nikon D2X	Nikkor 18mm f/3.5	f/8	1/15	400	n/a	n/a	24 × 16

Page	Image Name	Camera	Lens	F/Stop	Shutter Speed	ISO	Pano Image Count	Pano Levels	Dimensions in Inches
53	115 South Main Street, Buklin, Kansas	Nikon D810	Nikkor 35mm f/1.4	f/11	1/60	64	7	1	58 × 30
54	Train tracks along US 50, Kansas	Nikon D810	Nikkor 35mm f/1.4	f/11	1-15	64	15	1	96 × 26
56	Franklin's gulls or prairie doves, Kansas	Nikon D500	Nikkor 200–500mm f/5.6	f/10	1/250	10000	n/a	n/a	24 × 16
57	Cornfields in a drought year, Kansas	Nikon D2X	Nikkor 180mm f/2.8	f/11	1/80	100	n/a	n/a	24 × 16
58	Train near Holcomb, Kansas	Nikon D810	Zeiss 135mm f/2.0	f/11	1/60	64	8	1	67 × 20
60	Brick barn on Angus Road, Kansas	Nikon D810	Nikkor 85mm f/1.8	f/10	64	20	2	2	87 × 29
62	Neosho River, Flint Hills National Wildlife Refuge, Indian Hill, Kansas	Nikon D810	Nikkor 50mm f1.4	f/11	1/125	64	9	1	49 × 19
64	Amelia Earhart Bridge over the Missouri River, Atchison, Kansas	Nikon D810	Zeiss 135mm f/2.0	f/10	1.3	64	7	1	46 × 19
66	Sorghum harvest, Mitch's Farm, near Protection, Kansas	Nikon D810	Zeiss 135mm f/2.0	f/13	1/500	320	6	1	67 × 20
68	Loading sorghum, Mitch's Farm, near Protection. Kansas	Nikon D810	Zeiss 135mm f/2.0	f/14	1/500	320	6	1	67 × 20
70	7th and Main, Route 66, Galena, Kansas	Nikon D810	Nikkor 85mm f/1.8	f/10	1/200	64	6	1	65 × 34
71	*Amelia Comes Home*, by John Cerney, Atchison, Kansas	Nikon D810	Zeiss 135mm f/2.0	f/11	1/100	64	22	2	58 × 26
72	Aurora, Nebraska	Nikon D810	Nikkor 50mm f/1.4	f/10	1/250	64	6	1	30 × 19
73	Truck and shed, Hyannis, Nebraska	Nikon D810	Nikkor 85mm f/1.8	f/10	1/320	64	16	2	29 × 27
74	Freight train, Doc Lake, Nebraska	Nikon D810	Nikkor 85mm f/1.8	f/10	1/320	320	16	1	50 × 18
76	Cows in the mist, Nebraska State Highway 83	Nikon D810	Zeiss 135mm f/2.0	f/9.3	1/45	200	7	1	78 × 22
78	Rail yard, Alliance, Nebraska	Nikon D810	Zeiss 135mm f/2.0	f/10	1/125	64	18	2	52 × 25
80	Fields and clouds along Nebraska State Highway 61	Nikon D700	Nikkor 35mm f/1.4	f/11	1/60	200	9	1	51 × 16
82	Planted fields, Nebraska State Highway 73	Nikon D810	Zeiss 135mm f/2.0	f/11	1/100	64	6	1	47 × 19
84	Nebraska Northwest Railroad	Nikon D750	Nikkor 35mm f/1.4	f/8	1/400	100	7	1	40 × 34
85	Doernemann Farm, Colfax County, Nebraska	Nikon D810	Nikkor 85mm f/1.8	f/13	1/40	64	7	1	60 × 40
86	Empty corn cribs along Nebraska State Highway 79	Nikon D810	Nikkor 50mm f/1.4	f/9.0	1/200	64	18	2	50 × 20
88	Trees along Nebraska State Highway 12	Nikon D810	Zeiss 135mm f/2.0	f/9.0	1/60	31	7	1	43 × 19
90	*Carhenge*, by Jim Reinders, Alliance, Nebraska	Nikon D750	Nikkor 35mm f/1.4	f/8	1/320	100	12	1	92 × 35
92	Castle Rock Ranch, South Dakota	Nikon D600	Nikkor 85mm f/1.8	f/11	1/800	250	12	1	72 × 23
94	South Dakota ranch after winter storm Atlas, State Highway 16A	Nikon D600	Zeiss 28mm f/2.0	f/14	1/250	200	9	1	64 × 23
96	Early snow, South Dakota State Highway 36	Nikon D600	Nikkor 85mm f/1.8	f/11	1/800	100	14	1	94 × 29
98	Hereford cattle, South Dakota	Nikon D500	Nikkor 200–500 mm f/5.6	f/8	1/800	2500	n/a	n/a	24 × 10
99	Huron City Park, South Dakota	Nikon D810	Nikkor 50mm f/1.4	f/14	1/20	64	8	1	43 × 20
100	Bear Butte, South Dakota	Nikon 600	Nikkor 180mm f/2.8	f/11	1/640	200	13	1	75 × 22
102	Car carrier along South Dakota State Highway 385	Nikon D600	Nikkor 180mm f/2.8	f/10	1/100	200	9	1	65 × 18
104	Abandoned homestead, South Dakota State Highway 34	Nikon D700	Nikkor 50mm f/1.4	f/8	1/250	100	12	1	56 × 16
106	Cave Hills Lutheran Church, 1928, South Dakota	Nikon D600	Nikkor 35mm f/1.4	f/13	2"	100	11	1	42 × 15
107	Sylvan Lake, Custer State Park, South Dakota	Nikon D810	Nikkor 35mm f/1.4	f/8	1/200	64	9	1	88 × 35
108	Sunset along South Dakota State Highway 385	Nikon D600	Zeiss 28mm f/2.0	f/10	1/13	50	10	1	51 × 25
110	Pronghorn antelope in the Black Hills, South Dakota	Nikon D810	Zeiss 135mm f/20	f/5.0	1/80	64	16	2	52 × 26
112	Pond near Pringle, South Dakota	Nikon D810	Nikkor 50mm f/1.4	f/13	1/100	64	16	2	46 × 25
113	Yellow-bellied marmot, Black Hills National Forest, South Dakota	Nikon 800E	Zeiss 135mm f/2.0	f/13	1/15	100	21	3	50 × 44
114	Cloud formation along South Dakota State Highway 37	Nikon D810	Zeiss 135mm f/2.0	f/10	1/80	64	14	2	57 × 22
116	Roughlock Falls, Spearfish Canyon, South Dakota	Nikon D810	Zeiss 135mm f/2.0	f/16	1/5	64	18	2	93 × 41

Page	Image Name	Camera	Lens	F/Stop	Shutter Speed	ISO	Pano Image Count	Pano Levels	Dimensions in Inches
118	Female bighorn sheep, Badlands National Park, South Dakota	Nikon D7100	Nikkor 70–200mm f/28	f/9.0	1/500	280	n/a	n/a	24 × 16
119	Rocky Mountain goat, Harney Peak, South Dakota	Nikon D7100	Nikkor 70–200mm f/28	f/9.0	1/500	160	n/a	n/a	24 × 16
120	Farm on Vanoker Road, South Dakota	Nikon D600	Nikkor 85mm f/1.8	f/11	1/800	100	8	1	50 × 23
122	American bison, Custer State Park, South Dakota	Nikon D600	Nikkor 85mm f/1.8	f/11	1/250	320	10	1	68 × 24
124	Trees and hills along the Wildlife Loop, Custer State Park, South Dakota	Nikon D810	Zeiss 135mm f/2.0	f/9.0	1/125	64	6	1	48 × 16
126	The Needles, Black Hills, South Dakota	Nikon D600	Zeiss 28mm f/2.0a	f/13	1/30	100	11	1	74 × 30
128	White-tailed deer, Custer State Park, South Dakota	Nikon D7100	Nikkor 70–200mm f/2.8	f/9.0	1/500	320	n/a	n/a	24 × 16
129	Deer caught in early snowfall, South Dakota	Nikon D7100	Nikkor 70–200mm f/2.8	f/2.8	1/500	160	n/a	n/a	24 × 16
130	Storm, Highland Ridge, South Dakota	Nikon D810	Nikkor 50mm f/1.4	f/8	1/60	64	22	2	62 × 28
132	Bison bull, Custer State Park, South Dakota	Nikon D500	Nikkor 200–500mm f/5.6	f/8	1/2500	900	n/a	n/a	24 × 16
133	Yellow mounds, Badlands National Park, South Dakota	Nikon D600	Nikkor 35mm f1.4	f/11	1/400	250	12	1	46 × 26
134	Bison and moon, Wind Cave National Park, South Dakota	Nikon D750	Nikkor 35mm f1.4	f/8	1/250	500	7	1	53 × 18
136	Bison, Black Hills, South Dakota	Nikon D500	Nikkor 200–500mm f/5.6	f/8	1/2500	4000	n/a	n/a	16 × 24
136	Bison calf, Black Hills, South Dakota	Nikon D500	Nikkor 200–500mm f/5.6	f/8	1/1600	18000	n/a	n/a	16 × 24
137	Grand Lodgepole River National Grassland, South Dakota	Nikon D810	Nikkor 50mm f/1.4	f/10	1/200	64	6	1	68 × 40
138	Pronghorn antelope, Wildlife Loop, Custer State Park, South Dakota	Nikon D600	Nikkor 180mm f/2.8	f/11	1/400	250	7	1	71 × 24
140	Brink's Farm, South Dakota	Nikon D700	Nikkor 35mm f/1.4	f/8	1/250	200	10	1	64 × 22
142	Profile, Mount Rushmore National Memorial, South Dakota	Nikon D810	Zeiss 135mm f/2.0	f/10	1/160	64	8	1	50 × 22
143	Deer, Black Hills National Forest, South Dakota	Nikon D7100	Nikkor 70–200mm f/2.8	f/5.6	1/1000	800	n/a	n/a	16 × 24
144	281 Diner, Stickney, South Dakota	Nikon D810	Nikkor 50mm f/1.4	f/10	1/100	64	13	1	82 × 21
146	Church along South Dakota State Highway 34	Nikon D700	Nikkor 35mm f/1.4	f/11	1/250	200	7	1	27 × 18
147	Friendly horses along North Dakota State Highway 22	Nikon D300S	Nikkor 80–400mm f/4.5-5.6	f/5.6	1/1250	400	n/a	n/a	16 × 24
148	Giant hay roll along North Dakota County Road 4531, the Enchanted Highway	Nikon D700	Nikkor 35mm f/1.4	f/11	1/100	100	11	1	66 × 24
150	Silos, barn, and clouds along North Dakota State Highway 16	Nikon D810	Nikkor 50mm f/1.4	f/11	1/250	64	9	1	55 × 21
152	Coming into Finley, North Dakota, on Highway 32	Nikon D600	Nikkor 85mm f/1.8	f/16	1/30	100	14	1	82 × 19
154	Old house on North Dakota State Highway 8	Nikon D810	Nikkor 50mm f/1.4	f/10	1/160	64	8	1	47 × 17
156	Railroad crossing near Chaseley, North Dakota	Nikon D700	Nikkor 50mm f/1.4	f/19	1/30	160	n/a	n/a	24 × 16
157	Prairie dog pups, Half-Way Lake National Wildlife Refuge, North Dakota	Nikon D500	Nikkor 200–500mm f/5.6	f/8	1/4000	1250	n/a	n/a	24 × 16
158	Pond off North Dakota State Highway 16	Nikon D810	Nikkor 85mm f/1.8	f/13	1/40	64	8	1	52 × 17
160	Jim Olsen's sprayer along County Road 4805, , North Dakota	Nikon D810	Nikkor 85mm f/1.8	f/11	1/80	64	7	1	45 × 16
162	Ash Road, North Dakota	Nikon D600	Nikkor 35mm f/1.4	f/11	1/80	100	11	1	68 × 27
164	American bison calf, Little Missouri National Grassland, North Dakota	Nikon D500	Nikkor 200–500mm f/5.6	f/9.0	1/2000	2800	n/a	n/a	24 × 16
165	Wild horses, Theodore Roosevelt National Park, North Dakota	Nikon D500	Nikkor 200–500mm f/5.6	f/8	1/4000	4500	n/a	n/a	21 × 16
166	Trotter's Church, North Dakota (Black and White)	Nikon D810	Nikkor 50mm f/1.4	f/11	1/200	64	9	1	88 × 40
168	American bison herd in the grasslands, North Dakota	Nikon D810	Nikkor 85mm f/1.8	f/10	1/800	500	9	1	54 × 19
170	Leland Dam, North Dakota	Nikon D810	Nikkor 85mm f/1.8	f/11	1/60	64	28	2	70 × 24
172	Wild horses, Little Missouri National Grasslands, North Dakota	Nikon D500	Nikkor 200–500mm f/5.6	f/8	1/2000	2500	n/a	n/a	24 × 16
173	Storm over Forest Road 2, Little Missouri National Grasslands, North Dakota	Nikon D810	Nikkor 50mm f/1.4	f/10	1/125	64	6	1	37 × 20

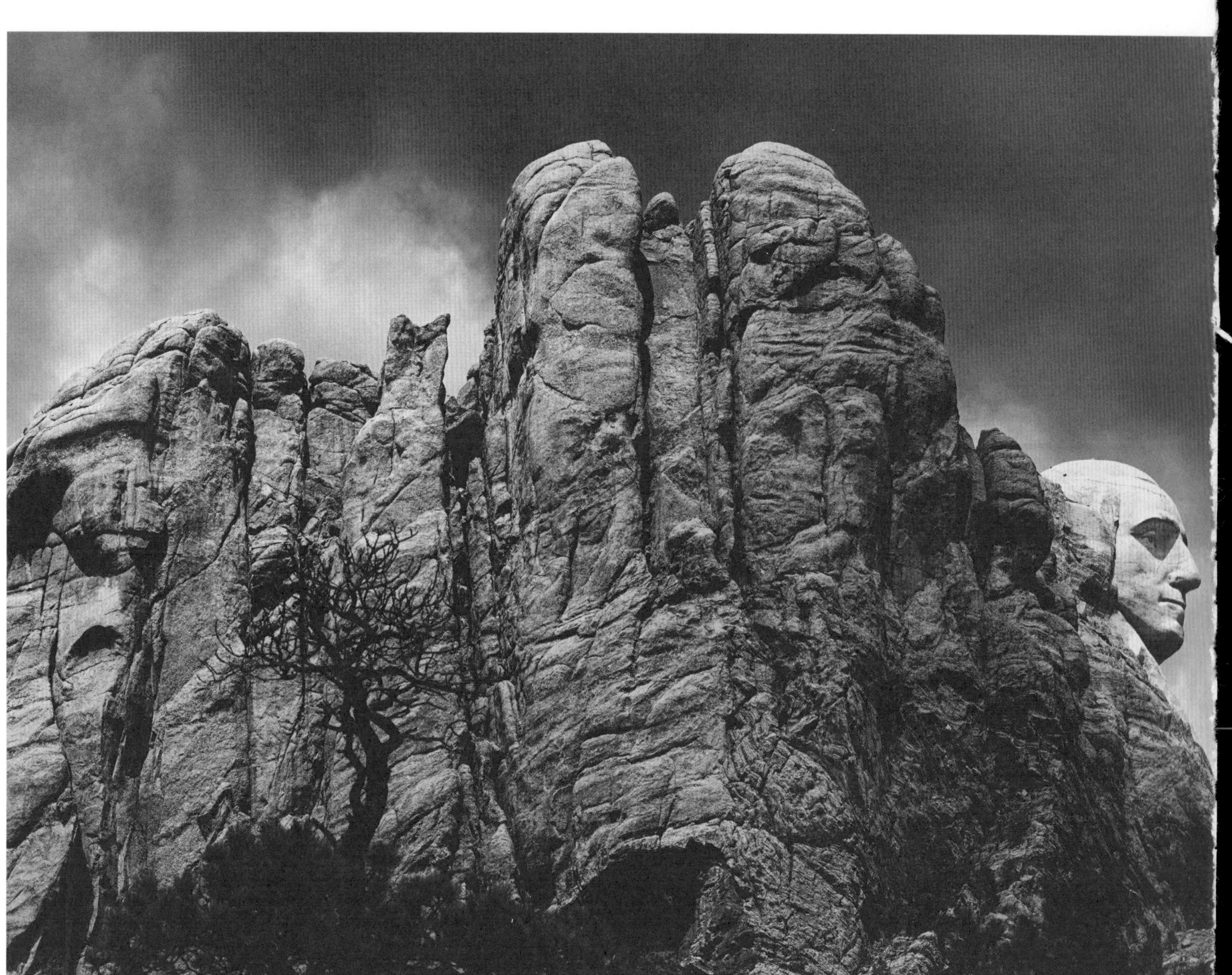